unInvited

THEORIES OF REPRESENTATION AND DIFFERENCE
General Editor, Teresa de Lauretis

unInvited

CLASSICAL
HOLLYWOOD
CINEMA
AND
LESBIAN
REPRESENTABILITY

Patricia White

INDIANA UNIVERSITY PRESS
BLOOMINGTON AND INDIANAPOLIS

This book is a publication of
Indiana University Press
601 North Morton Street
Bloomington, Indiana 47404-3797 USA

www.indiana.edu/~iupress

Telephone orders   800-842-6796
Fax orders   812-855-7931
Orders by e-mail   iuporder@indiana.edu

The paper used in this publication meets the minimum
requirements of American National Standard for Information
Sciences—Permanence of Paper for Printed Library
Materials, ANSI Z39.48-1984.

Manufactured in the United States of America

Library of Congress Cataloging-in-Publication Data

White, Patricia, date.
    Uninvited: classical Hollywood cinema and lesbian representability / Patricia White.
        p.   cm. —(Theories of representation and difference)
    Includes bibliographical references and index.
    ISBN 0-253-33641-4 (cl: alk. paper). —ISBN 0-253-21345-2 (pa: alk. paper)
    1. Lesbianism in motion pictures.   I. Title.   II. Series.
PN1995.9.L48W54   1999
791.43'653—dc21   99-35744

1   2   3   4   5   04   03   02   01   00   99

For Cynthia, my companion

Contents

SIX
On Retrospectatorship
194

Acknowledgments

This book has been a long time in the making; it feels like a collective effort. Teresa de Lauretis, with unmatched intellectual and personal generosity, has been teacher, editor, friend, and brilliant inspiration. The perceptiveness of Rhona Berenstein's careful comments on my dissertation and on chapter drafts was matched only by the impeccable timing of her interventions and the fine example of her work. Judith Mayne's scholarship and mentorship have sustained my commitment to film studies. Lisa Cohen has given me a decade (and counting) of intellectual companionship; phone calls with her have resolved many a sticking point. Todd Haynes's friendship and his films have infused this project with life. Leslie Camhi, Ann Cvetkovich, Elaine Freedgood, Joy Van Fuqua, Cathy Greenblatt, Chantal Nadeau, Debra Keats, Lisa Kennedy, Helen Lee, Frances Negrón-Muntaner, Fatimah Tobing Rony, Jennifer Terry, and Sharon Ullman are genuine genies, smart luncheon companions, reliable correspondents, and true friends. I was lucky enough to have on my dissertation committee Victor Burgin and Stephen Heath, and to have D. N. Rodowick to introduce me to film theory and politics. To the good offices of Judith Halberstam, Gayatri Gopinath, and José Muñoz I owe thanks and places to work during steamy, distracting New York summers. Marlene McCarty lent her keen eyes and talent to my design dilemma. And I'd like to thank my stars.

Several organizations nurtured me, my work, and friendships that will remain with me for life: thanks to my co-workers at Women Make Movies, to its inspired director Debbie Zimmerman, to the board and staff of the New York Lesbian and Gay Film Festival, and especially to Robin Vachal. Thanks

Acknowledgments

to Sasha Torres, Lynne Joyrich, Phillip Brian Harper, and Sharon Willis of the Camera Obscura collective, to the members of the Faculty Working Group in Queer Studies at NYU, B. Ruby Rich and GLQ, and to my cohort at the Wesleyan University Center for the Humanities for challenges and insights. Bringing it all back home, my colleagues at Swarthmore College — Betsy Bolton, Bruce Grant, and Sunka Simon — are astute critics and great company. To Nora Johnson's wit and openness I owe an enormous debt; she's read 500 pages and countless drafts on demand. I sincerely thank the students I've had the privilege to teach and learn from at Swarthmore. Pat Walter reminded me weekly of the insights of everyday life. My parents George and Donna White have always been wonderfully encouraging, even when I said I wanted to get a Ph.D. in the History of Consciousness. Since I started to write the first paper from which this book emerged, Cynthia Schneider, my love and counsel, has been there with good faith, good sense, and timely reminders that sometimes movie sisters really are just sisters. There isn't a word here she hasn't tenderly wrenched out of me. Now I don't have the words to thank her.

During a semester's postdoctoral residency at the Humanities Institutute at SUNY Stony Brook, supported by the Rockefeller Foundation, I began shaping this book. Swarthmore College generously granted me a Blansard Fellowship and a leave that allowed me to complete it.

An earlier version of Chapter 3 appeared in *Inside/Out: Lesbian Theories, Gay Theories,* edited by Diana Fuss (New York: Routledge, 1991). A substantial portion of the material in Chapter 5 was published as "Supporting Character: The Queer Career of Agnes Moorehead" in *Out in Culture: Lesbian, Gay, and Queer Essays on Popular Culture,* edited by Alexander Doty and Cory Creekmur (Duke University Press, 1995).

Introduction

In the film version of Carson McCullers's *The Member of the Wedding* (Fred Zinnemann, 1952), Frankie Addams (Julie Harris) plans to accompany her brother and his bride on their honeymoon. Twelve-year-old Frankie, an opening female voice-over tells us, is an "unjoined person": "[F]or a long time she had not been a member of anything." Just what kind of relation of belonging her brother's wedding presents for her, an unregenerate tomboy, is a question both elaborated and deferred by the film. Berenice (Ethel Waters), Frankie's primary caregiver and companion, teases her: "Frankie's got a crush, Frankie's got a crush." But although such a taunt may be familiar as a means through which a queer child recognizes her difference, Berenice is not implying that Frankie's crush is on her brother's fiancée. She knows that "Frankie's got a crush on the wedding." Somehow Frankie's longing and her difference find a support in the preposterous and painful wedding fantasy. How is her desire finally "joined" with knowledge about her nature in the memory and mastery of that summer's events? How is the spectator engaged by the unfolding of this scenario of longing in and through the film?

The Member of the Wedding is a trenchant tale of the process of reaching for an identity through a social ritual. What Frankie intuits as an ambivalent invitation to the wedding is not unlike the relationship of spectators with marginalized social identities to classical Hollywood cinema. For it is a truism of film theory that the ideal spectator/subject addressed by classical cinema—with its system of "suture," its narrative legacy from the bourgeois novel, its ideological investment in rendering natural and thus reproducing the status quo, its commodity status, its fetishistic structuring of the gaze, its hierarchy of image over sound, its single-point perspective, its required suspension of disbelief, its "realism"—is male. Implicitly, this ideal spectator or invisible guest is Western, white, and straight as well. Like the wedding, the cinema is, Teresa de Lauretis argues, a technology of gender (the weddings with which so many Hollywood films conclude celebrate this project) (*Technologies of Gender* 13; see Freeman). As such it must work broadly and individually; it requires our attendance. "Outsiders" too may have a "crush" on the movies, be wedded to the promise of the cinema. Frankie's fantasy—"My brother and the bride are the we of me"—is a sort of primal scene, in which the subject represents her exclusion from the very scene of her own conception. Similarly, queers are engendered within normative psychosocial matrices like the cinema and the family—and discover their difference there as well. If *The Member of the Wedding* issues an invitation to a queer spectator, it is because at the same time that it expresses the longing to conform, it also enacts a fantasy of autonomy and difference. Three outsiders—an adult Black woman, a sissy white boy, and his preteen tomboy cousin—figure the gap between hegemonic representation (the idealized picture of happiness that is the white wedding) and those who are dispossessed of the image. Frankie goes "breaking into weddings" just like we do.

Uninvited traces elusive representations of lesbian desire and difference in films of Production Code Administration–era Hollywood. I open with *The Member of the Wedding* because it enacts for me the affect and identification that writing about the movie past entails, together with a critique of, a distance from, that past. This distance represents the possibilities of lesbian viewing in our very different present.

The Biograph in Autobiography

Frankie's investment in the wedding may be matched by an immediate spectatorial investment in the film—an identification with Frankie's look, her alienation, and her fantasizing, or she might be our younger self before the cinema, over-identifying, loving naively. Looking back and looking on, we painfully perceive her inevitable disappointment, even recognize that she is a freak. The voice-over the film version of McCullers's text opens with is at once authorial and autobiographical: "It happened that green and crazy summer when Frankie was twelve years old," registering the passage of time and an unspecified "it." In this double relation, in which the past joins up with the present, the film's structure provides a model of the lesbian spectatorship with which this book is concerned. What does it mean to like *this* movie, to identify with it, to remember it, to be a fan of Julie Harris or Ethel Waters or Brandon de Wilde, to want to be a member of their group? Something happened some "green and crazy summer" when one saw this film (or another like it). A later experience of queer knowledge and desire makes the affective memory meaningful.[1]

I remember obsessively scrubbing my elbows when I was about thirteen; somehow the sight of Frankie's filthy elbows had gotten under my skin. Spending hours watching old movies on television, I (dis)identified with Frankie's introspection, awkwardness, and verbosity just as intensely as other lesbians remember having done with her tomboyishness. *Rebecca* and *Letter From an Unknown Woman* were also in heavy rotation on the Las Vegas channel that I watched as an adolescent, and their unformed heroines made a vivid impression upon me. My best friend and I modeled outfits on the schoolgirl dresses Joan Fontaine wears in the beginning of the latter film when she first takes the plunge into a lifetime of unrequited desire and ecstatic isolation. As different as were their gender presentations, the heroines of *Letter from an Unknown Woman* and *The Member of the Wedding* shared a conviction that they were represented in scenes that erased them. Thankfully, I was just as unrealistic.

"How can film theory address itself to the emotions films evoke," Annette Kuhn asks, "to the ways in which such emotions enter into people's fictions of the past, their own past? Any affective response to a film—and indeed recollections of such a response even more so—threatens to elude attempts to explain or intellectualize" (237). Kuhn describes her own vivid recollection of the post-war British film *Mandy* (Mackendrick, 1953), in which a deaf girl finally speaks her own name, thus transcending her isolation and joining her social world. A few years after teaching *Mandy*, a context in which her remembered identification with the child-heroine could not be given expression, Kuhn burst into tears when the film came up in conversation. She comments:

> The tears had come, unbidden and insistent, from some part of Annette that was decisively not the film scholar, nor even the cinephile. The grownup's conversation had been interrupted by something inappropriate and other—a child's response, troubling and hard to ignore. . . . [C]an [these responses] be brought together in our endeavors to understand how films engage our emotions and our fantasies? Does the naive, the untutored, the everyday response have anything to offer the professional, the academic, the intellectual one? (236)

What had not been grasped in analysis was point of view—the fraught representation of the little girl's subjectivity in the film and its answer in the child-spectator. Of the latter Kuhn remarks, "The child had certainly been moved—changed—by this film. . . . She was to find those sounds and images, and the feelings evoked by them, insistently memorable, held . . . like a compelling dream, a vision, outside and beyond the everyday" (234). Kuhn implies that her viewing of *Mandy* represented a passage to social and subjective integration parallel to its heroine's. The moments in the film she isolated, remembered, function, she suggests, like symptoms or dream symbols, subject to laws of displacement, secondarization, condensation—readable insofar as they are overdetermined by the life of the subject.

Kuhn's essay is somewhat reticent about what is at stake in her film—content that only reinforces, I would venture, the charge of the memory. For *Mandy*, like *The Member of the Wedding* or *The Wizard of Oz*, enacts an intense drama of *not* belonging, of abandonment and difference. Such films might be particularly insistent in outsiders' memories of popular cinema: memories, histories, fictions of the past, in which learning to speak one's name might be especially fraught, in which individual identity is conjoined with the taking on of a loaded social name.[2]

If the affect attached to a personal film favorite can be the basis for becoming a film theorist or a filmmaker, this book argues that it can also constitute the basis for community identification. Vito Russo, in his vivid and moving appearance in *Common Threads* (Jeffrey Friedman and Rob Epstein, 1990), the Academy Award–winning documentary on the Names Project's AIDS Memorial Quilt, displays a quilt square memorializing his close friend Jeffrey Sevcik. The square is designed around Sevcik's all-time favorite movie: *The Member of the Wedding*. When Russo, whose *The Celluloid Closet* touched so many lesbian and gay film viewers' lives, died of AIDS not long after *Common Threads* was released, this interview segment was screened at his memorial service at San Francisco's landmark Castro Theater. It was followed by the intensely emotional scene from Zinnemann's movie in which Waters sings "His Eye Is On the Sparrow" to de Wilde and Harris. A number of clichés came together in this moment of shared pathos—gay male culture's tribute to "old movies," the use of African American music as a sign of expressivity or metaphor of oppression—but the specificity of the text, and the cultural space that made its resignification as a text of mourning for lives lost to AIDS possible, gave evidence of some of the rich identifications that American movie history facilitates.

Through Russo's presentation of his friend's passion for the movies in the context of his own, the film's memory became significant for the group there to mourn him. This group came to represent the gay and lesbian film *audience* that has been constituted in part by Russo's scholarship on film history, the work his anecdote from *Common Threads* stood in for. My own adolescent memory of *The Member of the Wedding* was somatic, not intellectual, and it was the kernel of my sense of belonging at Vito's service. *Uninvited*, like any contribution to the field of lesbian and gay film studies, is indebted to Vito Russo's *The Celluloid Closet*. It also emphasizes the experiences—affective, private, subcultural, public—from which that work emerged.

Cinema is public fantasy that engages spectators' particular, private scripts of desire and identification. Equally at stake in spectatorship are the way organized images and sounds psychically imprint us and the way they mediate social identities and histories. Because Hollywood films are part of public culture that addresses women, and because they do so through representations of Woman invested with desire, they work with material—cultural and psychic—that engages lesbian fantasy. Without projecting our current experiences of lesbian identity and sociality onto the past, still we can recognize that mass culture spoke to women in ways influenced by the historical emergence of lesbian culture and the forms it has taken. Hollywood films have in part constructed our desire; the work of our readings of these films and the discourses and practices surrounding them is to construct the conditions of our own representability.

The retrospective dimension of spectatorship persists even in a current mass cultural climate in which the terms of lesbian representability and of "membership" have shifted drastically. Not only have lesbian representations proliferated, the audience for them has itself become visible—at least as a consumer demographic. Today's unprecedented lesbian and gay media visibility illuminates the reading practices that formerly sustained viewers in the face of invisibility.

Uninvited is indebted to the work on lesbian and gay representation in film that has emerged in the last decade, much of it part of the intervention in heteronormative disciplinary knowledges known as queer theory. It also took shape in relation to "nonscholarly" practices: traditions of gay male cinephilic writing such as Parker Tyler's *Screening the Sexes*, Jack Smith's "The Perfect Filmic Appositeness of Maria Montez," and Boyd MacDonald's *Cruising the Movies* and the work of independent lesbian and gay film and video artists and media arts organizations.[3] The most generative matrix, to the debates and claims of which this book is primarily addressed, is twenty-five years of work in feminist film theory. I shall briefly sketch the provocations this book takes from these theoretical contexts before turning to a brief summary of its individual chapters.

On the first page of her major contribution to queer theory, *The Epistemology of the Closet*, Eve Sedgwick claims that "major nodes of thought and knowledge in twentieth-century Western culture as a whole are structured—indeed fractured—by a chronic, now endemic crisis of homo/heterosexual definition, indicatively male, dating from the end of the 19th century" and further that this crisis "has affected our culture through its ineffaceable marking particularly of the categories secrecy/disclosure, knowledge/ignorance, [and] private/public" (11). Is mass culture, though perhaps not always credited as a "major node of thought and knowledge," structured by this epistemological crisis? Born at the turn of the last century, cinema is certainly a formative *experience* of twentieth-century Western culture. Classical Hollywood cinema, regulated by a self-censoring agency and a rare set of favorable economic conditions, works along the faultlines of Sedgwick's binarisms—secrecy/disclosure, knowledge/ignorance, private/public. Mass entertainment is a "feminized" sphere, though as a realm of consumption it is governed by a male-dominated, capital-intensive industry. Cinema plays out its epistemologies of sexuality around new forms of visibility of the female body. Does popular cinema then secure male-dominated heterosexuality, containing the "crisis" that Sedgwick locates within high culture? Or does it put pressure on the very constructions of agency and sexual subjectivity, knowledge and doubt, as indicatively if not exclusively male? *Uninvited* indicates that queer theory needs to consider more closely the relationship between lesbianism and femininity—what might be called the problem of female homo/heterosexual definition—in the commercialized "women's culture" of classical cinema. Certainly queer theory's understandings of sexual identity based on object choice and/or gender identification, and the attendant distinction between identification and desire, are central to theories of cinematic spectatorship.

Feminist film theory builds a vision of "sexual difference" in cinema around differential relations of desire for and identification with "woman as image" (Mulvey, "Visual Pleasure") and narrative goal (de Lauretis, "Desire in Narrative"). According to foundational texts such as Laura Mulvey's "Visual Pleasure and Narrative Cinema," Claire Johnston's "Women's Cinema as Counter Cinema," and Mary Ann Doane's "Film and the Masquerade," the female form and the apparatus that produces it as lure are mastered by male fetishism. The female spectator is excluded from a position of desire in "male" movies, and in "women's films" she is thought to mimic her screen surrogates' woes. Even when overly schematic, these feminist understandings of the gendered processes of spectatorship show how psychic structures are engaged and produced in patriarchal representations, and the limitations of strict sexually differential models of spectatorship have been addressed through work on cinema's engaging of fantasy as "mise-en-scène of desire."[4] The theory of fantasy allows for an understanding of how films mediate between the psychic and the social and traces the play of identification in practices that involve invisibility as well as visibility.

Feminist cultural and historical studies of film have gone beyond looking at the text and the subject constructed through its codes and enunciation, noting that women have actively been solicited as spectators by the film industry since its early days. This historical and cultural work takes female audiences and their contradictory experiences of texts as its subject. It is influenced by the theorizing of race, representation, and strategies of oppositional viewing, and these feminist studies have in turn influenced lesbian and gay studies. The idea that subcultural groups can "appropriate" mainstream mass media is by now clichéd however, and lesbian and gay film studies still needs to develop an adequate methodology for determining how this process works and what it accomplishes. Too often claims for "subversive" viewing practices ignore the insights of psychoanalytical accounts of spectatorial identification and specific textual features. *Uninvited* urges that psychoanalysis be retained. While it remains difficult to conduct empirical work on lesbian and gay spectators, we can reconstruct some of the discourses that intersected with film texts to broaden our analysis of how gender and sexuality were constructed by the cinema. Studies of stars, costuming, reception, source material, and authorship can all introduce traces of a lesbian historical presence that the narratives of the films exclude.

Drawing on and interrogating queer and feminist film theory, as well as cultural studies of classical cinema, this book looks at both the pleasure classical Hollywood films continue to give contemporary lesbian spectators and the ways in which those films and the social technology of Hollywood have constructed our very psychosocial identities and possibilities of self-representation. *Uninvited* identifies and analyzes some of the sites in which lesbianism, as a social identity under construction in twentieth-century U.S. mass-mediated society, registers effects in studio-era Hollywood films. The prohibitions mandated by the Production Code Administration could not eliminate all lesbian "inference." The personae of important female stars and the knowledges, meanings, and identifications generated by their fandoms, both historical and contemporary, constitute a crucial site for lesbian meanings. The conventions of the woman's picture for representing female homosociality, subjectivity, and difference—particularly in the subgenres of the gothic and the maternal melodrama, with their troubled depiction of women's relation to domestic and heterosexual ideology, are another site of contradiction. Finally, the practices of stereotyping governing the roles of supporting actresses intersect in interesting ways with the construction of lesbian types. Classical Hollywood cinema's terms of vision, narration, and address privilege normative and hierarchical racial and national ideologies, male discursive authority, and heterosexual hegemony. And yet, as a popular cultural form identified with the "feminine" world of commodity culture, emotion, romance, and entertainment, Hollywood cinema is diverse and unpredictable in its influences and the social and psychic needs to which it speaks. Contradictions within the definition of femininity characterize the sites I have isolated and influence spectatorial identifications. Readings of what I shall define as "femme films," women's pictures that sustain lesbian inference—such as *These Three* (William Wyler, 1936), *The Haunting* (Robert Wise, 1963), *Now, Voyager* (Irving Rapper, 1942), and *All About Eve* (Joseph Manciewicz, 1950)—attempt to trace these contradictions.

The Motion Picture Production Code formalized Hollywood's normative vision by stating what could *not* be stated or shown in the movies, and "sex perversion" was among these prohibitions. Arguably, the Code thus instituted a regime of connotation: If it was intended to help the movies instruct the public in middle-class, even traditionally "female," morals, in the process it taught viewers how to read in *particular* ways. If homosexuality dares not speak its name in the classical cinema, the visual medium allows for other signifying strategies. Chapter 1, "Reading the Code(s)," explores the discursive results of censorship, demonstrating how the representational paradigm of lesbian contagion can be read into Code-era Hollywood films when gender inversion—the other way in which lesbianism was commonly understood in the United States in the 1930s in popular literary and medico-scientific discourses—was not representable.

Textual analysis, and more specifically "reading against the grain," has been a central methodology in ideological studies of Hollywood film. But the conditions of lesbian representability also depend upon the intertextuality of Hollywood films. The studio system worked with a limited number of genres, stars, directors, and other creative personnel, through which patterns of signification were established, and it adapted already familiar source material and exploited its product through a range of promotional discourses. Sometimes homosexual content that was prohibited on-screen was available to audiences through publicity or other intertexts. Reading formations evolve in relation to extra-cinematic practices such as gossip and subcultural codes as well as these intertextual matrices. Chapter 1 looks at the discursive patterns that coexisted historically with the systemic censorship of lesbian themes.

Although it heterosexualizes its heroine, the Greta Garbo vehicle *Queen Christina* (Rouben Mamoulian, 1933) draws upon the paradigm of lesbian masculinity or inversion popularized by sexology and by Radclyffe Hall's novel *The Well of Loneliness*. However well-suited the female invert might be to be a romantic hero and subject of desire, the trope relies upon a visible transgression of gender codes that would not be attempted under Hollywood self-censorship. The film changes the biography of the queen, both in order to make an acceptable vehicle for its valuable star and in illustration of the ambiguity essential to a star persona—for it was Garbo's own mannishness and lesbian style that motivated the selection of the lesbian queen's life as suitable material in the first place. *These Three* (William Wyler, 1936) is also a deliberate heterosexualization of source material—Lillian Hellman's hit Broadway play *The Children's Hour*, which is set in the female institution most prone to "environmental lesbianism," the girls' school. A reading of the censorship files and press coverage around this adaptation shows the struggle to restrict the play of connotation. This was especially difficult since the whispered rumors (which are all the audience really gets of lesbianism in the original text) circulate in similarly unstable fashion in the screen adaptation.

Rather than "reclaiming" *These Three* as a lesbian film despite the distortions of censorship, I am interested in exploring what it meant in terms of lesbian representation that it was heralded by *Variety* as a "femme film." As a woman's picture, the film addressed itself to female audiences and was set in a women's world—here the girls' school, locus classicus of the reproduction of lesbianism. The film supports a hypothesis that the kinds of residual lesbian discourses in Code-era films are influenced by the way cinema was marketed to gender-differentiated audiences. Lesbian identities and styles emerged in relation to a massive deployment of mass culture (including the cinema) to encourage female consumerism and to emphasize women's "to-be-looked-at-ness" (Mulvey, "Visual Pleasure"). How did the woman's picture genre imagine the limits of the female homosociality this implied? Scholarship on the woman's picture has hardly addressed this question. Reconstructing available models of lesbianism through the process of *encoding* delimited by the Production Code gives a historical basis to contemporary lesbian spectatorship—not by arguing for intentionality in representations of the past, but by indicating how mass culture shaped particular conditions of emergence and intelligibility.

Chapter 2, "Lesbian Cinephilia," explores more specifically how spectatorship shapes our desires by looking at how viewers make use of and rejoin past representations to present experience. This chapter expands on the implications of the cinematic institution's display of femininity (especially through the star system) and its address to female fans—but shifts the focus to self-identifed lesbian viewers. Their anecdotal testimony to the subjective importance of particular stars, and what I identify as a new "genre" of lesbian videotapes that appropriates images from classical Hollywood cinema to similar ends, serve as evidence for a theoretical reformulation. Contrary to the idea that "the gaze is male"—one of the most durable tenets of feminist film theory—these accounts and artifacts demonstrate lesbians' visual pleasure—even fetishism—at the movies. Relating my concept of lesbian cinephilia to key texts on spectatorship by Christian Metz and Laura Mulvey, I challenge mimetic models of identification and desire based on "sexual difference" theory. I propose that the theory of fantasy can help us understand how public, social representations intersect with private, subjective positions of desire and identification and that these video works and biographical episodes themselves propose fantasmatic scenarios.

The names of Garbo, Dietrich, Hepburn come up persistently in lesbians' accounts of their favorite stars alongside more contemporary and more idiosyncratic choices. These icons are privileged because of particular aspects of their star images—constructed in part through extraordinary films —but also because discourse about them has contributed to subcultural formation. Contemporary tapes such as *L Is for the Way You Look* (Jean Carlomusto, 1991) and *Freebird* (Suzie Silver, 1993) reproduce their authors' investments in particular stars and images and address their spectators as lesbians. The relationship between fetishism and fantasy, stills and moving images, pictures and stories, is further elaborated through analysis of the video *Meeting of Two Queens* (Cecilia Barriga, 1991) in which Garbo and Dietrich "co-star." I argue that these texts, like stories about spectatorship, build group identifications. The exhibition of such works in the context of lesbian and gay film festivals—which also provide, through retrospective programming, encounters with classical Hollywood as a still living past— makes particularly clear how concrete audiences serve as contexts for such identifications.

The lesbian spectator that these videotapes testify to has been all but invisible in the primary formulations of feminist film theory. But this invisibility has surprising effects; the potential eruption of desire between women haunts psychoanalytic attempts to formulate theories of female spectatorship. The gothic and ghost films considered in Chapter 3, "Female Spectator, Lesbian Specter," give evidence of anxiety about sexual identity—and its familial and domestic "haunts"—that disrupts the visual regime and narrativity itself. The heroine's unacknowledged desire for a dead woman produces scary effects that are unmistakably part of the appeal of the genre to its female audiences. The faulty assumption that the female spectator does not have the ability to invest the look with desire leads to analogous disturbances in feminist theoretical discourse.

Narrativity in a film like *Rebecca* (Alfred Hitchcock, 1940) works to position the heroine (and the spectator who identifies with her) in relationship to a desirable female object. Yet the genre enacts prohibition against their representation *together*, since one of the women is dead. The question of representability is announced in *Rebecca*'s central conceit of an unnamed narrator-heroine and in the influence exerted by the unseen Rebecca over her. The argument of Terry Castle's *The Apparitional Lesbian* that the ghostly is one of the primary tropes of lesbian (in)visibility is supported in American cinema by the intertextual resonance of later films with *Rebecca*'s motifs. In *The Uninvited* (1944) the ghosts are real and in *The Haunting* (1963), there is actually a lesbian character. Yet neither "the haunting" nor homoeroticism is restricted to one character, as the very existence of a genre indicates. Freud's definition of paranoia as a defense against homosexuality may account not only for the heroines' desire, but for the theoretical erasure of lesbian spectatorship in certain formative theoretical texts.

Genre provides the viewer with a set of expectations, it allows the studio to take shortcuts, it offers variations on a fantasmatic script. Another sub-genre of the woman's picture, the maternal melodrama, casts the relationship between women not in the mode of absence but in terms of a very definite presence—a maternal figure—although this presence may nevertheless involve disguise. Ever popular, the maternal melodrama constructs bizarre female-centered domestic arrangements that are heavily invested with affect—between women on-screen, between screen and audience, between critics and the films. Contrary to readings that stress the sincerity and transparency of such films, Chapter 4, "Films for Girls: Lesbian Sentiment and the Maternal Melodrama," revels in their baroque opacity. Like the iconic status of the stars discussed in Chapter 2, the centrality of the mother here foregrounds the cinema's appeal to a female spectator through a female image. Drawing on the psychoanalytic theory that these films cry out for, I argue that while their thematics are undeniably oedipal, through triangulation among women they play out a struggle to have or be something else besides a mother. Maternal melodramas thus afford a fascinating "cover" for representations of lesbian difference and desire.

A cycle of Bette Davis melodramas including *Now, Voyager* (1942) presents a common scenario of intergenerational education. I relate the variations of the films to the education and differentiation of the female viewer by the genre itself. The quintessential heroine of women's fiction—the governess—is the metaphorical and sometimes literal central figure of this "generic fantasy." The governess represents "something else besides a mother" for the girl; she also forms an interesting couple with the mother. Women's pictures do not interpellate every female spectator, let alone every lesbian, but their radical revision of the patriarchal family, the romantic couple, and female destiny in the personae of their central female stars extend an invitation to fantasy.

The inheritance of mid-century Hollywood films from nineteenth-century paradigms of women's culture and relationality represents an articulation of new identities with older forms of female homosociality. Lesbianism is both enabled and contained by the familial and sentimental models—much as definitions of lesbianism are contained within reference to the maternal in traditional psychoanalytic and even in contemporary feminist accounts. By addressing an important category of the femme film, this chapter elaborates the relationship of female homosociality to lesbianism within queer theory; it also questions the tendency in straight feminist theory to defuse lesbianism by using it as a metaphor for female bonding.

The female world of the melodrama is overpopulated by pleasurable clichés. Chapter 5, "Supporting 'Character'," considers our enjoyment of the formulaic quality of Hollywood narratives by focusing on the types of women who populate the margins of the movies, women who are defined over and against the leading lady. Such "asexual" characters are as close as Hollywood gets to indicating "deviant" gender presentations and the sexual identities they sometimes imply. Such characters help us distinguish theoretically and practically between *women* and "Woman," a diacritical operation essential to locating lesbian subjectivity (see de Lauretis, *Alice Doesn't*). Supporting characters also encode class, body type, age, ethnic, and racial differences often minimized in classical Hollywood; often the tensions of these social differences are displaced to sexual contrasts. I discuss several figures whose specialization in particular types resulted in an oppositional coherence, reading their films together with other discourses that shaped their personae, including gossip about their affective and sexual preferences.

Agnes Moorehead, my central example, who specialized in the spinster aunt/shrew, performed with an extravagant theatricality across several distinct mass culture media: radio, film, and television, and over several decades. Two other performers' careers allow me to touch briefly on types less well represented in the rest of this study. Beginning in the late 1940s,

Mercedes McCambridge played bullies, often murderous ones; she was an effective Hollywood "butch." The violence that characterized her is associated with post-war misogyny and an iconography of sexual minorities, which McCambridge performed with panache. Ethel Waters's great screen performances came late in her breakthrough career as an African American singer and actress. While her roles restricted her to a "mammy" type—albeit partaking of a new post-war "liberal" discourse—her star persona revised this type. Her relationships with white women enacted particular racialized sexual logics. Waters was read through her reputation as a singer; audiences had varying degrees of access to the specificity of sexual discourses that constructed that reputation.

In the course of Hollywood's routine translation of social relations into personal relationships, romance and sexual tension become the bearers of other kinds of difference. If Hollywood is a family romance, there are many skeletons in the closet. Tracing "types" of female difference gives evidence of historical changes in the boundaries of hegemonic femininity. In spectatorial engagement with these figures, visual codes dominate narrative significance, sometimes subverting Hollywood realism. The characteristic two-shot that pairs a star with a supporting actress marks the diversity within the category of "woman" and provides an oblique angle of desire on the image of femininity the star represents. The ubiquitousness of the "dykey" supporting actress figure is a testament to lesbian presence in classical Hollywood—she's a ghost in the machine.

Chapter 6, "On Retrospectatorship," returns to the question of how the movies have made the subject position from which I'm reading them today possible. Building on my argument that genres and stars function fantasmatically, both subjectively and culturally, I begin with two texts by gay men that show how the female star becomes inscribed in the fantasy life of a spectator. Next I read *All About Eve* as an allegory of lesbian spectatorship. The structure of repetition and regress that the film sets up (Margo Channing must step aside for her biggest fan Eve, who is vulnerable to the machinations of her fan club president Phoebe) figures the retrospective construction of lesbian difference through our encounters with the products of an industry and a historical formation that privileged a sexualized image of woman (the star) and endowed her with significant cultural authority. While the film is not so utopian as to suggest that the star and the fan could form a couple, it makes a lesbian subject visible. Eve is more successful in breaking into the scene of her desire than was Frankie in *The Member of the Wedding*. I use the idea of "retrospectatorship" to diagnose a nostalgic impulse in spectatorship theory; to name my own use of classical film history; and to describe the irreducible play of past and present, the joining of audiences and artifacts, in the subjective and (sub)cultural experience of viewing and writing about films.

Like the concept of the uncanny in Freud's analysis—when we somehow feel we recognize what's unfamiliar—uninvited meanings reside within the ambivalent relationship of cinematic femininity and lesbian desire. Visual representations of lesbianism in classical U.S. cinema were censored, not extended the protections of freedom of speech. A seemingly inverse process of censorship is at work in the Freudian definition of the dreamwork. By the term "considerations of representability" Freud named a "requirement imposed on the dream-thoughts" by the censoring agent whereby even the most abstract words and concepts are transformed to "make them capable of being represented by . . . visual images" (Laplanche and Pontalis, *Language of Psycho-Analysis* 389). Despite the efforts of industry censors, in the visual language of cinema, lesbianism makes a dreamlike, uncanny appearance. In my title *Uninvited* I invoke the unauthorized reading practices of invisible guests as well as a number of figures—the ghost, the governess, the supporting character, the fan—who meet the considerations of lesbian representability in the Hollywood woman's picture. I hope to show that such inferences and coded figures are uninvited not because they are forbidden entry but because they are already at home.

When Joseph Breen of the Production Code Administration scrutinized the script of *The Member of the Wedding*, he cautioned that "the interruption of the wedding sequence should be handled with care and restraint so as not to be too broad."[5] I turn in the next chapter to what the industry censors might have understood of the significance of such an interruption.

unInvited

The Lesbian said about it, the better.
—HEYWOOD BROUN

1

Reading the Code(s)

A project addressing lesbianism and the classical Hollywood cinema imme-diately confronts a paradox. "Sex perversion or any inference to it is forbid-den," stated the Motion Picture Production Code, which by studio consen-sus governed Hollywood film production from 1930 through 1968.[1] Thus during an intensive period of the shaping of the modern lesbian social subject, homosexuality was not denoted on the nation's film screens. It is this legacy of absence that this study's focus on spectatorship and representability (rather than representation) addresses. Even the play of connotation was forbidden by the Code; the awkward formulation ("inference to," rather than "reference to" or "implication of") implies an attempt to legislate the *viewer's* potential impression of homoerotic content. Yet Freud and Fou-cault, in their own epistemologies of sexuality, have taught us that what is actively prohibited can nevertheless be inferred from its discursive effects. I argue that the Code's very prohibition of certain subjects generates visual and narrative codes that structure spectatorial "inference" about the exis-tence and force and significance of desire between women, in the movies and in the social formation. To understand how this works, we must consider the overdetermined relationship between representations of the female body and connotations of sexuality in our culture, as well as the ways Hollywood endeavored to address female audiences—in effect making a place for women as "dreamers" in film texts. In other words, we must understand the gendered and engendering implications of censorship practices.

Close textual readings and intertextual reconstructions allow us, much

1

like Freud's interpreter of dreams, to reconstruct social "dream thoughts" behind the cinema's "dream language" of pictures and sounds, despite the actions of the very real censor that governed the content of films. The industry's censorship administration recommended conventions that favored certain kinds of resolution, demanded involved negotiation over the letter and spirit of the Code, and even suggested ways to get around the Code's provisions. These processes of encoding can be reconstructed to reveal occluded possibilities that underlie the politically and libidinally invested process of decoding.[2]

Although the moments of encoding and decoding are historically disjunct, contemporary strategies of reading the traces of lesbianism in Code-era Hollywood films can help revise understandings of the historical implications of the "exclusion" of homosexuality from U.S. cinema to formulate the relationship between reading against the grain and the history of sexuality.[3] The language of exclusion tends to imply that there was some kind of clear-cut, historically stable "lesbian" content that existed elsewhere—in subcultures, in concrete individuals—and to adhere to a "repressive hypothesis" about movie censorship. I argue that the cinema as an institution did indeed contribute to the social construction of what we recognize today as lesbian identity—and not only through negative actions that made lesbianism invisible, abject, or pathological. Instead, the construction of lesbianism occurred primarily within, rather than despite, the movies' highly *visible* and regulated constructions of femininity, and through their appeal to female audiences. Hollywood's conscious, varied, and inventive attempts to represent and appeal to female subjectivity and desire, particularly through the production of "women's pictures" and through their ancillary promotional discourses, inevitably introduced the potential for lesbian inference. The world of women that was constructed on the screen and in the movie theater and in fan magazines may not have admitted the female homosexuality that was increasingly regulated in homosocial institutions such as girls' schools and women's colleges, but the cinema was an institution that "educated" far more girls. Censorship worked with other discourses, including the consumerist, romantic, and domestic discourses of a feminized mass culture, to define lesbianism even as it sought to repress its representation. In this chapter, films with intertextual lesbian significance (such as those adapted from literary sources depicting female homosexuality) will be addressed to see how censorship affected their textuality and their reception at the time. Reconstructing the conditions of lesbian representability in several films from the 1930s (as Hollywood stabilized in the years after the coming of sound and the institutionalization of self-censorship) will help to formulate a concept of genre rather than image as central to lesbian represent-ability and provide a matrix for interpreting the classical-era representations that are addressed in subsequent chapters.

Hollywood studio product was the nation's most significant mass cul-tural discourse for the first half of this century; at the height of Hollywood's cultural hegemony in 1946, ninety million Americans attended the movies weekly. Because women were considered a crucial part of motion picture audiences from the beginnings of the industry—according to *Motion Pic-ture World* women formed 83 percent of movie audiences in 1927 (Koszarski 30)—specific film genres and stars were constructed for and addressed to women, and to what were presumed to be women's interests.[4] To condense the scholarly work on this important topic: this appeal was an ideological operation that worked to maximize profit and to define and maintain par-ticular women's roles as consumers, sexualized spectacles, and domestic subjects within a patriarchal, white-dominant, culturally imperialist nation. The moralist, nationalist, and normative provisions of the Production Code make this ideology quite explicit.[5] At the same time, the address to female audience members was accomplished despite codes of cinematic narration and vision that centered a controlling male subjectivity, gaze, and agency and strictly circumscribed women's sphere.[6] But as Richard Dyer stresses in *Only Entertainment*, formulating a position common to many cultural crit-ics, mass culture must address real wishes and desires, real contradictions, even if the solutions it offers are individualized or ineffable or commercial —this is its utopian dimension. Definitions of femininity, agency, subjectiv-ity, homosociality, and homosexuality and their American cultural forms were contradictory, and the cinema fashioned its visceral appeal on this basis.

For feminist cultural critics, mass culture represents a realm in which women, denied political power, have a paradoxical public presence and voice. In *Babel and Babylon*, her study of silent cinema spectatorship, Miriam Hansen has proposed that cinema potentially offered an alternative public sphere for women—especially immigrant women—as it foreground-ed clashes among discourses and roles: "The styles of a heterosocial moder-nity promoted with the new leisure culture changed the definitions of female identity in relation to the family, superimposing the values of moth-erhood and domesticity with the appeals of pleasure, glamour, and eroti-cism" (117). The same social forces that put Hollywood's regime of censor-ship by self-regulation into place at the end of the silent era continued to shape attempts to reach and fashion female viewers with a gendered con-sumerist appeal. Hansen posits that the stabilization of classical-era cinema, with its address to a unified (male) subject, reduced and managed this heterogeneity. Arguably, however, the sphere of cinema consumption remained contestatory, and modernity's range of new identities and new modes of sexual expression, including homosexuality, could not be reversed by the cinema's consolidation of middle-class, middle-American domestic ideology in the classical period.

Usually, feminist claims about the utopian elements of mass culture's appeal to women remain attached to a profile of the female audience member that is presumptively heterosexual, signaled by gender conformity, familial role, the ability to purchase goods and services, and access to public leisure forms. Popular culture is said to foreground contradictions in her life by speaking to her "desire," but that desire is left curiously uninterrogated. By focusing on immigrant women Hansen specifies this generic female viewer, and by highlighting the transition from homosocial to heterosocial leisure activity she foregrounds the *construction* of heterosexuality through practices of mass culture consumption.[7] Although lesbian identities and desires are often at odds with the gendered roles and structures reinforced by mass culture's representations and institutions, even non–gender normative (butch) identities are nevertheless constructed within them. If this is true for individuals (as the example of viewing *The Member of the Wedding* illustrated), it is also arguable historically that shifts in social forms of leisure contribute to new public identities and eventually—while it must remain speculative here—to new social movements based on those identities. I believe that female homoeroticism is one of the contradictions that mass culture speaks to through its glamorous and charismatic female stars and the seductive women's world of the women's picture.[8] While occasionally feminist film scholars such as Jackie Stacey have acknowledged homosexual "components" of female spectatorship, the field has neglected the social dimension of the institutionalization of female spectatorship and its potential coincidence with lesbianism as an emerging cultural identity. In one of the first feminist analyses of "images of women," Molly Haskell demanded: "What more damning comment on the relations between men and women in America than the very notion of something called the 'woman's film'?" (153). From a less heteronormative position, Haskell's is an important insight. But queer cultural studies, vigilant about rejecting the desexualization that presumably shapes woman-identified realms as distinct as nineteenth-century romantic friendship and the second-wave feminism of the 1970s, has also largely overlooked women's culture in its mass mediated forms as a determinant of lesbian identity (though it has attended to the consumer pleasures of specific fandoms, for example). We must look beyond the patriarchal and heteronormative context in which the "separate sphere" of mass-mediated women's entertainment arose to locate a site of rich public and private experiences that have shaped our gendered definitions of homosexuality.

In 1930, one 19-year-old subject of the Payne Fund studies researching the social influence of motion pictures described her fondness for pictures set in women's colleges: "From them I gained an enthusiasm to come to college. . . . I have dreamed of going to war. . . . The excitement—shall I say glamour?—of the war has always appealed to me from the screen. Often I have pictured myself as a truck driver, nurse, HEROINE!" (Blumer 63). How might lesbian identities have evolved historically in relation to gendered consumerist discourses generally and in relation to fantasy consumption in the form of images and stories offered by the movies in particular? The cinema fostered new kinds of homosociality within the heterosocial sphere of commercialized leisure, and they are infused with homoerotic impulses. Another respondent—a 16-year-old white high-school junior— testified: "I have one girl friend that I love a good deal. She and I have been kissing each other 'hello' and 'good-by' for some time. It is on her that I make use of the different ways of kissing that I see in the movies" (45). Certainly the highly codified forms of film entertainment offered to women work to patrol the boundaries between heterosexual and deviant femininities by evoking homoerotic desires that can be channeled to consumption (of fashion, makeup, movie magazines, etc.). What is properly called lesbian spectatorship evolved in conjunction with lesbian social identities. Yet as Charles Eckert implies in a study of the dreamlike incorporation of commodity tie-ins in 1930s cinema, the movies' mise-en-scène of femininity and consumer culture remained dynamic and excessive. For the designers and merchandisers, he writes: "Out there, working as a clerk in a store and living in an apartment with a friend, was *one girl*—single, nineteen years old, Anglo-Saxon, somewhat favoring Janet Gaynor" (105). Cultural studies that champion spectatorial practices need to be more attentive to the differences within the female audiences whose contradictory needs and dissatisfactions are addressed through mass cultural narratives, both in order to understand the homoerotic expression allowed to historical female spectators and to delimit the conditions against which lesbian positions were formulated. After all, even Janet Gaynor was subject to the Hollywood rumor that her marriage to costume designer Adrian was a "Twilight Tandem, lavender cover-up" (Anger 171).

Enough women fashioned lesbian identities from the shifting social and cultural possibilities of the era that by the 1930s recognizable lesbian types

5

were depicted in popular medical and scientific discourses and in fiction and theater. The movies hinted at similar constructions that censorship both prohibited and structured in new ways. If the leisure culture of modernity replaced "separate spheres" with heterosociality and shifted definitions of public and private, both social systems were structured by binary conceptions of gender. Hence homosexualities formed in relation to mass culture (and its intensive construction of femininity as image) are also highly *gendered*. Today, at the end of cinema's first century, "lesbian" is an intelligible social identity, visible on the nation's television and movie screens. This visibility did not simply appear as a new historical phenomenon, dependent on second-wave feminism and the post-Stonewall gay rights movements as a decisive break with the past. Rather these movements catalyzed subjects whose social visibility was formed in relation to mass culture's politics of the visible, to the movies' contestations of heterosexuality and homosociality and their contradictory structures of address.

The readings of films, stars, and genres in this book take full advantage of our historical displacement from the moment of the encoding of these films, drawing on our contemporary experience of lesbian identity, desire, and self-representation. If we are to locate such signifying strategies in cinema's historical role in the construction of sexuality in the United States, we must reconstruct the gender and erotic discourses and prohibitions that were operative at the time. While the idea of reading against the grain has become a commonplace in film studies, symptomatic readings have only recently been allied with an attempt to historicize the place of the movies in the history of sexuality in the United States. Homosexuality can now be recognized as a "structuring absence" in the decoding of classical Hollywood texts (as the critics of *Cahiers du cinéma* considered the class struggle to be in their textual readings of the early 1970s).[9] While I would argue that any social history must work with an explicit theory of representation and some concept of textuality, it is almost impossible not to use this methodology in lesbian/gay history; the difficulties of working with an archive that isn't there have been theorized by scholars engaged in that project (see Terry's "Theorizing Deviant Historiography"). A study such as this one attends to the rhetoric and textuality of films and to intertextual and extra-cinematic discourses in order to establish the mutual imbrication of historical lesbian identities and the cinema. I suggest that same-sex female desire is central to how the movies work institutionally and historically despite the absences and erasures mandated by the Production Code. (In the next chapter I look more closely at the movies' psychic centrality in personal history.)

Acknowledging that the historical emergence of homosexual identity was made possible by some of the same forces that shaped American cinema (urbanization, routinization of work, and commercialization of leisure) does not in itself suggest a method for locating the traces of that existence in the cinema. Paradoxically, censorship is one site of the inscription of social formations of sexuality in particular texts; this chapter looks at where semiotic codes and the Production Code intersect. Industry self-regulation as conducted through the Production Code Administration (PCA) after 1934 was the product of multiple institutional and social forces. It was undertaken through close scrutiny of the letter and spirit of the Code and of every film considered for U.S. and international release—interpretations were contested and meanings negotiated. Understanding the role of censorship practices in constructing the meanings of lesbianism requires decoding strategies—the emphasis of this book—as well as historical contextualization. I turn now to a brief consideration of the methodological usefulness of Freud's and Foucault's work on the productive aspects of censorship in sexuality for a consideration of the Production Code's prohibition of "sex perversion or any inference to it."

In *The Interpretation of Dreams,* one of the most important twentieth-century works on hermeneutics, a book written at the dawn of cinema's era, Freud contends that in order to evade the dream censor and represent the fulfillment of a wish in dream content, dream-thoughts must meet certain "considerations of representability" (*Rücksicht auf Darstellbarkeit*). This aspect of the dreamwork entails turning abstract ideas into picture form: "A dream-thought is unusable so long as it is expressed in an abstract form; but when once it has been transformed into pictorial language, contrasts and identifications of the kind which the dream-work requires, and which it creates if they are not already present, can be established more easily than before between the new form of expression and the remainder of the material underlying the dream" (375). Historically, motion pictures were not afforded the protections of freedom of *speech*; they were deemed a business pure and simple and thus as open to censorship as the ideas that seek expression in a dream. But the dreamwork's particular property of evading censorship by relying on images rather than language is an apt image for desires prohibited from narrative codification or verbal acknowledgment in the movies. Certainly the cinema has often enough been compared to a dream.[10] Although one must certainly question the extent to which a *viewer's* wish can find fulfillment in an industrial product like a movie—dreamed up by someone not herself—and although it might be somewhat reductive to suggest that lesbianism is part of a social "unconscious" that evades the censors to find representation in cinema, it does seem that female same-sex desire frequently meets imagistic "considerations of representability" in classical cinema. Freud's phrase and his description of the dreamwork provide a suggestive analogy for how what is prohibited by the Code or ideologically excluded from dominant representation, what is unnamed, may nevertheless signify on screen. And Freud's model of interpretation suggests that we follow the paths of association laid down by the dream elements to reconstruct how particular representations came to condense and distort aspects of experience and of psychic longing.

In volume 1 of *The History of Sexuality*, Foucault traces how prohibition generates discursive effects. His account of censorship as *productive* of knowledge and of sexuality as an object of knowledge, like Freud's notion of the dreamwork, has quite precise application to the regulation practices of studio-era cinema. In fact, even motion picture industry practitioners recognized censorship as a set of codes for producing meaning, and particularly sexual meaning, and indeed for producing readings. As director of the Studio Relations Committee, the body that preceded the Production Code Administration in coordinating between the studios and the Motion Picture Producers and Distributors Association (MPPDA)'s standards, Colonel Jason S. Joy saw his work as establishing conventions "from which conclusions might be drawn by the sophisticated mind, but which would mean nothing to the unsophisticated and inexperienced" (quoted in Maltby, "The Production Code" 40).

As Richard Maltby documents in an account of the problem of literary adaptation for the movies, contemporary commentators on censorship also recognized that the Code encouraged, rather than denied, inference. In 1930, the *Nation* editorialized:

> The suggestion of everything which [MPPDA director Will Hays] has attempted to suppress has diffused itself through every scene, and the mind of the audience is encouraged to play about every idea that cannot be stated. (quoted in Maltby, "'To Prevent'" 116)

Foucault's concept of the "perverse implantation" effected by the proliferation of regulatory discourse on sex would seem to describe what the *Nation* saw happening under the PCA. "Sex perversion" is at once everywhere and nowhere in the movies. If the Code went so far as to prohibit inference in this case, it is because "sex perversion" is associated with a kind of representational contagion.[11]

Under Foucault's model we might expect to "find" lesbianism in the movies despite, or rather because of, its exclusion. But we are even left to *infer* that lesbianism is included under the rubric of "sex perversion," and therefore excluded from Hollywood films, because the varieties of prohibition are not enumerated in the Code. (The "unspeakable" nature of sexual perversion allows us to infer that it is not only homosexuality, but fetishism, sadomasochism, bestiality, pedophilia, etc. that this "particular application" of the Code forbids.)[12] However, the undifferentiated designation "sex perversion" has very differential gendered specifications; the generic "sex pervert" is male. This raises a central epistemological question of this study, and of lesbian theory more generally: To what extent is lesbianism subsumed under male definitions of sexuality? Lesbianism remains unnamed and invisible in the Code, as it often does when allied with male homosexuality (Foucault's pervert certainly reads as male), because sexuality is separated from gender in a manner that makes masculinity the unspoken standard.

At the same time, the fact that lesbianism remains unnamed suggests that it cannot be localized and thus contained within the designation "sex perversion." Even if this covers both a "minoritized" identity and a "universalized" type of act, to use Eve Sedgwick's categories for how sexual identity is discursively configured, the common representations of these identities and these acts are both male. As Judith Roof (among others) has argued, the relationship of lesbianism to agency and to representation—indeed its epistemological status in discourses of sexual definition (those generated by queer theory as much as those that queer theory interrogates)—is unstable. If lesbianism appears as something other than "sex perversion," and sex perversion does not necessarily encompass lesbianism, what considerations of representability must it meet in classical cinema? In addressing this question, what consideration must be given to the hypervisibility of women in classical cinema and to its characteristic representations of femininity? Analysis along the axis of gender is necessary.

The two "lesbian" films that bookended the dates of the Production Code Administration's reign—*Queen Christina* (Rouben Mamoulian, 1933) and *The Killing of Sister George* (Robert Aldrich, 1968)—both evoke definitions of lesbianism as gender inversion (and thus as *visible* difference) that would largely disappear from Hollywood film during the intervening period. While these films can help us to understand what the Code regulated, they are not evidence of some lesbian reality that existed "outside" censored Hollywood but are themselves very mediated representations whose censorship negotiations indicated what modes of lesbian representation the Code favored. The first film stands—with Marlene Dietrich and Katharine Hepburn's drag acts in their early 1930s films (discussed in more detail in

9

Chapter 2), as a source of *iconic* representation—a dream image of an imagined lesbian past. The gothic trappings of *The Killing of Sister George* have enhanced its status in debates over "negative" lesbian representations. While later in this chapter I am going to classify Code-era representations of lesbianism as "femme films," I'm not suggesting that the movies simply repressed "butchness" and compromised with more palatable representations of female-identified lesbianism, representations that could "pass." Certainly *Queen Christina*, by generic definition and in its visualizations of the body of the female star, is a femme film.

On December 28, 1933, MGM's Garbo vehicle *Queen Christina*, a biopic on the seventeenth-century lesbian Swedish monarch, opened in New York, to the annoyance of newly appointed Code overseer Joseph I. Breen, who had rejected the film. Breen had warned Louis B. Mayer that the film was in "definite violation of the Code."[13] On January 11, 1934, a jury of studio executives voted unanimously to approve the film over Breen's objection. This was not exactly a victory for freedom of sapphic expression, however. Although in this case the producers exercised dissent within their own self-regulatory body, their action clearly still served the interests of the industry, guaranteeing the release of an expensive production. In March 1934 the Production Code Administration was officially set up under Breen and the window of negotiation that had existed in the few years since the adoption of the Code in 1930 was closed; notably, the provision for an override of an MPPDA (known as the Hays Office after its director since 1922, Will Hays) decision by "Hollywood Jury" was eliminated and a new chapter in industry self-regulation began. Although *Queen Christina* in part provoked this particular reform, the film was not understood as particularly scandalous. There had been only the mildest comment from the censoring body on lesbian "inferences." The Queen's declaration that she had no intention of dying an old maid—"I shall die a bachelor!"—was deemed overly suggestive. The heterosexual love plot prevailed in the censors' reception of the script, and its indiscretions were targeted, despite the fact that the film mobilized everything about Garbo's already highly codified persona that connoted gender inversion. Although we might speculate that the Queen's delicious butch-femme kiss with her lady-in-waiting (and historical inamorata) Countess Ebba Sparre (Elizabeth Young) might have been eliminated had it been the Hays Office rather than the Hollywood Jury that gave it final approval, the film's "controversy" was not named at the time as having to do with lesbian content. *Queen Christina* was a phenomenal success.

The detailing of "sex perversion" does not seem to have been an especially pronounced preoccupation of the Code's drafters, although provisions about sexuality in general were. The term was carried over into the Code drafted by Father Lord from Will Hays's earlier list of "Don'ts and Be Carefuls," which he had culled from state and local censor boards. Censorship and moral campaigns and a patchwork of review processes had surrounded the movies since the days of the nickelodeon theaters in the century's first decades, and at the time the adoption of the Code as a mechanism of industry self-regulation, there was considerable risk that federal regulation would be imposed. This is not the place to attempt a full accounting of the events surrounding the beginning of the PCA. Briefly put: enforcement of the Code's provisions came about only after a widely publicized campaign by the Catholic Legion of Decency. Catholic alliances with WASP middle America at this moment, according to commentators such as Maltby and Black, were a power move against the Jewish moguls who led the Hollywood oligopoly and against the urban definition of early cinema. These campaigns also effectively mobilized women and the rhetoric of maternalism—especially pronounced in the WCTU's campaign of "mothering the movies"—had a large voice in reform movements of the period; such moral values would inform the centrality of domestic ideology to Hollywood film (see Parker). Amid this political and ideological jockeying, there is no evidence that lesbianism was a flash point for the advocates of censorship, although female sexual expression more generally, most notoriously in the persona of Mae West, certainly was, as Mary Beth Hamilton and Ramona Curry have detailed. And as the very important 1927 raid on "indecent" Broadway shows (which included not only West's *Sex* but also the English-language production of Edouard Bourdet's *The Captive*) demonstrated, lesbianism could indeed be regulated under "sex perversion" clauses and mobilize the zeal of censors against "dangerous" female sexuality. Lesbianism did become an important negotiating point in the revision of the Code in the early 1960s, when "tasteful" depictions of sexual aberrations—notably *The Children's Hour*—were permitted for PCA consideration (see note 1).

Although *Queen Christina* remains unique in Hollywood film history for the degree to which it "embodied" a sexological and subcultural persona—the invert—censors appear to have ignored its lesbian "inferences," perhaps because the star/fan "understanding" that the inferences exploited was extremely profitable. The film's seventeenth-century heroine is in fact a twentieth-century new woman. At the other end of the Code's time span, however, lesbianism was met with distaste. When in 1968 the PCA was finally reconfigured as the Code and Ratings Administration, giving us the

11

ratings still in use with some modification today, Aldrich's film adaptation of Frank Marcus's play *The Killing of Sister George* received the first X rating given to a "respectable" production. This time the controversy was clearly about lesbianism: Aldrich was told that even the removal of the sex scene (in which Coral Browne approaches Susannah Yorke's left breast "like an ichthyologist finding something that has drifted up on the beach," in Renata Adler's vivid *New York Times* description) would not have changed the determination (Leff 273). The rating "allowed" the film to be released in the United States, but effectively prevented it from being seen because major newspapers would not carry advertising for an X-rated film. The film flopped; its depiction of lesbianism was received—overdetermined—as "sex perversion." At the end of the film, Sister George, its stigmatized butch figure, has lost her lover and her job; if when she begins to moo on an empty TV set (practicing for her next role as a cow on a children's show) she lacks the grace of the solitary Queen Christina sailing into the void, both seem to echo Stephen Gordon's anguished cry on behalf of inverts at the end of *The Well of Loneliness.*

I cite *Queen Christina* and *Sister George* not as solitary examples (though they are examples of lesbian solitude) nor as evidence of a flourishing lesbian "presence" in the 1920s and on the eve of Stonewall that was suppressed under the Code during the intervening years, because the films demonstrate that censorship works through multiple channels and codes. Still less are they examples of some kind of butch authenticity that gave way to a duplicitous "femme" model of representability; both represent a tension between lesbianism as a "type of person" and lesbianism as a potentiality of genre. They are tangible examples of negotiation around particular aspects of lesbian representability—cross-dressing and historical and biographical erasure in the case of *Queen Christina* and butch-femme styles and sex itself in the case of Sister George—that the Code constrained in its own way. The "victory" of *The Killing of Sister George* over the Code's reign was not the product of a liberal drive to show what was missing; rather the adoption of the ratings system was only one marker of a irreversible fragmentation of the film market at the end of the studio era that permitted address to "mature" audiences. No longer was there a "general" audience to which films such as MGM's *Queen Christina* could address itself. It is within this generalized address that specific films of the classical era made a specific pitch to historically emergent lesbian identities.

The PCA's crackdown on "sex pictures" in the beginning of the 1930s reflected a wider cultural conservatism that accompanied economic depression, but it was also a strategy to construct a mass audience (it was not so much that the "minority" was excluded, but that it was incorporated, transformed). Mass culture effects not only the formation of national identity and the consolidation of heterosexual hegemony, but it also gives ambiguous or contested representations their widest audiences. The female homoeroticism that *Queen Christina* managed to incorporate by virtue of its genre, star, and production values continued to function throughout studio-era popular cinema in general. Part of the project of this book is to suggest the historical contours and codes of an absence of denotation.

Femme Films

As Andrea Weiss has noted in a survey of the small number of lesbian representations in U.S. and European films of the 1930s, "images of cross-dressing and gender inversion on the one hand . . . and a feminine-identification involving a female object choice, on the other, were concurrent images in the cinema, and the former never entirely gave way to the latter" (17). The "invert" who fits into a clear sexual typology and the female environment in which lesbianism spreads correspond with the major and sometimes conflicting paradigms of female homosexuality in medical, psychological, and cultural discourses of the period.[14] *Queen Christina* is a unique example of the former in classical Hollywood cinema; but I want to suggest that it is also consistent with the latter. It is characteristic of the movies made during the heyday of the studio period to encourage female object choice in women and men of whatever gender identification.

Queen Christina in essence tells the same story as Radclyffe Hall's *The Well of Loneliness*—with the crucial exception that Queen Christina doesn't declare herself an invert! (And regrettably the film doesn't depict its heroine's exploits after she arrives in Paris as did Hall's novel.) Both heroines are raised as boys amid wealth and social prominence and dogs, horses, and books; they experience strong identifications with dead fathers and are fastidious about the men's clothing they favor. After they are jilted by their first female lovers, the two protagonists find great love, which causes them to be exiled from their birthright. They each end up as solitary expatriates who strongly resemble Christian martyrs. There are scenes of late-night reading in each: Stephen Gordon pores over the nineteenth-century sexologist Krafft-Ebing and Queen Christina laughs aloud at Molière's anti-marriage jokes. I would go so far as to compare two extraordinary episodes of intense autoeroticism before the mirror. The sequence in which Stephen confronts her body "so strong, so white, so self-sufficient" in the mirror (*Well* 186–87), which Teresa de Lauretis analyzes in *The Practice of Love* (209–

13) as a fantasy of castration, contrasts with Garbo's gaze into the mirror after her famous caressing of the furniture at the inn. "This is how the Lord must have felt when he beheld the world he had created," Garbo declares, a line that was of great concern to the Hays Office. Christina's declaration of self-knowledge—by virtue of its heterosexual post-coital mise-en-scène, is of course the more acceptable. Hall's novel was a bestseller in 1929; there is strong evidence for reading *Queen Christina*, made four years later, as the closest thing yet to a film version of what remains the quintessential lesbian novel.

But as I noted, Garbo was not pegged by industry censors as a congenital invert. In her Adrian-designed courtier clothes, she looks today the very dream of the "mythic mannish lesbian," whom Esther Newton describes as a figure who allows the lesbian to become visible as a sexual agent.[15] The censors' main objection to gender play in *Queen Christina* lay in the valet's reaction to finding the Spanish ambassador and the young "nobleman" (Garbo in drag) behind drawn bed curtains. But in the intimation of male homosexual activity, no one had forgotten that this was Garbo. She thus "reads" as safely (if illicitly) heterosexual with the ambassador *and* as unmistakably butch. In allowing the transgression, the industry seemed to acknowledge how "right" it was for Garbo. Drag appears to be a guise in which her female fans could adore her anew. *Queen Christina* is a star vehicle, a costume drama—a woman's picture.[16] It was within a feminized genre that the lesbian paradigm ostensibly most distant from a "female identification" model—the paradigm of the "heroic invert"—could make it to the Main Street screen.

In *The Epistemology of the Closet*, Eve Sedgwick usefully delineates two competing models of homosexual definition. One would join male and female "sex perverts" in a "gender-integrative" manner (2); the other "gender-separatist" model would align homosexuality with homosociality. While the former would seem to be acknowledged in cinematic discourse by the Code's prohibition of "sex perversion," the question of inference, markedly difficult to forbid, favors a gender-separatist definition of lesbianism—a definition in relation to femininity and female homosocial forms. Not only was this paradigm operative in Code-era Hollywood cinema, but the movies have also discursively shaped this definition of lesbianism in ways that have not yet been accounted for. Lesbian visibility is veiled in the feminine display that is the cinema's primary dream language rather than embodied in the cross-gender identifications offered by the invert or the butch (which is not to say that the latter is not an available *spectatorial* identification). Within specific practices of promotion and consumption, and the debates on good taste and domestic (feminine) values that underpin censorship practices, what I am calling a "femme" paradigm of homoerotic representation developed. The films discussed throughout *Uninvited* are "femme films."

My use of the term femme without its conventional companion butch is meant to function in several ways. It carries the conventional queer meaning of a lesbian position defined in terms of feminine gender construction—but is not derived from or dependent upon the term butch or a butch presence. It approximates Weiss's "feminine-identification involving a female object choice" paradigm and encompasses several configurations of lesbianism related to women's culture: the nineteenth-century "female world of love and ritual"; all-female institutions such as colleges and convents and other sites where the proximity of women is cause for social concern; and the domestic and familial sphere. Unlike the gender inversion, gender-integrative paradigm, the femme paradigm covers the world of the women's picture: institutions such as schools and prisons and hotels for women, but also the home—and the world of movie consumption and fandom. My perspective dissociates these sites and practices from an exclusive and exclusionary association with heterosexual femininity.

The term femme is also borrowed from the language of the trade press. *Rebecca* was touted as a "brilliant picture with special appeal to femmes." *Variety* found the term a handy noun-adjective for the not much longer words "woman," "women," "female": describing, for example, *The Old Maid* as "heavy femme fare," *Mildred Pierce* as "Boff lure for femme trade," Dorothy Arzner as a "femme helmer," or the inmates of *Caged* as "the femme cast, completely deglamorized."[17] The term thus has a complicated relation to historical usage that corresponds with the model of "retrospectatorship" with which this book is concerned. To bring out the queer connotations in the usage—and in women's films—may appear a somewhat presentist gesture. Reading back is inevitably reading into. But although I don't think that all women's pictures can be converted to lesbian meanings by today's readers, I do believe that lesbianism was a horizon of experience shaping film reception for some spectators and the production of some films of the genre during the period. I wish to evoke a structure of feeling that corresponds to a generic *possibility*. The tension between lesbian femme and femininity *tout court* that is captured in the term works in two ways. Female homosocial forms work to fortify the divide between straight women and lesbians and to exclude lesbian difference; in this sense Hollywood never made lesbian films. Yet homosexuality is engendered within and against definitions of femininity. The possibility of designating particular films as femme films is opened up by a retrospective gaze; at the same time that gaze has been made possible by some Hollywood women's pictures and the social work they performed for their viewers. Finally, I would reject as imprecise Weiss's claim that in films set in female environments, "lesbianism takes the form of female identification" (17), for it is the representability of desire as distinct from identification that distinguishes what I am calling femme films from women's films.[18] Whether and where lesbianism might come to view in mass-mediated female homosocial forms is a central problem not only for interpretation but for twentieth-century U.S. popular culture itself. From this perspective, a film such as *The Killing of Sister George* might be understood not only as an exploitation of subcultural cachet in the immediate post-studio era, but, together with Aldrich's other films *Whatever Happened to Baby Jane?* (1964) and *The Legend of Lylah Clare* (1968), as revisions of what melodrama, the female star body, and nostalgia are capable of.

Considerations of Representability

When representation is forbidden, where do we look? In the overabundance of feminine representation in classical Hollywood films, how do we *cherchez la femme*? Visual coding, extratextual information, and intertextuality all structure our inferences; although they obviously work together, they will be separated for the purposes of this analysis. In the article "Seen to Be Believed" Richard Dyer shows how in dominant representation visual typing of lesbians and gays simultaneously functions as ideological shorthand and allows for recognizability. Such visible types are rendered meaningful through subcultural discourses and ultimately draw on the sexological discourse of inversion or "inbetweenism." There are few examples of visually coded butches or inverts in Code-era films until the 1950s, but in Chapter 5 I will develop this discussion of typing with regard to supporting actresses. Within the femme paradigm, visual coding proceeds not through types of persons but through point of view structures, composition, costume, and aspects of performance more generally.

Extratextual information might include biographical elements; for example accounts of the historical Queen Christina's lesbianism and cross-dressing were available to contemporary viewers and to the producers of the film, and countered the revisionist biography it depicted and amplified its visual codes.[19] While extratextual lesbianism doesn't mitigate the fact that the movie queen's fate is sealed by a heterosexual love affair, it reminds us that the negotiation of meanings took place on several levels of production and contemporary reception.

The condition of lesbian representability in classical Hollywood cinema that I want to focus on in some detail is intertextuality. Familiarity with lesbian texts obviously characterizes our present-day spectatorship of classical Hollywood films, which occurs in the context of our current definitions of lesbianism as a social phenomenon. But intertextuality refers not only to the way spectators of whatever historical juncture read films through other texts but also to the way that conventions for encoding lesbianism were available to film producers and hence generated further intertexts. In Freud's description of considerations of representability, images are more readily suited to express associations than words. Specific images are also overdetermined in dream language; this is another way of talking about intertextuality. Finally intertextuality conveys how representation is at work not only in cultural artifacts but in self-representations, historical inscriptions, and acts of decoding.

Intertextuality functions in a specific way in cultural commentary on lesbianism in the 1930s as a strategy of indirection and inscription. Reviewers were just as likely to refer to lesbianism by naming a text that was known to deal with love between women as to use the word itself. Today we are struck by how few lesbian representations made it to the screen under the Code, and, faced with these silences, we tend to privilege a few treasured examples. These texts are nodes that express networks of meanings, they are not isolated. To be sure, mainstream commentators of the period had a limited repertoire of references for lesbianism, but when they named names they too communicated shared associations about lesbian representability. The generic conventions or structures of feeling of femme films were shaped in part by intertextual references in promotional discourse and critical debate.

Although *Queen Christina*'s plot resonates intertextually with Hall's novel, when the film's producer Irving B. Thalberg suggested to Garbo's friend screenwriter Salka Viertel that putting a hint of lesbianism into the film might be "interesting," the intertext he invoked, according to Viertel's memoirs, was neither the actual queen's life history of relationships with women nor Hall's quintessential lesbian novel, but the quintessential lesbian film *Maedchen in Uniform* (Germany, 1931). "Does not Christina's affection for her lady-in-waiting indicate something like that?" To make sure we know what "that" is, Viertel describes the film: "it had been directed by a woman, my former colleague at the *Neue Wiener Bühne*, Leontine Sagan, and dealt with a lesbian relationship" (175). Thalberg asked Viertel to "keep it in mind." "Pleasantly surprised by his broadmindedness," she recounts, "I began to like him very much" (175). *Maedchen in Uniform* is a femme film that depicts the lesbian attraction between the orphan Manuela and Fraulein Elisabeth von Bernburg, "beloved by all," and it represents most of the resonances and potential of the paradigm. I will return to the maternal inflection of the femme paradigm in Chapter 4, but it is worth noting here that in the 1920s and 1930s Freud and his followers were busy constructing oedipal and pre-oedipal explanations of female sexuality (including lesbianism) and that such definitions were available at least to culturally sophisticated authors and reviewers and to some viewers.[20] Although the film doesn't depict contemporary German lesbian subcultures, it references Weimar cultural and sexual politics in its conditions of production and in its allegory of sexual freedom and, in the solidarity of the schoolgirls with the persecuted Manuela, gives a glimpse of a collective identity resonant with the politicized gender and sexual identity movements that emerged in pre–World War II Germany. But most familiarly, *Maedchen in Uniform* is set in a girls' boarding school. In her important essay "Lesbian Intertextuality," Elaine Marks traces this topos as the favorite site of lesbian fictions; her model can be extended to encompass non-French and film traditions.

"The title *Maedchen in Uniform* and the story associated with it have thus become symbolic, as it were, of Lesbianism, as far as motion pictures are concerned." This is not the pronouncement of a lesbian and gay film historian but of Breen's personnel, in an unsigned memo dated February 12, 1936, reporting on the Production Code Administration's denial of a "purity seal" that would permit the film's re-release. What might it mean that *Maedchen in Uniform* is symbolic of lesbianism as far as motion pictures are concerned? *Maedchen's* intertextual American heir was the quintessential lesbian play, Lillian Hellman's drama of boarding school scandal, *The Children's Hour*, then being adapted for film and for the PCA as Samuel Goldwyn's *These Three* (directed by William Wyler, 1936).[21] Thus the most important instances of female "sex perversion" commented upon by film censors and the press involved what Havelock Ellis referred to as "artificial lesbianism"; the protagonists were not noticeably mannish; and the texts had high-culture trappings. These femme film tropes would continue to govern lesbian representability until after World War II.[22]

Breen rejected repeated requests from John Krimsky and Gifford Cochran, who held U.S. distribution rights to *Maedchen in Uniform*, to re-release the film with the PCA seal. Summing up this position, the memo invoked "the spirit of the Code":

> The letter of the Code specifically prohibits the presentation of scenes and episodes that tend to arouse sexual passion or morbid curiosity. The spirit of the Code precludes the development of any theme whatever possessing the flavor of sexual irregularity or perversion. The fact that the Code does not name perversion, only enhances the implied condemnation.

The last sentence quoted asserts that an implied condemnation is more authoritative than an explicit one. It also suggests that not naming some-times enhances a meaning, that it is the "spirit" of a text that prevails — an argument quite similar to the one I am making about inference. Yet this same sentence is crossed out in pencil — I presume because someone in the PCA office knew the "letter" of the Code. Perversion *is* indeed named, although the precise perversion in question is not — "naming" perversion acts as a perverse implantation. This play of condemnation, the explicit and the implicit, what is under erasure and yet named — though equivocally — follows a Foudcauldian logic in which prohibitive and promotional dis-courses are entwined. The memo continues thus: "In our judgment, *Maed-chen in Uniform* in part portrays an abnormal and perverse love between two females: a girl pupil and her teacher. The inference of Lesbianism is pain-fully apparent even in the expurgated English version. It can not be ex-plained away." In this particular case, lesbianism explicitly counts as sexual perversion. As Breen wrote to Krimsky and Cochran, "You will recall that the German version . . . was definitely tagged as a picture with the definite flavor of sexual perversion (lesbianism)"; the parenthetical specifies the tag and the flavor (October 4, 1935). The *Maedchen in Uniform* correspon-dence is one of the only times the term lesbianism was enunciated by the PCA — and the film itself was thereby taken out of circulation.

However, the debate on *Maedchen in Uniform* shows how bound up the discourse of inference is with the problem of lesbian representation:

> True it is, that many people may see the present version and not get from it any suggestion of perversion, but in our unanimous judgement, the suggestion is definitely and specifically there — there is no possibility of escaping it. And because we caught this point, we felt that the picture was not acceptable, and definitely in violation of the Production Code. You have only to see the picture, yourself, to catch the point in issue.

The circumlocution here illustrates the different registers of epistemologi-cal indirection through which lesbianism travels: a "definite suggestion," *if* caught by a spectator (who is forbidden from "seeing the picture him or herself") constitutes a definite violation — of the letter and spirit of a code.

Krimsky and Cochran countered with an argument that, although unsuccessful, put into play the discourse of *quality*, which, I argue, provided cover for the "suggestions" of lesbianism that survived in Code-era Hollywood. In their first attempt to appeal, the distributors noted that the PCA's "decision is a contradiction to the universal acclaim this picture has had throughout the world, and the endorsements it has received from educators, clergymen, social workers and the general public." The PCA's susceptibility to such argument might be seen in the almost apologetic tone of the agency's prior refusal to approve *Queen Christina*, given that film's exceptional quality; "We recognize, of course, that the production is an outstanding one from an artistic standpoint. We are cognizant of its importance to the industry, both because of the splendid manner in which the picture has been written, directed and played, and also because it is remarkably free from vulgar offensiveness. . . ." Independent distributors evoking artistic or pedagogical merit could not equate "quality" with large-budget, important pictures as MGM had done. Obviously the MPPDA, as a trade association, was interested in protecting industry products. *Queen Christina* was an "A" production and ultimately lesbian connotations would survive as one of its qualities.

Despite the adamant refusal of the PCA to allow the re-release of *Maedchen in Uniform*, the film was quite different from the type of "sex picture" that excited public censure and contributed to Breen's appointment.[23] In the early 1930s "women's pictures" meant "sex pictures," according to Darryl F. Zanuck at Warner Bros. (quoted in Leff 36). By the end of the decade "women's pictures" meant something quite different. They represented the reinstatement of the domestic ideal. What definitions of femininity were in play as "tasteful" women's films replaced scandalous ones (ones depicting heterosexual promiscuity)? Historians of sexuality have traced how the intensification of discourses on female sexuality in the 1920s, fostered by scientific sex research, the popularization of psychoanalysis, suffrage, and urban modernity, stigmatized as lesbians women who had previously been widely admired and culturally prominent but were not heterosexually defined (see Franzen; D'Emilio and Freedman; Smith-Rosenberg). New women could not return to what had previously been havens of homosociality.[24] When the film industry "cleaned up" the urban sex picture it attempted to oppose the domestic ideal to modern sexuality, but in doing so it revived forms of homosocial culture that were now suspiciously sexual.

The femme film I'd like to discuss in this regard, *These Three*, attempts to remove the lesbian stigma attached to the girls' boarding school. It acts as a vehicle for Hollywood's return to "female" values, one whose depiction of past forms of homosociality had already been "sexualized" by wider cultural discourses. In the ultimately "successful" cooperation between the producer and the Hays Office in the production of this quality women's picture, lesbianism was rendered paradoxically invisible and intelligible.

A Reverse *Maedchen in Uniform* Angle: Perverse Implantation and *These Three*

In a well-publicized attempt to suppress publicity, the Hays Office forbade Samuel Goldwyn from filming Hellman's hit play *The Children's Hour,* enacting homophobic panic around a work whose very subject is homophobic panic.[25] A MPPDA reviewer dispatched to the play's opening night reported the film "thematically unfit for the screen." As *Variety* describes the play's premise, evil young Mary Tilford "invents a tale about the two femme teachers who run [her] school. They're lovers, she tells grandmother." When all of the girls are withdrawn from the school, the teachers, their livelihood destroyed, sue, unsuccessfully, for slander. Karen Wright breaks off with her fiancé under the strain of the scandal, and finally Martha Dobie confesses that she does feel "that way" about Karen and promptly runs off and shoots herself. Goldwyn went ahead with the purchase of the sensational property, but only after submitting a lengthy treatment to the Hays Office "substituting a straight triangle." He agreed to: 1) change the title, 2) avoid mention of the play in the publicity campaign, and 3) "remove any suggestion of 'Lesbianism.'"[26] The Hays Office's quotation marks around lesbianism are apt, for Hellman's play is not about sexual relationships between women, but about "lesbianism" as a signifier—one that, even under erasure (it's never pronounced, even in the play) has material effects.[27] The substitutions required of the film version multiply the contradictions of the play; what remained unspoken is declared unspeakable, only to resonate as—to borrow the British release title of the 1961 film version—the loudest whisper. In the case of this adaptation, censorship drew attention to a text that is already *about* the question of lesbian representability.

If *The Children's Hour* was in such blatant contradiction of the Code, why did Goldwyn seek to produce the play? Certainly the industry was eager to profit from audience familiarity with a work—or with a title—and industry self-regulation through the Hays Office was about film *production,* not prohibition. In "'To Prevent the Prevalent Type of Book,'" Richard Maltby characterizes Hollywood as an apparatus of affirmative culture, for which the problem of unsuitable source material—the "sophisticated" subject matter of the Broadway stage and the modern American novel—was a significant arena of contestation.[28] Although lesbianism raises particularly interesting challenges for screen adaptation, Hellman's play was by no means the only literary property of which the MPPDA was wary, as Maltby's work shows.

According to Maltby, industry practices of adaptation were not so much about the demands of a different artistic medium as they were about strategies for creating mass culture that would offend as few as possible. Conflicts that arose with authors were embedded in the fundamentally different interests and social functions of New York literary professionals and of Hollywood-produced mass culture. The film industry's role was to reach the American market with stories that conformed to expectations, whether those expectations were about genre or the moral compensation that was spelled out in the Code. In other words, "faithful" adaptation was not in Hollywood's interest: "rendering the objectionable unobjectionable [in Hays's words] was . . . a feature of the complex negotiations involved in dissemination of a culture of consumption" (Maltby, "'To Prevent'" 114). Lesbianism would have no place in this culture of consumption as Maltby outlines it, especially given that one of the devices most germane to Hollywood's hegemonizing project was the buildup of the romance plot leading to the heterosexual clinch ending—there is even one written into *These Three*. The new cultural product made of Hellman's play for screen presentation was indeed addressed to a mass audience, envisioned largely as female, and the incoherence at the heart of Hellman's representation of lesbianism was put into broad circulation. The film—like the women's picture more generally, I argue—popularized a "lesbianism" that couldn't be detected or located, but that was nevertheless "communicable." Thus while I agree that Hollywood does fundamentally different cultural work than literature, I'm not sure that its consumer product is as banal or uncontested as Maltby implies.

In an important essay that my discussion here builds upon, Chon Noriega addresses the phenomenon of Code-era adaptation of lesbian and gay literary texts and argues for a more historicized practice of lesbian and gay film criticism. To date, Noriega notes, "the emphasis has been on 'subtexting' censored films from a singular presentist perspective" (21). He points out that these subtextual meanings are historically encoded. Print reviews were permitted to speak of homosexuality even when the movies, which had no First Amendment protections, were not. Noriega takes into consideration the "'frame of reference' that reviewers disseminated to moviegoers," the way they "put the question of homosexuality before readers." He emphasizes that:

[i]t is this discursive fact that "subtexting" overlooks, since, as Michel Foucault argues, such an approach depends upon the notion of unmitigated repression that it alone transgresses. . . . The question, then, becomes not whether certain films have—in retrospect—gay and lesbian characters, subtexts, stars, or directors as an anodyne to censorship, but how homosexuality was "put into discourse," and the role that censorship played as "an element that functions along the things said." (21)

These Three, whose adaptation was widely commented upon at the time, serves as one of Noriega's most revealing examples. What was the pressure to "adapt" lesbianism to mass taste?

Hellman herself rewrote her play for the screen, replacing the child's accusation with an allegation of an affair between Martha and Karen's fiancé Joe Cardin (the rumors are thus provoked by Martha's unrequited love for *him*). As *Time* puts it, "the rumor charges one of the teachers with normal rather than abnormal misbehavior." Because even fairly mild forms of normal misbehavior were prohibited under the Code, Hellman's task of finding something "shocking" to replace lesbianism was in some sense a rather easy one. However, because the allegation of a straight love triangle did not really shock, the frisson of an implied *ab*normality was preserved despite the change. *Time* goes on: "This trivial change strengthens rather than weakens the story, makes it entirely fit for the consumption of all cinemaddicts with the most rudimentary knowledge of the facts of life." This evaluation seems to concur with Maltby's idea of Hollywood's address to the small-town consumer, whose cultural knowledge was also rudimentary, who was no more than a "cinemaddict." A middle-brow morality would congratulate the film for its high-brow cachet (it's a Broadway adaptation) *and* for its populist sensibility (rejecting "sophisticated" urban tastes) without acknowledging that even rudimentary knowledge of the "facts of life" might include lesbianism. The voices of reform welcomed the adaptation of *These Three*: The national preview chairman of the Daughters of the American Revolution praised it as a "highly entertaining clean dramatization" (PCA file on *These Three*, February 14, 1936), without noting its rather unflattering portrait of so-called guardians of morality. By all accounts the substitution of the straight triangle either "improved" upon the play or it didn't affect it—lesbianism, heterosexuality, what's the difference?[29]

Time's claim that the change demanded by the Code was merely "trivial" points to the insubstantial nature of lesbianism, unsubstantiated in the text of the film. In another sense, however, the change *is* trivial: the circulation of rumor and gossip around the female couple occupies the same discursive field in the adaptation; the relationship between utterance and referent is always in question.[30] Later assessments frequently judged *These Three* superior to Wyler's subsequent "faithful" film adaptation (again scripted by Hellman and produced by Goldwyn)—and in one sense this is a homophobic judgment. But in another, it recognizes that the later film's "liberal" openness cannot simply be valorized—there is no imaginable version of this text in which a prohibition about naming lesbianism would not be operative. *The Children's Hour* (1961) was one of several early 1960s films that provoked the emendation of the Production Code permitting "tasteful" representations of homosexuality. In it, Martha's admission of her feelings for Karen is followed by "tasteful" suicide by hanging.

In her essay on the 1961 film version of *The Children's Hour*, Julia Erhart traces the itinerary of the lesbian signifier: "'Lesbianism' remains unspoken throughout the entirety of the film. . . . [T]he word is not voiced once during the film's course, and all mentions of or allusions to it occur through a barrier, off-screen, in the distance, or in a whisper" (92–93). *The Children's Hour* is an important text in the configurations around lesbian representability that Lynda Hart calls a "paradox of prohibition" (3) and Judith Roof describes as a "lure of knowledge" in her book of that title. Erhart argues that the text's movement from epistemological uncertainty to the discursive production of lesbianism through Martha's taking on of the signifier and "coming out" relates to the changing medical and popular discourses on lesbianism particular to the late 1950s. Martha is not a homosexual "kind of person" but suffers from a kind of sickness.

If the banishment of actual lesbianism from *The Children's Hour* is what the film, ultimately, is about, how much more central to the censored 1936 version is this presence of the absence? What features of Hellman's original text characterize the constraints on the representation of female homosexuality operative *in the 1930s* (later adapted—with more or less resonance—to the early 1960s)? We need to look at censorship as much more than a one-time "no." The case of the production and adaptation of *The Children's Hour* allows us to scrutinize parameters of lesbian representability across a thirty-year history of commercial mass culture and self-regulation. Most histories of lesbian and gay film include *These Three* only as an example of suppression, an "unfaithful" adaptation of a prior text that is then construed as somehow pure. Yet the composite text—the play, both films, the reception of all three—has much to tell us about how lesbianism is discursively produced: lie, secret, rumor, confession, performative speech, protected speech, forbidden inference, invasion of privacy, and publicity. These logics reinforce and undermine each other.

To turn from the self-censorship of the 1961 adaptation to the censored 1936 version then: What is to stop Mary's *j'accuse,* her speech act under erasure—"I can't say it, I must whisper"—from *connoting* lesbianism? In answer to Mrs. Tilford's demand to know *what* "things" she saw and knows, Mary simply intimates, "funny things." What bad things go on at an all-girl school? "You've said this thing; now we'll force you to come out with it," Karen and Martha challenge Mrs. Tilford (yet the court scene in which the alleged libel is presumably specified is not shown). Making the accusation unspeakable, or unshareable as a public utterance, conflates it with, refers back to, lesbianism itself. The censors who wish to prevent "inference" in relationship to lesbianism must trust in this instance that inference will lead viewers to lesbianism's replacement.[31] "We are defending ourselves against lies" the women say, with only too much truth. Even the Hays Office must have seen that being (falsely) accused of having an affair with your friend's fiancé hardly justifies all the publicity (and then Martha is proven innocent of the accusation of heterosexual activity).

The more liberal press referred condescendingly to the Hays Office's requirements and, as Noriega points out, gave *These Three* the publicity hook to Hellman's play that the studio had been expressly forbidden from exploiting. Indeed, *The Children's Hour* was still running on Broadway when the film, heralded by the *New York Times* as "one of the finest screen dramas in recent years" (March 19, 1936), opened in February 1936. The film encoded lesbianism within the ranks of the Hollywood "quality picture" addressed to a female audience. It is this aspect of the film's reception, rather than the praise of the reformers or the auteurists that interests me. Was the management of female homosociality more central to the problems of 1930s cinema than Maltby, and those who speak of the female audience's desire only in terms of consumerism, allow for?

By the time *The Children's Hour* opened on Broadway, concern that lesbianism was running rampant in women's colleges and girls' schools had become a trope, in popular fiction as well as in scientific and cultural commentary, as Sherrie Inness thoroughly documents in *The Lesbian Menace.* Just as the child's accusation allowed Martha to come out, the reliance of the film adaptation upon its viewers' inferences pointed right back to lesbianism as what could be learned in/from the girls' school. Goldwyn knew what he was buying. In 1897, Havelock Ellis had mentioned "the school as by far the most auspicious environment for artificial lesbianism" a quality shared by prisons, factories, and other sites of working-class "contagion" (see Fuss, *Identification Papers*). If the Broadway text referred to a recognized social problem, its adaptation was located within one of the few sites of female homosocial culture that is *not* associated with lesbian contagion—the movies.

Variety described Hellman's play as one that "takes up the matter of girls' schools from a reverse 'Maedchen in Uniform' angle." Although the review's explanation of this comparison does not turn on lesbianism, the "signified" is contagious: whereas the German film featured "[c]lean children and nasty surroundings," here "it's a nasty psychopathic child and that child's effect on a previously happy seat of learning." "Nasty" may refer to authoritarianism and sadism in the respective texts—but of course lesbianism is not *not* connoted. The film adaptation would bring a more specific meaning to the cinematic metaphor adopted by the *Variety* reveiwer when the "reverse angle" on girls' schools was presented as *heterosexual* scandal.

The most important result of the translation of the text from stage to screen is arguably not its middle-brow "censorship" but its inscription within a women's genre. *Variety* greeted the film as "an extraordinary offering for women especially" (February 22, 1936). The film becomes "femme" fare in more than one sense. Martha is demasculinized ("two femme teachers" in *Variety*'s words) and *These Three* has all the elements of a woman's picture: a tale of the vicissitudes of love, with a female protagonist, set in a woman's world, and aimed at a female audience. Joe is a central character in Hellman's original, so again her rewrite was easy; Martha remains jealous of the *relationship* and looks stricken when they speak of each other or their marriage is mentioned. But without discounting the importance of Joe, I think we could be as justified in reading the eponymous triangle as including Mary Tilford. Mary Tilford's "sadism" (she forces her schoolmate Rosalie to swear to be her vassal) was another problem for the PCA—and this unnatural child is the relay of the *film's* unmentionable source material.[32] In an odd description of Karen's response to Martha's avowal in the play— "Karen decides to dismiss the matter realizing the fantastic story of the 'Maedchen in Uniform' is in reality the truth"—a reviewer uses the German phrase/title to underscore the truth that the fantastic story is about lesbianism. If *Maedchen in Uniform* is the prototype of screen lesbianism, young Mary is clearly tainted by these intertextual references. Like the bad seed of the 1956 film of that title, the connotation of the female child's rotten nature is hard to separate from the corruption of sexual perversion (indeed one relishes such connotations). The "reverse angle" (the *excitement* attached to lesbian contagion) is perhaps suggested in that the only time homoeroticism is explicitly referred to in *These Three* is when Mary accuses Rosalie of sticking up for Miss Dobie—her "crush." *All* of the work's female characters—including Lily Mortar (Martha's aunt and the source of statements

that are twisted by Mary) and Mrs. Tilford—are implicated in the circulation of knowledge and counterknowledge. The girls' school, as Diana Fuss
illustrates in her work on identification, is the perfect setting of the erotics of
learning and of learning about eroticism.[33] Perhaps the censors intervened
not only to prevent the (female) audience from "catching the point in issue"
but from catching the vice as well.

It is Martha's self-declaration that makes *The Children's Hour* so persistently interesting to lesbian viewers, her death that makes it so troubling.
The ending of Hellman's play presented a problem for reviewers whether
they were homophobic or not: "It isn't necessary to bring Mrs. Tilford back.
It isn't even necessary for one of the girls to shoot herself, but that might be
passed by," the *Variety* reviewer of the play opines. If the lesbian fatality is
easily dismissed by this reviewer, it is precisely what the 1936 adaptation,
alone among incarnations of the text, is able to bypass in "passing" the
censors.

For if *These Three* proceeds inexorably to the formation of a heterosexual couple at the fade-out—the inference of marriage was the Code's all-
purpose answer to the heterosexual passions ignited with banal regularity by
Hollywood narrativity—Martha remains an awkward third. The film tacks
on a perfunctory reunion between Karen and Joe, set in an Austrian village
decorated with as much Wiener kitsch as the studio could muster. Their
reunion and kiss are applauded by a number of older male "Austrians" who
resemble nothing so much as Hollywood executives—rarely has heterosexual consensus looked so manufactured. But doubling this resolution is an
ending more emotionally and narratively consistent with what has gone
before. *Martha's* story ends with a visit to the home of the tearful Rosalie,
who confesses her lie and receives a tender kiss from her "crush." Martha
becomes a true women's picture heroine as she departs, under the gaze of
Mrs. Tilford, to a destiny unknown to us. If the content of her "coming-out"
speech to Karen has been altered to fit the "straight triangle," the impact of
her self-realization has not; in this sense the film's ending is all hers.

The very fact that *These Three's* Martha doesn't have to die shows how
gratuitous and calculated queer movie deaths are (the Code requires that
crime and vice must be paid for). Thus one of the most remarkable effects of
the screen prohibition of homosexuality was that it couldn't include overt
homophobia either. Having the lesbian pass for straight in this film saves her
life.

We've already noted that the film successfully "passed" for straight
among the Daughters of the American Revolution. As the *Hollywood Reporter* wrote, "By all standards, this is a great woman's picture. It may annoy

some of the male members of its audience who will not trouble themselves to understand it. But the women will come in droves, impelled by word of mouth. And when you get the women, you get the world" (February 22, 1936). Goldwyn, Hellman, and Wyler's envisaging what would have been (unfilmable as) a "lesbian film" as decidedly a *woman's* film renders "woman" a less transparent marketing or representational category than it has been suspected of being. The droves of women envisioned here are "impelled" to see a film whose actual subject matter and derivation were conveyed not by the film's promotional campaign but by word of mouth (that didn't extend to male audiences). In the text the "word of mouth" on the two femme teachers impels a different mass response—hysteria, censorship, the shutting down of the school for girls through the moral agency of Mrs. Tilford and the other mothers. But the rumors also lead one of the teachers to recognize her desire.

The vision of women "impelled" by a rumor of lesbianism to engage in a particular kind of consumption (see this movie!) allows us to reconceive the cultural work performed by the women's picture. *The Children's Hour* and its adaptations are *about* lesbianism and lying as well as illustrations of them. If the censoring of the text is a kind of "lying" about its original content in a different circuit of signification and in a context of mass reception, then perhaps the film is "lying about lesbianism" (and the prevalence of lesbian activity) only, as Mary does, to produce it.

Feminist film studies that have focused on the women's picture have presumed that the spectator-subject was heterosexual. The fact that censoring the inference of lesbianism in Mary's accusation made *These Three* into a successful women's picture would seem to support this assumption. But I'm arguing that Hellman's text would have been one anyway—what is at stake is whether and where the line can be drawn between the discursive work of the lesbian play and the femme film. In this tracing of the discourses surrounding the key "lesbian" texts and intertexts produced during the period of consensus formation around the Code, I imply that despite its absence on the screen, lesbianism, which existed in the social formation as an emerging identity, as a subject of debate (about literary works, about women's education, about modern marriage, for example) was being constructed intertextually, and in a paradoxical relation to visibility—not through the "mythic mannish lesbian" who wears her desire on her sleeve, but as something male members of the audience couldn't even be troubled to understand. Yet large numbers of women appear to have "caught" it.

2

Lesbian Cinephilia

"I have loved the cinema, I no longer love it. I still love it," writes Christian Metz in *The Imaginary Signifier* (79), describing the disposition of the film theorist as a kind of disavowal. Disavowal—the holding of two contradictory beliefs—is the psychic defense that accompanies the perversion of fetishism, which in Freud's definition entails countering the "knowledge" of castration through "belief" in the phallic substitute, the erotically invested fetish. Metz makes an analogy between the fetishist's defense against lack and our belief in the cinematic illusion. "I know very well (that 'it's' not really there)," the formula for disavowal goes, "but (I believe it is) just the same." Laura Mulvey's essay "Visual Pleasure and Narrative Cinema" made explicit the assumption that the spectator so described, like Freud's fetishist, was male (and presumptively heterosexual), and that it was the carefully controlled representation of the female body that guaranteed cinematic pleasure. Metz's metapsychology of spectatorship justly came under critique for its idealism, technological determinism, and masculinist bias. But Mulvey's own dictum "woman as image, man as bearer of the look" (19), became emblematic of the fixed gendered and heteronormative categories that characterized feminist theorizing about spectatorship for more than a decade.

To understand the specificities of spectatorial positions inflected by gender, race, class, national identity, sexual orientation, etc.; to grasp the social reality of diverse audiences and reading formations; to recognize the "multiaccentuality" of the text, cinema studies has increasingly turned to

29

accounts of the practices of film reception. Yet reliance upon accounts of so-called "oppositional" viewing often leaves out something of the stubborn libidinal pull of cinema that psychoanalytic theorizing illuminated and that Metz invokes in the first person. Moreover, lesbian viewing practices have not been easily envisioned within these more commonsense approaches to the possible intersections between disempowered social groups and the movies—in part because until very recently we just haven't been visible, even as an audience. While there has been an increase in work on female audiences and consumer culture, such material can be gender normative and often excludes the erotic. And while all types of "sex perversion" were barred from on-screen depiction during the reign of the studio system, there is obviously a vigorous tradition of claiming the movies—the melodrama, the musical, the B movie, the diva—in gay male cultural practices such as camp and drag. The tendency to include lesbians under gay male cultural rubrics makes almost as little sense with regard to cinema as it does with regard to sex. We cannot be presumed to share in either the spectacular subculture of gay male camp or in the conspicuous consumption of female audience demographics. But we may do both.[1] I still love the cinema. And I'd like to retain a more everyday understanding of film fetishism, updating the gender of Christian Metz's words: "To be a theoretician of the cinema, one should ideally no longer love the cinema and yet still love it . . . not have forgotten what the cinephile one used to be was like, in all the details of her affective inflections . . . not have lost sight of her, but be keeping an eye on her" (15, pronominal gender altered).

Clearly we need to bring attention to psychic mechanisms and social practices together in discussions of lesbian spectatorship: after all, lesbianism is both a social identity and a psychosexual investment in loving women. One goes to the movies and can evaluate what one sees there "as a lesbian," at the same time that something in the cinema experience calls forth, confirms, and specifies lesbian identities. I think it makes a kind of intuitive sense to link "gynophilia"—love of women—with cinephilia—love of movies, to recognize that cinema's stock-in-trade, the eroticized image of Woman, is also addressed to us. This spectatorial position entails its own forms of disavowal.

Lesbian cinephilia came out of the closet in what can be seen as a genuine genre of lesbian independent video in the early 1990s. Kaucyila Brooke and Jane Cottis's hilarious guided tour of lesbian subtexts in classical films, *Dry Kisses Only* (1990), and Cecilia Barriga's assemblage of Garbo and Dietrich clips in *Meeting of Two Queens* (1991) scramble Hollywood's heteronormative codes through strategies of citation. Video technology allows these artists to express their love of cinema even while tearing it apart. Fairly straightforward documentaries such as *Jodie: An Icon* (Pratibha Parmar, 1996) and *We've Been Framed* (Cheryl Farthing, 1990) air lesbians' testimony to their enjoyment of the cinema on the BBC. More formally sophisticated work such as Jean Carlomusto's *L Is for the Way You Look* (1991), Suzie Silver's *Freebird* (1993) and *The Look of Love* (1998), and Sadie Benning's *It Wasn't Love* (1992) engage popular cultural icons and idioms, both predictable and quirky, in complex performances of contemporary lesbian identity and collectivity.[2] By generating and in essence theorizing audience affect, these tapes construct new terms of lesbian visibility— intertextual and social, spectatorial and authorial. As mainstream media flirts with what Danae Clark calls commodity lesbianism, these independent works, programmed in lesbian and gay film festivals, begin to shape a counterpublic from an audience. They also serve a pedagogical function for younger audiences less familiar with Hollywood lore. Central issues of spectatorship theory—the semiotics of stars, identification, fantasy, and fetishism—are framed in lesbian terms by the textual and reception practices of these works.

Don't Let's Ask for the Moon—We Have the Stars

Bette Davis/Charlotte Vale's famous admonition to Paul Henreid/Jerry at the end of *Now, Voyager* (Irving Rapper, 1942), "Don't let's ask for the moon—we have the stars," yields a rare form of pleasure for viewers of classical Hollywood film. It announces the film's rejection of heterosexual closure and the heroine's desire for something else. It is a cliché, but it carries a great deal of affect. For lesbian spectators the gesture makes clear that what Charlotte proposes is not settling for less, for a substitute object, but aspiring to one different in kind—why ask for the moon, indeed, when we *want* the stars?[3] It is also a reminder, all the more effective because it is Bette Davis who tells us so, that if the resolutions offered by Hollywood much more frequently fall short of sustaining our desire, lesbians have always had the *stars*. . . .

This was particularly evident in the 1990s, when a number of female celebrities came out, in effect making their lesbian *audiences* visible—although mainstream speculation about whether such self-identification would hurt the stars' commercial credibility seemed to disavow the fact that lesbians were part of the "general public" who bought film tickets. The possibility of such naming only makes more public a mode of relating that always had a paradoxical relationship both to visibility and to identification. Ask a

31

dyke of the right generation about a straight star such as Katharine Hepburn or Sigourney Weaver, and she will most likely respond enthusiastically. If a star is successful not, or not only, because of individual "talent," but because her image manages cultural contradictions, as Richard Dyer suggests in his seminal study, *Stars* (38), certain star images codify conflicts around female gender and sexual identity that emerge in particular historical and social contexts, conflicts in relation to which lesbians also identify themselves and their desires. This may hinge on qualities of gender presentation—the appeal of Hepburn's and Weaver's sometimes butch stance—that have erotic or identificatory appeal, and/or on more conventional erotic coding or "charisma" (Dyer 35). Desire is, after all, what Hollywood banks on.

Female homoerotic desire is in a sense foundational to the star system, which as common (and marketing) sense would have it, appeals primarily to women.[4] Within the contours of an historically homosocial phenomenon, specific lesbian practices can be discerned—these have to do with many elements of the star phenomenon, including gossip and now outing and coming out, and also with the particularities of the media texts that contain certain star images (or fail to) and the junctures at and discourses through which they are received. Some of the most interesting lesbian spectatorial practices are attested to, explored, codified, and reproduced in very material ways in video works that appropriate images of Hollywood stars. The tapes draw, in turn, on lesbians' narratives of their crushes on stars, emphasizing the psychic dimensions of spectatorship.

Not surprisingly, lesbian fandoms haven't been extensively theorized or documented. Certainly lesbians have not been as visible as gay men or straight women as movie fans. But it is also only recently that stars have become central to feminist film studies, and that lesbianism has been considered in theories of sexual difference. Stars are clearly the mainstay of popular discourse on the cinema. Correcting a bias that held their study to be impressionistic and unscholarly, the work of Dyer and others has found in the phenomenon of stardom a rich source for cultural commentary. The complex ideological work performed by a particular star image frequently provides ways for marginalized groups to negotiate a pleasurable response to dominant cultural productions that would seem to exclude them. Donald Bogle's important work has transformed the way we think of African American stereotypes by its focus on performers who could not be contained by such roles. Recent studies of Carmen Miranda (Roberts) and Sessuye Hanakawa (Kirihara) read and reclaim these typecast figures for histories of Latin American and Asian American spectatorship, respectively. And Bette Davis,

Charlotte Vale's impersonator, has a gay male following whose practices could sustain tomes of cultural comment.[5]

One of the important emphases in recent feminist work on spectatorship is the insistence on the privileged relationship between women audiences and stars, particularly female stars. Bette Davis's popularity with female audiences determined the production schedule at Warner Bros. in the 1940s. A disempowered social group that comprises more than half the population, women are subject to massive (and differentiated) management—a function consumerism attempts to perform. Certainly, the extent to which sexual desire is implicated in commodity desire deserves further consideration, and stars would appear to be a key mechanism in this metonymy. Maria Laplace and Jackie Stacey, drawing on Dyer's work, have astutely described the contours of Bette Davis's appeal to female audiences in the 1940s. Laplace notes her appearance primarily in the woman's picture genre, in roles displaying a kind of "independence" familiar from the heroines of women's fiction and promoted during the war years. Studio publicity constructed Davis herself as this kind of woman, and her image was circulated in the fan magazines to promote consumer morale during wartime. Davis's idiosyncrasies as a performer and the intelligence and frustration they seemed to project emerge in some of the comments made by Davis's actual fans, the focus of Stacey's study. If lesbian and gay audiences are unmentioned in these feminist works, it is in part because they are concerned with the 1940s reception context or with fans' present-day memories of those years. Yet aspects of the Davis persona that encourage less direct identifications (available, I think, to queer audiences at the time and from which queer histories of Bette Davis spectatorship derive) are underplayed in feminist readings that focus on general notions of the female audience.

When lesbians talk about their love affairs with the movies, there is an intractable insistence on the subjective relation to female stars. Julie Andrews, Jean Arthur, Jodie Foster, Eartha Kitt, Susan Sarandon, Hannah Schgylla, Barbara Stanwyck—the list is both extensive and selective, the preferences idiosyncratic and overdetermined. As an adolescent, I pinned pictures of Garbo and Louise Brooks on my wall, and Lizabeth Scott and Gloria Grahame stare down at me now. Crushes on particular stars, or "identifications" with them, cross-gender alliances and genre predilections, unprecedented and stock emotional responses, are the data of lesbian spectatorship theory. What does a crush on a star mean? What can we learn from an analysis of *how* lesbian spectators and critics talk about and represent their relationships to stars? How are aspects of a star image rendered meaningful to this process, recognizable to others? Which stars are privileged in lesbian discourses and practices of fandom, and why? Can we distinguish between reactionary and transgressive meanings? The terms of the mediated relationship of lesbians to popular culture are currently being reworked in practices of *self*-representation that avoid undertheorized assumptions about our "subversive" viewing practices.

Quoting movies (by incorporating Hollywood film footage) and drawing upon and transforming familiar anecdotes attesting to the affective investment of lesbians in particular filmic scenarios, lesbian video productions actually construct new scenarios though their own performance. I hope to do more than provide evidence that avid lesbian fans exist; I want to show how representations of spectatorship become ways of communicating and constructing contemporary lesbian cultural positions. The emergence of works such as *Dry Kisses Only, Meeting of Two Queens,* and *L Is for the Way You Look* at the moment of mainstream lesbian visibility known as "lesbian chic" signals a shifting relationship between contemporary lesbians and mass culture that cannot be reduced to commodity identity. Although it is certainly not rare to see Hollywood film clips in video art in the 1980s and 1990s, these works are characterized by earnestness and humor in their citational practices; the images and clips are rather more fetishistic than postmodern. Predictably, certain images and stars from classical Hollywood recur—these new roles become part of the cultural discourse Dyer calls the "star text."

In *Dry Kisses Only*, their witty assemblage decoding lesbian "subtexts" in classical Hollywood films, Kaucyila Brooke and Jane Cottis dramatize a *dyke's* obsession with the star on whom perhaps the strongest claims of gay men and straight women spectators have been made—Bette Davis. Brooke performs—with a twist—the big confessional scene in the dressing room from the beginning of Joseph Mankiewicz's *All About Eve* (1950), definitively outing that classic's eponymous, crypto-queer heroine. Unlike the original film, in which Eve (Anne Baxter) makes up a heterosexual past and a hard-luck story to gain entrée to the inner circle of Broadway star Margo Channing (Davis), the New Eve of *Dry Kisses Only*, wearing Baxter's distinctive "raincoat and funny hat," tells her coming-out story. Shots of Brooke are cleverly intercut with reaction shots of Davis, Thelma Ritter, and assembled company, who are moved to tears by her narrative. As in the original film, Eve's story gets the intended results. When she concludes, Margo's voice-over relates: "That night, we sent for Eve's things. The honeymoon was on."

This Eve's "true" tale of heroism, heartbreak, and homophobia (touching on the historical emergence of San Francisco's lesbian community during World War II) demonstrates that lesbian plots fit the codes of melodrama quite nicely—as Birdie (Ritter) says, "Everything but the bloodhounds snapping at her rear end!"—though it took forty years to film it this way. Only one aspect of the original Eve's tale was true, and it provides the key to the lesbian reading *Dry Kisses* performs: her confession of compulsive spectatorship, her fanaticism. Whereas Eve Harrington told of attending Margo Channing's performances "every night, every matinee," Brooke's character testifies that it was Bette Davis films that sustained her lesbian imaginative life in the post-war years. That is, in this contemporary reflection on classical Hollywood's encoding of female homoeroticism, the character's deliberate diva devotion becomes the key criteria for lesbian identification. I am using identification here in the sense of identifying this character as a lesbian, and in the sense of lesbians' identifying with her. The fact that this fan's discourse is imagined in a plausible historical context, through the tried and true devices of the coming-out story, makes it an even more compelling tale. This brief segment from *Dry Kisses Only* exemplifies the clandestine, complex nature of lesbian viewing: how tenacious we are, and to what lengths we will go to insinuate ourselves into the picture. But even as Eve is outed, it is her strategic storytelling, not her "true identity," that *Dry Kisses Only* re-enacts.

In the central section of Jean Carlomusto's *L Is for the Way You Look*, a group of lesbian friends recount in turn their versions of spotting, scoping, and swarming around singer Dolly Parton after a performance by the lesbian comic Reno at a downtown New York performance space. As Douglas Crimp aptly observes, this segment of Carlomusto's tape deals with "the communities we form through . . . identifications":

> The emphasis on signifiers of Dolly's feminine masquerade—huge hair, tiny miniskirt—by a group of women whose masquerade differs so significantly from hers, implicates their identifications and their desire in difference. (312)

Watching the story travel and become embellished, the tape's viewer is interpolated as a crucial link in the chain of sapphic gossip.

In *Group Psychology and the Analysis of the Ego*, Freud offers female fans as a perfect example of "a group of individuals who have put one and the same object in the place of their ego ideal and have consequently identified themselves with one another in their ego" (48). Freud writes:

> We have only to think of the troop of women and young girls, all of them in love in an enthusiastically sentimental way, who crowd around a singer

> or pianist after his performance. . . . [I]n the face of their numbers and the consequent impossibility of their reaching the aim of their love, they renounce it, and instead of pulling out one another's hair, they act as a united group, do homage to the hero with their common actions, and would probably be glad to have a share of his flowing locks. (52)

Although here the performer's gender is male, the fetishized "flowing locks," strike me as an appropriate "signifier of feminine masquerade." Carlomusto's tape allies the mechanism of group identification in a fandom with forms of political collectivity based in identity. For one fan, confirmation for rumors of Dolly's lesbianism is found in the fact that she, like the fans, was a member of the audience: "I'm a dyke and I'm here, so she could be a dyke too."

Suzie Silver's *Freebird* performs an even more spectacular reversal of the relationship between lesbian fans and star icons. In the first sequence of the tape, Silver, wearing white tie and bright red lipstick, delivers a mildly obscene mock Oscar acceptance speech. She is warmly applauded by a whole troop of enthusiastically sentimental present-day divas—Catherine Deneuve, Jodie Foster, Sharon Stone, Geena Davis, Susan Sarandon—their reaction shots intercut from an actual awards ceremony. The tape draws on the recognition of the place of these particular mainstream actresses in lesbian fandom (by now, because of specific roles), with the aim of making contemporary lesbian culture itself recognizable—putting it into the public domain, as it were.[6] Through these tapes, private histories of consumption are points of departure for public interventions. Carlomusto's tape chronicles an emergence into politics through activist videomaking, and *Freebird* comments indirectly on the commodification of lesbianism in mainstream movies by showing a lesbian who would *not* be depicted in them.[7]

Carlomusto's opening voice-over of *L Is for the Way You Look* speaks for the dykes interviewed in her piece as well as for those to whom it is addressed: "I can trace an entire history of my life from the age of about five on as a series of crushes on movie stars, television personalities, and rock goddesses." Freudian psychoanalysis asserts that "It is by means of a series of identifications that the personality is constituted and specified" (Laplanche and Pontalis, *Language of Psycho-Analysis* 205). Our relationships to stars go beyond identification. The same-sex star crush narrative, with its complex negotiation of identification and desire, idealization and recognition, is particularly revelatory for queer subjects. Simply put, when you recognize your lesbianism through movies and movie stars, you identify your desire. Stories about stars facilitate the construction of lesbian identity through identification with others who share one's preferences.

Star Signs

A series of interviews conducted in 1978–79 by Judy Whitaker for *Jump Cut's* landmark special issue on lesbians and film has been one of few sources cited in work on lesbian spectatorship. Rather than as evidence, the narratives deserve to be read symptomatically. Whitaker asked nine lesbians who grew up in the 1950s and 1960s about particularly influential film-going experiences, favorite films and stars, patterns of viewing and iden-tification. (Similar interviews are included in Cheryl Farthing's *We've Been Framed* and present a fairly consistent, updated narrative of adolescent same-sex eroticism "caused" by the movies.) Films such as *All About Eve*, *Rebecca*, and *Calamity Jane* are cited, as well as encounters with the overt lesbian portrayals of *The Children' s Hour*, *The Fox*, and *The Killing of Sister George*. The memories of these generations include the standard clas-sic Hollywood stars—James Dean, Marilyn Monroe, Katharine Hepburn, Greta Garbo, and Marlene Dietrich—but differ, I think, from a generic nostalgia narrative. For the role of memory here is to retrieve (or to invent) a transgressive scene of adolescent awakening rather than to confirm a culturally "preferred" position.

Not that these accounts don't display the repetitive banality of much fan commentary. But I think this rituality is akin to the self-evident teleology that Biddy Martin has detected in coming-out stories in general. In her essay "Lesbian Identity and Autobiographical Difference(s)" Martin cites Bonnie Zimmerman's observation of the "radically rationalistic rewriting of per-sonal history" of coming-out stories, adding, "hence the often formulaic and noncontradictory quality of some autobiographical writing; hence, too, the forms of moralism and voluntarism that inhere in such demands for the identity of sexuality, subjectivity, and political stance" (280). Martin goes on to critique these assumptions about autobiography, particularly by attention to different, contestatory writing strategies of lesbians of color and anti-racist white lesbians sensitive to the relational and provisional aspects of identity, language, and power. Given the anti-patriarchy stance of the cultural femi-nism that generated many of the more moralistic coming-out tales, lesbians' stories of popular culture already have a refreshingly iconoclastic, tellingly trivial quality. As photographer Deborah Bright notes in an essay on her own viewing history, written to accompany her series of photomontages "queer-ing" Hollywood female icons, sharing such stories can provoke a transgres-sive "whoop of recognition" in other lesbians (154). They might share in Martin's best-case scenario of the function of the coming-out narrative:

> Rendering lesbianism as natural, self evident, original, can have the effect
> of emptying traditional representations of their content, of contesting the
> only apparent self evidence of "normal" (read heterosexual) life course.
> Lesbian autobiographical narratives are about remembering differently,
> outside the contours and narrative constraints of conventional models.
> Events of feeling that are rendered insignificant, mere "phases" . . . when
> a life is organized in terms of the trajectory toward adult heterosexuality,
> marriage, and motherhood become differently meaningful in lesbian sto-
> ries. They become signs that must be reread on the basis of different
> interpretive strategies. Whether the emphasis is on a tomboyish past, on
> childhood friendships, or on crushes on girl friends, teachers, or camp
> counselors . . . these narratives point to unsanctioned discontinuities be-
> tween biological sex, gender identity, and sexuality. (279)

An affinity with Katharine Hepburn or James Dean may function transpar-
ently in a progressive narrative toward recognition of one's butch dyke
identity, but this is in the context of an identification of and with cultural
constructions of spinsters and rebels, rather than with dutiful wives and
daughters.

Jackie Stacey's *Star Gazing* provides a model for reading women's statements about their memories of stars, and her work can help us think about
how lesbian accounts differ from the processes of female spectatorship
generally. Stacey's primary data is in the form of letters received in response
to her solicitation in British women's magazines asking readers for accounts
of their favorite Hollywood stars of the 1940s and 1950s. She is concerned
with "the diversity of processes of identification, including forms of desire"
(159), and the specific tie between women and female stars is emphasized.
"The spectator/star relationship significantly concerns forms of *intimacy
between femininities*" (172).

Stacey categorizes her range of material into several kinds of identification, broadly dividing them into two categories. "Cinematic identificatory fantasies"—devotion, worship, transcendence, inspiration—are proper
to the act of spectatorship and appear to be based primarily on difference
from the star ideal, and "extra-cinematic identificatory practices"—imitation and consumption—attempt to close the gap between subject and star
even as they take place outside cinema. Her first set of categories would
seem to bear most directly on lesbian accounts. One letter writer remarks: "I
wanted to . . . tell you of my devotion to . . . Doris Day. . . . I saw *Calamity Jane*
45 times in a fortnight and still watch all her films avidly. My sisters all
thought I was mad going silly on a woman . . . but I just thought she was

wonderful" (138). The worship of Day is not surprising; she was one of the top box office draws of the 1950s. But this woman singles out in her fanaticism Day's cross-dressing role in the biopic of a legendary lesbian. Though her sisters worried about the attachment, the only word she can find for her feelings is "wonderful." Indeed, Day, and *Calamity Jane* in particular, in which the star sings both "Secret Love" and a duet with another, feminine, character called "A Woman's Touch," are regularly cited by lesbians as crucial cinematic texts. In *We've Been Framed*, one woman recounts going to see this childhood favorite at a women-only screening. She was flabbergasted when the leather dykes sang along to "Whip Crack Away!"

For Stacey, a lesbian critic working on "non gay" material in this instance, the process of spectatorial *identification* includes "forms of desire" like her informant's. However, this assimilation presents problems for thinking about lesbian viewing. First, "overidentification" with the image has been posited as the sole position open to the female spectator, who lacks the "distance" to desire, a position that in avoiding homoeroticism condemns female spectatorship in general to an impossibility. Second, while sexual desire is not the only affect lesbians experience at the movies, sometimes identification with the female star is wholly absent. At the very least, differences in gender identification among lesbians make any unifying theory of the psychic processes in play unworkable. For lesbians to construct their identities in relation to stars as culturally reinforced norms of heterosexual femininity, a specific set of cultural contradictions needs to be negotiated.[8]

Stacey insists on the homoerotic potential of all women and of female sociality. For Diana Fuss, who in "Fashion and the Homospectatorial Look" makes a claim for the eroticism of female spectatorship in general, a poststructuralist critique of assertions of lesbian identity takes precedence over accounting for how one goes about constructing and living such an identity. It is in her interest to deny the specificity of a psychic process (women's desire for women) to one a priori group. As fraught as the concept of identity is, I *am* concerned with spectators who identify as lesbians rather than those susceptible to what Stacey calls "feminine fascinations." This is an endeavor for which, for all its care, *Star Gazing* does not lay the groundwork. For one conclusion might be that the cinema successfully manages and contains the "homerotic" response it evokes by channeling it into heterosexual constructions of femininity.

Certainly the commonsense meaning of identification, so frequently invoked in fan accounts, does not clarify matters. In Whitaker's introductory remarks, she implies that her subjects didn't really "get" the idea of identification, by which she meant "associate closely with" (33). The women mixed the term up with affection and sexual desire, slipping between being "fond of," desiring, relating to, and lusting after different figures.

> Whitaker: Would you fall in love with characters you identified with? Like Katherine [*sic*] Hepburn?
> J.A. Marquis: I'd for sure be intimidated by Bette Davis. I'd feel I was on very thin ice. (35)

Through this very confusion, the interviews end up presenting self-contradictory, partial accounts of the intersection of subjective fantasy and the social institution of cinema.

"[Film] did give me the context in which to play out all these ideas, fantasizing romantic encounters and playing one of many roles, always switching around when it got too hot in one seat. . . .[F]ilm had a central role in allowing me to come to terms with lesbian sexuality" (34), says Anna Maria, one of the women interviewed. Again, since most women are ostensibly achieving normative identities even if they are responding to transgressive aspects of the stars' personae and performances, Anna Maria's response is an uninvited one. It points to a fundamental and by now familiar contradiction in the social and subjective function of cinema; it is a capitalist tool of dominant patriarchal ideology and an outlet for frustrations with that system and discontent among those who attend its performance. If the "homoerotic" feelings of women who are well socialized find expression there, perhaps women who refuse those culturally prescribed positions can even confirm their erotic identities in relation to its expressions of visual and narrative pleasure.

Anna Maria's response to another of Whitaker's leading questions illustrates the play of identification and dis-identification in lesbian spectatorship:

> You asked, "Did I make myself be Spencer Tracy?" That's the rub about growing up a lesbian and trying to put yourself in the film situation in some way. You're attracted by these women and yet you don't fit in—an incredible contradiction for me. At times I'd identify with a character. Other times I'd float outside the situation, sort of watching the effect this attractive woman was having on me. I'd imagine Katherine [*sic*] Hepburn and Spencer Tracy together, or sometimes I'd be Katherine [*sic*] Hepburn. And I might be sort of behind Spencer Tracy but I wouldn't *be* Spencer Tracy! (34)

Anna Maria's comments are typical, and not only in their invocation of Hepburn. Anna Maria loves the cinema; yet she recognizes the "rub," the resistance put up by her spectatorial position. Put another way, she articulates the lesbian quandary of finding oneself both within and outside the technology of gender deployed in filmic narratives and by the cinematic apparatus itself.[9] Her desire is solicited by the cinema, but not represented therein. Thus Anna Maria experiences "an incredible contradiction"—not only on the level of story, where lesbian desire finds no obvious support, but also on the level of address. She struggles with a film "situation," a setting in which heterosexual complementarity (the very mode of production of the technology of gender) couples narrate closure with ideological forms such as the romantic "team" of Hepburn and Tracy.

In contrast to the binaristic model of gender identification and attendant "heterosexual" object choice—if you "like" Katharine Hepburn, you must "be" Spencer Tracy—implied by Whitaker's original question and presumed in Laura Mulvey's influential notion of the female spectator as "transvestite" in her essay "Afterthoughts on 'Visual Pleasure,'" Anna Maria formulates her youthful spectating as a series of permutations not governed by direct gender correspondence but determined nevertheless by her social and libidinal location.[10] Indeed, her shifting and contradictory affective involvement in and distance from the scene of desire as enacted specifically in those Tracy-Hepburn movies and cumulatively in her filmgoing experience recall theoretical accounts of the structure of *fantasy* in spectatorship.

As Laplanche and Pontalis write in "Fantasy and the Origins of Sexuality," and as many film theorists have subsequently quoted: "Fantasy . . . is not the object of desire, but its setting. In fantasy the subject does not pursue the object or its sign; [s]he appears caught up [her]self in the sequence of images" (26, pronoun altered). In the most immediate sense, such a conceptualization allows us to detach processes of identification and desire—which are both involved but which are not collapsed—from an assumed correspondence between spectator and like-gendered character, an ideology of sexual difference governed by a heterosexual teleology even more relentless than that of Hollywood. Anna Maria's taking up of active and passive roles, available positions in representation, indicates that identifications, cinematic and subjective, are shaped by narrative patterns, ideological forms such as genre, stars, consumption, modes of the visual, and the erotic. They are also shaped by immediate social and autobiographical—including unconscious—factors. Far from suggesting that the fantasmatic qualities of film allow any spectator to take up any identificatory position at will, regardless of their gender or sexual identity or the specific text or context (a criticism leveled by Stacey and de Lauretis, among others, at much theoretical work on fantasy), Anna Maria's comments offer a fairly precise description of her lesbian viewing fantasy. And "the subject is invariably present in these scenes," Laplanche and Pontalis insist (*Language* 318).

A brief look at Freud's "A Child Is Being Beaten," the text upon which many film theorists, as well as Laplanche and Pontalis themselves, have based their work on fantasy, might help clarify the usefulness of the concept to determining the specificity of modes of lesbian spectatorship. With its dynamic model, Freud's analysis has been immensely useful in complicating the rigidly binaristic positions of gendered identification and desire previously (if also polemically) legislated in film theory.[11] Beneath the fantasy's conscious formulation in the simple, but oddly impersonal phrase, "a child is being beaten," Freud uncovers versions of the fantasy (entailing genital love of the father and its punishment/substitution in the beating) in which the subject's position and erotic aim as well as the gender of the actors undergo certain consistent permutations. "A Child Is Being Beaten" relies on the accounts, not unlike the "interviews" I am looking at here, of four different female subjects who share the non-subjective version of the beating fantasy that gives his essay its title. (Freud also discusses the cases of two male patients that he links explicitly with homosexuality.) The children's fantasies are sparked by encounters with erotic structures in fiction (that is, symbolically structured texts give form to unconscious fantasies), again recalling our lesbians' "uses" of films. The girls' conscious fantasies constituted "an artistic superstructure of daydreams" that often subjected many boys to elaborate punishment scenarios (190).

Freud's reading of the beating fantasy has proved of such interest to film theorists because of its direct link to spectatorship—an ingenious spectatorship that, moreover, is paradigmatically female. Pressed by Freud to say where *she* was in her fantasy, one of his informants came up with a provisional answer: "I am probably looking on" (186). Freud claims she "turns herself in fantasy into a man, without herself becoming active in a masculine way, and is no longer anything but a spectator to the event which takes the place of a sexual act" (199). Though critics such as Mary Ann Doane take a pessimistic view of what Freud calls the girl's "renunciation of her sex" (*The Desire to Desire*, 294–95), more interesting interpretations are conceivable. Remember that for feminist film theory the woman has rarely been anything but a *spectacle*. To play both author and spectator, and to obtain erotic gratification by at the same time creating a male stand-in and "causing" his physical punishment, is a relatively empowering response to a male representational regime. Although the girls may have "accomplished a more thoroughgoing work of repression" (128) than their male counterparts in disappearing from the scenarios they make up, they seem to have produced more inventive and more lastingly rewarding fantasies. The beating fantasy would seem to be a way of claiming power and control when one is literally not in the picture—a useful trick for queer kids.

Like the fantasizer, Anna Maria is "floating outside" her movie scene, "probably looking on," locating herself "sort of behind" a figure in the scenario. But far from desexualizing her, her fantasies construct her own conditions of pleasure. The scene offers a script for appropriating to herself a definition of her lesbian sexuality, albeit retrospectively, from the vantage of an adult feminist lesbian identity.

In her series "Dream Girls," Deborah Bright casts an ingeniously literal visualization of "subjective" fantasy in the idiom of "public" film culture. "Dream Girls" is a series of altered film production stills featuring female stars of the lesbian pantheon. In one image, Bright visualizes her own adolescent fantasy in strikingly similar terms to Anna Maria's fantasy, putting herself in the Hepburn-Tracy "scene" even as she's literally "behind" it as its author (fig. 1). Inserting her own butch figure in the picture, Bright disrupts the inert, clichéd quality of the movie still, offering a reading of the exclusion of lesbians from such a "picture." She appears in the person of a chauffeur, sullenly waiting for Tracy to give Hepburn a good-bye peck on the cheek, a supporting character on her way to romantic lead status (see Bright 152). In two other images from the series involving the thus over-represented Hepburn, Bright "reads" the star's persona through different mise-en-scènes derived directly from that persona's evolution across films: one shows Bright's character with the girlish 1930s Hepburn in an evening gown, Bright's riding boots suggesting an aristocratic role-playing "sapphic" couple of the era; another image depicts career-girl Hepburn, who doesn't seem to mind her butch lover (Bright) showing up at the office. The fit between the iconography of the stills and historically specific "dyke" codes is striking.

As Bright herself points out, her photomontages are "one-liners," with no pretension to postmodern pastiche or the distanciation of much appropriative art. In fact, preserving and transferring cornball affect, giving (sexual) meaning to nostalgia, seem to be her intent. The photos literalize the common understanding of identification as "seeing oneself in the picture." Her title captures the paradox of stars for lesbians; they are the answer to your dreams—*dream on*.

The insistence of invocations of Hepburn is worth exploring. Where do the knowledge of lesbians of Hepburn's importance and their experience of her appeal come from? If there is indeed a shared fantasy of Hepburn, there must be a pedagogy through which Hepburn's meanings and her films come

1. *Deborah Bright, untitled from "Dream Girls" series, 1990. The artist's own presence in the driver's seat adds another dimension to our perception of the Spencer Tracy/Katharine Hepburn "team." Courtesy the artist.*

to reside in lesbian popular memory to a degree to which those featuring, say, Jean Arthur (who was rumored really to have been a lesbian), do not. Attempts to account for the appeal of the most commonly invoked Hollywood stars are of variable usefulness in their analyses of their star images; collectively, they raise crucial epistemological questions.

In "Lesbians and Film," commissioned for Dyer's pioneering book, *Gays in Film*, Caroline Sheldon cites the independent women of the 1930s and 1940s and the stars who portrayed them as the foundation of dyke film culture. She singles out Marlene Dietrich's flirtations with women in her cabaret numbers in *Morocco* (Josef von Sternberg, 1930) and *Blonde Venus* (von Sternberg, 1932), Greta Garbo in male garb kissing her lady-in-waiting in *Queen Christina* (Rouben Mamoulian, 1933) (figs. 2 and 3), and Katharine Hepburn's cross-dressing role in *Sylvia Scarlett* (George Cukor, 1936), as having particular resonance and appeal in lesbian culture. She, in turn, quotes Janet Meyer, writing in the publication *Dyke* in 1976:

> Most lesbians I know feel a strong response to these women on screen. The qualities they projected, of being inscrutable to the men in the film and aloof, passionate, direct, could not be missed. They are all strong and yet genuinely tender. In short, though rarely permitted to hint it, they are lesbians. (quoted on 18)

Similar language is used much later by Margie Adam, writing after Garbo's death in 1990, "I knew, right down to my molecular structure, that the shimmering beauty with such a jawline up there on the screen was a dyke, just like me" (quoted in Mayne, *Cinema and Spectatorship* 163). Such assertions may be illuminating primarily for the libidinal investment they reveal.

Andrew Britton, author of an exhaustive study of Hepburn, justly calls invocations of the "gender ambiguity" of certain female stars a "critical commonplace" (*Katharine Hepburn* 39), and is particularly dismissive of Meyer's claims that the 1930s icons "were" lesbians.[12] Britton provides a case history that reads the particularity of the star image: across her films, publicity discourses, critical accounts, historical vicissitudes, and accrued meanings. He claims:

> Katharine Hepburn is the only star of the classical cinema who embodies contradictions (about the nature and status of women) in a way which not only resists their satisfactory resolution in a stable, affirmable ideological coherence, but which also continually threatens to produce an *oppositional* coherence which is registered by the films as a serious ideological threat. There is no star so many of whose films seem systematically dedicated to expressing animus against her. (1)

Although many stars embody contradictions about what it means to be a woman (this is a primary function of stardom), Hepburn, according to Britton, does so most saliently. Britton analyzes in detail the potential challenge of the Hepburn image to conventional meanings of femininity: her physical appearance and athleticism, her sartorial style, the undermining of patriarchal power in her films, her autonomy. He also emphasizes the ways in which that challenge is contained by her films (through narrative "correction" of her independence, the neutralization of feminist resistance as headstrong individualism, her casting in a cycle of "pathetic spinster" roles), promotional discourses (highlighting upper-class privilege and eccentricity, the romance with Tracy), and her public persona (her status as "American institution," and, I would add, her homophobia in interviews).

2. *The pleasure of the cliché. Marlene Dietrich in the top hat and tails she wears in* Morocco *(von Sternberg, 1930).*

3. *Greta Garbo as Queen Christina kisses her lady-in-waiting (Elizabeth Young) in Rouben Mamoulian's 1933 film.*

According to Britton, the massive effort to "place" or contain the feminist Hepburn shows that the contradictions she embodies are meaningful. Obviously "lesbianism," as an occluded signified of "gender ambiguity," and a connotation of feminism in the 1930s as it is today, contributes to the coherence of the oppositional meanings, giving a name to the ideological threat and to the widespread appeal of her persona. While Dietrich's performances might carry stronger connotations of sapphic sexuality, they are reconcilable with major components of her image: European/decadent/perverse. Hepburn relies upon a stronger impression of the "inadvertent lesbian verisimilitude" of physique, stance, and gesture (Ellsworth 57). Any surfacing of the lesbian connotations of the Hepburn image would threaten to expose the disavowal on which it is based. *Sylvia Scarlett*, in which Hepburn cross-dressed and found herself in both lesbian and gay male sexual situations, was hostilely received. Britton's reading of Hepburn is a sophisticated cinephilic tour de force; the average dyke's "take" on Hepburn is more likely to have been derived from postcard images and late-night movie encounters than a familiarity with the radical project of the 1930s oeuvre and the way it was undermined in the later films. Yet, as Meyer, Bright, and Whitaker's subjects indicate to me, Hepburn, Dietrich, and Garbo are actively *read* by lesbian audiences, who resist the recuperative operation that replaces the stars' lesbian connotations with "something else."[13]

The acts of cut-and-paste fetishism performed by Bright, the video artists, and lesbian autobiographical narratives become a way of resolving the contradiction between desire and denial, delectable image and depressing story. In this way they are diagnostic of lesbian cinephilia. In her groundbreaking work on the lasting visual appeal of butch director Dorothy Arzner, Judith Mayne stresses the lure of the iconic image: "Some cinematic images have proven to be irresistibly seductive as far as lesbian readings are concerned" ("Lesbian Looks" 103). She lists the by-now-familiar triumvirate of star turns—the pivotal scenes from *Morocco, Queen Christina, Sylvia Scarlett*—continuing, "some images have been cited and reproduced so frequently in the context of gay and lesbian culture that they have almost acquired lives of their own" (103).[14] They seem to seduce independently of the film texts, which work to contain any lesbian implications through heterosexual narrative resolutions.

The insistence that certain images signify "differently," on an iconographic and fantasmatic level, is an antidote to banal assumptions that particular stars are of interest to lesbians primarily as "strong women," as narrative or real-life "role models"; that lesbian spectators consciously appropriate such images and willfully assign independent meanings to them, or that the appeal of these stars can be named by an equivocating reference to their "androgyny." Such isolated images "hold" the spectator through an effect something like what Roland Barthes has called the "third meaning." "The [third] meaning has something to do with disguise" ("The Third Meaning" 58) Barthes writes, identifying the quality with *stills* from Eisenstein's films. We might link this function—in these three examples at least, to the "third sex" appeal of a historically specific representation of the crossdressed, "mannish" lesbian, as well as to the codifications of glamour in studio cinematography and portraiture. Bright's images of butch drag play upon both stillness and disguise as well, but they remain conscious wishfulfillments. I am not arguing for some ineffable "lesbian sensibility" here in these icons; I think that there is a system of cultural reference at work.

"Depending on your point of view," Mayne writes, "lesbian readings of isolated scenes are successful appropriations and subversions of Hollywood plots, or naive fetishizations of the image" (103). Mayne's remarks encourage us to understand the "lives" of these images as subcultural histories of citation—practices not unrelated to camp, the privileging of style and mise-en-scène in reception, or the method in political criticism of locating moments of "rupture" in dominant texts. The images have the commonsense currency—and curious opacity—of the cliché as they become inserted into narratives of identity and cultural recognition. But they also embody the detachability and mobility of the fetish—naivete is a form of disavowal.

Mayne notes "a striking division between the spectacular lesbian uses to which single, isolated images may be applied and the narrative of classical Hollywood films, which seem to deaden any such possibilities" (105). Yet such remarkable films as *Queen Christina* and *Sylvia Scarlett* cannot be said to kill off their lesbian possibilities for every spectator, to embody a Hollywood classicism that successfully reproduces a heterosexual position for the subject. And the insistence of a particular image repertoire cannot be fully explained just as "using images." Perhaps there is a third possibility.

Barthes writes, "the third meaning structures the film *differently* without . . . subverting the story. . . . [I]t is at the level of the third meaning . . . that the 'filmic' finally emerges. The filmic is that in the film which cannot be described, the representation which cannot be represented" (64). I want to look at how memory captures the "filmic," erecting a fetish or a visual sign that generates an alternative narrative: "The [third] meaning is the epitome of a counternarrative" (63). Before I discuss counternarrative further, I'd like to turn to a case of lesbian cinephilia in which it is the *look* that hooks, a case that provokes a reexamination of film theory's proclamations on fetishism and the male gaze.

Card-Carrying Lesbian Fetishist

One of the women interviewed for *Jump Cut*, identified as "Gladys," an African-American lesbian born around 1950, offers a spectacular example of a lesbian "use" of a specific cinematic image. Gladys identifies von Sternberg's *The Blue Angel* (1930) as "without a doubt the first film that had a lot of impact on me as a kid," and recalls the scene in which Marlene Dietrich made a lasting impression upon her:

> I can . . . remember vividly the school boys planting her promo cards—not a picture of her naked but nude enough with a little feather covering her bottom half and you blow it and you'd see it all. I just thought that was fantastic. How wonderful it would be to blow it up and see Marlene Dietrich's—pudendum! (35)

The described scenario is a sort of cinematic primal scene of that famously men-only perversion, fetishism, as it involves a glance at the female genitalia that is deferred. The designated fetish is prototypically the last thing seen before the supposedly horrifying sight of the "castrated" woman's—pudendum. According to Freud the fetish "is not a substitute for any chance penis, but for a particular quite special penis"—the maternal phallus ("Fetishism" 215). It serves to memorialize the moment before the male subject recognizes castration, to preserve his belief in the maternal phallus, even as the substitution confirms his "knowledge" of its "absence." Freud notes, "Velvet and fur reproduce the sight of the pubic hair which ought to have revealed the longed for penis" (217). Here the feather is the metonymic stand-in that protects the indeterminacy of Dietrich's endowment. The feather fetish later returns in Dietrich's Medusa-like headdress in *Shanghai Express* and in other costumes. While it has been claimed that Dietrich is the cinema's premier phallic woman, Gladys is equivocal on this point: "Dietrich has substance," is all she'll say (35).

"When the fetish comes to life, so to speak, some process has been suddenly interrupted," Freud explains, "interest is held up at a certain point" (217). In *The Blue Angel*, the promised view is withheld from the nondiegetic spectator. Gladys, however, remembers herself gleefully imagining the actual sight. Her "interest" in the cinema is held up, fixated, on this originary scene of spectatorship and involvement in the female body. Gladys's enthusiastic response is just the opposite of a scenario of dread. She sees this picture, knows she is without it and wants to have it—to paraphrase Freud's account of the little girl's reaction to her discovery of the anatomical distinction between the sexes (188). "You'd blow it and you'd see it all!" What is memorialized in Gladys's story is not only her understanding of what it means to be a girl, but of what it means to like them.

The dramatic pause in her delivery, "How wonderful it would be to blow it up and see Marlene Dietrich's—pudendum!" sets up the unexpected word choice with the technique of a joke teller. What is hidden in that pause, what process is being interrupted? Was Gladys too expecting to see the maternal phallus? Or is she relating the process whereby she confirms that the woman is precisely *not* castrated (as Irigaray might note, not defined in phallic terms within a visual economy)? Her pause in selecting a word for genitalia can be read as a hesitation to use the term "pudendum," whose meaning, "something to be ashamed of," Gladys clearly rejects. It may be shameless to say, but I can't help but think that in the context of this formal interview, she was simply checking the urge to blurt out: "How wonderful it would be to blow it up and see Marlene Dietrich's—pussy"—the urge to *apelle un chat un chat.* . . . This lesbian cinephile is intransigent in the face of an attributed "castration"; yet her pleasure is still structured on the disavowal of loss.

For Gladys knows very well that if she had it for her own, the promo card would not really reveal it all. The image is precisely a promotion, promising an image of woman upon which even the cinema, from which the body is necessarily absent, cannot deliver.[15] Moreover, what is in question is not any chance pudendum, but one particular quite special one—Marlene Dietrich's. Mystery and inaccessibility are the foundation of this particular star's image, well dramatized in the spectacularly delayed entrance in this, her star-making debut film (we are forced to linger, with the schoolboys, over the card before we get to see the actress herself). Gladys's return to Dietrich, who, she is convinced, has substance, is made of flesh, not cardboard or celluloid, enacts a desire to see that which cannot be recovered in the full field of vision.

In "Visual Pleasure and Narrative Cinema," the influential essay by Laura Mulvey that relegated women to a kind of spectatorial exile, Dietrich served as the very model of the image of woman constructed to gratify the "fetishistic scopophilia" of the male spectator. Gaylyn Studlar's revision of the Mulvey model argued that it was a *masochistic* male spectator position that was constructed by the von Sternberg films with Dietrich. Studlar also conceded that this cycle of films sets up "a system of looking that elicits both female spectatorial identification with and desire for the powerful femme fatale" (248). But Gladys would reject this formulation: "There was no identification," she insists. It was "like looking at a magazine. You can't call that love, it's lust!" (35).

Peter Baxter's essay on *The Blue Angel*, "On the Naked Thighs of Miss Dietrich," takes on the question of fetishism and re-enacts its mechanism by himself disavowing sexual difference. He too uses an isolated, "spectacular" image to illustrate his argument:

> The commentary which englobes the film, reflecting and fixing its position in the discourse of society, includes in one place and another that famous still of Lola leaning back, grasping her knees, on the stage of the Blue Angel. . . . It should be obvious by now that this pose arrests the instant of fetishization, the instant before the child's glimpse of the female genital organ. (35)

Commenting on an attempt by censors to black out the suggestion of Dietrich's "pudendum" in one widely circulating version of the still (fig. 4), Baxter detects the failure of such an attempt in the proliferation of phallic symbols remaining within the frame (that is, the top hat, the dangling bird) that signify castration. He concludes, "Perhaps most awkward of all, however, for the censor's task, is the direction of Guste [the other woman]'s gaze, which ensures from inside the still what the eye outside the still will be drawn to" (25). This assertion is a somewhat awkward one for Baxter, for, having failed to take the gender of the spectator—or the child—into account, he is unable to acknowledge the difference of the gaze "inside," the *woman's* gaze. Why can she look with impunity, and precisely *not* at Dietrich's fetishized thighs and garters, which is all the viewer sees in the uncensored version of the still? Aptly, this "most famous of all Sternberg's stills" (Herman Weinberg, quoted in Baxter 25), which captures a woman's frank stare, is reproduced yet again, in its uncensored version, as illustration to Gladys's interview in *Jump Cut*. Both the censored and the uncensored versions of the still give evidence of a female, even lesbian, gaze arrested there but disavowed by the male critic.[16] Gladys can distinctly "remember Dietrich singing with her leg up on a chair" (35).

Gladys's favorite scene from the film is remarkably similar to the little girl's autoerotic fantasy analyzed in Freud's "A Child Is Being Beaten." In her fantasy the girl takes the spectatorial position—"I am probably looking on"—as a group of schoolboys are disciplined by their male teacher. Gladys does not, in fact, forget the narrative context in preserving the erotic charge

4. *Dietrich as Lola-Lola in* The Blue Angel *(von Sternberg, 1930). This is the censored version of the still.*

of the image. She remembers the boys in the schoolroom planting the card in another student's notebook, where it will inevitably be discovered and the bearer punished. It is nameless boys who are punished for their illicit looking—not her. The fact that her surrogates are male does not seem to give Gladys pause. When Whitaker asks Gladys, "Did anybody ever tell you that you shouldn't have those kinds of reactions?" she replies, "No, I was a real quiet child. . . . My brother went to films but he could have cared less about what I saw. . . . I can remember going home and thinking about those movies forever and ever and ever, not modeling myself after them but carrying them around . . . It would take three years of psychoanalysis to bring it all up" (35). In this account, Gladys becomes the film's paradigmatic spectator. Like the character Guste within the film, she looks and gets away with it.

I think Gladys's memory can help us rethink the tension between spectacle and narrative that Mayne detects in lesbian viewing practices. It centers on the postcard fetish, which thematizes the paraphernalia of star promotion; it circulates *within* this narrative much like a movie still or glamour portrait circulates outside it—it is thus staged, literally *mise*-en-scène, put on stage. Gladys's impression of Dietrich was not "isolated," "selected" or "appropriated" naively. Rather it "comes to life"—becomes a *moving* picture—because it is overdetermined. It is encoded by the studio's promotion of Dietrich in 1930 as "the woman all women want to see," and by lesbian sartorial codes in the 1920s and since, it is fully subjectivized by the narrative and the viewing situation. We may not have to make a decision between the seductions of isolated images and the subversion of plots, between purely stylistic and conventionally narrative codes, between the stars and the moon, in theorizing a lesbian relation to classical Hollywood cinema. Like the fetishist, we might have it both ways.

Popularized "lesbian" images such as the cross-dressing moments from *Queen Christina*, *Sylvia Scarlett*, and *Morocco* neither subvert nor are they neutralized by the films that include them. Iconic codes work with and against the narratives of specific films as well as intertextually and across the star persona to confirm and convey lesbian spectatorial possibilities. The "spectacular" dimension of lesbian signification is further narrativized by the citation of such images in subcultural and critical discourses such as movie autobiographies, photomontages, and videotapes. The sartorial splendor of Dietrich's tails complements the narration of identity and community performed by the genre of Dietrich tales.

Endless Love

A low-budget compilation tape by Spanish video artist Cecilia Barriga takes the appropriation of fetishized moments of star performance to its extreme and shows that these isolated images do have narrative context and consequence for lesbians by constructing a counternarrative around their implications. The title of this cinephiliac exercise, *Meeting of Two Queens* (1991), refers both to the roles of its heroines—Garbo as the lesbian Queen Christina of Sweden and Dietrich as the debauched Catherine the Great in *Scarlet Empress* (von Sternberg, 1934)—and to the estimation in which the stars are held by the videomaker and her presumed lesbian and gay audience of address. By removing the sound and splicing together resonant gestures and poses from the signature roles of the two actresses; linking point-of-view structures; and scrutinizing costumes, settings, and props to develop an alternative erotic economy, Barriga's tape fulfills what John Ellis calls the "invitation" of the star image as does no other film (1).

Uninvited

As Jane Gaines points out in an analysis of *Queen Christina* and its commodity tie-ins, "the unbounded opulence as well as the absolute power of monarchy [is], for the female viewer, an abundant and favorite fantasy" (51). Barriga's lesbian fantasy doubles our pleasure. If *Queen Christina* enacts the ultimate sacrifice for impossible (though nominally heterosexual) love, *The Scarlet Empress* shows us the heartless mistress of wanton pleasure. The solemn pageantry of Christina's coronation is intercut with Catherine's coolly lascivious review of her troops. Through Barriga's intercutting we can imagine that Catherine is being presented as a taunting seducer in the court of the vulnerable Swedish monarch.

To dream up a vehicle for *two* queens, a vehicle co-starring Garbo and Dietrich, is to cut neatly across the heterosexual hegemony of cinema. The Hollywood apparatus sets up women to become Woman; each female star is an emblem of uniqueness. Probably no two divas make this more apparent, and are, consequently, less likely to have female co-stars than Dietrich and Garbo (despite, or because of, the lesbian connotations of their images). Fan magazine articles of the early 1930s registered their claims to singularity as rivalry between the stars. Yet their "otherness" is actually similarly figured, around constructions of the (phallic) maternal, foreignness, and female narcissism and thus uniqueness. (That they were not rumored ever to have slept *together* also seems telling in this regard. But Mercedes de Acosta reports having relationships with both.) Barriga's tape is divided into a series of vignettes accompanied by "silent film" music, separated by intertitles introducing the action ("The Meeting"), naming a highlighted motif ("The Hat," in which the most outrageous concoctions of Travis Banton — Dietrich's designer at Paramount — and Adrian — Garbo's at MGM — go head to head), or providing the setting ("The Library"). In most of these segments the stars are juxtaposed in a pattern of strict alternation. This amounts to more than a mirroring of twin constructions of Woman, like the studio-manufactured rivalry between the two in the early 1930s, or a catalogue of campy details of mise-en-scène, costume, and performative excess. For what and how the two actresses signify is in tension; elements of each star's persona inform the syntagmatic progression, and the alternation culminates in a narrative coupling. Dietrich's coy masquerade is opposed to Garbo's sincere expansiveness. Characteristics of their acting styles and preferred codes of lighting and cinematography facilitate the cutting: Dietrich's shaded and mysterious downward look complements Garbo's heavenward gaze and thrown-back head. We have a butch-femme scenario where we might not expect one. Garbo's direct, reckless passion versus Dietrich's calculated sensuality; Garbo's threatened loss of control versus Dietrich's subtle but definite exercise of it; Garbo's face, Dietrich's legs; even, perhaps, Garbo's secret lesbianism and Dietrich's fickle, flaunted bisexuality. When the stars are "sutured" in the frame together in a segment such as "Dialogue," their role-playing is sustained in a flirtatious manner.

Cumulatively, *Meeting of Two Queens* offers a story of unhappy love. This we would expect—and demand—from Dietrich's habit of betrayal and Garbo's penchant for tragic sacrifice. One of the most exquisite pleasures of *Meeting of Two Queens* is precisely its refusal of a happy ending. After an ambiguous title that proclaims "The End" is revealed as simply the last of the series of intertitles introducing the discrete segments, there is a final vignette. As Dietrich kisses the woman in the bar from *Morocco*, Garbo (as Anna Christie) watches, drowning her sorrows in whiskey and ginger ale and anxiously puffing on her cigarette as if to underscore oral deprivation. Next Dietrich takes a drag on her cigarette, affecting indifference as Christina sweeps Ebba into a meaningful embrace. These overinvested girl-girl kisses from Hollywood history don't tell the whole story, the tape implies, and invites our imaginations.

These shots are followed by images of both stars in the arms of some of their innumerable, unmemorable, male costars. This is not only "the end" of their fantasized affair but "The End" according to a cinema script in which the woman swoons in the man's arms at the fade-out. The ultimate tragedy and betrayal is on the level of cinema itself. The final set of images begins with Dietrich weeping, pathetic on account of its very improbability. A tear rolls down her cheek, to dissolve into an image of Garbo's incomparable visage. A brief dissolve from her face back to Dietrich's is less a *Persona*-esque merging of feminine identities than an insistence that the "narrative image" of this film include *both* women. The tape's last shot is taken from the fade-out of *Queen Christina*, a lingering, famously inscrutable close-up of Garbo's "snowy solitary face," the face that Barthes has described as "almost sexually undefined, without however leaving one in doubt" ("The Face of Garbo" 721). The quoted image, Garbo's face as metaphor for the screen itself, recasts such questions of definition and doubt within lesbian terms.

Yet it is the tape's penultimate scene, entitled "Alcove," that seduces most completely. Viewers of *Queen Christina* will remember the episode at the snowbound inn in which the queen, traveling the countryside in drag, is compelled to share a room with Don Antonio, the stranded Spanish Ambassador (John Gilbert), a scene whose male homoerotic implications were registered in the film and, as I mentioned in Chapter 1, by the censors. When she reluctantly takes off her jacket, the revelation of her true self instantaneously provokes the fade to black that signifies sex in Hollywood movies. Into the disrobing scene (purged of Gilbert's intrusive reaction shots) Barriga cuts footage from von Sternberg's 1931 espionage film *Dishonored*, in which Dietrich performs a coy and very effective striptease of her own. Attentive viewers of *Queen Christina* will remember a flirtatious blonde serving maid who offers to help the disguised queen remove her boots, markedly preferring Garbo to Gilbert. In *Meeting of Two Queens* Dietrich arrives on the scene to make good the serving maid's proposition. The "peasant" costume she removes in *Dishonored* is no less a masquerade than Christina's lower-class male drag—donned solely for the purposes of seduction. Dietrich rolls down her stockings, checking the effect of her display, as Garbo sheepishly lays aside her sword. Dietrich unbuttons her bodice (fig. 5) as Garbo roughly unfastens her jacket (fig. 6).

The curious spectacle of Garbo's undressing in *Queen Christina* has itself been memorialized as something of a critical fetish. Charles Affron notes, "After Christina removes her jacket, the barest alteration of posture is only one step removed from the previous ambiguity, and is not at all conventionally feminine" (cited in Gaines 59n) and Gaines adds, "While Christina's downcast eyes and coy pose suggest 'modesty,' she stands yet fully dressed as a man" (59). Such ambiguity is dispelled in the re-making of the scene in *Meeting of Two Queens*. In a gesture of erotic capitulation, Garbo removes her dashing masculine outer garb to reveal—a passionate, vulnerable butch. Whether she's a woman is not in question; the suspense is about how much she will take off. Her masquerade bespeaks that "deeply Lesbian language of stance, dress, gesture, loving, courage, and autonomy" that Joan Nestle identifies in butch-femme roles (100). Just as the naked Dietrich (framed from the shoulders up) raises her eyes in a look of calculated surrender and Garbo relaxes her defiant pose we see the aforementioned title: "The End."

Although the video goes on in this final segment to enact the melancholy loss of one woman to the other, it does offer Garbo and Dietrich at the brink of consummation as the last image before the actual words "The End." There is structured ambiguity in the video's resolution. It has it both ways —inevitable loss and secret presence—the promise of lesbian cinephilia. The video enacts the meeting of two "scenes," in the sense of settings of desire, which correspond to two remarkably resonant and enduring star images. It also joins the "scene" of the individual's (clearly the artist's, certainly

5. *In Cecilia Barriga's* Meeting of Two Queens (1991), *Marlene Dietrich unbuttons her bodice.*

6. *Garbo unfastens her jacket (*Meeting of Two Queens, *Cecilia Barriga, 1991).*

this viewer's) fantasmatic investment in the cinematic image with the sub-cultural "scene" in which practices of transgressive spectatorship circulate —through gossip, stories of coming out with the stars, and the production and appreciation of such video homages.

The Fetish Is Dead; Long Live the Fetish

"What you are about to see is a true story of love and devotion," video artist Jean Carlomusto prefaces the Dolly Parton sequence from *L Is for the Way You Look*. That sequence, which deals with the lesbian public, with the question of audience, is introduced with an image more evocative of the private dimensions of spectatorship. The intertitle is followed by a brief clip showing the beatific face of Jennifer Jones in *The Song of Bernadette* (Henry King, 1943). The young nun is having an ecstatic spectatorial experience, a vision of a woman—of the Virgin Mary in fact. Carlomusto adds computer graphics to encircle the icon and trace the direction of Jones's gaze in multicolored blips and arrows. (Later, an iris-out from this madonna to *the* Madonna, pop star, makes explicit the connection between religious epiphany and female fandom.) The actress who plays the virgin is unbilled, but it's a (literal) cameo appearance by a miniaturized Linda Darnell, a Twentieth-Century Fox star at the time.

Coincidentally, one of Deborah Bright's montages also features Linda Darnell. Darnell is gazing at herself in the mirror, a narcissistic scenario female spectators have been told we are destined to replay. But Bright restages this mirror scene, placing herself behind Darnell and superimposing her own face over the male co-star's reflection which also appears in the mirror. She might be read as that "transvestite" female spectator, getting a little bit of distance from the reflected glory of womanly masquerade.[17] Except that Darnell is in drag here too, and the butch Bright is helping her with her tie (fig. 7), which disrupts the more predictable mappings of lesbian desire onto heterosexual scenarios. Darnell is an eccentric choice, one that displays that tangle of taste, chance, compulsion, and personal history that characterizes our addiction to the cinema and our object choices alike. Despite the fact that our contemporary encounter is mediated by television, home video, and commercial appropriations—and that female celebrities from other media crowd the lesbian pantheon—the classical Hollywood look and the cult of its female stars still structure lesbian fetishism. The artworks I've looked at here have an important pedagogical function in communicating this aspect of lesbian culture, this way of seeing.

7. *Deborah Bright, untitled from "Dream Girls" series, 1990. Linda Darnell and the artist. Courtesy the artist.*

Was It Love?

"From the sample of 458 motion-picture autobiographies written by high-school students it has been found that . . . in 66% there is distinct evidence and mentioning of day-dreaming as a result of motion pictures" (Blumer 59). This data was gathered in the Payne Fund Studies and was published in 1933 and used as part of the justification for more stringent regulation of the movies. One "Female 17, white, high school senior" claims: "I practiced love scenes either with myself or with a girl-friend. We sometimes think we could beat Greta Garbo, but I doubt it." Such daydreaming is now incorporated into modes of lesbian self-representation, for example in the videos Sadie Benning made while still a high school student.

"We didn't need Hollywood," Benning says in her tape *It Wasn't Love*, recounting her misadventures with a juvenile femme fatale: "We were

Hollywood." Benning's justly celebrated pixelvision tapes, constructed and set in her bedroom in her mother's house and composed of poses and references drawn from popular culture, are exemplary of the kinds of things baby dykes do with the legacy of classic movies.

"I no longer love the cinema; I still love it," was Christian Metz's statement of the position of the film theorist. Benning's title also smacks of the fetishist's disavowal. "It wasn't love," states a line of text at the end of the tape. "But it was something." Or, as "Gladys" might say . . . "It was lust."

3

Only one aspect of the optical effect appears distinctly and massively, and that is heterosexuality. Homosexuality appears like a ghost only dimly and sometimes not at all.

—MONIQUE WITTIG, "ON THE SOCIAL CONTRACT"

Female Spectator, Lesbian Specter

Genre and Deviance

What have been considered the very best of serious Hollywood ghost movies—*Curse of the Cat People* (Gunther Von Fritsch/Robert Wise, 1944), *The Uninvited* (Lewis Allen, 1944), *The Innocents* (Jack Clayton, 1961), and Robert Wise's 1963 horror classic *The Haunting*—are also, by some uncanny coincidence, films with eerie lesbian overtones. Masquerading as family romance, these films unleash an excess of female sexuality that cannot be contained without recourse to the supernatural, or indeed the unnatural. Of course, the best of Hollywood lesbian movies are always in some sense "ghost" movies. If the apparitional trope characterizes lesbianism's paradoxical place in modern culture generally, as Terry Castle argues in *The Apparitional Lesbian*, it operates quite palpably in the visual field of the cinema. Feminist theoretical work on female spectatorship and women's genres has drawn upon theories of the cinematic apparatus to project an image of femininity defined by lack and negativity. Lesbianism is the ghost in the machine, a sign of the body, desire, the other woman. The spectral presence of lesbianism in this genre, on the one hand, and in feminist theories of spectatorship, on the other, can be detected in the defense against homosexuality, which Freud believes characterizes paranoia.

The Haunting, the most explicit of these films, was produced after the Production Code Administration was permitted in 1961 to consider approving "references to sex aberrations" that "are treated with care, discretion and restraint" (quoted in Russo 205). Female homosexuality is manifested in the character of Claire Bloom rather than in a supernatural manifestation. Yet homosexuality, like the haunting itself, still does its work *implicitly*, behind the scenes. As the paradigmatic ghost film, *The Haunting* foregrounds lesbianism as a problem of representability.

In *The Haunting* two women are the only ones, among many people said to be "touched by the supernatural" who were originally invited, who agree to take part in a psychic experiment in a haunted New England mansion. As explicitly deviant women, they are asked to bear witness to an other power, an alternative reality. They join their host Dr. Markway (Richard Johnson), the pompous anthropologist-turned-ghostbuster, and the wise-cracking future heir to the house, Luke (Russ Tamblyn), who is skeptical of any unusual goings-on.[1] A truly terrifying sojourn with the (female) supernatural at Hill House leaves one woman dead due to unnatural causes and the spectator thoroughly shaken.

Although it was regrettably, though perhaps understandably, eclipsed by the two Oscar-winning films Wise directed before and after *The Haunting*—namely *West Side Story* (1962) and *The Sound of Music* (1964)—the film will maintain its place in cinematic history for two reasons. First, its lesbian character: Bloom appears as what is perhaps the least objectionable of sapphic stereotypes—the beautiful, sophisticated, and above all predatory lesbian.[2] Although not herself a fashion designer (a favorite lesbian profession), her wardrobe is by Mary Quant, she has ESP, and she shares top billing with Julie Harris, a star who from her film debut in *The Member of the Wedding* to her role as the hysterically frigid wife in another queer Carson McCullers adaptation, *Reflections in a Golden Eye* (John Huston, 1967), her incongruous casting as James Dean's love interest in *East of Eden* (Elia Kazan, 1955), and her one-woman show *The Belle of Amherst* has insistently been coded "eccentric." In *The Haunting*, Harris adds the characterization of a spinster aunt (see Chapter 5 on this type).

The second reason for which *The Haunting* is remembered is its effectiveness as a horror film. Like its source, Shirley Jackson's *The Haunting of Hill House*, the movie is adept in achieving in the spectator what Dorothy Parker calls "quiet, cumulative shudders" in her blurb on the back of the book. At least one reliable source pronounces *The Haunting* "undoubtedly the scariest ghost movie ever made," and the film is generally cited as a classic of its genre (Weldon 307). It is clear that reason number two is related to reason number one—*The Haunting* is one of the screen's most spine-tingling representations of the disruptive force of lesbian desire.

The at-first-glance disconcerting alliance between horror and lesbianism that *The Haunting* exploits so effectively can be traced through the evolution of classical Hollywood cinematic genres in response to problems of representability. The horror genre has been claimed in film criticism as an ideologically progressive one on several grounds. Concerned with the problem of the normal, it embodies the abnormal in the figure of the monster. In her influential feminist interpretation, Linda Williams has noted a potentially empowering affinity between the female victim and the monster in classic horror films, an identification that gives expression to female transgression. The omission of any mention of lesbian desire in this configuration is striking given her thesis: "clearly the monster's power is one of sexual difference from the normal male" (87).[3] Subsequent work by feminist and queer critics has explored the propensity of horror films to encourage identifications across gender lines and explore perverse sexualities.[4]

Horror can be seen to have an affinity with homosexuality beyond its queer cast of characters or its insistent thematic elaboration of difference in the representation of predatory or sterile desires. For horror puts in question the reliability of perception. Such an epistemological question is bound up with the representation of homosexuality. The question is not only whether "something else" exists, but in what forms its difference can be grasped — horror works the far side of this equation, inventing both "things" and the means of revealing or concealing them. As film theorists such as Mary Ann Doane have insisted, the structure of the look in cinema supports an epistemological drive. The adequacy of representation (the classical continuity system, for example) shores up the adequacy of the one who looks — who is understood since Laura Mulvey's work to be male. The epistemological doubts that stalk both the cinematic look and assertions of heterosexuality and male mastery are uniquely mobilized in horror films that imply nightmarish alternative realities.

The horror genre manipulates codes specific to the cinema — camera angles that warp the legibility of the image and the object of the gaze, framing that evokes the terror of what lies beyond the frame, sound effects that are not diegetically motivated, unexplained point-of-view shots that align the spectator with the monster or with something else — for effect and affect.[5] This play on representational adequacy, on the border, on the anxious reversal of subject and object positions, on the drama of emergence into the field of vision, has specific resonance for a theory of homosexual representation at the margins.

The ghost, or somewhat more abstractly, the haunting, seems to be particularly suited to exploit such questions of visibility. Why is it a disembodied variant of horror that is so frequently associated with femininity (and hence with the epistemology of lesbianism)? Williams considers the horror genre to discourage the female (heterosexual) audience's gaze: "Whenever the movie screen holds a particularly effective image of terror, little boys and grown men make it a point of honor to look, while little girls and grown women cover their eyes or hide behind the shoulders of their dates" (83). Yet the representation of the female gaze within the film is central to horror's effects. In *The Desire to Desire*, Mary Ann Doane reads Williams's argument about the affinity of woman and monster in terms of her own notion of the woman's problematic (and narcissistic) relation to the look: "Female scopophilia is a drive without an object . . . what the woman actually sees, after a sustained and fearful process of looking, is a sign or representation of herself displaced to the level of the nonhuman" (141–42).

Interestingly, Doane here uses a discussion of horror to theorize the female gothic, which addresses a female audience much more explicitly than does the horror film. A genealogy of *The Haunting*—and of the haunting of classical cinema by lesbianism—leads us to Alfred Hitchcock's *Rebecca* (1940), a key example of the female gothic, a genre that as a whole is concerned with heterosexuality as a institution of terror for women.[6] *Rebecca* is also a site of interpretive struggle in feminist film theory, and lesbianism functions as a spectral shadow in these debates. Although *Rebecca* is not overtly about the supernatural, its ghostly lesbian overtones become real ghosts in *The Uninvited*, a film explicitly marketed in the spirit of *Rebecca*. A consideration of what's at stake in the heroine's relationship to dead women in these two 1940s films provides significant insight into *The Haunting* and its challenge to heteronormative theorizations of narrativity and the gaze.[7]

Tania Modleski's influential reading of *Rebecca* argues that the film's appeal to the female spectator lies in its staging of the difficulties of the female oedipal drama, in which the little girl is asked to renounce her active desire for the mother for a passive position of soliciting the love of the father ("Never to Be Thirty-six Years Old"). The film's nameless, motherless heroine (Joan Fontaine) is obsessed with her precursor, a dead woman who is more vivacious than anything in the film. At every turn the heroine, who is coded as clumsy and childlike, is made to feel her inadequacy to this figure, with whom she presumes her husband is still in love. The oedipal script compels her to identify herself with the powerful maternal imago represented by Rebecca—even, Modleski argues, to substitute her body for the other woman's, most remarkably so when she dresses up in a costume (itself modeled on the dress worn by an ancestor whose portrait hangs at Manderley) that Rebecca had worn before her. The heroine takes the place of Rebecca not only by marrying Maxim de Winter (Laurence Olivier), but by handling and living among her things, preserved in fetishistic detail by another vivid and powerful female figure, Mrs. Danvers (Judith Anderson). Indeed the heroine's desire is channeled toward Rebecca as a powerful presence-in-absence by this other woman, who enjoys a peculiar and intense relation to her former mistress and who functions as a sort of regent of Rebecca's reign at Manderley.

In order to achieve the "goal" of Freud's story of femininity, adult heterosexuality, in which the woman takes her place as complement of the man, mirror of his desire, the second Mrs. de Winter must depose the first, the mother. Yet not only is this victory rather empty, Modleski argues—for all of Rebecca's positive and attractive qualities must be devalued, and the heroine must ask to be loved precisely for her own supposed lack of any such qualities (52)—it is also incomplete: Rebecca cannot be vanquished. She inhabits, Modleski asserts, "the blind space of patriarchy" by virtue of her very unrepresentability. This dynamic of visibility figures a specifically cinematic power as well. "The beautiful, desirable woman is not only never sutured in as object of the look, not only never made a part of the film's field of vision, she is actually posited within the diegesis as all-seeing" (52). Rhona Berenstein, in revisiting *Rebecca*, explicitly associates her invisibility with lesbianism. Ultimately the heroine's desire is not fully directed toward the man, as evidenced by her compulsive return in her dreams to Manderley (87).

At the opposite end of the spectrum is Mary Ann Doane's analysis in her key study of the woman's film of the 1940s, *The Desire to Desire*. For Doane, *Rebecca* "establish[es] the image of an absent woman as the delayed mirror image of a female spectator who is herself only virtual" (175). This is a rather dour prognosis for the second Mrs. de Winter and the female spectator whose identification her quest solicits, but it is characteristic of the limit-case kind of argument Doane is at pains to construct for the woman's film. For Doane, the classical Hollywood woman's film, in its almost mimetic relationship to psychoanalytic accounts of the "impasse" of female subjectivity, works very efficiently to dispossess women of the gaze and of a proper desire. In *Rebecca* the woman's literal absence echoes a conceptual impossibility.

The differences in these interpretations can be illustrated in the critics' discussions of the scene in the boathouse on the night that Rebecca's body is recovered from the sea. Maxim recounts to the heroine the story of his first wife's death and reveals the secret of his true feelings for her. As he narrates the tale the camera tracks around Rebecca's boathouse hideaway as if following the events of the night she died. Finally this shot is assigned to the heroine's point of view. For Modleski, "the camera pointedly dynamizes Rebecca's absence. . . . Most films, of course, would have resorted to a flashback at this moment, allaying our anxiety over an empty screen by filling the 'lack.' Here, not only is Rebecca's absence stressed, but we are made to experience it as an active force" (53). In contrast, Doane argues that this scene in *Rebecca* constructs "a story about the woman which no longer requires even her physical presence" (171).

The divergent readings of *Rebecca* and of the boathouse scene deploy the association between femininity and lack differently and have different implications for the representability of lesbian desire within feminist theoretical models. Doane's reading, however compellingly it may illustrate the repression of women in a patriarchal symbolic order, privileges negativity in a way that makes lesbianism *specifically* impossible to envision: the heroine and Rebecca are seen as undifferentiated echoes of an abstract "woman" constructed in negativity (that Mrs. Danvers is erased entirely in Doane's reading shows how this abstraction is supported only by certain types of women). Even the PCA picked up on the associations in this film between absence and indirection and lesbianism, as the emphasis in a memo to producer David O. Selznick indicates: "Sex perversion, *or an inference of it*, will not be allowed."[8]

Modleski, to be sure, does not proffer a lesbian reading of the film. For example, in judging Rebecca's mocking laughter at men, as recounted by Danvers, to be simply "playful," Modleski seems not to get the joke. Her vivid evocation of Rebecca's sexual daring is disappointingly revealed to refer to marital infidelity, although, as Berenstein points out, Max's reference to the "unspeakable" nature of Rebecca's confession to him draws out the connotation of homosexuality (88).[9] Most importantly, Berenstein concludes in her critique of Modleski on this point, "In order for queer sexual desires to be removed from the domain of heterosexual identification processes, Rebecca's status as a maternal figure must be separated from her role as an object of female sexual desires" (90). Indeed one is struck by what seems a common, euphemistic, move of psychoanalytic feminist criticism in the easy association of both Rebecca and especially Danvers with "the mother," when neither of them exhibits even remotely maternal qualities.

Yet in addition to distinguishing between these roles, we must elucidate their paradoxical dependence in dominant representation (including critical discourse). In Chapter 4 I will discuss in more detail how in classical cinematic narratives the place of the "maternal" may answer to considerations of lesbian representability. In the present context, the conflation with the maternal object that Berenstein bemoans positions Rebecca as in effect even "more" than the object of "an adult woman's attraction for another" (17). Rebecca's unpresentability is bound up with her function in the place of the mother—as the narrative and specular lure of "woman" for the female, and more particularly, for the lesbian subject's desire. Berenstein characterizes her essay as, in part, "an attempt to render Rebecca corporeal" (26). This making visible, giving body to the spirit of the text, is an important function of lesbian criticism. Yet the fact that Rebecca is not en-visioned may signify more than homophobic negation. Through its inscription in narrative, perverse *desire* itself, rather than its object, is made representable.

Rebecca holds our desire because she is in the place of what de Lauretis calls the film's narrative image. De Lauretis derives this concept from Modleski's reading of the film as female oedipal drama, which she argues prompts a "re-examining [of] the notion of specularization in the context of a figural narrative identification" (*Alice Doesn't* 152). Ironically the power of the invisible Rebecca is still invested in her function as "image." De Lauretis defines figural narrative identification as a double identification with the figure of narrative movement and with the figure of narrative closure, an identification that "seduces" the female spectator. In *Rebecca*, de Lauretis writes:

> the heroine . . . functions not as a mirror, a flat specular surface, but rather as a prism diffracting the image into the double positionality of female oedipal desire . . . [and] narrative identification: "Rebecca," as self-image and rival, marks not only the place of the object of the male's desire, but also, and more importantly, the place and object of a female active desire (Mrs. Danvers's). The portrait here is not . . . simply a mirror reflection of its viewer or the image the viewer must become, according to the ideological operation by which all women are represented as (reducible to) woman; for the film narrative works precisely to problematize, to engage and disengage, the heroine's—and through her, the spectator's—identification with that single image. (152–53)

What de Lauretis implies here, but fails to name, is that through this process "Rebecca" stands for more than self-image and rival or maternal object for the heroine. She is the object of the heroine's desire as well as that of Mrs. Danvers's—and indeed this triangulation is a condition of representability.[10]

Rebecca figures as insistently in feminist film theory as does Rebecca in the second Mrs. de Winter's psyche—and often the reasons why are similarly misrecognized. That *Rebecca* is a lesbian film—and invisible as such—is the condition of its almost uncanny recurrence in a critical discourse that, Berenstein shows, "traverses the edge of queerness, but does not call [it] by its proper name" (92). "Rebecca" has stood in for that proper name. Films that follow in *Rebecca's* footsteps show that female audiences share the fascination of feminist critics—a fascination dependent upon the fact that they don't always know what they're in for. If the specter of lesbianism in *Rebecca* is raised primarily in the question of visibility, *The Uninvited's* stress on the difficulty of defining the relation to the mother emphasizes that piece of the representability equation.

In Paramount's *The Uninvited*, the fact that the dead woman returns as a "real" ghost, not just a memory, anticipates the supernatural phenomenon of *The Haunting*. The film's advertising campaign exploited its uncanny similarities to the Oscar-winning Hitchcock film of 1940, touting the novel by Dorothy McArdle from which it was adapted as "the most fascinating mystery romance since *Rebecca.*" The films invite comparison in many respects, revealing how particular generic elements provide a home for lesbian undercurrents in the female gothic. Like *Rebecca, The Uninvited* thematizes the undue influence exerted over its young heroine by a dead woman and by the seaside house she once inhabited. In the later film the heroine's fascination is directly identified as love, rather than being veiled over as some fantasy of persecution. But the condition of this unveiling is that the object of her attraction becomes literally her mother. The film thus dramatizes how the female oedipal narrative functions as a support for another story, a lesbian desire that is both evoked and covered over.

A brother and sister from London, Rick and Pam (Ray Milland and Ruth Hussey) buy a house on the Cornwall coast, ignoring rumors that it is haunted. They befriend the granddaughter (Gail Russell) of its former owner, who now lives in the village. On her first visit to her new friends at Windward House, this girl, Stella, falls into a trance and runs to the edge of the cliff overlooking the sea. It is revealed that her mother had plunged to her death at precisely this spot when Stella was just a baby. Yet while resting from the close call in her former nursery, Stella thrills to the realization that her mother's presence is reaching out for her in the house. She spurns Rick's advances: "I can't think of you—not while *she's* out there." The dual nature of her supernatural experience—sometimes gentle, sometimes aggressive—plays throughout the film. "She has been waiting for me," Stella says, "In some queer sort of way I always knew it."[11]

Her grandfather calls in her mother's former companion Miss Holloway to remove Stella from danger and she is taken to the Mary Meredith Retreat—named for Stella's mother. But Miss Holloway's sinister intentions are revealed when she permits Stella to return to the house and to whatever threatens her there. Stella finds the house empty but for her grandfather. When the specter of Mary appears to them, he dies of fright, but the others return in time to save the young woman. The puzzle is finally solved when it is revealed that Stella is the daughter not of Mary but of Carmel, a Spanish model who lived in the home and posed for her artist father. Carmel has been reaching out from the grave to protect Stella from the evil designs of the unnatural Mary, who had actually been trying to kill the other woman's child when she fell from the cliff to her own death. The true mother's ghost seems to be satisfied at delivering her daughter to the arms of the hero, and Rick takes it upon himself to vanquish Mary's ghost: "It is time somebody faced that icy rage of yours!" he shouts, brandishing a candelabra at the retreating apparition.

The division between good mother and bad is the classic stuff of psychoanalysis, and the film follows the script of the "family romance"—"phantasies of a particular type, by means of which the subject invents a new family for [her]self" (Laplanche and Pontalis, *The Language of Psycho-Analysis* 160). Stella is if anything more childlike than the heroine of *Rebecca*, an impression reinforced by Rick and Pam as the protagonist couple whose interest in her reads as parental. Leona Sherman and Norman Holland note, "One might find in the gothic two versions of mother: a nurturing mother who should be trusted and a sexual mother who should not" (290) and argue that the gothic castle shelters a range of associations with the mother and with the body (287–88). Stella recounts a dream about the nursery: "I'd be lying there and it would be dark and cold and frightening, and then a little flame would come, just a tiny point of light, so big [she gestures with her thumb and forefinger] and I'd be warm. Then someone would put it out." The dream suggests the *jouissance* of association with the mother and the trauma of separation from her. Carmel's ghost is retroactively associated with experiences of warmth, the smell of mimosa, sobbing, and finally laughter—the sensual cues and rhythms that Julia Kristeva might identify with the semiotic, the preoedipal closeness to the mother. In contrast, Mary is externalized, associated with prohibition, distance, and the cold studio at the top of the house—and her ghost takes visual rather than aural form.

But if the film's task is to dampen Stella's excessive desire for the mother and to bring about the resolution of the heterosexual romance through this exorcism, the split between the two "mothers" results in a remainder that can't neatly be resolved. Stella must transfer her affection from one "mother" to the other. The film's trailer sets out the alternatives (neither of which depends on the hero, it could be noted): on the one hand "the breathless beauty of a haunting love," and on the other, "the heart-clutching dread of a nameless horror." We only know of their presence by what happens to the body of the heroine. The efforts to oppose the two women and to attribute to them opposite qualities—good/evil, warmth/coldness, light/darkness, love/hate—are confounded and ultimately redouble the discourse of the *sexual* mother. The bliss Stella feels at Windward is attributed to Carmel: "I wanted to see the dawn with her. I could feel her presence everywhere—and there was something else . . . something I've never known in my whole life." At another point she is discovered unconscious in Mary's haunt, the studio, and the film doesn't fill in the offscreen events that led her there. While the overdetermination of the maternal scenario would seem effectively to lay to rest the lesbian phantom that haunted *Rebecca* (there were no actual mothers in the earlier film at all), the fact that motherhood itself is occasion for epistemological doubt threatens to reinscribe a lesbian thematic (one that the fantasy of *two* mothers supports). The splits and doublings in the film permit no coherent lesbian reading of Stella's desire, but they raise its specter again and again.[12]

The implication that such excessive love signifies lesbianism is facilitated by the film's intimations of the adult lesbian desire between Miss Holloway and Mary. Miss Holloway tenderly extols Mary's beauty and goodness and reminisces about the plans they used to make as if they had been a couple. As in *Rebecca*, the relationship between the two women takes on its full significance only after one is dead. This reinforces the morbidification of lesbian desire, but also endows it with the romantic and tragic qualities of an impossible love that transcends death. And the formidable Mrs. Danvers is clearly the prototype for Miss Holloway. In *Rebecca*, when the young bride arrives at Manderley, a steely glance from Mrs. Danvers causes her to drop her gloves, and later the older woman very nearly convinces the younger to jump to her death. In *The Uninvited* Miss Holloway is endowed with explicit powers of hypnosis, successfully commanding Stella to sleep; she later sends the girl back to Windward and the cliff in the belief that the sea—and Mary—will claim her. Ultimately, when the truth about the dead women they protect is revealed, both women go mad.

Like Rebecca, Mary is ultimately revealed to be something other than who everyone thought her to be, and her unnaturalness is finally detected through her rejection of her reproductive role. Rebecca claimed she was pregnant in order to provoke Maxim into killing her; it was really cancer that was growing in her. Mary, far from being the tender mother who brought little Stella a night light, "feared and avoided motherhood," we are told. Mary's lesbianism and sterility are signified by her coldness: the arctic blasts in the studio, her "icy rage" and self-control. When Stella learns about Mary she remarks, "There was always something fighting in me that couldn't be calm like Mary."

The suggestion that Stella's relationship to Mary might be of the same passionate nature as Miss Holloway's desire for her dead companion is indicated by the identical portraits the women have of her. Both speak to their portraits—Miss Holloway assures hers: "They shall never find out, my darling." The two portraits hint at Mary's duplicity; the facade of proper womanhood hides her lesbian, nonreproductive self. If Stella's portrait, like the portrait that figures so centrally in *Rebecca*, signifies the "narrative image" of the female oedipal drama, the second, *identical* portrait suggests that there exists another version of the girl's story. Despite everything the narrative does to abject Mary, to make the revelation of her unworthy, unlovable nature its "gimmick," she is present everywhere, doubled in Miss Holloway, in Carmel, and in Stella, and refracted in the double portrait and in her own ghostly apparition that itself eerily echoes the flowing white gown in which she was painted. Although the decision to actually *depict* Mary's ghost in the film would seem to test spectatorial credulity with its fakeness and to restrict the "signified" of the film's haunting by lesbianism to a single figure who can then be mastered *visually*, nevertheless the specter can't be pinned down. If Rebecca can "revel in her own multiplicity," according to Modleski (54) precisely because she is never represented visually, so can "Mary," despite the phony-looking ectoplasm. Like Rebecca, Mary is never portrayed in flashback or photograph; according to the pressbook for *The Uninvited*, one actress sat for the portrait(s), another provided the ghostly voice, yet another was used to film the spectral apparition.

Now if *The Uninvited* ultimately lays its ghosts and its conflicts to rest, there are nevertheless some threatening undercurrents. When Stella talks of her loyalty to and longing for her mother, Rick may label her sentiments "horrible, unhealthy stuff," but the film never condemns this excess. His attempt to kiss her, to force "healthy stuff" upon her, is resented bitterly: "You shan't make me forget her." At the film's conclusion Stella still has a maternal memory to defend. Rick's final confrontation with Mary's ghost smacks of queer-bashing: "What do you want? It's Stella, isn't it? It's too late, we're on to you!" He laughs that the revelations about Carmel have given her "saintly legend rather a black eye." This invocation of physical violence underscores the homophobic impulse, but a black eye can hardly intimidate a ghost. Rick's bravado is undercut by the film. Stella notices that his encounter has left him shaking. He cracks a conventional misogynist joke: "I've had a narrow escape. *She* could have been my mother-in-law." The joke is funny because Mary is a scary ghost, but the prospect is scary to Rick because Mary is "funny." And after all, at the film's conclusion, Stella has successfully returned to Windward House, the haunt of her "mothers."[13]

The Uninvited is itself a reading of *Rebecca* that highlights the female oedipal dynamic and the lesbian identity of the dead woman suggested in the earlier film, inviting an understanding of the gothic genre to which both belong as a lesbian oedipal drama. In the gothic narrative, the heroine's look is central yet unreliable, precisely because the female object sought by her gaze is withheld. This narrative can be seen to encode the dramas of desire and identification at stake in female spectatorship and the lesbian excess that haunts them, to remind us that we can't always believe our eyes.

Secret Beyond Theory's Door

A lesbian specter can be said to have haunted feminist film theory as it developed in the 1980s, in particular to stalk the female spectator as she was posited and contested in that discourse. The "problem" of female spectatorship took on a dominant and in a sense quite puzzling position in feminist film theory (a field, after all, pursued in the main by avid female filmgoers), which in some instances denied its very possibility. Laura Mulvey herself, revisiting her widely read "Visual Pleasure and Narrative Cinema" in an essay called "Afterthoughts on 'Visual Pleasure and Narrative Cinema,'" explains: "At the time, I was interested in the relationship between the image of woman on the screen and the 'masculinization' of the spectator position, regardless of the actual sex (or possible deviance) of any real live movie-goer" (12). This parenthetical, "or possible deviance," is one of the few references to sexual orientation in the body of psychoanalytic film theory. Yet within the binary stranglehold of "sexual difference" theory, lesbianism is so neatly assimilated to the "masculinization of the spectator position" as to constitute an *im*possible deviance. In asserting the female spectator's narcissistic over-identification with the image (Doane), in describing her masculinization by an active relation to the gaze (Mulvey), or in claiming that the film's fantasy encourages identifications that disregard the viewer's gender and sexuality (Bergstrom), feminist film theory has been unable to envision women who looked at women with desire. The avoidance of this evident reality at times seemed to enact the defense against homosexuality that Freud posited was at the very heart of paranoia. If the female spectator "is" the image, she cannot desire the representation of woman that supports that image. Her masculinization denies her distance from the dominant, male, desiring position. If her sexuality is not considered determinative of her spectatorial orientation, it does indeed make no difference. Female spectatorship may well be a theoretical "problem" only insofar as lesbian spectatorship is a real one.[14]

In *The Desire to Desire* Mary Ann Doane addresses female spectatorship in relation to the gothic, which she aptly designates the "paranoid woman's film." Doane argues that the figuration of female subjectivity in the woman's film is characterized by a deficiency in relation to the gaze, a metonymy for desire itself. Within this framework "subjectivity can . . . only be attributed to the woman with some difficulty" (10), hence "female spectatorship . . . can only be understood as the confounding of desire" (13)—or at most as the desire to desire.

The gothic subgenre's privileged status in Doane's book corresponds to its ambiguous position within the woman's film genre. Related to the "male" genres of film noir and horror "in [its] sustained investigation of the woman's relation to the gaze," the gothic is both an impure example of the woman's film and a "metatextual" commentary on it (125–26). "In their hyperbolization of certain signifying strategies of the woman's film, they test the very limits of the filmic representation of female subjectivity for a female spectator," Doane argues (125). I would suggest that it is lesbianism that is figured by these "limits." The "paranoid woman's film" is inadvertently privileged in another sense. For, via Freud's definition of paranoia, the specter of homosexuality makes a rare appearance in Doane's text. The process by which it is exorcised is intimately bound up with Doane's definition of female spectatorship.

Paranoia and Homosexuality

For Doane paranoia is strikingly articulated in the film gothic because of the visual medium's ability to externalize and project. Doane offers a lengthy discussion of psychoanalytic descriptions of paranoia, but she qualifies Freud's identification of paranoia with a defense against homosexuality as a merely "technical" definition of the disorder (129). Freud himself was "driven by experience to attribute to the homosexual wish-phantasy an intimate (perhaps an invariable) relation to this particular form of disease."[15] Perhaps it is homosexuality's relevance to a critical account of the gothic genre that Doane's discussion of paranoia represses. She writes:

> Yet, there is a contradiction in Freud's formulation of the relationship between paranoia and homosexuality, because homosexuality presupposes

> a well-established and unquestionable subject/object relation. There is a
> sense in which the very idea of an object of desire is foreign to paranoia.
> (129–30)

Homosexuality is foreign to the definition of paranoia that Doane wishes to
appropriate to describe the gothic fantasy.[16] "Because Freud defines a passive homosexual current as feminine, paranoia, whether male or female,
involves the adoption of a feminine position." This assimilation of homosexuality to the feminine effectively forecloses the question of the difference
of lesbianism when Doane later turns to Freud's "Case of Paranoia Running
Counter to the Psychoanalytical Theory of the Disease." In it Freud writes:

> The relation between paranoia and homosexuality had so far been easily
> confirmed by my own observations and analyses and by those of my
> friends. But the present case emphatically contradicted it. The girl seemed
> to defend herself against love for a man by transforming the lover straight-
> away into a persecutor: there was no sign of the influence of a woman, no
> trace of a struggle against a homosexual attachment. (99–100)

We can recognize a gothic plot brewing here. And given the genre, we can
be assured we *will* find, as we delve into the past, signs of the influence of a
woman.

In this case, which is said to run "counter" to psychoanalytic theory of
paranoia on the point of an apparent *absence* of homosexual desire, the
primal fantasy that Freud ultimately uncovers as confirmation of his hypothesis (the homosexual wish made clear by the discovery of a same-sex
persecutor and behind her, a same-sex love object, the mother) is read by
Doane as the female patient's "total assimilation to the place of the mother."
Desire between women is subsumed by female identification, "assimilation." Doane writes that

> the invocation of the opposition between subject and object in connection
> with the paranoid mechanism of projection indicates a precise difficulty in
> any conceptualization of female paranoia—one which Freud does not
> mention. For in his short case history, what the woman projects, what she
> throws away, is her sexual pleasure, a part of her bodily image. (168)

In forming a delusion as defense against a man's sexual advances and in
breaking off relations with him, the woman is seen to be throwing away her
pleasure.

For Doane homosexuality is too locked into the subject/object dichot-
omy to have much to do with paranoia. Femininity represents a default in
relation to the paranoid mechanism of projection—"what [the woman spec-
tator] lacks . . . is a 'good throw'"[17]—precisely because the woman cannot

achieve subject /object differentiation. The "contradiction" between homosexuality and paranoia, and the "precise difficulty" inherent in female paranoia are related by a series of slippages around a central unspoken term, lesbianism.[18]

"Homosexuality" appears in Doane's text only furtively; female subjectivity is its central focus. Yet, strikingly, it is an account of "lesbian" desire that is used to summarize Doane's position on female spectatorship:

> The woman's sexuality, as spectator, must undergo a constant process of transformation. She must look, as if she were a man with the phallic power of the gaze, at a woman who would attract that gaze, in order to be that woman. . . . The convolutions involved here are analogous to those described by Julia Kristeva as "the double or triple twists of what we commonly call female homosexuality": "I am looking, as a man would, for a woman"; or else, "I submit myself, as if I were a man who thought he was a woman, to a woman who thinks she is a man." (157)

Doane has recourse to what only Kristeva could call "female homosexuality" to support a definition of female spectatorship that disallows homoeroticism completely—lesbianism and female spectatorship are abolished at one "twist."[19] Female subjectivity is analogous to female homosexuality, which *is* sexuality only insofar as it is analogous to male sexuality. The chain of comparisons ultimately slides into actual delusion: "a woman who thinks she is a man." In what seems to me a profoundly disempowering proposition, the very possibility of female desire as well as spectatorship is relinquished in the retreat from the ghost of lesbian desire. As we shall see, a similar path is traced in *The Haunting*. The impossibility of lesbianism's coming into view, the lack of terms with which to grasp it, results in the textual dispersion of terrifying and unexpected disturbances.

A House Is Not Her Home

"An evil old house, the kind that some people call haunted, is like an undiscovered country waiting to be explored. . . ."

The male voice-over—Dr. Markway's—with which *The Haunting* opens, will have, for some viewers, an uncanny resonance with the description of woman as "the dark continent." The further association then set up between signifiers of femininity and of the domicile would not be unusual: in cinema it appears in genres from the western to the melodrama. Doane cites Holland and Sherman's précis of the gothic formula: "the image of woman-plus-habitation and the plot of mysterious sexual and supernatural threats in an atmosphere of dynastic mysteries within the habitation" (124). It is the uncanny house that the heroine is forced to inhabit — and to explore.

Freud's essay on the uncanny draws on the literary gothic, particularly the work of E.T.A. Hoffman. He associates the uncanny sensation with an etymological overlap between the definitions of the uncanny, *das Unheimliche*, and its apparent opposite *das Heimliche* (literally, the homey, the familiar), ultimately identifying this convergence with "the home of all humans," the womb. In this account the woman provokes the uncanny; Freud gives us no elaboration of what her experience of it would be. It is this underexplored, shadowy realm into which the cinematic subgenre of the female gothic enters.

In the threatening family mansions of the gothic, and in *The Haunting*'s evil old Hill House, a door, a staircase, a mirror, a portrait are never simply what they appear to be. The title of Fritz Lang's *Secret Beyond the Door* sums up the enigma of many "paranoid woman's films," in which a question about the husband's motives becomes an investigation of the house (and of the sexual secret of a woman who previously inhabited it). In *Secret Beyond the Door* the husband is an architect whose hobby is "collecting" rooms in which murders have occurred; beyond one door the heroine finds a replica of her own bedroom (fig. 8).[20]

Hill House, too, reflects the obsessions of its builder, we are told. "The man who built it was a misfit. He built his house to suit his mind. All the angles are slightly off; there isn't a square corner in the place." Visitors become lost and disoriented, doors left ajar close unnoticed. The film's montage exploits this as well, disorienting the spectator with threatening details — a gargoyle, a doorknob, a mirror — and unexplained camera set-ups and unmotivated movements. Yet as a house that is literally haunted, Hill House poses another secret beyond its doors, one of which the architect himself is unaware. Hill House is uncanny *for the woman*. The advertising art for the film (fig. 9) depicts a female figure trapped in a maze beneath the outline of the house. Architectural elements are integrated into the title design. Thus the aspect of the house, its gaze, are crucial in the film, as they were even for the novelist who, as Shirley Jackson's biographer recounts the story, "plowed through architecture books and magazines" until finding a picture of the perfect house for her tale, only to discover that her great-grandfather, an architect, had designed it (Oppenheimer 226).

Hill House is a projection not only of the female body, but also of the

8. *Joan Bennet,* Secret Beyond the
Door *(Fritz Lang, 1948).*

9. *Advertisement for* The Haunting *(Robert
Wise, 1963).*

female mind, a mind that, like the heavy oak doors, may or may not be unhinged. A reading of the terrors of Hill House as a reflection of the heroine's disintegrating mental state could certainly be supported by both film and novel. And yet consider Jackson's—dare I say?—paranoid reaction to finding her name in the index of Jeanette Foster's *Sex Variant Women in Literature*, in which another of her tales, ostensibly about a schizophrenic woman, had been characterized as "an eerie novel about lesbians."

> I happen to know what *Hangsaman* is about. I wrote it. And damnit it is about what I say it is about and not some dirty old lady at Oxford . . . Because (let me whisper) I don't really know anything about stuff like that. And I don't want to know. Yes yes . . . I know, I read Freud. But there has got to be a point where I dig in my heels and decide who is going to be the master, me or the word. (Oppenheimer 232–33)

Jackson's recourse to rather circular proofs—she is paraphrasing Humpty Dumpty—suggests that lesbianism and signification itself are eerily linked for her: "[I]f the alliance [between the two women] is unholy then my book is unholy and I am writing something terrible, in my own terms, because my own identity is gone and the word is only something that means something else" (233). The biographer steps in to explain that Jackson's books are "about separate personalities—separate women—who are actually one. . . . The relations among these splintered parts, familiar, affectionate, cozy, intimate, were meant to be the relations among parts of one single mind—and to have that misread as lesbianism horrified her" (233). The *heimlich*—that which is familiar, affectionate, cozy, intimate—becomes *unheimlich*, uncanny, lesbian, the cause of "horror" to the horror writer.[21]

Robbers, Burglars, and Ghosts

The relationship between the representation of woman and the space of the house is not simply a generic requirement of the gothic. In "Desire in Narrative," Teresa de Lauretis analyzes Jurij Lotman's narratology and his reduction of plot types to just two narrative functions—the male hero's "entry into a closed space, and emergence from it." Lotman concludes:

> Inasmuch as closed space can be interpreted as "a cave," "the grave," "a house," "woman" . . . entry into it is interpreted on various levels as "death," "conception," "return home" and so on; moreover all these acts are thought of as mutually identical. (quoted on 118)

And de Lauretis sums up: "the obstacle, whatever its personification, is morphologically female and indeed, simply, the womb" (*Alice Doesn't* 119).

The sinister slippage in the chain of spatial designations from grave to house to woman lends a narrative progression to Freud's uncanny. Given the conflation of "woman" with the space rather than the subject of narrative, and given the identification of heterosexuality qua conception with the very prototype of narrative progression and resolution, it is no wonder that the lesbian heroine (and her spectatorial counterpart) are so difficult to envision.

Insofar as the cinema rewrites all stories according to an oedipal plot, when the woman is the hero, her story is told as the female Oedipus, as we have seen with *Rebecca*. To reiterate, the heroine's conflicting desires for the mother and for the father are put into play only to be "resolved" as the mirror image of man's desire. De Lauretis proposes in "Desire as Narrative" that as the story unfolds the female spectator is asked to identify not only with the two poles of the axis of vision—feminist film theory's gaze and image—but with a second set of positions, with the figure of narrative movement, and the figure of narrative closure. Of the latter, de Lauretis writes: "The female position, produced as the end result of narrativization, is the figure of narrative closure, the narrative image in which the film, as [Stephen] Heath says, 'comes together'" (140).[22] We can recognize the "narrative image" as fundamentally an image of heterosexual closure, or, in Lotman's equation, death.

The narrative work of classical cinema can thus be defined as the visual playing out or narrativizing of space (the house, the grave, the womb) that articulates femininity with the image (femininity *as* image). *The Haunting* is one of the exceptional Hollywood films that frustrates the hero's "entry into a closed space" and stages a story of deviant female subjectivity, of the *woman*'s return precisely as a struggle with the topos of the home. One publicity still for *The Haunting* shows the iconography of the "image of woman-plus-habitation" gone awry, overlaying multiple images of the heroine and the house in a collage-like effect, encapsulating the film's narrative as one of female and domestic fragmentation.

The Haunting tells the story not of Theodora (Claire Bloom), the invited researcher who is definitely a dyke, but of the other guest, Eleanor (Julie Harris), a woman whose sexuality—like that of the heroines of *Rebecca* and *The Uninvited*—is latent, not necessarily, not yet, lesbian. Her journey is articulated as female oedipal drama almost against her will, and is resolved, with her death, as a victory of, exactly, the house and the grave (perhaps the womb). "Now I know where I am going, I am disappearing inch by inch into this house," she finally recognizes in her eerie voice-over. My reading of the film will attempt to trace the "haunting" of Hill House as it shifts between homosexuality and homophobia.

As a ghost film, *The Haunting* dramatizes not only the woman's "deficiency in relation to vision" (as Doane characterizes the female gaze), but a deficiency in relation to visibility or visualization. In *The Haunting* we never see the ghost, though we do see the lesbian. Which is not to say that we "see" lesbian sexuality. *The Haunting* is "not a film about lesbians," the common disavowal of mainstream producers of lesbian- and gay-themed films, as Vito Russo documents. It is (pretends to be) about something else. I would consider "something else" to be a useful working definition of lesbianism in classical cinema.[23] It is precisely the fact that the "haunting" is unseen, that there are no special effects, that renders *The Haunting* the ultimate ghost film.

> Robbers, burglars and ghosts, of whom some people feel frightened before going to bed . . . all originate from one and the same class of infantile reminiscence. . . . In every case the robbers stood for the sleeper's father, whereas the ghosts corresponded to female figures in white nightgowns. (439)

What is immediately striking in this passage from Freud's *Interpretation of Dreams* is the dissymmetry between the referents of the two dream symbols. Burglars and robbers stand quite definitively for the father. Ghosts are a figure of—a figure. Not "the mother," perhaps a governess, a nurse, or a sister (fig. 10).

"Scandal, Murder, Insanity, Suicide"

Dr. Markway's voice-over resumes after the opening credits of *The Haunting*. The story of Hill House as Dr. Markway envisions it—literally envisions it, for his narration is accompanied by a sort of prologue or flashback sequence—is the story of women and the grave. The mansion, built by one Hugh Crain "ninety-odd—very odd" years ago, is the site of the deaths of four women, which are enacted for us: Hugh Crain's two wives, his daughter Abigail (who lived to old age in the house), and her paid companion. This prologue sequence supplies us with a surplus of cinema's "narrative image"—*female* scandal, suicide, murder, and insanity—before the drama even begins to unfold. It is as if all the visual power of cinema (exceeding Dr. Markway's as narrator) is amassed to contain the threat that whatever it is that haunts Hill House poses.

Dr. Markway hides his interest in the supernatural under the guise of science; his true object of study, like that of Freud, another "pseudo" scientist, is deviant femininity. He designates one room of the house the "operat-

10. *Claire Bloom and Julie Harris appear as "female figures in white nightgowns," in* The Haunting *(Robert Wise, 1963).*

ing room"—"that is, the center of operations," he reassures his female guests. Suave, paternalistic, Dr. Markway is yet somehow lacking in relation to the law—or at least the laws of Hill House. (In contrast is Theodora's ESP, which affords her privileged knowledge of "the haunting" and of Eleanor. She's thus a better analyst than the doctor as well.) Dr. Markway admits, when asked to reveal the laws of psychic occurrences, "[Y]ou'll never know until you break them." His laughably inadequate readings of the goings-on in Hill House ("I have my suspicions"), his lectures on the preternatural (that which will some day come to be accepted as natural), his efforts to measure the "cold spot" become more and more readable as fumbling attempts to explore the "undiscovered country" of female homosexuality. In this light his disclaimer about the supernatural—"don't ask me to give a name to something which hasn't got a name"—is also a disclaimer about knowledge of "the love that dares not speak its name." He rejects the word "haunted," preferring "diseased," "sick" and "deranged"—pathologizing, anthropomorphizing and, I would argue, lesbianizing the haunted house.

When his version of the story of Hill House includes the proclamation: "It is with the young companion that the evil reputation of Hill House really begins" we are prepared, indeed invited, to speculate about what the scandal attached to the companion might be.[24] It is onto the fates of the four female characters/ghosts, most crucially that of the companion who is extraneous (subordinate) to the nuclear family, that Eleanor Vance maps her oedipal journey, her crisis of desire and identification. As narrativity would demand, she starts out in the place of the daughter. Yet she is a grown-up daughter, a spinster, who leaves her family home—her mother has recently died, and as the maiden aunt she lives in her sister's living room—to "return home" to Hill House.

Eleanor and Theodora were invited to Hill House by Dr. Markway in the hopes "that the very presence of people like yourselves will help to stimulate the strange forces at work here." They are the only persons "like themselves"—who have had paranormal experiences—who accepted the invitation. The doctor's interest in Eleanor's case was sparked by her child-hood poltergeist experience—a shower of stones that fell on her house for days. Eleanor at first denies—"I wouldn't know" (about things like that)—what her brother-in-law calls the "family skeleton," the secret of "what [her] nerves can really do." In the internal monologue accompanying her journey to the house (a voice-over that recurs throughout the film, giving the specta-tor an often terrifying access to her interiority) Eleanor refers to herself as homeless. She has never belonged within the patriarchal home and its family romance. Her "dark, romantic secret" is her adult attachment to her mother, which she angrily defines as "eleven years walled up alive on a desert island." Eleanor is thrilled at the prospect of "being expected" at her destination; for the first time something is happening to *her*. (She never dares expect that she will *make* something happen.) More is "expected" of her than she dreams . . .

Things That Go Bump in the Night

When Eleanor arrives at Hill House she is relieved to meet one of her companions. "Theodora—just Theodora," Claire Bloom's character intro-duces herself to Eleanor, adding, "The affectionate term for Theodora is Theo." "We are going to be great friends, Theo," responds Eleanor, whose affectionate name "Nell" Theo has already deduced by her keen powers of

11. *Eleanor (Harris) and Theo
(Bloom) resolve to become
friends—"like sisters?" in* The
Haunting *(Robert Wise, 1963).*

extrasensory perception that are exercised most often in reading Eleanor's mind.[25] "Like sisters?" Theo responds sarcastically (fig. 11).[26]

Theo recommends that Eleanor put on something bright for dinner, sharing with her the impression that it is a good idea always to remain "strictly visible" in Hill House. On their way downstairs, they have their first supernatural experience, during which Eleanor shouts, "Don't leave me, Theo," and Theo cries out, "It wants you, Nell." After they have joined the others Eleanor proposes a toast: "I'd like to drink to companions." Theo responds with obvious pleasure and the camera moves in to frame the two women. "To my new companion," replies Theo with inimitable, elegant lasciviousness. The toast, like their relationship, alas, remains unconsummated, for Eleanor continues—"except I don't drink." Eleanor clearly is the main attraction for both the house and Theo, each finding in her what Theo calls a kindred spirit. The film, resisting the visualization of desire between women, displaces that desire onto the level of the supernatural, Theo's seduction of Eleanor onto the haunting. Numerous shots of both women

12. *Harris and Bloom as "lesbian spectators" in* The Haunting *(Robert Wise, 1963).*

looking in horror at—nothing—figure the problem of lesbian representability and spectatorship at once (fig. 12).

The process whereby the apparition of lesbian desire is deferred to the manifestation of supernatural phenomena is well illustrated by a sequence depicting the events of the first night spent by the company in Hill House. Theo accompanies Eleanor to the door of her bedroom, and offers to come in and arrange Eleanor's hair. Although Eleanor refuses Theo's advances, the women end up in bed together anyway, but not according to plan. Eleanor, realizing with a mixture of relief and anxiety that she is alone after Theo's departure, locks her door ("Against what?" she muses) and drifts off to sleep. A shot of the exterior of the house, and a dissolve to a shot from the dark interior at the base of the main staircase are accompanied by a faint pounding that rises in volume. Eleanor stirs and, half-asleep, knocks in response on the wall above her bed: "All right, mother, I'm coming." When Theo calls out to her in fear, Eleanor realizes her mistake and rushes into

Theo's adjoining room. Huddled together in Theo's bed throughout the protracted scene, the women withstand an unbearably loud knocking that eventually comes to the door of the bedroom. Finally the sound fades away, and Eleanor runs to the door when she hears Luke and the doctor in the hall. The men enter, explain they had been outside chasing what appeared to be a dog, and ask whether anything has happened. The women burst into laughter, and after catching their breath, sarcastically explain that something knocked on the door with a cannonball. Luke remarks that there isn't a scratch on the woodwork—"or anywhere else," and the doctor soberly intones: "When we are decoyed outside, and you two are bottled up inside, wouldn't you say that something is trying to separate us?" The sequence ends with ominous music and a pan to Theo's face.

The knocking that terrorizes the women takes up an element of the film's prologue—the invalid Abigail pounds with her cane on the wall to call the companion who fails to come, sparking malicious town gossip that she had somehow or other murdered her mistress. At this point in the film we are already aware that Eleanor harbors guilt about her own mother's death; what this scene makes explicit is the exact parallel between the scenarios, down to the knocking on the wall that Eleanor later admits she fears she may have heard and ignored on the fatal night, which puts Eleanor in the position of companion (servant, sexual partner, murderer?) vis à vis her own mother.

> When a wife loses her husband, or a daughter her mother, it not infre-quently happens that the survivor is afflicted with tormenting scruples . . . which raise the question whether she herself has not been guilty through carelessness or neglect of the death of the beloved person. No recalling of the care with which she nursed the invalid, no direct refutation of the asserted guilt can put an end to the torture. (80)

Freud concludes in this discussion from *Totem and Taboo* that a repressed component of hostility toward the deceased is the explanation for these reproaches, and similarly for the "primitive" belief in the malignancy of spirits of dead loved ones: the *projection* of that hostility is feared aggression from the dead. Projection is of course the mechanism of those suffering from paranoia who are "struggling against an intensification of their homo-sexual trends." In paranoia, Freud tells us, "the persecutor is in reality the loved person, past or present" ("A Case of Paranoia" 99).

Eleanor's psychosexual history is strikingly similar to that of the subject of Freud's "Case of Paranoia Running Counter to the Psychoanalytical Theory of the Disease"—a thirtyish woman living with her mother who forms a paranoiac delusion to defend herself against the attentions of a man.

In both cases, the loved person, then, the persecutor, is the mother. Much has been made in film theory of the form the patient's delusion took in this case: that of being photographed, sparked by an "accidental knock or tick" that she hears while visiting the man in his apartment. The visual and the auditory, the camera and the click, are the two registers of which the cinema is composed, rendering it analogous to paranoid projection (Doane 123). The noteworthy point of Freud's case history is his reading of the instigating cause of the delusion: "I do not believe that the clock ever ticked or that any noise was to be heard at all. The woman's situation justified a sensation of throbbing in the clitoris. . . . There had been a 'knocking' of the clitoris." "In her subsequent rejection of the man," Freud concludes, "lack of satisfaction undoubtedly played a part" (104–105).

The knock recurs in this scene from *The Haunting* with the force of a cannonball (proportionate to the force of Eleanor's repression, manifested before in the violence of the poltergeist against her mother's home) and intervenes precisely at the moment of the intensification of homosexual desire, during its visualization. It is a knocking that on the manifest level can be read as the ghost of Abigail looking for a companion, or on a latent level as the persecution of Eleanor by her own mother in conjunction with her taking of a new lover. (That is, Theo. If we are reluctant to read this as a quasi–love scene I offer as anecdotal support the fact that, despite its centrality, it was cut from the version I saw on TV.) Like Freud, the men suspected that there had been no noise at all. Love between women is considered unspeakable. It is inaudible and invisible—it doesn't leave a scratch. I do not contend that the laughter Theo and Eleanor share over the men's ignorance is triumphant; in fact the scene most literally transforms homosexuality into homophobia by replacing sexuality with fear. When the doctor pompously acknowledges that "something" is separating the girls from the boys in Hill House, he resolves to take precautions. "Against what?" Eleanor asks, naively, for the second time in this sequence. For the camera tells us it is Theo, some*one*, not some*thing*, who separates the doctor and Eleanor.

The next morning Eleanor awakens a little too excited by her first experience of the supernatural. Over breakfast, her hair arranged in a new style as if in response to Theo's wish, she claims to be "much more afraid of being abandoned or left behind than of things that go bump in the night." This does not appear to be entirely true, for her feeling of excitement is accompanied by her turning away from Theo as potential love object and toward the doctor, whose paternalistic interest in her Theo calls "unfair." When asked what *she* is afraid of, Theo responds, "of knowing what I really want." Her words make Eleanor uncomfortable on several levels. Eleanor misreads her own desire, as I suspect some feminist film critics would, as desire for the man, that is, the father. Theo's attitude toward her rival is manifested with knowing sarcasm, telling Eleanor she "hasn't the ghost of a chance" with the doctor. A production still (fig. 13) depicts Eleanor's relationship to the doctor in an ambivalent embrace. Actually, he has just caught her as she is about to fall backwards over the railing. She had been staring up at the turret, and in a rapid zoom from the point of view of the tower window, she has been virtually pushed by the camera, the house itself, and the implied gaze of a (female) ghost. Eleanor's turning toward the father smacks indeed of "a defense against a homosexual wish," and she literally begins to see Theo as a persecutor. The very forcefulness of this defense supports a reading of the night of knocking as a seduction scene.[27]

13. *The heterosexual embrace. Dr. Markway (Richard Johnson) catches Eleanor in* The Haunting.

More Than Meets the Eye

The defense against homosexuality is mirrored on the level of the film's enunciation; when the supernatural events of the second night bring the women together the cinematic apparatus emphatically separates them. The women are sleeping in beds pushed next to each other. Dr. Markway (taking precautions) has advised the women to move in together. ("You're the doctor," Theo responds.) Before turning out the light Eleanor snaps at Theo homophobically, "I told you I was tired." When Eleanor wakes to mysterious sobbing noises she holds on tightly to Theo's hand. She finally manages to turn on the light and the camera pans rapidly from the divan where Eleanor now rests to Theo's bed on the opposite side of the room. Eleanor, horrified, realizes it was not Theo's hand she was holding but that of some ghostly companion. It is not the "supernatural" alone that is responsible for this mean trick. The cinema itself seems to render the women's physical contact (albeit merely handholding) impossible. A cinematically specific code — and a disruptive one at that, the swish pan — intervenes to separate the two women from each other and to render the viewer complicit. The spirit actually complies with the letter of the Production Code Administration's recommendations: "[W]e think that a scene showing the two girls together in the same bed, even though nothing happens, would be of the highest imprudence. It seems to us that this scene should be re-dressed so as to put the two in twin beds."[28]

In a scene that encapsulates the "oedipal" drama of Hill House and thus the conflict over Eleanor's proper identification, the cinematic enunciation works *with* the supernatural in allowing a lesbian reading. The four guests literally find their "family portrait" in a massive group statue meant to represent St. Francis curing the lepers, who are all represented by female figures. The women notice that the statue seems to move when they look away, a classic "uncanny" effect. Luke remarks that the configuration reminds him of a family portrait of the historical inhabitants of Hill House, Hugh Crain looming above his wives, his daughter, the companion, and a dog. Theo maps the current group onto the statue and thus onto the original group, designating Eleanor as the companion, herself, tellingly, as the daughter — "grown up," the doctor as Hugh Crain, and Luke, the ostensible oedipal hero, as the dog. Luke, startled, indicates with a glance at the women that with this put-down he has finally caught on to Theo's sexual orientation, commenting that "more than meets the eye" is going on in Hill House. This phrase, referring to lesbianism, applies equally to the supernatural events of

The Haunting. Immediately after the group leaves the room, "more" meets the eye of the spectator—the camera zooms into two of the female figures, one of which clutches the other's breasts from behind. It is the camera and not the statue that moves, but the effect is analogous. This privileged view is a cinematic flourish, and a key to a reading, implicating Eleanor in a lesbian embrace through the figure to which she corresponds, and suggesting that the female forces of Hill House are beginning to close in on her.

"You're the monster of Hill House," Eleanor finally shouts at Theo, several scenes later, coming closer to the truth than she knows. It is at the culmination of this denunciation scene: "Life is full of inconsistencies, nature's mistakes—you for instance," that Mrs. Markway, not inconsistent with the violent invocation of normativity, makes her entrance. Coming to persuade her husband to give up his nonsense, she embodies the missing element of the family portrait, marking the futility of Eleanor's attempt to identify herself with the wife's position and in effect preventing Theo's relationship with Eleanor as well. In another still (fig. 14), the psychic im-

14. *Mrs. Markway (Lois Maxwell)
materializes. With Harris in* The
Haunting *(Robert Wise, 1963).*

89

portance of the mother to Eleanor is represented by her spatial subordination to Mrs. Markway.

The materialization of the wife at this point in the film seems to be part of the process whereby cinema—like the house itself, which calls Eleanor home through literal writing on the wall—demands its tribute of the heroine. On this "final" night of Eleanor's stay, she imagines she has killed off the wife/mother when Mrs. Markway, a skeptic, becomes "deranged" by Hill House herself and disappears from her room. She had insisted on sleeping in the nursery, Abigail's room, "the cold rotten heart of Hill House," whose door had remained locked before opening spontaneously on the night of her arrival. Mrs. Markway then appears unexpectedly to scare Eleanor (ultimately to scare her to death) on two additional occasions.

First she interrupts Eleanor's intense identification with the place of the companion's suicide, the library. Eleanor's haunting by the wife is quite logically played out over the architecture of the house, which is fantasmatically inflected with Eleanor's own psychic history. Eleanor sums up her subjective crisis: "So what if he does have a wife, I still have a place in this house. I belong." As Eleanor runs through the house, she is frightened by her own reflection; we hear loud creaking and crashing, and the image rocks. She thinks, "[T]he house is destroying itself, it is coming down around me." Eleanor had been unable to enter the library before, overpowered by a smell she associates with her mother, but tonight she seems to be called there. The *unheimlich* part of this home is transformed to a *heimlich* one. And Eleanor is able to embrace the identification with the companion she had earlier refused in her hopes of playing daughter or first or second wife. Eleanor climbs the library's spiral staircase as if induced by the camera, which makes the dreamlike ascent before her. The companion had hung herself from the top of the staircase (hence the "call" of the turret window earlier), and the camera has prefigured these later ascents in the prologue's terrifying enactment of this death. "I've broken the spell of Hill House. I'm home, I'm home," Eleanor senses. The doctor "rescues" her when she reaches the top, yet just as she turns to descend, Mrs. Markway's head pops into frame through a trap door above. Eleanor faints, and the screen fades to black.

It is now that the doctor, futilely, decides to send Eleanor away from Hill House. For he misrecognizes (as an hallucination) her recognition of the wife. Yet for once she has actually *seen* something that we, importantly, also see. She is terrorized, at the very moment of her identification with the companion, by the apparition of the heterosexual role model, the wife. Eleanor comprehends the displacement of her oedipal drama (the substituting of herself for the mother, or for the first wife of the gothic) by the inverted drama of Hill House. "I'm the one who's supposed to stay. She's taken my place." And Eleanor dies, ironically, literally in the wife's place. For the "narrative image" figured in the film's prologue—the death of Hugh Crain's first wife—her lifeless hand falling into the frame, after her horse rears, "for no apparent reason" at the approach to the house—is now offered as the narrative image of the film. The shot is repeated exactly after Eleanor's car crashes into the very same tree, her hand falling into the frame. The first wife died before rounding the corner that would have given her the gothic heroine's first glimpse of the house; Eleanor cannot leave the gaze of Hill House. She crashes, apparently, to avoid hitting Mrs. Markway, who, for the second time, suddenly runs across her path.[29] Mrs. Markway appears as agent of a deadly variant of heterosexual narrative closure. Eleanor is not allowed to live or die as the companion; incapable of living as the wife, she is tricked into dying in her place.

But it is a ghost film, and *The Haunting* goes beyond the image of death. The final image is properly the house—the grave, woman?—accompanied by Eleanor's voice-over (or rather the voice of Eleanor's ghost) echoing these words from the opening narration: "Whatever walked there, walked alone." Prying the narrative image from its oedipal logic and usurping the authority of the male voice-over and its third-person narration, Eleanor transforms the words: "We who walk here, walk alone." Eleanor finally belongs—to a "we" that we know to be feminine and suspect might be lesbian—"we who walk alone"—and the house belongs to her and her ghostly companions.[30] The "haunting" exceeds the drive of the cinematic narration to closure, diverting cinematic codes—using voice-over to indicate the presence of the ghost—to suggest "something else."

The Haunting goes beyond the woman's story as female oedipal drama enacted in the gothic. In that genre, we recall, the protagonist's search for the "secret" of a dead woman is facilitated (or impeded) by a key figure, an older, often sinister character, variously the housekeeper, the nurse, or, in some other capacity, a "companion" to the dead woman. This gallery of crypto-lesbians, played by the formidable likes of Judith Anderson and Cornelia Otis Skinner (figs. 15 and 16), are a compelling reason for the young woman, recently married and suspecting it might have been a mistake, to realize that it *was* one. The companion is central to the psychic history of Hill House. Indeed the character function provides a mapping and an iconography of female homosexuality throughout the gothic genre. These figures intervene crucially in the threatened collapse of the heroine's identity onto that of the other woman, opening up the space of desire by

15. *Judith Anderson as companion with Joan Fontaine in* Rebecca *(Alfred Hitchcock, 1940).*

16. *Cornelia Otis Skinner as companion in* The Uninvited *(Lewis Allen, 1944).*

triangulating the relationship with the dead woman/"mother." They signify through their unnatural affection a potential di- or perversion of the heroine's desire from the straight and narrow oedipal path.

In *The Haunting* a crucial transformation has taken place with the manifest appearance of lesbianism. The other woman, the object of the heroine's desire ("Rebecca" as precisely unrepresentable in that film), and the companion converge in the quite material figure of Theodora, who is emphatically not the mother. The film most forcefully represents the collision of the female oedipal narrative with "something else."

The Canny Lesbian

The heroines of *Rebecca* and *The Uninvited* oscillate between the two poles of female oedipal desire—desire for the mother and desire for the father. Mrs. Danvers sets the "sick" house on fire and dies there, joining the ghost of Rebecca who, as Modleski reads it, "haunts" her (51),[31] and Miss Holloway goes mad, sending Stella to Windward House, cackling "It's all straight now." And if Eleanor's trajectory, as heroine and spinster, assimilates these two variants, Theo simply grows up—like Abigail, the daughter before her—and lives to tell of the terrors of Hill House. In developing a feminist film theory that would incorporate Theo, we might recall the model of spectatorship she offers in the film. Telepathy, to lesbians and gay men as actual readers and viewers, has always been an alternative to our own mode of paranoiac spectatorship: "Is it really there?" The experience of this second sight involves the identification of and with Theo as a lesbian. As for *The Haunting*, it's a very scary movie, even a threatening one. As Leonard Maltin's TV movie guide recommends, "See it with a friend." Or, perhaps, a companion.

4

Films for Girls: Lesbian Sentiment and Maternal Melodrama

"Oh Jerry, don't let's ask for the moon," says Charlotte Vale, a little impatiently, "We have the stars." When Bette Davis delivers her immortal line at the end of *Now, Voyager*, making a rhetorical gesture quite characteristic of the woman's picture, our spinster is plainly refusing heterosexual "fulfillment." But what exactly is she opting for instead? In this film's rich cosmology of desire, how do we interpret "the stars"? Is Charlotte picking the ugly-duckling little girl she met in the sanatorium over Jerry, the girl's father? Is this a slippage guided by Freudian logic (baby = penis) or a more affirmative choice of a female object? Surely I'm not suggesting that there is something *sexual* about her relationship with 12-year-old Tina? Irving Rapper's *Now, Voyager* (Warner Bros., 1942), adapted by Casey Robinson from Olive Higgins Prouty's 1941 novel,[1] enjoys popular enthusiasm as well as feminist and even mainstream critical acclaim as a high-water mark of the wartime woman's film and one of Davis's defining performances.[2] The film is exemplary, too, of the woman's picture's ambiguous invitation to lesbian fantasy—of the convergence of the perverse and the sentimental that melodrama allows.

Ultimately Charlotte's gnomic utterance tells us something about, and in, the language of melodrama, and it is within the universe of the woman's picture that the film must be interpreted. In its idiom the gesture, the glance, the cry, the musical motif, even muteness itself, speak louder than words—

but what these effects are saying we can't, precisely, say. This reliance on the unspeakable opens melodrama to queer effects. "We have the stars"—an indirectly named, mutually understood, infinite and dispersed gratification —stands for the crypto-lesbian satisfactions of this film and its generic sob sisters. As the camera tilts toward the window and the stars in the film's last shot, riding the swell of Max Steiner's score, we are transported to woman's picture heaven, where such extravagant affect is appropriate, where men and their attempts to understand or fit in are dismissed with offhand, definitive grandeur, and the feminized spectator is granted a sort of private audience with the star. This is *an ending*, something art manages rather better than life. *Now, Voyager*'s "happily ever after" unites girl and fantasy-governess through the sound of music itself. How we decide the sense of this ending has more to do with feeling than saying.

Most frequently, *Now, Voyager*'s ending is read within two prominent thematics governing the women's picture: the sacrificial and the maternal, often seen to work in tandem and both loaded with affect. Proper Bostonian Charlotte "gives up" the married man she met on the luxury cruise ordered as part of her recovery from her mother-induced nervous breakdown, but finds a peculiarly feminine consolation by nurturing his child. In a misreading that is characteristic of feminist film theory's early approaches to the woman's picture, Barbara Creed accepts that since "Charlotte resists the temptation to engage in a full-blooded affair with Jerry," the film's ending represents her "capitulation" to the patriarchal order and its conventional roles for women (30). Nancy K. Miller classifies the heroine's text that does not end in marriage as dysphoric. But the film's figural power, its refusal of literal meaning along with conventional closure, "queers" these interpretive claims about its ending—an ending whose "radicalism" and/or "perversity" is applauded by theorists gay and straight, avowedly feminist or not.[3]

In her chapter on the 1940s maternal melodrama in *The Desire to Desire*, Mary Ann Doane notes that "a discourse of the obvious . . . grounds an understanding of the maternal in terms of the sheer ease of its readability" (71); hence the affective resonance of these films in the immediate recognition of the pathos of maternal sacrifice. In *Now, Voyager* the readability of the maternal is at once taken for granted as the condition of sentiment and, in a manner that the film's explicit engagement with psychoanalysis and the question of sexual identity foregrounds, radically in question. What can be seen as Charlotte Vale's "coming-out" narrative is obviously governed by an intense struggle with her own tyrannical mother. But the film is not a conventional maternal melodrama. Charlotte herself is precisely *not* Tina's or anyone else's mother and whether and what she may have sacrificed depends on how one *reads*—the stars, for example. The film involves a *performance* of maternal feeling that opens up a space within the woman's picture for a different version of the daughter's story (fig. 17). Unlike the gothics and ghost films discussed in Chapter 3, in which we are asked to identify with a heroine who is struggling with an absent figure in the place of the mother, in the maternal melodrama the mother figure is very much present, and she's portrayed by the star. Because *Now, Voyager*'s heroine functions as both daughter and "governess," or surrogate mother, she helps us to locate different possibilities within the oedipal plot. Because she's played by Bette Davis, the film illuminates similar scenarios in a cycle of her related Warner Bros. films of the period.

For spectators like me, *Now, Voyager* addresses the "untold want" mentioned in the lines by Walt Whitman that Charlotte is given as her motto:

17. *Tina (Janis Wilson) and Charlotte (Bette Davis) share vanilla ice cream in* Now, Voyager *(Irving Rapper, 1942).*

"Untold want by life and land ne'er granted, / Now, Voyager, sail thou forth to seek and find." Considering this film in the context of the intergenerational female relationships in Davis's other films, and in the broader context of the maternal melodrama, I argue that fantasmatic revisioning, the mise-en-scène of "untold want," is part of the work of the woman's picture as an historically evolving genre and that this labor both engages and engenders spectators. The associations of "genre" with both gender and generation are illuminated by the woman's picture's staging of "maternal" scenarios. These bizarre female-centered domestic arrangements become heavily invested with affect—between women on-screen, between screen and audience, between critics and the films. Raising the question of lesbian representability in the context of "obviously" familial attachments and rivalries, women's pictures can revise female oedipal fantasy, drawing upon the precedents of sentimental women's fiction and romantic friendship to figure the desire to have or be "something else besides a mother"[4] and to stake out a contested homosocial space in mass-produced consumer culture.

I first set up some of the spectatorial possibilities offered by the maternal melodrama through revisiting film theory's characterizations of the genre. A genre that concerns itself with the problem and contradictions of woman's place, her connection with other women, her fit with the public sphere or her role in the symbolic realm, involves the disruptive and transformative possibility of lesbian desire. In the second half of the chapter I turn to the cycle of Davis films to define a peculiar pattern—a kind of lesbian family romance—that has not yet emerged in discussions of the maternal melodrama. Noting the curious way in which the maternal and lesbianism are bound up with each other in popular psychoanalytic as well as feminist theoretical discourses, I will propose the governess as a trope that governs the fraught relationship between homosociality and lesbianism (linking the family oedipal triangle with socialization) and connects traditional idioms of women's culture with emergent sociosexual identities in commercial culture marketed to women at midcentury.

Return to the Maternal Melodrama

The woman's picture—films with female protagonists addressed to female audiences—has served a distinct need among the proliferating forms of twentieth-century mass entertainment, from the first perceptions of the importance of women in the filmgoing public to today's Lifetime cable network, whose motto is "Women Are Watching." In her influential argument about nineteenth-century American literary culture, Ann Douglas locates the seeds of consumer-based mass culture in the "feminization" represented by the domestic novel of the mid-nineteenth century. The influence of domestic discourse on Hollywood film is enormous, particularly when industry self-regulation attempted to incorporate moral values traditionally associated with the feminine sphere.

If feminist critical attention has been insistently directed to the woman's film, it has by no means found the genre an unequivocally progressive one. Categories such as passivity, masochism, and the "de-eroticization" of the female body guide Doane's benchmark study of 1940s woman's films, begging the question of how the films could have been and are experienced as pleasurable and even empowering to the women viewers to whom they were addressed. John Fletcher, in his introduction to a special issue of *Screen* devoted largely to gay male readings of melodrama, remarks: "One is tempted by the relentlessness of Doane's survey to identify the paradigm of the woman's film she offers as a kind of 'spinster machine,' but it would be truer to say that it is the bachelor machine pathologically locked into the impossible attempt (given its premises) to render a female subjectivity and spectator-position that it can only immobilize, violently cancel, disembody or render absent: a failed trans-sexual operation" ("Versions of Masquerade" 56). Fletcher's description vividly renders the implications of a theory of "sexual difference" that allows for only one female spectator-position, understood only as the absence of masculinity.

Clearly, feminist critics participate in what could be called the "homo-sociality" of the genre. Yet there has been remarkably little discussion of the dynamics of desire between women in the films themselves or in the social forms of their production, reception, and commercial and critical promotion.[5] Rather than offering explicit depictions of lesbianism, the genre *addresses* — in both senses — women's desire for women. This recognition has important consequences for our understanding of heteronormativity and popular culture and the possibilities of lesbian representability and self-recognition within its forms. The films themselves figure their address to women in their fraught portrayal of relationships among women.

Certainly the maternal melodrama is a site where the question of lesbian visibility is dramatized as one of interpretation, reading, and the "authorization" of discourse. If psychoanalytic accounts of female homosexuality have stressed an "explanation" (obviously unsatisfactory yet tenacious) based on the mother-daughter relationship, these films flirt with the possibility in rather blatant fashion, leaning on aesthetic resources and genre conventions. If heterosexual feminist theorists have recast the mother-daughter bond as a safe haven from both patriarchy and, consequently, from the troubling implications of adult female sexual orientation toward women, as I shall discuss below, the scenarios in these films nevertheless resist such containment.

In fact, because women's pictures of the studio era are the object of such extensive feminist criticism, they can be used to test the limits and investments of straight feminist theory. Can lesbian desire emerge from the structure of desire that "mothering" entails in fictional narratives?[6] What does it take to activate the potentiality for representing female desire for "something else besides a mother"? In psychoanalytic terms, these films stage the possibility that women's desire might be defined in terms of a female object: they present a perverse fantasy. In relation to classical cinematic genres that privilege the male Oedipus, they demonstrate the repercussions of making female subjectivity central. The excesses, contradictions, and incoherences of the woman's picture demonstrate not the impossibility of female desire, but its multifarious forms and distortions. For feminist theory, a lesbian reading of the maternal melodrama can test heterosexist assumptions by putting into play different iconic, emotional, and fantasmatic registers within privileged and conventional narratives of maternal "bonding." In addition, judgments about the progressiveness and "excess" of melodrama can be refocused to account for different economies of expressivity. Even lesbian theory's presumptions about the signifiability of same-sex desire (for example in the visibility of the "inversion" or butch-femme model) can be interrogated through the genre. The rituals of sexuality enacted under cover of the "female world" need no longer slide down the lesbian continuum into desexualization even under Hollywood censorship. If popular forms give expression to ideological contradiction, women's genres that struggle to resolve themselves in favor of female heterosexuality inevitably put female homosexuality into play.

Christian Viviani first typologized the maternal melodrama of the 1930s in his important 1979 essay, "Who Is Without Sin?," opening with the following claim: "Melo must be moving, and thus it has recourse—not to the grotesque, as many believe—but to situations, feelings and emotion which everyone has experienced at one time or another. . . . In this perspective, it is only natural to grant a privileged place to maternal sentiment" (83). Like their stage precedents, Viviani claims, maternal melodramas succeeded in "touching the spectator by appealing to the 'Oedipus' in him which asked nothing better than to rise to the surface" (83). Not until the end of the essay does Viviani remember the female viewer (to whom the genre specifically appealed) in a formulation of deceptive symmetry: "What male viewer has never dreamed of being fondled by a desolate and arousing mother with the face of a Constance Bennett, a Kay Francis, a Marlene Dietrich, an Ann Harding? What female viewer has not dreamed of herself looking like an Irene Dunne, a Barbara Stanwyck, a Sylvia Sidney?" (98). Viviani gives us the standard distribution of male and female positions in terms of having and being, although here in relation to the female star's face rather than to the phallus. His rhetorical questions are open to revisionist answers, however.

Concerned both to lay down the groundwork for the inscription of the mother's point of view and the possible coming into expression of the mother-daughter relation, E. Ann Kaplan traces the social, philosophical, and literary heritage of discourses of the mother in film. She concurs with Viviani that the maternal melodrama per se, with its fantasy of the sexual mother's exclusive dedication to her child, her sacrifice and redemption through reunion, is a male and normative fantasy: "The appeal to the female spectator is Oedipal from the other direction, as it were, and relies on female internalization of patriarchal constructs. It permits the Oedipal fantasy of replacing the lost penis with a boy child, and in addition, vicarious iden- tification with an idealized Mother-figure which women, as historical sub- jects in the cinema, can never live up to" ("Mothering, Feminism and Representation" 125). Kaplan's statement presumes that the female specta- tor aspires to *be* the maternal ideal, and women are thus automatically rallied to "identification" with the female character, the star, in a scenario governed by a strict heterosexual logic.[7] As a more expansive understanding of identification suggests, the female spectator has identificatory options other than gendered mimesis or merger with the mother. If we uncouple the mother-son pair, we might recognize that the long-suffering, almost phan- tasmagorical, mothers of the silent and early classical periods may appeal to the Oedipus in *her* as well, giving us opportunities to imagine possibilities of being and having another relation to desire for women that the cinema would seem to exploit, and, in giving mother roles to its biggest stars, to render almost literal.

The vicissitudes of representations of mother-love in early classical Hollywood cinema were in fact closely related to contestations over movie morals. In her excellent study of censorship and Hollywood's "fallen wom- an" cycle, *The Wages of Sin*, Lea Jacobs historicizes changes in maternal representations as the Code's authority was being negotiated in the early 1930s. Jacobs notes that feminist critics of the maternal melodrama "have called attention to the way in which the films tend to define motherhood in opposition to female sexuality" (85). (The heteronormative logic behind this observation assumes that in the absence of overt heterosexuality there is *no* sexuality.) Jacobs suggests a different interpretation of the opposition between maternity and (hetero) sexuality since in fallen women films featuring illegitimate children the overdetermined melodramatic trope of the long-suffering mother was able both to replace (as a theme in the narrative) and to *signify* illicit heterosexuality. Jacobs concludes that "the emphasis on motherhood in and of itself provided a way of managing or controlling what the MPPDA considered the potentially offensive aspects of female deviance," for motherhood "provided the cornerstone of a moralizing discourse which defined the woman's place in terms of her function within the domestic sphere" (90). Through a study of negotiations over von Sternberg's *Blonde Venus* script, which ultimately allowed for a fair amount of "deviance" within the governing maternal scenario (Dietrich becomes a cabaret star and a prostitute in order to support her child), Jacobs demonstrates how such a strategy was a logical product of "a system which favored the development of indirection or allusive forms of representation" (105).

Jacobs's argument—that censorship and industry self-regulation generated a set of narrative and aesthetic codes that structure the audience's "inference" of the forbidden—is very provocative for a reading of lesbian representability in classical cinema. In particular, the maternal could be read as a convention or accommodating structure for the signification of female homosexuality under the regime of censorship, although for Jacobs female "deviance" means heterosexual activity outside marriage (often for money or status). The consequence that homosexuality would be unrecognizable within such a commonsense—or strongly normalized—discourse as mother-love of course cannot be overlooked. Yet Jacobs's contention that the nineteenth-century form of the maternal melodrama is recruited to the work of moral regulation in the twentieth—with ambiguous results—suggests to me that the "mother" in these films could be someone other, the genre a node at which the contemporary emergence into public discourse of "deviant," non-heterosexual female identities might make itself felt.

Kaplan's book distinguishes as "maternal women's pictures" a group of melodramas whose use of a female rather than a male child marks a more multivalent and possibly resistant address to female spectators than films such as *Blonde Venus*. Arguably some of the finest exemplars of the woman's film—certainly those that have been most elevated by critical and popular attention: *Stella Dallas* (King Vidor, 1937), *Now, Voyager* (Michael Curtiz, 1946), *Mildred Pierce* (Michael Curtiz, 1945), and both versions of *Imitation of Life* (John Stahl, 1934 and Douglas Sirk, 1959) are concerned with a romantic attachment between mother and daughter. Although even these films admittedly do not ultimately show the "genuine" mother-daughter relationship Kaplan would like to see, this may be, from a lesbian point of view, precisely the point. In "'Something Else Besides a Mother,'" Linda Williams asserts, in response to Kaplan's reading of the film's final eradication of the mother's subjectivity, that *Stella Dallas* is a "mother-daughter love story" (302).[8] The film, a remake of Henry King's 1925 adaptation of Olive Higgins Prouty's best-selling novel, depicts a working-class woman's decision to give up her teenage daughter "for her own good," allowing the girl to go to live with her wealthy father and his new wife and to make a socially advantageous marriage (though we have little guarantee that it will be more successful than Stella's disastrous one).[9]

Williams argues that "The female spectator tends to identify with contradiction itself—with contradictions located at the heart of the socially constructed roles of daughter, wife *and* mother—rather than with the single person of the mother" (314). The "double vision" (316) that takes in both the mother and the daughter's positions can be understood as a fantasmatic identification with the scenario or mise-en-scène of mother-daughter division. The critical question raised by *Stella Dallas*, as Williams frames it, is, "What happens when a mother and daughter, who are so closely identified that the usual distinctions between subject and object do not apply, take one another as their primary object of desire? What happens, when the look of desire articulates a rather different visual economy of mother-daughter possession and dispossession?" (302). Stella (Barbara Stanwyck) scoffs at the idea of dating, announcing that her daughter Laurel (Anne Shirley) "uses up all the feelings I've got." Laurel in turn declares, "[A]s long as my mother is alive, my place is with her!" It is worth attending to Williams's language in the question she poses, for the equivocation of the meanings and proximity of identification and desire—*primary* desire seems to mean close identification and to exclude *sexual* desire—raises the question of women's desire for women only to foreclose it.

Although Williams's model of contradiction opens up space for critical *reading* as a central process of spectatorship (and thus contests Doane's characterization of the female spectator's overidentification with her like in the maternal melodrama in particular) it nevertheless still presumes that the relationship between women—on-screen and between screen and audience—is one of likeness. When Williams next credits Nancy Chodorow's analysis of parenting for "point[ing] the way to a new value placed on the multiple and continuous female identity capable of fluidly shifting between the identity of mother and daughter" (306), much of the critical distance she has established collapses in language that has by now become a cliché. Furthermore, her attempt to liken the dynamics of identification in *Stella*

Dallas to Luce Irigaray's "female homosexual economy" and to Adrienne Rich's formulation of the "lesbian continuum" (307) diffuses the sexual meaning of the lesbianism thereby invoked by aligning these concepts with Chodorow's decidedly heteronormative view of mothering. Williams explains, "Whether or not a woman's sexual preferences are actually homosexual, the mere fact of 'lesbian existence' proves that it is possible to resist the dominating values of the male coloniser . . ." (307). Although she does acknowledge the "lesbian existence" in Rich's subtitle, sexual preference makes little difference. The way she continues her statement: "[T]he mere fact of 'lesbian existence' proves that it is possible to resist the dominating values of the male coloniser with a more nurturing and empathic relationship similar to mothering," makes one doubt lesbian specificity and take the quotation marks she's put around "lesbian existence" literally.

Williams continues: "The importance of both Irigaray and Rich is not simply that they see lesbianism as a refuge from an oppressive phallic economy—although it certainly is that for many women—but that it is a theoretical way out of the bind of the unrepresented, and unrepresentable, female body" (308). At best actual lesbianism is a refuge; considered expansively, it points a way out of a feminist theoretical bind. A better example of what Teresa de Lauretis in *The Practice of Love* calls "the seductions of lesbianism" for 1980s straight feminist theory could scarcely be imagined. Here the "lesbian metaphor" allows the signification of a female desire and hence a spectatorial position otherwise rendered "impossible" in Lacanian-influenced feminist film theory, but at the same time it shelters lesbian sexual difference under a benign maternal umbrella.

Indeed for straight feminist criticism, the importance of "mother-daughter love stories" like *Stella Dallas* is their figuring of the pre-oedipal relationship with the mother—not lesbianism—"as a refuge from an oppressive phallic economy"; they offer precious glimpses into a prelapsarian realm.[10] The signifying materials of film melodrama—emotion, rhythm, music, and gesture—are particularly apt for reductive appropriations of Chodorow's emphasis on "fluidity" of boundaries or of the Kristevan concepts of *chora* or the semiotic realm.[11] Besides the impossibility of recovering "authentic" female subjectivity or presymbolic gratification in products of industrialized mass culture, there is another problem with a strictly "pre-oedipal" reading of the genre. Critics' consideration of the bond between mother and daughter as one of mutuality and nurturing (passivity, dependence, identification) quite often misses the emotional emphases and perverse pleasures of the films—whose vision of "pre-oedipality" can be closer to that of the sadomasochistic maternal relations described by Helene Deutsch or Melanie Klein.

Stella Dallas illustrates these definitional problems, as it dramatizes a romantic mother-daughter intimacy that I would read as enjoyably excessive but not as lesbian and then gestures toward a horizon of difference in the mother's self-realization. Stella and Laurel seem to gaze at each other with the blind eyes of lovers, and the mise-en-scène emphasizes their exclusive involvement with each other. We see, after all, two adult actresses caressing each other—performativity cuts across the codes of mother-daughter intimacy. Today's spectators can draw upon Stanwyck's long career (and gossip about her affective and sexual orientation), and in 1937 viewers might reflect that Anne Shirley, in adopting her professional name from her breakthrough role as the eponymous *Anne of Green Gables,* carried over its juvenile and tomboy connotations. One moving scene occurs after Stella and Laurel have abruptly cut short their stay at an expensive resort where Laurel had met her first boyfriend. On the train, in a mute melodrama moment, the two women, neither sure whether the other is awake, hear the society girls discussing the scandal of Stella's appearance. When Laurel climbs down into her mother's train berth to spend the night in mother's arms, the moment is given melodramatic emphasis as an affirmation of a relationship that is incompatible with bourgeois standards of good taste. As pleasurable as these visual codes are, the relationship is safely within definitions of mother-daughter merger (fig. 18). But the scene marks a turning point in the narrative.

Immediately after the fade to black, Stella goes to visit Helen (Barbara O'Neil) her husband's new wife, severing the dyadic relationship by entering into a social contract with another woman as the third term. As the two women realize their unspoken "sympathy" with each other, they excitedly move closer and closer together until their physical attitude speaks, in melodramatic fashion, louder than their words. The interest in each other depicted in this extraordinary tête-à-tête seems to go beyond a mutual capitulation to the ideology of maternal renunciation. Doane writes that the women's instant recognition here is based upon the fact that "all mothers share the same predicament" (77), but it is precisely Helen's difference— particularly her class status and her style—that excites a crush in Laurel, facilitates the alliance, and *moves* both the spectator and Stella (in her case literally). Robert Lang goes so far as to characterize Helen Morrison as "phallic," and his description of her as evocative of the type of the New Woman is revealing: "To Laurel, Helen is like a goddess in one of her mythology books. What we see is a tall, flat-chested, square-shouldered, handsome woman with short, dark hair, wearing a blazer" (142). Doane is correct in noting that the women's immediate understanding of each other

18. Stella (Barbara Stanwyck) and Laurel (Anne Shirley) share a train berth in Stella Dallas *(King Vidor, 1937).*

mimes the way the melodrama solicits its female audience. But their bond is not immanent but social and symbolic. Through their transfer, the "essential" qualities of mothering are shown to be at once generalizable (any woman can perform them) and arbitrary (which is the "real" mother?).

Stanley Cavell, writing about thematizations of "the world of women" in what he provocatively calls "the melodrama of the unknown woman," reads the scene with Helen as something more than a scrap of sentiment cast to women who are asked to cheer on their own abject compliance with patriarchy:

> Stella's mutual recognition . . . with the mother to whom she discovers she can entrust her daughter, nominates the woman at the same time as the

> mother Stella never had, from whom she receives, so I read here, a mutuality of gifts, authorization to try the world on her own terms; from which it follows that Stella's gift of and for her daughter . . . is precisely not self-sacrifice, while the other woman does not, ironically, quite know what she herself is giving. ("Ugly Duckling" 280)

Although it is hard to know quite what Cavell understands this exchange to entail, I'll take up his suggestion that the project of the melodrama of the unknown woman involves a "search for the mother" (280). His invocation of Stella's mother (and he obviously doesn't mean the character played by Marjorie Main in the film) reminds me of a formulation of Julia Kristeva's that has received considerable attention. Kristeva writes, "By giving birth, the woman enters into contact with her own mother; she becomes, she is her own mother. She thus actualizes the homosexual facet of motherhood, through which a woman is simultaneously closer to her own instinctual memory, more open to her own psychosis, and consequently, more negatory of the social, symbolic bond" (*Desire in Language* 239). Kristeva both expropriates the "homosexual" (in order to designate narcissism and mothering) and pathologizes it. But Stella is not giving birth to but giving away her daughter, and she thereby secures, rather than negates, a new kind of social bond (as Cavell's use of the term authorization suggests). It is in this exchange, rather than in some inchoate experience of maternal sentiment, that spectators participate through the pathos of this moment.

The female triangle in *Stella Dallas* and other maternal melodramas seems to me more adequately described by Kaja Silverman's revision of Kristeva's work on the "homosexual-maternal facet" in *The Acoustic Mirror*. Silverman responds to the romanticization of the pre-oedipal realm in feminist psychoanalytic writing through a return to Freud's writing on the *negative* (or inverted) Oedipus complex. In Silverman's account, the female subject sustains both an identification with and a desire for an *oedipal* mother, a mother possessed of language, desire, and symbolic agency (102). This relation of desire is "negative" not only because of the lack and loss — symbolic castration — that constitute the mother as object of desire (and thus initiate the negative Oedipus complex in this Lacanian reading), but because of the acute cultural devaluation of the feminine position and of homosexuality (120–24). Silverman's locating the negative Oedipus in the symbolic introduces the mechanism of desire along with a social setting, but calling it oedipal rather than pre-oedipal does not mean that we can base a model of lesbian desire upon it. Silverman's feminist project is the restoration of a female position (here identified with the mother on a symbolic level) that is not robbed of all discursive power. By recasting the pre-oedipal relation as the negative Oedipus complex, and by considering the commonality of the latter to all women (rather than just to inverts) it "becomes possible to think of all sorts of discursive and relational strategies for activating the fantasmatic scene which corresponds to maternal desire, one which the symbolic does its best to . . . deny . . . representational support" (124). Paradoxically, the industrial-commercial category of the woman's picture would seem to be just such a representational support.[12]

In *The Practice of Love* de Lauretis adopts the term "discursive consent" from Helene Deutsch's work on a symbolic function associated with the mother as a concept that can go further than Silverman's idea of a "primary love for the mother" and "permit" lesbian sexuality. De Lauretis extends the idea of discursive consent to the realm of representation, to cinematic practices (75). The gesture of giving up one's child, entrusting it to another woman, usually grandly and pathetically orchestrated, occurs so frequently in the women's picture (*Torch Song, Dr. Monica, That Certain Woman, The Old Maid, To Each His Own, The Great Lie, Three Secrets*) that the spectator can hardly ignore its pleasures.[13] The genre appears to give its "discursive consent" to a disavowal or rewriting of the maternal and of domesticity.

What interests me is not only how through the ritual sacrifice the heroine escapes a maternal destiny while capitulating to maternal ideology, but how she uses the child to form a connection with another woman that limns a new identity. The last, memorable, shot of Vidor's *Stella Dallas* signifies an undepictable "beyond," as Stella strides toward us, tears streaming down her face, her destiny unknown.[14] Lesbian identities were available in this period although they were occluded in the cinema. If the ideological investment in marriage and the family that the women's picture was part of attempted to deny them, this ideology was far from seamless—the emphasis on the female family in the women's picture authorized the homosociality at the center of the genre.

Elsewhere in the genre there is a non-domestic mise-en-scène for the post-sacrificial moment. In the earlier film version of *Stella Dallas*, the overwrought Stella takes refuge in the ladies' waiting room at the train station directly after her visit to Helen. She's watched very closely by a woman whose flashy dress indicates her similarity to Stella in class status, if not in her dubious profession. The stranger offers the apparently inconsolable Stella a cigarette, and Stella puts it in her mouth and lights it end to end with the cigarette in the other woman's mouth. A fade to black gives the gesture—which resembles a kiss—an elliptical significance, though nothing else is made of this scene. The shot echoes with Stella's connection to Helen in the previous scene. But the silent version of *Stella Dallas* suggests that such sympathy, and women's motives, need not be reduced to shared maternal feeling. The washroom "pick-up" scene doesn't occur in the book — the anonymous woman inhabits the semi-public world Stella chooses, while Helen and Laurel define domesticity.

In numerous maternal melos of the early 1930s mothers go off and become prostitutes or opera singers or gamblers once they are unburdened of child rearing (*I Found Stella Parrish, House on 56th Street*, etc.). The fantasmatic force of this trope is marked in sumptuous clothes and exotic locales. *Blonde Venus* (Marlene Dietrich) affords the most suggestive example of the spectacular rise. Helen Faraday finally voluntarily relinquishes her son to his father, who contemptuously pays back the money she had procured for his operation from her liaison with Nick Townsend (Cary Grant): "It represents my life's work," Ned Faraday tells her pompously. Helen gets drunk and ends up in a women's flophouse. Helen dramatically mimes her husband's inflated gesture, and ironizes the economics of mothering, by handing over the sum to another destitute woman and repeating his line. She vows to find herself a better bed. A "success" montage of Paris nightclub marquees heralding the performances of Helen Jones immediately follows, culminating in her wildly successful cabaret performance — in drag! From the inadequate bed of the ladies-only welfare hotel she has arrived in a Paris where she flirts with chorus girls.

The explicit presence of lesbianism is rare in the women's picture and can be attributed to the Dietrich persona's association with decadent European nightlife and the lesbian trope established with her first U.S. film *Morocco* (von Sternberg 1930). Yet I'm tempted to read such connotations in the structurally similar trip Bette Davis takes abroad in *That Certain Woman* (1937), the actress's first collaboration with gay writer-director Edmund Goulding.[15] A dissolve joins the pathetic private moment of her grief after she has sent her child away to the onscreen title: "Monte Carlo!" Where Stella's journey was unimagined, we find a chicly dressed Davis, having traveled unaccompanied throughout Europe, presumably making the most of her "loss," trying the world on her own terms.

The return to domestic ideologies made necessary by censorship of the "sex picture" in the early 1930s meant that there were fewer depictions of female association in the public sphere, in the city. However, similar to the manner in which the pre-oedipal, once experienced through the oedipal (as it must be to be symbolized) is never again "innocent" — the return to domestic relationships among women after a pathologization of female association in the public sphere cannot be cleansed of sexual possibilities.

The mother-daughter relationship acquires connotations of excess connotations and by the late 1940s is represented in a pathological way.

Doane notes that maternal melodramas made in the 1940s are rarely "pure" examples of the genre as defined by Viviani during their heyday in the early 1930s. *Mildred Pierce* (1945), as a melodrama–cum–film noir, is often cited for its generic schizophrenia. This dilution of the sentiments of sacrifice (or their splitting off onto the figure of the idealized mothers of films such as *Mrs. Miniver* and *Since You Went Away*), the rupture created by the clash of generic conventions, may enable the emergence of the lesbian connotations of the scenarios that are staples of the genre. The pathology of Mildred's (Joan Crawford) excessive fixation on her elder daughter Veda (Ann Blyth), whose affections she actually courts and whose monstrousness aligns her with representational strategies that depict lesbianism, is underscored by the death of the younger, "normal"—though tomboyish—daughter. More explicitly than was possible in *Stella Dallas*, an appropriate adult female object, Mildred's unmarried friend and business partner Ida, signifies lesbian possibility. This reading is underscored in this case by the casting of Eve Arden, who became a household word through her portrayal of such roles. Although not actualized in the story, the lesbian connection with the "best friend" is presented as a "healthier" alternative to incestuous female homosexuality.[16]

Douglas Sirk's *Imitation of Life* is one of a cycle of 1950s and early 1960s remakes of classical Hollywood women's pictures updated to a new gender regime. Sirk's version raises a different set of questions through its equivocation around economic relations between the two mothers (as Marina Heung argues); when Annie (Juanita Moore) refers to saving money for "our kitty" she both covers over her status as servant in the house and suggests an unconventional domestic partnership between the women. If the playing out of 1950s misogyny separates the white mother and daughter in this version, an explicitly sexualized excess erupts elsewhere in Sarah Jane (Susan Kohner), who has no natural relation to speak of with the surrogate white "mother" she emulates.[17]

Critical interest is tied to the emphasis the films give to the mother-daughter relationship, but I would argue that that relation is resistant not only to heterosexual romance in the films (a "sacrifice" feminist critics often bemoan), but also to feminist attempts to contain it in a definition of nurturing female bonding. Unlike the films discussed in Chapter 3, in which lesbian desire was paradoxically made present through figures of absence, in these films lesbian representability is both dependent upon and precluded by the discourse of maternal presence. As Doane points out, maternal ideology rests on the mother as *there*, as given. A mother is "obviously" a mother; her feeling for her daughter "is" maternal, appropriate, natural, her actions toward her signifying as much. The economic relations inscribed in all of these films as mediating between mothers, daughters, and other women, and the representation of the mammy as second mother to the white girl (and as rejected maternal representation to the "passing" daughter in *Imitation of Life*) challenge these presumptions of immanence and presence.

Doane's further characterization of "[m]elodrama and the maternal [as] two discourses of the obvious which have a semiotic resonance . . . sign systems which are immediately readable, almost *too* explicit" (71) would seem to disqualify lesbianism's semiotics of the *implicit* from their signifying universe. But melodrama, the maternal, and the closet rely upon the unspoken, the gestural, the affective, the telling secret—upon connotation. And connotative codes tend to amplify one another, as D. A. Miller notes: "[I]f connotation, as the dominant signifying practice of homophobia, has the advantage of constructing an essentially insubstantial homosexuality, it has the corresponding inconvenience of tending to raise this ghost all over the place" (125). The woman's picture's scenarios of secret suffering, anonymous desire, immediate recognition, forbidden physicality—of perversion and excess—have definite queer appeal. Yet the homosocial domain of women's culture has gone largely overlooked by queer theory, relegated to a feminist analysis that, if it acknowledges lesbianism, analogizes it with forms of female bonding and thus contains its sexual difference. Lesbian desire is not an "aspect" of these films, but the hinge of an alternative experience and reading of them.

Another way to jar this presumption of maternal feeling as obvious (and obviously non-sexual) out of place is to attend to the effects of star discourses in the women's picture, which although central to popular accounts such as Haskell and Basinger, have been curiously de-emphasized in feminist theoretical studies of the genre (exceptions include LaPlace and more recent works such as that represented in Gaines and Herzog's anthology). In general, almost any major female star connotes "sexuality" as well as motherhood, if the latter can be said to signify as such in her films (in Crawford's and Dietrich's cases, the "real-life" maternal discourse was built up in the hopes that it would take the edge off their filmic personae). Qualities such as Davis's neuroticism and spinsterishness, Stanwyck's ineffable "butchness," Crawford's monstrous "masculinity," inevitably inflect their intimacy with other actresses on-screen.

Star personae are constructed intertextually and are put to work differentially by various texts and by various viewers depending on their cinematic literacy and predilections. I argue that the presence of the same actors recombined in film after film of a particular genre and used by the same writers and directors and designers (stars and genres as the studio system's capital) functions somewhat like the variations of fantasy discussed by Freud in "A Child Is Being Beaten." The permutations of the fantasy achieve the staging of a scene, not the finding of an object of desire, and in the history of the fantasy across its multiple forms, conscious and unconscious, lies the pleasurable negotiation of the oedipal complex for the girl. Genres and cycles are industrial and consumer categories, but they are also another level of cinema's inscription of fantasy as mise-en-scène of desire, and they depend on the presence of particular stars. The articulation of Bette Davis's star image with maternal discourse is accomplished across a cycle of Warner Bros. weepies from the late 1930s to the early 1940s; in this articulation the biological grounding or heterosexual causality of "mothering" is called into question. Davis's character is a spinster, a governess, or an adoptive mother; her image brings together the nineteenth-century Brontë-esque heroine, the passionate hysteric of psychoanalytic case histories, and the independent Bostonian and career woman constructed in her publicity.[18] The unusual process of female socialization depicted in the films can be said to be extended to and staged between spectators and the genre. Within this relation, I will argue, the implied viewer is constructed as a girl with a crush.

All About Bette

Like its competitors, Warner Bros. had banked on a cycle of maternal melodramas among its thirty-two "fallen women" films produced between 1930 and 1934 (Balio 247). Because the "proletarian studio" lacked proven female stars (even Barbara Stanwyck wasn't under exclusive contract), Kay Francis and Ruth Chatterton were lured from Paramount to suffer at Warner Bros., while Davis's early career there was being, notoriously, mishandled. Davis's objections to unsuitable material resulted in her widely publicized suspension, and the success of the lawsuit Warners brought against her when she attempted to sign with an English company quashed her rebellion. But two Academy Awards for Best Actress (1936 and 1938) and her growing critical reputation and box office popularity convinced the studio to feature Davis in better material—though again it would stick to formula when a winning combination was found. By the end of the 1930s Davis was the biggest female star at Warner Bros., and the studio's style of women's pictures had deposed MGM's glamorous and Paramount's sophisticated formulas. In fact the other studios were by this point featuring their major female stars in screwball comedy, a genre that is overtly concerned with the challenge of the formation of the heterosexual couple. This was not the project of the Davis films, and for a decade the studio featured Davis in an extraordinary run of high-quality women's pictures preoccupied with female identity, of which the developmental narrative in Now, Voyager is the most explicit example.

During her box office heyday in the late 1930s and early 1940s, Davis played exclusively in dramas. Her roles were split between "bitch" — Jezebel (1938), The Letter (1940), The Little Foxes (1941), In This Our Life (1942) — and sympathetic — Dark Victory (1939), All This and Heaven Too (1940), The Great Lie (1941), Now, Voyager (1942), Old Acquaintance (1943) — parts (which is not to say the bitches are not sympathetic). This oscillation informed and enhanced individual characterizations; Davis's performance style in Now, Voyager depends on the glimpse of fire beneath the restraint. Two "prestige" costume dramas, William Wyler's Jezebel (1938) and Edmund Goulding's The Old Maid (1939) articulated the Davis persona to (hetero)sexuality in the apparently contradictory ways signaled by their respective titles, but again the characterizations inflect each other at the point of reception. In his study of Jezebel, "A Triumph of Bitchery," Thomas Schatz argues convincingly that Davis's "personality and the Warners style were inexorably bound together, fused in that peculiar symbiosis of star and studio style that was so essential to the Hollywood cinema" (89). William Wyler's role in Schatz's case study is important — the collaboration between director and star, the emphasis on performance, was in tension with the pace of production at Warners but produced a successful bid for prestige. Indeed, Davis's work with Wyler is often considered her best (their affair is usually used to explain her enhanced artistry — not his). I would concur with Andrew Britton that the Wyler films, and Davis's persona constructed in them, are complemented by the cycle of weepies, which can be considered in rather different auteurist terms.

Edmund Goulding directed Dark Victory, The Old Maid, and The Great Lie, wrote the shooting script for Now, Voyager, and began work on Old Acquaintance. Like his fellow gay director, George Cukor, Goulding is recognized in standard film histories in coded fashion for his "way" with female stars but hardly granted auteur status. The alliance between the diva and the gay director allows for a distinctive negotiation of the border between the homosociality that I have argued characterizes the themes and address of the genre and the homosexual identities and epistemologies on its interpretive horizon.[19] In a comparison of Katharine Hepburn and Bette Davis, Andrew Britton looks at the contributions of their gay directors (as well as of writer Casey Robinson to the Davis films) in a framework that closely articulates the concept of genre with female star personae.

Britton notes "the Hollywood cinema provides numerous examples of films about female relatives—sisters, cousins, mother and daughter—bound together in passionate, destructive resentment and animosity" (*Katharine Hepburn* 49). A great number of the films of Bette Davis are apt to be of this variety. Hepburn's films, by contrast, more often depict supportive "and potentially lesbian" relationships with other women, whether within the family or in the context of a female community (*Stage Door*, LaCava 1935). Britton's richly detailed analysis could be said to describe the star's fantasmatic. Britton's comparison also conveys a much more sophisticated and textually and ideologically attentive version of Molly Haskell's typology of female characters/stars of the period as either superwomen—career women who compete with men in the public sphere—or super-females who exercise their influence, often destructively, within the home. Although Haskell's typology is derived from and serves to shore up women's relations to men (and the description of the superwoman in particular evinces anxiety around lesbianism), Britton's interpretation reveals lesbian resonances that allow us to value the exercise of power of a super-female like Davis differently, as a style of "femme" performance.

As I set out in more detail in Chapter 5 on supporting actresses, in a search for popular cultural traces of lesbian social identities it makes good sense to begin with the old maid.[20] The Davis cycle begins with *The Old Maid*. Zoë Akins's Broadway adaption of Edith Wharton's novella was characterized by *Variety* as "heavy femme fare," and reviews of the film touted its "special appeal to femme fans." As Britton defines the interaction of star and genre:

> While the consolidation of the thematic of *The Old Maid* as a peculiarly appropriate dramatic form for Davis cannot be simply ascribed to her— she cannot be said to be its "author"—her presence is the main determinant of its persistence. . . . The thematic of the old maid acquired a particular resonance and pertinence in the late 1930s and early 1940s, the period of Davis's greatest box-office popularity. Her stardom, in other words, is inseparable from a specific dramatic situation and its inflection. (72)

For Britton this "specific and consistent thematic" is derived from the nineteenth-century heroine's story, and consists of the figure of the old maid and the themes of illegitimacy and the mother's anonymity and friendship or

113

rivalry with another woman. Most important, it is worked out across a series of films. If maternal travails in early 1930s films justified the fallen woman's transgression, as Jacobs argues in *The Wages of Sin*, mothering in these Davis films seemed to sanctify the spinster heroine and her fraught relationship with other women. "Bette from Boston," as she was called in fan magazines, seems especially well suited to the "Boston marriage" of *The Old Maid*.

The Old Maid (1939) is set in the private sphere of nineteenth-century high society, what Carroll Smith-Rosenberg has dubbed the "female world of love and ritual" (while overlooking the kinky connotations of the term!). Charlotte Lovell (Davis) and Delia Lovell Ralston (Hopkins) are best friends and cousins raised by their grandmother in Civil War–era Philadelphia society who, after the convenient deaths and departures of various men in their lives—including the ubiquitous George Brent, with whom they are *both* supposedly in love—raise their children together. Because Charlotte's daughter Tina (Jane Bryan) is illegitimate, Charlotte conceals her identity as her mother, at first hiding the girl among other children in a home for war orphans she founds for this purpose, and then, after setting up a domestic life with Delia, fashioning herself as a stern, unfeeling "old maid" aunt to disguise her love for the girl. Meanwhile, the widowed Delia plays Tina's charming surrogate "mummy," thoroughly alienating the girl's affections and finally adopting her so that the girl can make a socially advantageous marriage. (Tina will thus avoid Charlotte's mistake of succumbing to premarital sex and her fate of becoming an old maid.)

On the eve of Tina's wedding, Charlotte confronts Delia: "Just for tonight, she's mine!" She enters the girl's bedroom to reveal her true identity, a speech act that would reveal her sexual secret. Tina turns from her dressing table when she hears the other woman enter behind her, posed very much as a bride on her wedding night—and is clearly disappointed that it is not "Mummy" who is coming to her. Charlotte realizes that this girl is not "hers" after all and renounces her intention to tell her a truth that is now in question. In return for her silence, Delia persuades Tina to give "Aunt Charlotte" her final kiss before driving off for her honeymoon, revealing to the girl only part of the story—that Charlotte had refused to marry in order to keep Tina by her side. After the wedding the two women go arm in arm back into the home they share.

Unlike Laurel in *Stella Dallas*, Tina is depicted as sexual, and the whole film is structured by family jealousies, indeed by an incest prohibition. Tina was conceived on Delia's wedding day when Charlotte ran off to console Clem (Brent) over Delia's marriage to a rich Ralston. Charlotte is always looking for the signs in her daughter's body and behavior of her own sexual transgression, and the girl also seems marked by the passion her father Clem felt for Delia and mirrors it in her own feelings for Delia. Delia reciprocates and Charlotte is jealous. The sexuality encrypted in Charlotte's self-consciously prudish persona inflects the supposedly "tragic" lack of alternative that binds together two unmarried women relatives who presumably hate each other. The girl vehemently accuses stern "Aunt Charlotte" of never having been young, never having known love, but Charlotte must keep her nature secret. Her history might explain her passion for the girl, but the film seems to suggest the inversion of cause and effect: that her passion for the girl explains her behavior. Clem is killed off perfunctorily (his usefulness to the woman's film complete after one sexual union resulting in pregnancy) and Charlotte lives in daily intimacy with Tina—thus Tina seems to have proleptically motivated the alliance with Clem. Delia's unnaturally strong love for Tina—ostensibly displaced from her feeling for Clem and displacing her own children—signifies a different life that she might have led. The social world (of "Old New York" in Wharton's novella) limits erotic possibilities and eroticizes limitations.

The prohibitions the two women suffer under are played out in their manipulations of weddings, "female" events that cement patriarchal power relations. The marriages entailed by weddings (or arranged or prevented by female machinations) are themselves barely shown; rather, the iconography of weddings consistently links female characters (figs. 19 and 20). When Delia finally adopts Tina and disenfranchises Charlotte it is, ironically, to give Tina the Ralston name and status so that she will be suitable for a socially prominent marriage. The daughter's destiny, like Laurel's, is disappointingly conventional and without emotional emphasis. At the beginning of the film, both Charlotte and Clem are "jilted," in a sense equally, by Delia—companions of youth who are left behind on Delia's wedding day—although it is Charlotte who is shown skipping out on Delia's wedding. When she is later set to marry Delia's husband's brother, Delia performs her most dramatic prohibition. She maliciously intervenes in Charlotte's engagement because she finds out about her cousin's relationship with Clem. Delia thus binds Charlotte to her through blackmail, earns her enmity, and expiates herself through their alliance, but also recognizes in Charlotte the "Bette Davis" destiny. Charlotte accuses: "You made me an old maid!" a truth-telling that could be addressed to her female audiences. The "old maid" is a name for the closet of the Hollywood woman's picture.

For Charlotte is neither "old" (her aging is disproportionate to Hopkins's) nor a "maid." Davis's grand Victorian spinster prefigures Gladys

19. Delia (Miriam Hopkins) as the bride in The Old Maid *(Edmund Goulding, 1939).*

20. Charlotte (Bette Davis) as the bride in The Old Maid *(Edmund Goulding, 1939).*

Cooper's interpretation of Mrs. Vale in *Now, Voyager*, and her performance is also a tour de force star turn, aging being a mark of skilled acting. But most notably, the identity is a constructed one, closeting both her sexual desire and her maternal feeling, which become indistinguishable in animating her persona. The film and Wharton's novella emphasize how meticulously Charlotte gathers the signifiers of her spinster identity around her. *The Old Maid* reaches back to a tradition of American women's history through American women's fiction, a tradition that remains implicit in the other Davis films. If historiographic debates have not yet decided the point of whether Victorian romantic friendships might have been experienced as sexual (since lesbian identity did not yet exist), complete "innocence" would be anachronous in the 1930s and might inform *The Old Maid*'s return to a depiction of Victorian femininity.

This is the first film in which Davis is teamed with a woman (although it is one of eleven films in which she is supposedly in love with George Brent) and the on-set rivalry between Davis and Miriam Hopkins is relished in movie lore. (Hopkins showed up on set in a replica of Davis's *Jezebel* dress to provoke her costar. Hopkins, a Southerner, had originated the role on stage.) Anecdotes about Hopkins's attempts to upstage her co-star during production are ubiquitously reported in the biographies and seem to have been exploited by the studio—most interestingly by reteaming the stars in *Old Acquaintance* five years later. Lawrence Quirk insists that Hopkins was infuriated by Davis's spurning her sexual advances (161, 257–58). As titillating as the lesbian rumor is, it demonstrates Judith Mayne's point about ambivalence in star discourse, for it clearly derives from a misogynist idea of lesbian desire (*Cinema and Spectatorship* 128–29).

The representability of lesbianism in homosocial spaces and genres is related to the question of "femme" intelligibility. The similarity of Davis and Hopkins, especially at the beginning of the film, gives way to difference as Charlotte emerges as a stereotypical old maid, which in turn produces Hopkins's femininity as a masquerade.[21] *The Old Maid* can only indicate the conditions of possibility of lesbian difference within homosociality—the more clearly the crypto-lesbian type of the spinster is drawn, the more suspect the relationship between the pair. Although the film is not about a liberatory desire or even feminist solidarity between the two women, the power dynamics are eroticized, and the triangulation of their relationship with their shared "daughter" performs the constraints of their bond as well as the limits of the genre. In the space of contemporary reception, a "lesbian" legacy can be decoded in the female world of love and ritual.

The Old Maid is considered by Viviani a sort of last gasp of the 1930s maternal melodrama, and some contemporary reviewers questioned whether even "the handkerchief trade" might find it old-fashioned. Frank S. Nugent wrote in the *New York Times*: "Unquestionably it is as dated as the Victorian morals code which scourges its heroine through eight or nine reels; in the rudest terminology, it is a tear-jerker." Oddly, Breen attributed a decline in treatments of the unwed mother theme about this time to greater popular disapproval (explaining to Warner Bros. his now more stringent reading of the extramarital sex in the script since approving Paramount's initial purchase in 1935 when the play was still running on Broadway).[22] Surely *The Old Maid* was no threat to public morals, but Breen may have intuited a genuine threat to normative femininity in the film's redeployment of Victorian codes—including those of romantic friendship—in the present juncture. (*The Children's Hour* seems to dramatize the juxtaposition of the 1930s understanding of lesbianism and the perception of romantic friendships at exactly the same time on the Broadway stage.) In other words, the film's fantasy is strong, especially with Davis to perform it. Nugent continues:

> But . . . dramatically it is vital, engrossing and a little terrifying. Miss Akins deserves something more than the epithet sentimentalist, unless it be applied in the sense one employs it to describe Emily Brontë. . . . Cathy's repressed love for Heathcliff, Charlotte's stifled yearning to manifest her love for her daughter—the two are much the same. No drama can be as tepid as "sentimental" implies when it is built on the cone of such an emotional volcano. (*New York Times* August 12, 1939 16:2)

Mother-daughter love, in the hands of the woman writer, is equivalent to heterosexual passion, and the critic of the paper of record seems to admit it.

Women's films like *The Old Maid* are populated with surrogate mothers, spinster aunts, adoptive daughters, perfunctory fathers, and gratuitous sons—their relentlessly domestic realm is subjected to all sorts of complications. If Aunt Charlotte had "come out" to Tina—given in to her "stifled yearning to manifest her love," what story might she have told? After a series of 1939 triumphs—from *The Old Maid* to the virgin queen in *The Private Lives of Elizabeth and Essex*, Davis held out for a suitable script. She found it in another costume drama, this one set in nineteenth-century Paris. Again this "prestige" production adapted a successful contemporary woman's work, Rachel Field's 1938 best-selling historical romance, based on her great-aunt's story. And its heroine's profession is eminently suitable for a woman of Davis's class background, intellect, and looks—for Henriette Desportes-Deluzy was a governess. The governess, like the maiden aunt, is an adjunct to the oedipal triangle, one whose presence cannot be reduced to the logic of kinship. Not only is it her role to educate young girls, her exemplarity as a passionate heroine is richly attested in the traditions of women's genres, implying a similar pedagogical relation to female readers and viewers. The governess is a key figure in the "lesbian" family romance—the fantasy of two mothers.

All This and Heaven Too

All This and Heaven Too (Anatole Litvak, 1940) tells the story of the unconsummated romance between Henriette Desportes-Deluzy and her employer, the Duc de Praslin (Charles Boyer), which causes her dismissal, national scandal, and finally her imprisonment on suspicion of abetting the murder of the mother of her charges (Barbara O'Neil). Exonerated of the crime, Henriette sails to America to take a position in an exclusive girls' school. At the beginning of the film, we find her facing a class of hostile schoolgirls who are gossiping maliciously about their new French mistress, "the notorious Mademoiselle D—." The most daring among them demands of her an explanation of the French word *Concièrgerie*. The film unfolds under the graphic sign of that most famous of women's prisons (metonymically under the sign of Marie Antoinette herself, the subject of a sentimental girls' cult) as the buttoned-up schoolmarm deliberately writes it on the blackboard, her eyes flashing with "Bette Davis" passion (fig. 21).[23]

The governess's tale of desire and destiny is embedded in the schoolmistress's diegetic task of winning the affection of the girls. Tears, embraces, and vociferous vows of loyalty in the last scene attest to the schoolgirl taste for precisely such a tale, delivered in clipped accents by a deceptively prim teacher of French. That is, an elaborate flashback, a mise-en-scène of desire, is staged for the spectator, who is placed in the position of an adolescent girl before her preferred schoolmistress. What this narrational device foregrounds is that this position, the spectator with a crush, is constructed by the woman's film generally. The motif of the young girl in the Davis cycle provides a diegetic representation of the viewer.

Just as the film encloses its tale within a circuit of intergenerational female desire, Field opens her novel with a preface addressed to Henriette. After avowing her frequent girlhood visits to her ancestor's grave she confesses: "My forefinger has grown none the less curious in the thirty more years that I have been tracing your legend from that inscription" (1). The enigma of her female ancestor, as in the plot of a gothic, is infused with

21. *The "notorious Mademoiselle D—" (Bette Davis) as a mistress of French in* All This and Heaven Too *(Anatole Litvak, 1940).*

sensuality and compulsion. "Curious forefinger" seems to link reading and writing to masturbation to romance. Field goes on, "You must have waked sometimes in the big Empire bed of polished mahogany that stands now in my room. . . . I, too, have lain wakeful in that same bed" (2). This understanding across female generations is depicted as mutual: "You were barren, who should have been the most fruitful of women. To you, children . . . were a passion, as absorbing as if each had been an unknown continent to be explored and charted" (4). Both the book's preface and the film's framing device thematize the structure of address of women's fiction and the women's film and specify the gendered address as particularly compelling to impressionable young girls.

The adaptation—again by Casey Robinson—reduces the bulging novel by eliminating the story of Henriette's life in America and hence her marriage to the Rev. Field (who appears, but peripherally, in the film).[24] The film is a sumptuous compendium of signifiers of nineteenth-century romance for mid-twentieth-century female audiences. The privileging of historical fiction as a genre of female fantasy (see Harper) is attested in the film's carefully researched mise-en-scène (see Custen 112, 115; McKee). In the film's text and context, such homosocial spaces as the girls' school, the nursery, and the women's prison adjoin contemporary ones such as the movie theater, and, increasingly by 1940, the workplace, and the military. Here are three daughters in crinolines, two of them of an age to share intimacies with and idealize their governess. The eldest (June Lockhart) is featured in a tearful bedside exchange with Henriette; the middle daughter (Virginia Weidler) accompanies her governess and her father to the theater to see the period's famous star, Rachel, and it is this public appearance that provokes the scandal.

Davis's hairstyle takes its cue from Field's comments on her great-aunt's portrait: "The thick chestnut hair was smoothly parted after the fashion made familiar by your contemporaries Elizabeth Barrett Browning and George Eliot" (3). Interestingly, the protagonist is likened to a female author, again strengthening the story's inscription in a female literary tradition (and indirectly allying Field herself with these women). Davis perhaps most resembles the prototypical Charlotte behind governess fiction—Charlotte Brontë. *Jane Eyre*, taken by Britton in "A New Servitude" as the prototype of *Now, Voyager*, was filmed by Selznick in 1944, and even *Rebecca* was an acknowledged attempt to update the Brontë classic (Sconce 145). *All This and Heaven Too* is also reminiscent of another of Brontë's governess novels, *Villette*. Britton recognizes in this continuity a project of feminist consequence:

> The Davis films are not concerned to construct a House of Correction for the spinster; rather, she becomes—like her antecedent, the governess of nineteenth century women's fiction (*All This and Heaven Too* makes the genealogy very explicit)—the focus of an obsessive concern with the problematic and contradictory nature of the normative female role (motherhood) and the organization of desire which it entails. (99–100)

The genealogy of the governess and the costume drama made Davis's "uncorrected" spinster persona possible and resonant in a period when women's autonomy and normative roles were undergoing ideological change.

Feminist commentators on Victorian gender ideology such as M. Jeanne Peterson, Mary Poovey, and Nancy Armstrong have noted that the governess threatened the divisions between public and private—male and female—social spheres as well as between the middle and working classes. She is both genteel and a servant, family member and outsider, working and domestic woman. The governess is required to be both unmarried and educated — but to prepare her girls for marriage and to "educate" them for domesticity.[25] Poovey suggests that "If the fallen woman was the middle-class mother's opposite, the middle-class governess was her next of kin, the figure who ought to ensure that a boundary existed between classes of women but who could not, precisely because her sexuality made her resemble the women from whom she ought to differ" (250). This "sexuality" is understood, however, in terms of the domestic ideal — the ideology of the white middle-class woman's passionlessness coupled with her innate maternal instinct. The governess's "position" is the performance of this ideology for wages. According to Poovey, "the governess not only revealed what the mother might otherwise have been; she also actively freed mothers to display desires that were distinctly *not* maternal, thus setting up the unsettling possibility that a mother's 'jealousy' and her energies might find an object other than the one 'nature' had decreed" (249). The governess is quite literally something else besides a mother for the child and figures social differences in the heart of the oedipal conflict, as her key role in several of Freud's case histories shows.[26] The similarity/difference threatened by the governess marks the tension of lesbian desire, not as the "real" meaning behind tensions in domestic ideology and the work it does in creating class distinctions — but as one of their forceful encodings.

These tensions are at the center of *All This and Heaven Too*. Through the very excess of her characterization, the Duchesse puts as much pressure as does the Davis persona on the concept of "woman's normative role" and the "organization of desire" supposedly entailed by motherhood in this film. Her excessive desires — like those of Rebecca — provoke her husband to murder. The Duchesse's diabolical animus toward Henriette, who displays nothing but patience and attentiveness toward her, recalls Freud's definition of delusions of jealousy in women. Erotic jealousy is the sole form of female paranoia he considers in his comments on the mechanism of the disorder. "'It is not *I* who love the women — but *he* loves them.' The jealous woman suspects her husband in relation to all the women by whom she is herself attracted owing to her homosexuality and the dispositional effect of her excessive narcissism. . . . [T]hey are often old and quite inappropriate for a real love relation — revivals of the nurses and servants and girl friends of her childhood" (34–35). The Duchesse's jealousy of the young governess seems to find an "appropriate" object in Henriette.[27] The failure of the romance between the Duc and Henriette to be consummated, as well as the film's refusal to exonerate the man, once again endorse the outcome of and pleasure taken in Bette Davis's singleness and "singularity." For the classic governess plot ends in marriage to the lord of the manor—here its gothic underside is invoked when it is implied that the Duc is the brutal murderer of his wife. After *The Old Maid*, the relationship with another woman seems as important to the Davis fiction as a Max Steiner score. Arguably, the ideological repercussions of the governess's autonomous erotic identity are felt in the mistress's fate. The inassimilable violence and unresolved mystery of the Duchesse's demise mark the attempt to contain excessive female desire.

Henriette, on the other hand, is remarkably restrained—her secret passion is spoken only in her narration of her tale. I have implied that the governess is the object of desire for the children—she replaces the mother in the family romance. The governess's social and imaginative status as a hybrid creature, erotic mother substitute, or expression of women's conflict in relation to domestic and sexual ideology, renders her a key figure in the Anglo-American lesbian imaginary.[28] To take one example, from a text that would seem not to require a *coded* lesbian type: in *The Well of Loneliness*, Stephen Gordon has a governess "of uncertain age, pale, with iron-grey hair, grey eyes, and invariably dressed in dark grey" (67). Miss Puddleton not only recognizes Stephen as an invert, but seems to have experienced some similar pathos in her own life: "And Puddle would flush with reminiscent anger as her mind slipped back and back over the years to old sorrow, old miseries, long decently buried but now disinterred by this pitiful Stephen. She would live through those years again, while her spirit would cry out, unregenerate, against their injustice" (112–13).

Dressed all in grey, Puddle resembles not only Bette Davis, but the governess whose case history Anna Freud recounts under the heading "A Form of Altruism" in her influential work *The Ego and the Mechanisms of Defense*: "What chiefly struck one about her as an adult was her unassuming character and the modesty of the demands which she made on life. When she came to be analyzed she was unmarried and childless and her dress was rather shabby and inconspicuous. . . . It looked as if her own life had been emptied of interests and wishes; up to the time of her analysis it was almost entirely uneventful" (124–25). According to Freud, this governess's quiet life affords some unexpected pleasures: "One would have expected to find that the repression was caused by a prohibition of sexuality" (124), but this is not the case. Rather her gratification is obtained from the "surrender of instinctual wishes to an object better qualified to fulfill them" (131), whether those wishes are betrayed in her "lively interest in her friends' clothes" (125) or the care of other's children, or they are more explicitly erotic or ambitious—and perhaps unseemly for a woman of her time and situation—and

thus become displaced onto men.[29] Such "altruism" has narrative consequences—certainly Puddle enables Stephen to fulfill her destiny. But it
might remind us of the passionate heroines of the women's picture who are
satisfied with "the stars" or indeed of the affective fulfillment attained by the
act of movie-watching itself.

The tragic side of such altruism is Charlotte's closeted fate in *The Old
Maid*, and, to a lesser degree, in *All This and Heaven Too*. The shared fantasy
of the Davis cycle discussed so far includes variations on the triangular
relationship among governess, mother, and child, a triangle crisscrossed by
desire and prohibition. Davis's character plays the governess/paternal pro-
hibitory role in *The Old Maid*, and she occupies the maternal role in *All This
and Heaven Too* and narrates to the girls the passionate history that she was
prevented from telling Tina in the first film. But most remarkable is the
variation whereby the old maid whom Charlotte Lovell transforms herself
into, with her stern carriage and plain dress—in short "Aunt Charlotte"—is
the persona whom Charlotte Vale transforms herself out of again in *Now,
Voyager*. The resonance of the moment in *Now, Voyager* when Charlotte
defines herself to Jerry, "I'm poor Aunt Charlotte and I've been ill!," is
amplified by the structuring role of the earlier film. The vicissitudes of
spinsterhood played out from film to film foreground the performance of the
role. Having lost Tina in *The Old Maid*, Bette Davis—when she's acquired
a fashionable wardrobe—plays "governess" to another Tina in *Now, Voyager*. The access to the daughter is prepared by the intermediate film, *All
This and Heaven Too*. In *Now, Voyager*, Charlotte herself has access to the
daughter *position*, and her mother, Mrs. Vale, is as severe as Charlotte Lovell
appeared to be. In repairing that relationship, *Now, Voyager* allows the
heroine to reproduce her desire as something new.

Telling the Untold Want

If we accept Britton's characterization of the Davis "motherhood" films
as in some sense sequels to *The Old Maid*, we can note how structures of
address and identification invite the spectator to participate in this revision,
so that what might be called the "governess" or "something else besides a
mother" fantasy is cast in terms that are both textually (and culturally)
determined and subjectively taken up. *Now, Voyager* is a revision of the
scenario of *The Old Maid* with a happy ending. *Now, Voyager* moves the
conflicts of the earlier film out of the explicitly Victorian setting, and yet
Charlotte doesn't have the options the 1940s might have granted her. Rather,
the mise-en-scène of her mother's house oddly preserves the genre's Victo-

rian origins as well as the ideology of separate spheres that shaped it. When Charlotte promises, "I shall buy a cat and a parrot and live alone in single blessedness," she is empowered by a nineteenth-century spinster precedent (fig. 22).

For despite Charlotte Vale's breathtaking transformation from awkward aunt and dutiful daughter to popular philanthropist and smart shopper in the film, she is first, last, and always a spinster. Charlotte's self-declarations may be laced with irony at first, but they are significantly similar before and after her physical transformation: "'Read it, Doctor—the intimate journal of Miss Charlotte Vale, spinster,'" she says before collapsing at the beginning of the film. Later she responds to Jerry's "'I don't even know yet whether it's Miss or Missus'" with "'It's Aunt. Most families have one, you know.'" But by the end of the film she has claimed this identity with dignity: "I shall never marry. Some women are not the marrying kind," rejecting the proposal of the wealthy Bostonian Livingston. Significantly, it is not the therapeutic consumerist culture that she chooses; rather, she remakes her mother's female world, establishing herself in her home and acting as benefactor to

22. *Spinster Charlotte Vale in* Now, Voyager *(Irving Rapper, 1942).*

125

Cascade.[30] Although she gets her makeover fairly early in the film, the *continuity* between the first segment at her mother's house and her later return is actually reinforced in fashion terms. She wears very similar "before and after" dresses of dark fabric printed with a white pattern that resembles a night sky full of stars.

It is her mother who attempts to stigmatize Charlotte's identity: "I should think you'd be ashamed to be born and live all your life as Miss Charlotte Vale." The discourse of shame and the explicit presence of psychoanalysis in the film suggest that we think of Charlotte's story in terms of the question of sexual identity. Certainly she presents herself as a "case," and the language of her breakdown is significant: "I am my mother's well-loved daughter. I am my mother's servant, her companion. My mother! My mother!" In fact it is her mother who has defined what it means to be Miss Charlotte Vale, and the film will recast that identity by transforming the family and/through the female couple. E. Ann Kaplan sees the film as anticipating the virulent mother-bashing that would become commonplace in the 1950s.

> It is only through the text's dehumanization of Mrs. Vale—its refusal of any sympathy or sensitivity to her subjectivity, her unconscious, her history/memory—that the text makes possible Charlotte's "freedom." The text insists on the central relationships being those of Charlotte and the surrogate fathers (the psychiatrist, the lovers); only by punishing Mrs. Vale sadistically, and forcing the spectator to hate her, can the narrative pry Charlotte and her mother apart, sever the mother-daughter bonding. ("Motherhood and Representation" 130)

In her identification of its "central relationships," Kaplan seems to get the film's preoccupations almost completely backward. Certainly *Now, Voyager* depicts the relationship between two adult women who share a home, wealth, social situation, and name as intensely fraught with jealousy and role-playing. As bearer of the Vale name, position, and wealth—and of a symbolic cane—Mrs. Vale is a usurper of the symbolic position of the father. But it is Kaplan's description that forces *its* reader to hate Mrs. Vale, by not admitting her centrality to our affective experience of the film. If the film "act[s] out a childlike hatred rather than empathizing with both parties in the dyad" (131), I would argue that this is because it is rewriting the idea of the symbiotic dyad—not in conformity with "a patriarchal fear of the mother" but in direct opposition to it.

It is hard to dismiss Gladys Cooper's bravura performance as "unsympathetic" or incidental to the film's effects; besides, she is significantly tamed in the course of the film by the nurse Dora (Mary Wickes), who contributes to the transformation of the terms of her cohabitation with Charlotte.[31] When Charlotte comes back from her cure, Mrs. Vale judges her ready to move into her father's room (and "take up a daughter's duties"), thus reading the daughter's trajectory more astutely than many critics have done; this is a return to a mother who is not pre-oedipal, but endowed with symbolic agency — although as a lawgiver she's being challenged. Mrs. Vale dies just as Charlotte says "If that's a mother's love I want no part of it" and Charlotte is quite convinced that her words "did it." I think we should accept a literal reading and take her relationship with Tina in light of her resolution to have no part of a mother's love. Finally, if Mrs. Vale is like Charlotte Lovell in *The Old Maid*, who misidentifies with patriarchal power and is tragically cut off from the daughter's recognition, the second movement of *Now, Voyager* reverses this identification and retrospectively answers the earlier film.

In *Now, Voyager*, Charlotte is no "Aunt Charlotte" to Tina; she captures the love she relinquished in *The Old Maid*. But she is no mother to her either.[32] Sitting around the campfire, in one of several scenes in which she is asked to name their relationship, Charlotte proposes a list of names for herself, "Carlotta, Charlie . . . even Aunt Charlotte." Tina chooses to call her Camille, Jerry's pet name for her. Cavell observes:

> Charlotte's relationship with Tina may be regarded either as the most disturbed or as the most therapeutic of all we are shown; as the one in which the conditions of unhappiness in this world are perfectly synthesized and reproduced for another generation, or in which they are specifically relieved, or modified. (*Contesting Tears* 142–43)

If the latter is true, perhaps this is precisely what is disturbing about the relationship. Charlotte's trip with Tina re-enacts her time spent with Jerry in Rio; there is a direct parallel between their camping and the first night the romantic couple spent together, stranded in the mountains in Brazil. The Hays Office scrutinized that scene closely: "[I]t will be absolutely essential that in the finished picture, it be quite clear that there has been *no* adulterous relationship between Charlotte and Jerry. . . . We again call your attention to the fadeouts."[33] Directing our attention to the fadeout of the camping scene, in which Charlotte sleeps with Tina in her arms, we find it prefigures another trope. At the close of the scene, the camera tilts up above the treetops to a shot of the stars, clearly connecting this moment with the film's invocation of the sublime in its final shot. Both Britton and Elizabeth Cowie, in "Fantasia," read the relationships to Mrs. Vale and to Tina as more crucial to the film than the romance or doctor plots.[34]

Cowie argues that beneath the "banal" fulfillment of erotic and ambitious wishes through Charlotte's romantic and social successes, "a far more 'serious,' seemingly 'perverse,' fantasy arises as the film progresses" (126). The work of the film's narrative results in "excluding the father in favor of the mother/child relationship . . . now represented as admirable, all-fulfilling" (177). "Such a reading," Cowie notes, "implies a homosexual desire played across the film" (177), giving access to

> another ("unconscious") scenario of desire, clearly Oedipal, but where the subject positions are not fixed or completed, Charlotte is both mother and daughter. . . . This is not Charlotte's fantasy, but the "film's" fantasy. It is an effect of its narration. . . . If we identify simply with Charlotte's desires . . . then the final object, the child Tina, will be unsatisfactory. But if our identification is with the playing out of a desiring, in relation to the opposition (phallic) mother/child, the ending is very much more satisfying. (178)

Cowie's is one of the most influential formulations of fantasy in film, and in a careful reading of "Fantasia" Teresa de Lauretis questions whether an unconscious fantasy can be said to exist "in" the film and in spectator homologously. The risk is that statements such as "the subject positions are not fixed or completed" would be extended from the gendered and oedipally determined axis specified here in Charlotte's taking up both "daughter" and "mother" positions, to argue that such positions are unfixed and incomplete for *any* spectator. Then Cowie's having named the "film's" fantasy as "seemingly" perverse takes on unintended resonance: the mother-daughter fantasy would hardly be perverse if it were hegemonic, and it would hardly be *perverse* if it were simply about their familial union.

Indeed, de Lauretis challenges Cowie's reading on more specific grounds. "What *homosexuality* can be fantasized," she asks, "in the masquerade of femininity, which is by definition addressed to men, or in a surrogate motherhood that reconstructs for the subject the pre-oedipal phallic mother?" (*Practice* 132). Charlotte, I would contend, does not masquerade, however (as Cavell says, she is always blurting out what her altered persona hides— "I'm the fat one," "These are an old maid's tears of gratitude"). And, as I've argued, it is something else besides a (pre-oedipal) mother that is reconstructed. De Lauretis's query prompted Cowie to revise her use of the term "homosexual" in a revision of "Fantasia": "Such a reading implies a desire played out across the film to have and to be the good mother . . ." (*Representing the Woman* 149). She explains the revision: "[B]y 'homosexual' I had intended a feminine homosexual desire. . . . [M]y attempt to sum up a sexual position of considerable complexity under this term is clearly inadequate.

What I wished to note here, however, was that the woman's desire, Charlotte's desire, is not conventionally heterosexual, though it may be perfectly feminine" (350 n55). Within Cowie's Lacanian framework, it is the impression of having made an appeal to an identity position that is regrettable. Although it is clearly important to specify the definition of "homosexual" one intends, Cowie implies that the complexity of the lesbian position she had located was not considerable enough to warrant further specification.

That lesbianism is consistent with Cowie's reading and can indeed be fantasized from a particular subjective position is the logical consequence of de Lauretis's insistence on the particularity of fantasy. It is the *surrogate* motherhood or "governessing" both depicted and enacted here (it is a film, not an intimate relationship) that enables its reconstruction of the "mother" as another (female) object of desire for the spectator who takes up the girl's position. This is what I think the intertextuality of the woman's picture and of star images authorize, certainly in today's spectatorship. In other words, the film's scenario joins a spectator's fantasy through the structuring action of genre.

Cowie is explicitly concerned with the problem of cinema as collective fantasy and suggests that genre conventions, mise-en-scène, formal qualities, structures of repetition and difference, and, we can presume, although she does not mention them, stars extend a particular invitation to fantasy to audiences. She asks: "How does the spectator come into place as desiring subject of the film? Secondly, what is the relation of the contingent, everyday material drawn from real life, that is, from the social, to the primal or original fantasies?" (168). The "everyday" material refers both to the forms of specific films and to the situation of viewers. The positions of desire of spectators, though indeed "contingent," are also, as I read de Lauretis's emphasis, specific to the subject. De Lauretis describes the *social* subject of fantasy as "one whose subjectivity and psychic configuration is effectively shaped, formed and re-formed—but also disrupted, fragmented, or shattered—by social discourses, practices and representations, as well as by a unique and singular personal history" (125). Just as the governesses of Freud's case histories insert themselves in familial relations in ways that introduce and inculcate social practices, so do movie genres structure patterns of desire.

The Great Lie

Goulding's *The Great Lie* (1941) includes what could be read as a sort of primal scene for the conclusion of *Now, Voyager* and its fantasy of Davis as surrogate mother/governess, for in it the Davis character literally has a baby with another woman. However, the co-parenting fantasy (which twists the much more plausible scenario of mistaken *paternity*) and the child itself are of less interest to the film than is the relationship between the "mothers" —this one leaves us asking for the moon. If the films discussed so far unite pathos and lesbian subjective investment in the perversion of sentimental women's forms, *The Great Lie* maximizes the pleasures of the "contingent" or secondary elements of Hollywood melodrama in its lesbian innuendoes.

The implausible chain of events is this: When Pete (George Brent) is informed that his drunken marriage to fiery concert pianist Sandra Kovak (Mary Astor) is invalid, he goes back to and marries his fiancée Maggie (Davis) and attempts to earn her trust (and that of Violet [Hattie McDaniel] who apparently raised her) by taking a responsible government position in aviation. His plane promptly goes down in the jungle and he is believed dead, which is inconvenient for Sandra, who's discovered she's pregnant after their one-night "marriage." When Maggie finds out, she rushes to Sandra and proposes—that the two go away together until Sandra gives birth to the baby, which Maggie will then pass off as her own; it will remind her of Pete. What would be an ellipsis in most films—the two women setting up housekeeping during the pregnancy in an isolated cottage in Arizona, away from reporters (Charlotte's sojourn in Arizona during her pregnancy in *The Old Maid* is not seen)—becomes the emotional centerpiece of this one. Sandra and Maggie's marked role-playing at the cottage—at one point Maggie has to slap the hysterical Sandra—raises to fever pitch several earlier confrontations between the women. Their physical contrast, significant eye contact, body language, barely contained emotion, and the film's largely dismissable dialogue, as well as its musical and point-of-view cues, provide ample material for Brooke and Cottis's re-editing of "lesbian" interludes in the opening sequence of *Dry Kisses Only*. Davis strides about in jodphurs for most of the film, while the much taller, dark-haired Astor sports an extraordinary butch coiff. Davis chain-smokes and paces outside while Sandra is in labor as if she were the baby's father.[35]

When Pete unexpectedly returns (literally out of nowhere, in his airplane), Sandra visits the newly reunited family, and the tension about her and Maggie's secret—"I'm sticking around until you tell him"—is palpable. Finally Pete demands, and it's a fair enough question: "What is going on between you two?" The film ends on a note of pathos and pleasurable sacrifice appropriate to the genre. With great dramatic flair, Sandra announces that she intends to leave the child with its mother and sits down at the piano to provide appropriate accompaniment (Tchaikovsky), or "melos" in its literal sense of music, to Davis's tearfully mouthed thanks. *The Great Lie* was made at the onset of World War II, after which a husband might very well have returned to find that things had changed since he went away. If *The Old Maid* works like and perhaps with *Now, Voyager* to unite the pathos of sentimental women's forms with lesbian spectatorial pleasure, *The Great Lie* maximizes the improbability of Hollywood melodramatic conventions. Not least ironic is its title, which refers to the ostensible heterosexual love triangle (allowing us to recognize, in Britton's words, "the reduction of the phallus to the indispensible George Brent" [*Katharine Hepburn* 78]) and, in this film, to maternal sentiment itself.

Old Acquaintance; or, More Bitch-Femme Role Playing

The affective intensity of the interactions of the female leads in *The Great Lie* is repeated in the film version of playwright John Van Druten's saga of female friendship *Old Acquaintance*, in which Davis and Hopkins are reteamed in a box-office ploy more common with male-female pairs. Elements of the film suggest that the formula of female rivalry and confrontation is also consciously repeated. If Davis's slapping Astor in the cottage in Arizona was an eruption of physicality in a surreal plot, a climactic scene in *Old Acquaintance* in which Davis shakes Hopkins and throws her down on a divan, an explosive outlet of pent-up emotion, is more dramatically necessary. Both moments easily work as camp, and the stories of Hopkins's on-set one-upmanship are played up in biographical sources. The Davis and Hopkins characters end up together once more, again after a daughter is married off. But most important, this time Davis's character's unmarried status is closer to the horizon of contemporary lesbian representability (signified in part by her clothing) than ever.

Old Acquaintance traces the lifelong friendship between two women and portrays female achievement in the public sphere. Kit Marlowe (Davis) is a critically acclaimed novelist and Millie Watson Drake (Hopkins) becomes an enormously popular romance author, partly in competition with and in imitation of her friend. The two women stand for competing models of femininity. Kit remains unmarried—she again gives up two suitors in this film—and is clearly figured as a New Woman through her dress, her work, and her repeated association with other women. The film's opening scene is set in the 1920s, and when Kit arrives at her hometown train station in a mannish suit and tie, she's hoisted onto the shoulders of a group of college girls as Millie looks on jealously (fig. 23). If the group serves as a stand-in for Davis's female fans, the schoolgirls of *All This and Heaven Too* have grown into a particularly vigorous set. A woman reporter (Anne Revere, Broadway's first Martha Dobie) in a smartly tailored suit, sent to interview Millie, sees Kit and expresses her keen admiration—and her contempt for Millie's brand of popular fiction. At another point in the film, after a narrative ellipsis, Kit is shown in uniform and glasses giving a radio address on the activities of the Red Cross with rows upon rows of women in uniform behind her. The inclusion of groups of women (college girls, the community of serious women readers for whom the reporter stands, the volunteer Red Cross) signify new social formations and serve as reminders of a female audience emerging as a presence in the public sphere during the war years.

Millie is endowed with exaggeratedly feminine attributes and is given to making digs about Kit's marital status that are rebuffed quite suggestively. Millie: "Are you engaged or something? Kit: "What do you mean, 'or something'?"; Kit: "You have a lovely daughter." Millie: "It's time you had

23. *Kit Marlowe, author (Bette Davis), is greeted at the train station in* Old Acquaintance (*Vincent Sherman, 1943*). *Millie Drake (Miriam Hopkins) at far right.*

one of your own." The half-hearted triangle that emerges around Millie's neglected husband (John Loder, who played the other suitor Charlotte rejected in *Now, Voyager*) is upstaged by the women's competition over Millie's daughter. In their climactic fight scene, Millie shouts that Kit, who has become her husband's preference, should take her daughter, too. "I could have, many times" Kit replies, the sort of statement more appropriate for a husband. By threatening to take her daughter, Davis's character recalls Delia's theft of Charlotte's daughter in *The Old Maid*. As in that film, the daughter in *Old Acquaintance* marries, and her conventional destiny contrasts with her mother's. Again, marrying off the daughter enables the conclusion of the film, in which the two women sit at home by the fire and toast their friendship.

If in this film the destiny Bette Davis's persona has been closeting seems open to her historical doppelgänger, the 1940s lesbian (and certainly to today's reader), once again the codes of sentimental culture and homosociality displace this emergence of a visible lesbian type with the film's romance plot. But the sentimental model offers pleasures that would otherwise be invisible—for example, reading Millie as a femme. Millie becomes a producer of women's fiction because Kit does it, but her recruitment results in a different style. Here the two models that I have been suggesting are in tension with one another—a homosocial world of ritualized passions, and a relationship between adult women that *looks* like lesbianism—are present on-screen at the same time, suggesting that conventions of sentiment might operate even in explicitly lesbian films. This film juxtaposes sentimental formulae and lesbian visual codes, the "female world of ritual" and a lesbian-identity model of visual and subcultural representability.

Britton notes that *The Great Lie* is "distinguished by a remarkable inversion of casting logic whereby Davis plays the 'Miriam Hopkins' role" (*Katharine Hepburn* 72). The "inversion" he remarks recalls the reversible, coexistent positions characteristic of subjective fantasy, but here the consistency, within which variation can be then discerned, is rendered by a historically specific star persona. Across her films Davis is the quintessential bitch and the quintessential spinster heroine, she both suffers and inflicts suffering, she can play the "Miriam Hopkins" or the "Bette Davis" role; her persona is constructed through this fantasy scenario. While the intense relationships between women are a source of pleasure, it is not on this level alone that her films may engage lesbian viewers (see my discussion of *All About Eve* in Chapter 6). *Now, Voyager* owes its pivotal place to its story of the daughter who grows up to be something else besides a mother—a role that I've identified with the figure of the governess—and authorizes the reproduction of another like herself. Thus the Hollywood genre and star systems mediate between private and public forms of fantasy.

Let me specify further the importance of the endings of these films in terms of what Terry Castle has described as "[a] kind of subverted triangulation, or erotic 'counterplotting,' that is in fact characteristic of lesbian novels," a "euphoric" ending in which the women get together and the marriage plot is thwarted (*Apparitional Lesbian* 74, 86).[36] In the last shot of *The Old Maid*, Hopkins and Davis turn and walk together, arm-in-arm, through their front door, which stands open center frame, the house's facade parallel to the plane of the screen. None of the film's four weddings held in this house was actually depicted from this classic point of view. Thus the film's last shot completes all of the weddings and answers the film's first shot, in which the heroines are dressed almost as two brides. Indeed, among the group of films discussed in this chapter, only in the almost overtly queer *The Great Lie* does Davis end up in a male-female couple. (Brent complained of his role in *The Great Lie*: "I'm used to playing second or third fiddle but this is too much!" [Quirk 222].)

The generic requirements of the cycle of Bette Davis's spinster and shared-female-parenting films are a mechanism of invitation to the lesbian spectator to "triangulate" a fantasy (which is played out in the violation and renewal of those conventions). In other words, the films present counterplots (heterosexual destiny is refused, men are banished), but just as importantly, the spectator is taught counterplotting as a reading strategy. It is not that these are lesbian films because women end up on-screen together in the last shot; rather, through their generic inversions the films activate a "maternal" fantasy that circumvents the role of the man and displaces that of the mother within a female world. Like Charlotte Vale, Charlotte Lovell and her cousin Delia inherit their money, home, and social standing from a matriarch, and in *The Great Lie*, Maggie's home is with her "mammy" Violet (Hattie McDaniel).[37] Yet the films also plot against the narrative of mother/daughter merger, through literal separation, disguise, and passion, and through the female third term. To ignore the "counterplot" thus generated is greatly to simplify the effects of women's pictures' address to female spectators. The aim of this reading of the "oedipal" problematics of women's pictures is to acknowledge the functioning of a genuine spinster machine in mid-century Hollywood cinema, one that potentially disengages the female spectator from heterosexual teleology.

Old Acquaintance ends with never-married Davis and divorcée Hopkins drinking champagne at home (fig. 24). Millie announces that she has begun

24. *Bette Davis and Miriam Hopkins toast their future in* Old Acquaintance *(Vincent Sherman, 1943).*

work on a book about their relationship and wonders how to end it. Would her readers find it too sad if the two heroines ended up just like this, in front of the fire? The film suggests otherwise and seems to invite us to remember that there is more than one reading of such an ending. The pair toast both their as-yet-unwritten future *and* its fictionalizing. Millie's *Old Acquaintance* might turn out to be the very film before us. After all, she knows what women readers want. The plot doesn't suggest what fictional treatment the author character played by Bette Davis would give the same material, and the possibilities are intriguing. But perhaps their story is more satisfying as a romance after all.

*They say what the audience
often feels, pricking the great bubble
of pretension which floats through
the morals of every movie. They are
disruptive elements. And they are very
good company. . . .*

5

*I shall look forward to a movie
composed entirely of the works of
supporting actors. And I expect it to
be good.*

— GILBERT SELDES, *ESQUIRE*, 1934[1]

Supporting "Character"

Sister George: The Character of Lesbian Representation

The main character of Robert Aldrich's *The Killing of Sister George* is a role-playing lesbian in more than one sense. In "real life" June Buckridge (Beryl Reid) is "George," a bawdy, domineering, cigar-smoking butch, whose younger lover Childie keeps house and collects dolls. As the country nurse "Sister George" on a TV soap opera, she is a character actress beloved by the public. Produced in 1968, on the verge of Stonewall and just in time to receive an X under the ratings system that finally replaced the Production Code, *The Killing of Sister George* is one of the first Hollywood films to represent lesbianism openly, and remains one of the most striking films to do so. The film may not offer lesbians positive role models, but it offers a model of the role of lesbians in popular culture—which has certainly not been a featured one. Yet, in making its main character a character actress, the film suggests that lesbians may always have been present in dominant cultural forms, accepted and loved by audiences in genres that never admitted of the existence of homosexuality.

The Killing of Sister George thematizes the continuity between the off-screen "masculine," tweed-suited dyke type and the on-screen "asexual," tweed-suited nurse type—the butch George is able to appropriate her moniker from her TV character—and demonstrates that the very construction of the "asexual" is a heterosexist one. Cheerful, good deed–doing Sister George travels about on a motor scooter; George cracks that anyone would be cheerful with 50cc's throbbing between her legs, mischievously alluding to a lesbian culture of motorcycles and other things mechanical (fig. 25). The drunken George makes a pass at a group of nuns in a taxicab in a scene that at once demonstrates her butch courage and visibility and wittily restates the theme of covert and overt types. George ought to be able to recognize a sister when she sees one. In the film's masquerade party scene—filmed on location and thus with extraordinary subcultural verisimilitude at London's Gateways Club, a lesbian bar—George and Childie dress up as Laurel and Hardy (fig. 26). This additional level of role-playing makes reference to a practice of comic typing that conceals homoerotic logic within a wildly popular and presentable mass cultural form.

The Killing of Sister George has often been accused of trucking in stereotypes.[2] Far from presenting George's profession—acting—as simply a reflection of the inauthenticity of her lesbian lifestyle, the soap opera role encodes in the film a very particular awareness of the operation of stereotyping in lesbian representation—including in identity as representation. The mutual dependence of role and individual, imitation and reality, theatricality and genuine emotion is the field, according to Jack Babuscio, of homosexual irony—of camp. One level of irony is that the lesbian actress plays a presumptively heterosexual character. A mainstay of camp is hyperbolic contrast—from a bulldyke playing a god-fearing, homespun country nurse, it is just a short step to the reading of the homespun country nurse as the very type of the bulldyke. It is the performer who unites in her image different signs of lesbianism, from the roles she plays and is considered appropriate for—"she's the type we're looking for"—and her "personal"/public life and style.

When chic BBC executive Mercy Croft (Coral Browne) takes a fancy to Childie and has the Sister George character killed off the soap, the question of the actress's visibility as a lesbian is preempted. The killing of Sister George is without question an act of homophobic violence; her scooter is run down by a ten-ton truck. (Whereas such a character could be gratuitously disposed of in a feature film, on a soap the death of a longstanding character is an event dreaded and hyper-invested with drama.) Despite the perfect disguise afforded her by her TV persona, George is too "out" by virtue of the stereotypical attributes of the "pathetic old dyke" that Mercy accuses her of being—her drinking, her coarse language and behavior. The rivals collide over the protocol of passing. There is a certain gleeful logic to the fact that George's boss is a closet case who controls representations (a logic played out in the phenomenon of outing). Ironically, while this lesbian cheats on the attributed heterosexuality of the cinematic signifier "woman" (see also, for example, James Bond lesbians such as Pussy Galore and

25. *Sister George (Beryl Reid) the television character, with her motorbike, in* The Killing of Sister George *(Robert Aldrich, 1968).*

26. *Childie (Susannah York) and George (Reid) as Laurel and Hardy in* The Killing of Sister George *(Robert Aldrich, 1968).*

Octupussy), she is as visually typed as are the Sister Georges. Mercy conforms to the "type" of the chic, tailored predatory lesbian (Dyer, "Seen to Be Believed" 8)—what Vito Russo calls the "hooded cobra, . . . excessive eyeshadow and dangling earring school of lesbian screen villain" (172)—whose tactics of innuendo and stealth require her invisibility and betray her lineage to the lesbian vampire (Dyer 12–13). *The Killing of Sister George* would seem to mark the end of a certain regime of lesbian representation, which the killing of Sister George encodes in the film. Yet the 1970s and 1980s were hardly witness to a rash of progressive portrayals of lesbians ushered in by the demise of the Production Code and lesbian and gay militancy. In the film, the turn away from the codes of butch-femme bar culture simply catapults us into Mercy's closet. At least George herself escapes the fate of Martha Dobie in *The Children's Hour*—her *persona* endures.

After being killed off the soap, the supporting actress is offered a starring role—on her own series no less—as Clarabell the Cow. In Frank Marcus's play, from which the film was adapted, Sister George was a character on a radio soap opera; the movie parallels the demotion from human to animal with the step down from on-camera to voice-over role. While the cow is clearly meant to be demeaning and misogynist, it affords a certain finesse to George's disguise. Think of the sex-role transgressions of children's television; *Pee-wee's Playhouse* featured the Countess, a talking cow in a tiara. Or think of the extraordinary character actress Hope Emerson, whose massive size prompted her casting as the sadistic prison warden in *Caged*, the circus strongwoman in *Adam's Rib*, and as the voice of Elsie the Borden cow. Interestingly, while disguising the transgressive bodies of "dykey" character actors, these animal roles are nonetheless motivated by their "deviant" looks. At the end of the film George, who had at first scornfully turned down the role of Clarabell, refusing to play "any part of a cow," begins to practice her "moos." Even in her humiliation lies a certain triumph. Her "unrepresentable" butch persona will still enter the homes of countless television viewers, her voice—associated throughout the film with transgressive speech acts—will be recognizable to her fans.

And Also Starring . . .

Agnes Moorehead was a familiar and popular television personality in her role as Endora on *Bewitched* (it ran from 1964 to 1972 and thus was on the air when *Sister George* was released), when in one of the last of some sixty film roles she provided the voice of the goose in the animated feature

Charlotte's Web (1971). It was not a degrading part, as Clarabell the Cow was meant to be—she co-starred with her "beloved friend" Debbie Reynolds, and Paul Lynde contributed to the barnyard fun. The role drew upon her roots in radio—what one reviewer described as her trademark "crackling, snapping, sinister, paranoic, paralyzing voice."[3] Before her television stardom as TV's preeminent witch, Moorehead reigned throughout the 1940s and 1950s as one of the most widely recognized and highly regarded supporting actresses in Hollywood cinema. Like George, she played "types"; she was the silver screen's definitive spinster aunt—one who easily made the transition to Technicolor glory. In accounting for the adaptability of her persona across a range of popular media (her public readings and recordings also met with great success), I believe that another element of Moorehead's star image must be considered. In an interview with Boze Hadleigh, "A Hollywood Square Comes Out," Lynde, a special guest star on *Bewitched* who played an "uncle" as inevitably and as memorably as Moorehead played an "aunt," remarks: "Well, the whole world knows Agnes was a lesbian—I mean classy as hell, but one of the all-time Hollywood dykes."[4]

Regardless of whether the lady really was a lesbian, the characterization complements her persona. It is no mere queer coincidence that Agnes Moorehead can be dubbed both one of the all-time Hollywood supporting actresses and one of the all-time Hollywood dykes. In what follows I will look at the convergence between marginal cinematic femininity and lesbian representation in Hollywood, discussing several inflections that correspond with certain actresses before coming back to a concluding section that reads the films and persona of Moorehead as my primary example. As apt a subject for hagiography as any, Moorehead is widely recognized and enormously popular. Endora, her best-known incarnation, has undisputed camp-icon status—gay audiences don't need to *appropriate* her—and *Bewitched* is a readily available popular cultural text. Moorehead even passes the cinema snob test, having been featured in films by auteurs such as Welles, Sirk, and Ray. In a sense, her ubiquity is such that she can be identified with the very media in which she triumphed, with the regime of popular entertainment itself. Thus she exemplifies what I contend is a systemic relation: the supporting character—at once essential and marginal to classical realism and its narrative goals—is a site for the encoding of the threat and the promise of homosexual difference. Elements of negative valence are strong in Moorehead's roles—Endora herself is the butt of a constant barrage of mother-in-law jokes. It is easy to read here the ideological stake in subordinating female difference—age, appearance, gender role—that is played out elsewhere with regard to race, ethnicity, and religion. Moorehead's persona is less "heartwarming" (and a somewhat later incarnation) than that of many a golden-age supporting actress—from Anne Revere to Edna May Oliver to Mary Wickes to Marjorie Main, and her witchiness is somehow less endearing than Margaret Hamilton's. This negativity is also, perhaps, her most subversive edge. I emphasize the star herself not to give undue weight to biographical data, nor to embrace a concept of transcendent talent or an attenuated auteurism. The Hollywood studio system, in exploiting and shaping the connotations of actors' personas through assignments and publicity, reinforces meanings latent in the types of roles supporting actors play and the type of "types" they are recognizable as.

The vast majority of overt gay characters are in fact supporting roles; while subject to myriad plots, they are unsuitable to heterosexual romance and the marriage plot (the organizing principle of the Hollywood universe) and must be assigned other functions. They must "support" lest they undercut, oppose, or emerge as a challenge. Their in-between narrative status frequently resonates with gender liminality: effeminate men and masculine women are conjured up at the boundaries of the model gender behavior of the stars. Tough dames such as Thelma Ritter might be recognized as queer types equivalent with the prevalence of sissy roles in the 1930s. Mercedes McCambridge's violent "butch" persona corresponds to a moment of pathologization of gender deviance in the 1950s and offers a rare example of female masculinity in Code-era cinema. The lack of "love interests" for supporting characters (the Hollywood cinema deems only one type of love of interest), and the fact that they are comic butts or are readily killed off sets them up as possible points of identification for lesbians and gay men (at least in the sense as "identifiable as"). It indicates, moreover, that signifiers of homosexual marginality have attached themselves to these roles even though they aren't explicitly "gay." Performance artist Lisa Kron's biographical note jokes, "It begins to dawn on her that 'character actress' is really a code word for 'lesbian.'"[5]

At the same time there is an intuitive connection between the narratively and visually marginalized and the socially subordinated. Any discussion of supporting characters turns definitively on the structuring absence of people of color from Hollywood film. Below I will look at some of the implications of the construction of racial and lesbian difference together, narratively and visually, by looking at the revisionist "mammy" roles of supporting actress/star Ethel Waters. Waters's associations as a singer bring a sexual style to the cinema that is in productive tension with normative white models. Because Hollywood tends to render questions of racial difference and national identity as family romance, relationships between African

American and white characters are often figured as sexual or filial. The mammy is a particularly condensed sign that takes on historically variable inflections and poses questions about the relationship between black and white women and the representability of African American lesbians.

That associations with a particular star impinge on reception and reading is confirmed by the long history of enthusiastic recognition extended to supporting actors in gay and other minority cultures. To grasp in what ways a star image (even a character actor's) might be received as "queer," or otherwise be available to non-hegemonic audiences, we need to understand star images as complex, contradictory signs. Richard Dyer's theoretical and methodological paradigms and case studies, Vito Russo's reclamation of sissy character actors such as Franklin Pangborn and Grady Sutton (and his oft-avowed adoration of Thelma Ritter), and tributes to Clifton Webb or Hope Emerson penned in the inimitable epigrammatic styles of Parker Tyler and Boyd McDonald constitute a rich critical inheritance in gay male culture. Donald Bogle's work on African American types and performers and a growing corpus on ethnicity and star images help queer readings decode racialized gender formations. The emblematic figures whose personae and films I'll discuss make marginalization a star turn: Ethel Waters exceeds liberal Hollywood's attempts to integrate her into its racial plots; Mercedes McCambridge is a supporting player who can be insupportable; Agnes Moorehead self-consciously presents herself as a character actress and an actress of character. The star text is a crucial intertextual dimension of a consideration of the narrative function of supporting characters in the heterosexual Hollywood regime. My account of the dimension of lesbian representability through supporting characters will thus be illustrated by these case studies at specific junctures.[6]

They Dare Not Love

What is it that supporting characters are meant to "support" if not the imbricated ideologies of heterosexual romance and white American hegemony permeating Hollywood cinema? In Bordwell, Thompson, and Staiger's *The Classical Hollywood Cinema*, it is noted that heterosexual romantic love provided the primary line of action in eighty-five of one hundred films sampled and constituted a line of action in ten of the remaining fifteen (16). In *The Woman at the Keyhole*, Judith Mayne critiques the offhand tone of this presentation of the "statistical" dominance of heterosexuality as drawing "more [from] the realm of the obvious than the explorable or questionable" (118). *Obviously* heterosexuality is more than a theme or a formal convention; it dominates narrative organization. Supporting characters are thus first distinguished by the fact that although they may participate in the romance plot, they generally are not its "beneficiaries." The title of gay creature-film director James Whale's last film provides their perfect motto: *They Dare Not Love.*

In Vladimir Propp's study of the dramatis personae of the Russian folktale, a model which has sometimes been extrapolated to cinema's narrative schemas, there is only one distinctly female role: that of the princess, and the "sphere of action" of the princess is not, in fact, characterized by much activity.[7] The female supporting character already violates a certain expectation of femininity. It hardly needs to be pointed out that age, race, appearance, nationality, and wealth delimit a very restricted field of females as suitable for the princess role. The non-princess may fill the role of donor, helper, or even villain. (The association with animals noted above probably derives from her function in the tale.) Basically, she is a witch—even mothers are unnecessary in and of themselves in the tale. She may delay, obstruct, or facilitate the plot and the goal of marriage. This leaves us with the paradox that women are often in fact not heterosexualized, for only a complementary and complimentary male desire can accomplish this. The threat thus posed may be registered in the fate of a supporting character. Her narrative function completed, she can be killed off or exploited for comic relief.

How can the relation of supporting characters to "main" or central, that is, to narratively heterosexualized and otherwise unmarked, characters be articulated? Homosexuality stalks the assertion of heterosexuality as its repressed underside. According to Judith Butler's influential formulation of the notion in *Gender Trouble*, gender identity must be perpetually performed; its "originality," as well as that of heterosexuality, is thus called into question. Although there is a comic tradition of a "doubling" heterosexual plot among supporting characters, just as often as not, they are not required to perform heterosexuality themselves, but to perform various functions that uphold its appearance as central. And yet if the romance plot is thereby thrown into relief, we can take note of how much trouble it takes, how much service, to pull it off. Finally, although narrative closure "cancels out" the romantic protagonists' desire in the final embrace, ending their stories, supporting characters may not be fully subjected to narrative closure. The same types come back again; their very continuity across texts foregrounds cinema's repetition compulsion and the need constantly to reestablish heterosexual normalcy in the same old stories.

As Stephen Heath describes the operation of narrativity, "The film picks up . . . the notable elements (to be noted in and for the progress of the narrative which in return defines their notability) without for all that giving up what is thus left aside and which it seeks to retain—something of an available reserve of insignificant material—in order precisely to ring 'true', true *to reality*" (*Questions of Cinema* 135). The supporting character is self-evident, a given; she helps the story get told. In a sense she speaks a social "truth" by representing "an available reserve of insignificant," if "realistic," types of women—mothers, shopkeepers, maids—black, white, or "other." The "realism" bolstered by the supporting character, like all realisms, is highly arbitrary and conventionalized. By the film's end she has literally been left aside, as for example Mrs. Holloway (Cornelia Otis Skinner) in *The Uninvited*, Dora the nurse (Mary Wickes) in *Now, Voyager*, Violet (Hattie McDaniel) in *The Great Lie*. For, as Heath economically puts it, "Narrative contains a film's multiple articulations as a single articulation, its images as a single image (the 'narrative image,' which is a film's presence, how it can be talked about, what it can be sold and bought on—in the production stills displayed outside a cinema, for example)" (*Questions of Cinema* 121). Supporting characters are sacrificed to the narrative image of heterosexual closure; their names may not be listed in the newspaper's television blurbs or their photographs included on the videotape box that delivers a "picture" to a potential viewer.

Thus attention to the function of certain types of female characters can throw into relief the single-mindedness with which the Hollywood system re-presents heterosexuality. For example, the discourse of lesbian desire introduced by housekeeper Mrs. Danvers in Hitchcock's *Rebecca* significantly undercuts the film's conventional "resolution"; insofar as the heroine or the spectator falls under her thrall, Danvers has exceeded her role in the plot (fig. 27; see Chapter 3). And while melodramatic pathos depends upon Jane Wyman's long separation from Rock Hudson in Sirk's *Magnificent Obsession* (1956), an alternative reading—or a different focus of spectatorial regard—might note that she spends this off-screen time in the company of her devoted nurse/companion, played by Agnes Moorehead, who offered Wyman support in four other films as well. A film may be dismissive of a minor player and portray her fate as gratuitous, but it may take less time and care to assimilate her to its ideological project than it would in the case of the female protagonist. In Hedda Hopper's column, "Bit Player Outshines the Stars," Moorehead remarks, "I sort of look at myself sideways on the screen." While this comment ostensibly refers to being leery of the on-screen image, even, perhaps, to cringing at the conservatism to which that image can be harnessed, it also suggests an astute reading of its liminal, and at times disruptive, function.

Narrative function cannot be separated from role (although a character may perform more than one function, or a function may be shared), and in the case of supporting roles this will most often be bound up with the notion of type. Typification in supporting actress roles can be related to its importance in lesbian and gay representability. In "Seen to Be Believed: Some Problems in the Representation of Gay People as Typical," Dyer writes:

> A major fact about being gay is that it doesn't show. . . . There are signs of gayness, a repertoire of gestures, expressions, stances, clothing, and even environments that bespeak gayness, but these are cultural forms designed to show what the person's person alone does not show: that he or she is gay. Such a repertoire of signs, making visible the invisible, is the basis of any representation of gay people involving visual recognition, the requirement of recognizability in turn entailing that of typicality. (2)

27. *Judith Anderson as a predatory lesbian in* Rebecca *(Hitchcock, 1940).*

Dyer looks at a range of visual types, noting the impact of the discourse of "in-betweenism"—the notion that homosexuals betray characteristics of the opposite gender—in typical representations of effeminate men and mannish women. There are even competing "dyke" types, he notes, citing both George's tweeds and her rival Mercy Croft's tailored suits ("Seen to Be Believed" 8). In turn, the codes of dress and behavior in gay subcultures are intelligible partly in relation to codes of popular culture. In this light, the oft-heard desire for non-stereotypical, "well-rounded" gay and lesbian characters in film may go against the very conditions of our visibility. As Perkins stresses, stereotypes are a structurally reinforced ideological phenomenon, "prototypes of shared cultural meanings," neither simply erroneous, nor unchanging, that can be manipulated and contested by the group about whom they are held (141).

How do lesbian stereotypes relate to the typing that makes ostensibly non-lesbian supporting characters legible iconographically and ideologically? Certain character types, particularly those connoting "asexuality" or "masculinity," have qualities that significantly overlap with those attributed to lesbians. Nurses, secretaries, career women, nuns, companions, and housekeepers—the field of Agnes Moorehead's characterizations—connote, if not lesbian identity, at least the *problem* of heterosexual identity. Like African American domestics, these characters are defined in relation to work (implying economic and social self-reliance) and with female communities.[8] Comic roles echo misogynist and homophobic derision, others literalize divergent embodiment, and "unfeminine" aggressiveness gives rise to the overtly sadistic lesbian characters of later exploitation films.

But as noted above, the semiotic overlap of these types with lesbianism is strongest in the lack of attribution of romantic attachment to men. This is often compounded by a sarcastic, flippant, or superior resistance to male values. Crotchetiness may be a low-level rebellion. If heterosexuality is attributed to them, it may be to comic effect. Performance can also establish the type as disruptive to the diegetic world or linear flow of the narrative. The supporting character is the representational locus where negative judgments of femininity—from flightiness to prudishness to condescension to female power—are deployed offhandedly, defining their deviance from normative roles. Even though these types are incidental, negative, comic or two-dimensional, they may have a utopian function. They expose the ideological stake in the maintenance of a narrow vision of femininity and foreground how bound up narrativity is in reproducing heterosexuality, in a closure that also guarantees white, middle-class hegemony.

Supporting character types are not entirely determined by historical period, although differences are meaningful. Russo's sissies, for example, are mainly a phenomenon of the 1930s, and the African American performers Bogle reads as playing "against" their servant roles were also active primarily during that decade. As for the possibility of encoding lesbian difference, early 1930s urban melodramas, musicals, and comedies offered probably the last context in which any viable urban social milieu could be signified: best friends, roommates, chorines, and golddiggers thrived in reference to new codes of sexual morality and female "contiguity." A gratuitous New Woman could walk through films of the pre-Code era for verisimilitude's sake. The 1940s registered sexual phobia in the threatening women of the workplace and the noir world, but often enfolded the extrafamilial supporting actress into the women's domestic drama. T. E. Perkins notes that stereotypes are strengthened at moments of social conflict and change, and indeed in the 1950s sex role stereotypes reached exaggerated dimensions (156). McCarthyism's attacks on homosexuals in government jobs and the rise of lesbian and gay subcultures contributed to wider recognition of lesbian and gay stereotypes. Yet, Hollywood was still not permitted to depict actual homosexuals, engendering an almost literal paranoia through the detachment of signifier and signified: one couldn't believe one's eyes. Aliens, communists, murderers, and homosexuals occupied the same semiotic field, and spinsters were also pathologized. During this period critically acclaimed character "stars" rendered superfluous or anomalous in films found homes on TV where a "type" could carry a show: Ethel Waters, Hattie McDaniel, and Louise Beavers could take turns "starring" as "Beulah," or Shirley Booth could parlay a Best Actress Oscar into series television portraying "Hazel" the maid. Eve Arden could carry the show as "our Miss Brooks." As ideological phenomena, and often as sites of ideological reinforcement, supporting roles have functional similarity yet different determinants and effects across periods and media.

Serving Ideology

Obviously, because narratives almost always contain supporting characters, no broad claims for their subversiveness or queer connotations can be made. Even as they work to repress or contain or normalize difference, they mark the place of the other. To argue that supporting characters can encode lesbianism in the most traditional of texts is to broach the question of the self-regulation of the textual system—to what extent does dominant ideology allow contradiction, to what extent does it require and reintegrate it? In positing the systemic nature of the arrangement of subordinate characters, their generalized function in relation to representations and social power, I by no means wish to assert some unchanging structure. Nor do I want to belabor probably unresolvable debates on the open or closed nature of Hollywood classicism, nor definitively to locate the "subversive"—whether in the subcultural reading or the progressive text, in textual contradiction or incoherence, or in some combination of all of these. However, I do want to have such debates open to the question of homosexuality as a source of ideological incoherence alongside the discourses of gender, race, and class hierarchy that determine dominant texts. For example, femininity must be at once subjugated and elevated; even the most blatant "sexist" structures—Claire Johnston's example is the mythologizing of the role of woman in John Ford's westerns ("Women's Cinema" 27)—can foreground the necessity and the operation of that containment. Homosexuality operates somewhat differently because it can be more conveniently "othered," cast out as pariah. At the same time, what Luce Irigaray calls (male) "hom(m)osexuality" can be seen as the ground of the patriarchal organization of power, and the potential eruption of lesbianism as a fissure in the construction of sexual difference itself (*This Sex*). While I certainly do not wish to assert an autonomous efficacy for representations of supporting characters in breaking with heterosexual ideology, their very centrality multiplies the sites at which friction can be located.

While it would be a mistake to appropriate representations as homosexual or even queer that are part of other structures of difference and domination, we should not underestimate the vampiristic operation of ideology, through which the negative connotations of one disempowered group's depictions can be siphoned off to "infect" another. The margins are the location of homosexuality in the classical text. We can acknowledge in supporting characters a site for a range of unpredictable effects, whether activated by "making strange" through the film's foregrounding the narrative conventions that require the marginalization of such characters, by the audience's "negotiated" or "oppositional" relation to a particular social or ethnic type, by the resonance with a performer's other roles or the flamboyance of performance. The phenomenon of supporting characters is a vast one that can be approached structurally, ideologically, and aesthetically. The films of a particular performer and those with which they can be contrasted provide a convenient means of isolating some of these effects and making visible patterns of marginality, functionality, and iconicity. These will be cut across—augmented, inflected or undermined, and ironized—by performance codes. Casting and performance are already a reading of type; the audience performs a reading on another level, informed by cultural and subcultural codes, spectatorial experience of the star in other roles, and subsidiary discourses. I want to trace an oblique sightline on classical cinema by making visible a portion of its "background"—the characters who proliferate but are not foregrounded or even thoroughly narrativized in Hollywood cinema.

Bruce Robbins's literary study *The Servant's Hand* can help define some of the methodological problems and theoretical urgency raised by attention to the "class" of supporting characters in classical narrative film. He first faces the problem of servants' remarkable literary recurrence and what he calls the "surprising and (to one trained as an historical critic) annoying sameness of these formal manifestations" (x). Buffoon and faithful retainer are found from Roman comedy through to the black stereotypes of "coons" and "toms" of U.S. minstrel shows and cinema. At first glance, the anachronistic qualities of literary servants would seem conservative, affirming an unchangeable, hierarchical social structure. Rather than real social relations being evoked by servants in readers, "all that is remembered is their effects, their momentary performance of useful functions. It is as expository prologues, oracular messengers, and authorial mouthpieces, rhetorical 'doublings' of the protagonist, accessories used to complicate or resolve the action, that servants fill the margins of texts devoted to their superiors" (x). The concept of a servant's "place" is ideological, economic, and functional; the visual deployment of such figures in cinematic representation underscores these spatially. (Indeed, character actors themselves have a different relation to Hollywood's organization of labor than do stars.)

For Robbins, the presence of the literary servant, a convenient, knowable figure of the other, is an ideological representation of the absence of "the people" from literary tradition. In this lies their ambivalent meaning. Robbins writes, "[A]t the very heart of realism is the scandal of a figure which both stands for the confrontation of [classes] and refuses to represent historical and social difference at all, which is merely instrumental and yet which seems to enjoy an uncanny life of its own, producing effects incongruous with its social position and moments of vision incongruous with literary functionality" (xi). Such a contradictory status also obtains, I would argue, for the supporting character in Hollywood cinema. But a class analysis will not explain this fully, even in the case of servant and worker characters; other familiars return as the uncanny. Robbins reads for the utopian moments when, for example, conventions of impertinent dialogue between servant and master, or scenes of recognition, assert the pressure of social relations.

Formal commonplaces are used to resist bourgeois hegemony and make possible the imagination of another order of social reality and power. My contention that lesbian possibility is encoded in the relatively static function of highly conventionalized cinematic types is surely a no less utopian claim.

These characters make visible that which is usually excluded, arrogate to themselves a narrative weight that skews the relations of closure, or simply draw spectatorial attention. The Hollywood supporting characters that interest me here—many of whom are in fact servants—are remembered for the functions that Robbins enumerates. They are an expression of cinema's novelistic and theatrical inheritance. Class, gender, and race function as major axes of exclusion and differentiation, determining particular narrative patterns as well as specific representational practices in cinema. I am particularly interested in the ways in which the construction—or notation—of femininity in the supporting character is played against the signification of class or racial or ethnic subordination to evoke the unrepresentable other of lesbianism.

. . . Mulattoes, Mammies, and Bulldaggers

One of the most pernicious strategies of Hollywood's containment of difference is the near-exclusive restriction of people of color and recognizably ethnic "types" precisely to supporting—and often servant—roles and the orchestration of audience identification to the white characters who are more highlighted. Manthia Diawara hypothesizes that a black spectator is split between identifications directed by narrative and a recognition or reading that rejects negative stereotypes and distorted histories (68). This is an important formulation of resistant spectatorship that implies that the cinematic deployment of types actually may make possible a critical vantage on the text. In the case of "visible minorities" it is important to the system that visibility itself be harnessed to typicality, so the repercussions of the presence of the "other" in the text are not too great, the representations too polysemic. It is in these roles that the basic ideological function of the supporting character can easily be seen as a normalization of hierarchy. While it is clear that supporting roles and stereotypes are a method of containment, it is also important to explore the resistant and inassimilable qualities of types, as well as why and how "stereotypes" originate about oppressed peoples and how they function over time.

In his influential *Toms, Coons, Mammies, Mulattoes, and Bucks,* Donald Bogle takes on the legacy of Hollywood's black stereotypes and offers a model of resistance and counter-reading. Bogle contends that all African

American actors have portrayed stereotypes, but particular talented performers have transcended their roles. Bogle's approach implicitly foregrounds
formal and narrative conventions and underscores the crucial role of reception—how the performance is read and interpreted, how the type is recognized as signifying. Yet Bogle leans heavily on unproblematized notions of
individual achievement; wavers between dynamic concepts of irony or critical reading on the one hand and static ones of expressivity, humanity,
essence on the other; and tends to downplay the ideological and aesthetic
determination and effects of these stereotypes.

In Hollywood cinema, African Americans and other people of color are
relegated to the sidelines; homosexuality also haunts the margins. Traits
related to the transgression of normative gender attributes, which could be
read as signifiers of gayness, may characterize stereotyped representations of
people of color. To understand how this occurs, the ramifications for both
groups—and particularly for lesbians and gays of color—and the efficacy of
this conflation for the system, we need to look at how racial stereotypes are
gendered and sexualized. A critical commonplace is the denouncing of
stereotypes of people of color as "asexual" precisely because they are relegated to supporting roles. Bogle's remark, "Black actors in movies were
generally denied black women, which was one way of making them sex-
less—therefore harmless—creatures" (81) shows the unreflective (hetero)-
sexism informing this sentiment. The equally strong tradition of the hyper-
sexual racial "other" leaves a remainder of perversion that might sometimes
be interpreted as homosexual. [9]

In "Dark Continents," Mary Ann Doane stresses that the woman's film
is really the "white woman's film." "When black women are present, they are
the ground rather than the figure; often they are made to merge with the
diegesis. They inhabit the textual sidelines, primarily as servants" (*Femmes
Fatales* 233). Doane suggests that melodrama's use of objects and decor as
vehicles of the white heroine's emotional externalization may be related to
the relegation of black servants to the domestic background.

> It would be less than accurate to suggest that white women are emotionally
> invested in their female black servants in the same way in which they
> overinvest in objects. Rather, the black servants often function as a kind of
> textual echo of the white female protagonists. . . . The intuitive knowledge
> or maternal power credited to the black woman acts as a measure of the
> distance between the white bourgeois woman and the nature or intuition
> she *ought* to personify. In these narratives, the black woman has no inde-
> pendent function. Which is to say, she is not awarded the status of a
> *character*. (240)

Bogle might suggest that, particularly as portrayed by a recognizable black performer, such a character is likely to spark other textual "echoes" that prevent her from merging altogether with the diegesis, especially for black audiences. (Hattie McDaniel in *The Great Lie*, for example—whom Doane does not name in her discussion of the film, despite the actress's prominent billing.) These characters may be brought to the foreground for lesbian viewers as well, either because of an attunement to the marginal—the supporting role, non-hegemonic feminine embodiments—or because of the character's peculiar and intimate relation to the heroine. If Doane fails to notice the potential erotic charge of the interdependence between white women and their servants, at the same time I wouldn't want to underestimate to what degree the sexualization of the interracial same-sex relation might disguise the hierarchical power relations of economic exploitation and racism in the same way that its sentimentalization does.

Black actresses are employed to "perform" race and class stratification in the service of "ringing true to reality"—an ideological reality in which African American women's service to whites as domestic laborers is naturalized. But it is impossible to separate race from gender in representations of black women. The common plaint that black women in film are frequently "defeminized" may imply that they become "simply" a racial signifier. As Hortense Spillers, bell hooks, and others have emphasized, dominant constructions of black femininity are indeed not "feminized" after the white model. Such stereotypes are not simply "inaccurate" but select and freeze differences operative and enforced in society. One of the primary ways black women characters bear the weight of sexual ideology is in their relationship of contrast with white heroines. Some elements of this distinctive gendering of black women in dominant texts may be keyed to lesbian stereotypes. Thus what is perhaps intended to disempower and "other" black women all the more—and often succeeds, in a consumer culture that valorizes white heterosexual femininity—can be read for other meanings, as a site of contestation.

Hortense Spillers's fascinating essay, "Mama's Baby, Papa's Maybe: An American Grammar Book," uncovers some of the determinants of the gendering of U.S. black women and the meanings of "matriarchy". Her essay begins:

> Let's face it. I am a marked woman, but not everybody knows my name. "Peaches" and "Brown Sugar," " "Sapphire" and "Earth Mother," "Aunty," "Granny," God's "Holy Fool," a "Miss Ebony First," or "Black Woman at the Podium": I describe a locus of confounded identities, a meeting

ground of investments and privations in the national treasury of rhetorical wealth. My country needs me, and if I were not here, I would have to be invented. (75)

These types, she notes, "are markers so loaded with mythical prepossession that there is no easy way for the agents buried beneath them to come clean." The black woman is a locus of "signifying property *plus*" (75). Spillers traces the cultural and representational repercussions of the fact that under slavery black maternity was "dispossessed," in practice rendered illegitimate as her children became slaves, and argues: "[T]his problematizing of gender places [the black woman], in my view, out of the traditional symbolics of female gender. . . . [W]e are less interested in joining the ranks of gendered female-ness than gaining the insurgent ground as female social subject. Actually *claiming* the monstrosity (of a female with the potential to 'name'), which her culture imposes in blindness, 'Sapphire' might rewrite after all a radi-cally different text for a female empowerment" (80).[10]

The relationships between black and white women in women's pictures that Doane comments on give little indication of this reverse discourse. However, the black woman is not merely an echo. Spillers writes, "We might say that African-American women's community and Anglo-American wom-en's community, under certain shared cultural conditions, were the twin actants on a common psychic landscape. . . . In fact, from one point of view, we cannot unravel one female's narrative from the other's, cannot decipher one without tripping over the other" (76). Drawing on Spillers's essay, Lauren Berlant looks at national identity and female embodiment in the novel and both film versions of *Imitation of Life*, which has by now become a *locus classicus* of feminist film criticism. All three versions of the text form a study of the expropriation of the black woman's body. Berlant demon-strates how her labor and her very bodily image — most explicitly in the case of the marketing of Aunt Delilah's pancake mix — are turned to benefit commodity culture and shore up national identity, a process in which the white woman is agent. As Judith Butler writes in yet another commentary on Sirk's version of the film, "*Imitation of Life* establishes the phantasm of femininity through certain exclusionary norms that suppress and subordi-nate blackness and maternity" ("Lana's 'Imitation'" 7). Yet the two versions of *Imitation of Life* attract so much critical attention because they offer the most sustained instance in classical Hollywood in which black and white women share narrative and domestic space and destiny.

Butler and Berlant are among the few commentators to read lesbian connotations in *Imitation of Life*. Berlant argues that John Stahl's 1934 adaptation in particular puts forth something of a utopian reading in its depiction of a remodeled female domesticity, "an affirmative female economy" (123). And Butler claims that "the scene over the kitchen table in which Annie announces her intention to continue to live with Lana [sic] is one of the most effective seductions of the film" (16). Marina Heung offers an important reading of Sirk's version of the film in terms of the relation of black domestics and their white female employers. She stresses that the conflict inherent in this relation is what the text's melodramatic genre conventions work to cover over: "[T]he possibility of cooperation between black and white women is a powerful fantasy in *Imitation*; the film tellingly ends with the image of final separation between its two protagonists, whose relationship with each other remains the deepest level of silence in the film" (39). Yet Heung remains silent about the potential erotic dimensions of the melodramatic depiction of such a relationship. Doane, as we have seen, stresses the white woman's function as pivot of representational politics around race and gender and does not read agency in the black servant's role.[11] Without imposing a closeted lesbian narrative on these films, we still can refuse to dismiss their radical female homosociality or to accept the assumption that desire between the women functions *simply* as another mode of capitalist exploitation or metaphor of white supremacy. In any case, it does not function simply.

The very proliferation of black servants in 1930s Hollywood films that encouraged Bogle's revisionist project would seem to warrant consideration. Robbins considers the prevalence of the servant trope in nineteenth-century realist British fiction and demonstrates that "rather than grapple with the new and exotic industrial worker . . . novelists turned to those vestigial, unrepresentative members of the same class who lived in their homes" (xi). At the same time the number of domestic servants was rapidly increasing to comprise the largest occupational group in nineteenth-century England— a group that was overwhelmingly female. A similar effect can be registered in the films of the 1930s, in which shifting realities of Depression-era race relations and migration made it to the screen as wish-fulfilling antebellum dramas or in depictions of white masters and black servants that nostalgically duplicated pre-emancipation paternalistic white supremacy. The contemporary reality of increasing numbers of black women employed as domestics during the period, and the social and psychical conflicts the phenomenon engenders, are also recast by these representations.[12]

The "mammy" figure is probably the most effectively anachronistic of African American types, an overdetermined role for black women in film, a catalyst for black activism around Hollywood movies, and center of an ongoing cultural conversation including African American visual artists, writers, and feminist theorists.[13] Because the mammy's work, if recognized as such at all, is associated with nurturing, it becomes the vehicle of the carryover of the "old order." The mammy stereotype resolves contradiction with Christian resignation, superstition, or blind devotion. Yet she is also an unmistakable image of power. More particularly, the "paternalism" she upholds is matriarchal, however ideologically interested and historically impacted that concept might be.

McDaniel, the most successful, recognizable, and distinctive interpreter of Hollywood "mammy" roles, is Bogle's primary example of a resistant performer. McDaniel's supporting actress Oscar for *Gone With the Wind* came at a time when African American protests against screen stereotypes were making a mark, and her performance was praised and her role faulted at the same time (Cripps, *Slow Fade to Black* 364–66). Bogle particularly values McDaniel's "backtalk"—a stage convention of the servant character discussed by Robbins—derived from the paradox of mutual dependence and understanding between mistress and servant (though profoundly asymmetrical in terms of power), a paradox which also puts pressure on that relation. "There was another life and point of view that was being suggested to me by Hattie McDaniel's rather hostile edge," Bogle explained in an interview with Lisa Jones (69). Indeed, "McDaniel scared her audience" (*Toms* 92). An opposing assessment is offered by Karen Alexander in "Fatal Beauties." Recounting her adolescent quest for a black female figure who could be identified with fully, she turns to the object lesson of leading lady Dorothy Dandridge. She rejects along the way "negative images" of "mammies born to serve. . . . The archetypes were the roles repeatedly played by . . . Hattie MacDaniels [*sic*] in films of the thirties and early forties, reaching their peak in the performance as the comically servile maid in *Gone With the Wind*" (50). McDaniel's characters' "relationships" were with white women, and they were protective, intimate, frank, and sometimes took place in a matter-of-fact sexual milieu (in *Blonde Venus* it is a brothel). She shared living quarters with glamorous white "mistresses" such as Jean Harlow and Barbara Stanwyck in her films of the 1930s.[14]

The many black maids derived from the mammy figure can signal the sexual transgressiveness of white women such as Marlene Dietrich or Mae West.[15] This operates in a manner similar to the effects of the iconography of racial difference in nineteenth-century French orientalist painting as described by Linda Nochlin: "[T]he conjunction of black and white, or dark and light female bodies, whether naked or in the guise of mistress and maid servant, traditionally signified lesbianism" (126). Yet as motherliness rather than sexuality defines the salience of the mammy stereotype, it comes to stand in its place; for example in innumerable scenes of black maids helping white women dress, the corset-scene from *Gone With the Wind* etched in the moviegoer's consciousness. Bogle describes McDaniel's world as a "topsy turvy one in which servant became the social equal, the mammy became the literal mother figure, the put-on was carried to the forefront of the action" (82). This invocation of the carnivalesque, with maternal feeling itself coming into question, suggests where a queer reading might begin. Thomas Cripps writes of the overt operation of ideology informing black depictions in Hollywood: "The interoffice memoranda recorded the endless game of outguessing the [Production Code Administration] man. Go as far as we like in shooting black maid and white mistress embracing in *Nothing Sacred* (1937), wrote Val Lewton to his boss, Selznick, providing we give no impression of equality" (10). Interestingly, the question of how far it was permissible to go was not toward sexual explicitness but toward equality. Is it because the women are unequal that Lewton didn't see sexuality? Or is there a risk that the expression of intimacy between women of different races might begin to look like equality, breaking down the roles black maid/white mistress? Miscegenation and sex perversion were explicitly forbidden by the production code, racial equality implicitly unrepresentable. Just what are we are looking at in this embrace?

In Chapter 4 I suggested that surrogate mother relationships in melodramas be read *against* a nurturant or literal mother paradigm to suggest a different social organization. African American women mothering white women represents a particularly loaded relationship in American cultural productions and runs along a different fault line of history and social power than does the white "governess" figure. In *The Great Lie*, it is Hattie McDaniel's character Violet who does the work of raising the child who is the object of the unusual exchange between two white women. In a sense Davis's character qualifies as a good mother by providing the child with the same good "mammy" who had raised her—another perverse fantasy. The role of Violet is clearly built upon the presence of the Academy Award–winning McDaniel, who contracted out to Warners for the film, and it "progresses" beyond the mammy type in her quasi-partnership with her co-star Davis. "The close confidantes grew closer," Cripps writes of the dawn of the war years, and notes that McDaniel's character "was plainly egalitarian and made the plot work" (367). The intimacy between the black and white women and the emphases of McDaniel's performance at the very least make the viewer conscious that their shared parenting of the child shadows the dominant "double mother" storyline.[16]

Now I wish to discuss a performer whose return to Hollywood in the immediate post-war period further shifted the inter-female nurturing mammy paradigm toward autonomous meanings. The ambiguity in relations among women in Ethel Waters's films is refracted through a star persona that entails constructions of African American female sexuality from popular music and performance rather than from white Hollywood film.

Ethel Waters

In Bogle's reading of types, the resistant performances of actors playing servants in the 1930s gave way to banal 1940s roles (such as McDaniel's boringly loyal maid in *Since You Went Away*, 1944). In 1942, Walter White of the NAACP had received a commitment from Hollywood studio heads to improve African American representation in cinema, and Southern stereotypes were particularly scrutinized (Cripps, *Making Movies Black* 376). The return to Hollywood in the post-war period by Ethel Waters, who as an extremely successful vaudeville and nightclub singer and Broadway headliner had made her first film—playing "herself"—in 1929, entailed a reworking of the mammy stereotype, overlaying conservative cultural nostalgia with a liberal veneer. *Pinky* and *The Member of the Wedding* in particular, I will argue, combine this reworking with a potentially resistant nostalgia on the part of the female protagonist (and spectator) for forms of female intimacy and authorization. Waters's reemergence in this period as an avatar of the mammy—Bogle calls her "an earth mother for an alienated age"— demands some accounting for.[17] The inflection of the type responds to ideological conflict over race and emergent political power among African Americans in the post-war period.

Waters's star status makes it difficult to read her as a stand-in for the "social issue" of race. Waters was never strictly a supporting actress; her film appearances, primarily in musicals, though infrequent, were generally "featured," if not top-billed, as in the black-cast *Cabin in the Sky* (Vincente Minnelli, 1943). (She is also the female "lead" in the "black" segment of *Tales of Manhattan* [Julien Duvivier, 1942]; thus there are segregated and integrated steps on the star ladder for black actors.)[18] Her performances combined the individuality of the realist characters she portrayed with her individuality as a star—with a history as a sensual, talented, and famous singer. Gary Giddins claims that "Waters, in many respects, was the mother of modern popular singing, the transitional figure . . . who adapted white theatrical styles to a black image" (63). Her galvanizing presence in a few film roles suggested a similar potential in that medium.

Edward Baron Turk points out that when Waters was consigned to the role of Jeannette MacDonald's maid Cleo in the wartime musical spy spoof *Cairo* (W. S. Van Dyke II, 1942), Waters's musical style, and the manner in which it was featured, went some way toward "equalizing" the disparity between the lead and the "companion, sidekick, confidante, friend role" (3). Turk notes that "MacDonald tailored her MGM persona by insisting that potentially competing female talent be written out of her screenplays. This is what makes the MacDonald-Waters connection in *Cairo* especially intriguing" (5). Perhaps Waters's "competing" talent was made acceptable by her "connecting" with the star on another level (though Cleo has a heterosexual romance subplot in the film). Compounding this potential eruption is what Turk notes as an ideological schema operating in the xenophobic film "in which otherness, and the fear it inspires, is not at all marked as black" (5). The "others" include the female Nazi leader "dark haired Mona Barrie, [who] is virtually coded as crypto-lesbian in her emotional coldness and severe fashion taste" (5–6). It is this character whom MacDonald is mistaken for in the vicissitudes of the film's plot. Thus blackness is secured for American authenticity and wholesome heterosexuality in a text otherwise marked by a homosexual symptomology raised by female difference and casting conventions.

Like Dandridge, but unlike many black women in film, Waters's star image was informed by a degree of white public knowledge about her "private" life. Her widely read 1951 autobiography *His Eye Is on the Sparrow* offered a prism through which her starring film role in *Member of the Wedding* was received, as Bogle argues (162). (The memoir concludes with her starring on Broadway in the stage version.) This image included extreme early poverty; success in Jazz-Age Harlem, on Broadway, and in Hollywood, alternating with prolonged periods of unemployment; scandal, conflict, and adversity; a strong will and autonomy; and a reputation for being "difficult" — notoriously on the set of *Cabin in the Sky*. A long excerpt from the memoir appeared under the title "The Men in My Life" in *Ebony* in 1952. Its first line promises, "This is a story about prostitutes, thieves, pimps, dope addicts and petty hustlers" (24). As a young girl, "sex didn't interest me much," Waters writes, "but there was nothing about it I didn't know" (25) and proceeds to portray herself as a sexual agent even when exploited by her husbands and boyfriends. The magazine's cover photo adds counterpoint to the title by depicting Waters with the head of her white female co-star in *Pinky*, Jeanne Crain, nestled on her shoulder. The image suggests respite from urban life and masculine hard use through the sanctified domestic type, but at the same time the voice of the article doesn't permit the reading of Waters as asexual that the movie type might encourage. Waters's depiction as a *subject* of (hetero)sexual desire in her singing was carried over to the frankness of the autobiography. And Hollywood allowed some hint of the expression of her sexual agency in non-narrative codes; in *Cabin in the Sky* (Minnelli, 1943) as the good Christian wife whose husband strays under the influence of Lena Horne, she reclaims her man in a remarkable dance number. In *The Member of the Wedding* she tells stories about the husband who satisfied her desires, while visually she's most memorably depicted with another white girl's head resting on her shoulder. The complicated relationship between white-washed Hollywood's inability to depict African American sexuality, the white woman's picture's use of black women to express the embodied aspects of mothering, and the conventions of the blues for expressing female desire and loneliness intersected in Waters's roles. Her movie pairings with women were thus fascinating condensations of cultural meanings.

Whether it was an aspect widely available to or apprehended by post-war viewers cannot be determined, but several accounts assert that Waters had been known as bi- or homosexual, at least during early periods of her life. In his study of the Harlem lesbian and gay subculture of the 1920s, "A Spectacle in Color," Eric Garber states that Waters was involved with women, though she wasn't open about it, unlike other blues singers such as Gladys Bentley (326).[19] And in her autobiographical essay in *Persistent Desire: A Fem-Butch Reader*, "My Mother's Daughter," Ira Jeffries recounts that when Waters had asked Jeffries's mother to tour with her, her grandmother had refused permission on account of "Ethel's reputation as a 'bulldagger'" (59, fig. 28). Another aspect of Waters's persona, her strong Christian identity, is threaded through all of her public presentations. The final "man in her life" discussed in the excerpt from *His Eye Is on the Sparrow* quoted above is the "God I first met through the gentle sisters of an interracial Catholic school in Philadelphia" (38), and Waters forcefully conveys the compatibility of her sexual and religious subjectivities. Her roles in *Pinky* and *The Member of the Wedding* are identified with an "earthy" Christian faith put into practice by her mentoring of the young female protagonists. In her later years, spent touring with Billy Graham's Crusade, she played "mom" to at least two white Christian women who wrote books of testimony about the transformative power of their relationships.[20] These slippages among familial, partnering, and mentoring relationships occur in the force field of a star persona that held together faith, sexuality, identifications with African American and white cultures, and, above all, self-definition.

Removed from the stock or comic mammies of the 1930s, Waters's

28. *Ethel Waters in drag.*

Academy Award–nominated "Aunt Dicey" in *Pinky* (Elia Kazan, 1949) was the first of three "realist" (though simultaneously highly stylized) portrayals of the southern black woman as survivor. *Pinky* was followed by *The Member of the Wedding* (1953) and *The Sound and the Fury* (1959), serious, and somewhat bizarre, literary adaptations. *Pinky* was the first of the post-war genre of "message movies" on black issues, made with high production values for first-run release, and it proudly wore its mantle of what Cripps calls "conscience liberalism" in *Making Movies Black*, his study of Hollywood after the NAACP agreement. Cripps traces the production history of the film and the ideological struggles both behind the scenes and encoded in the film among the different positions on integration, passing, and demands for social change. He basically pigeonholes the role of Dicey as a faithful retainer, the "dark grandmother who knows ancient things" (232), a throwback to earlier representations, and a conservative voice in the film.

As T. E. Perkins emphasizes, stereotypes are strengthened at times of structural change in a group's position, even as their meanings are contested (148). The film throws its weight with Dicey as a mark of its liberal humanism; she is undeniably its strongest African American representation (Pinky herself is played by white actress Jeanne Crain, a casting decision which has semiotic effects and exemplifies the irony in the "opportunity" the white-produced problem picture cycle offered African Americans). While Lorraine Hansberry listed "'Aunt Dicey,' complete in bandanna, who just 'loves old Miss Em' who has exploited her all her life" (460) among the film's "insults," Bogle finds Waters's "grandiose" performance transformative of the type, indeed the place "where *Pinky* shown through with brilliance." Bogle writes, "In the screenplay the character was a combination Tom and Mammy. . . . But Ethel Waters . . . exhibited ambiguities and contradictions that seemed to come from her own personal experience" (152). He cites Waters, together with Poitier and Dandridge, as the key figures of 1950s black cinematic representation. The timeless, wise, long-suffering, heroic, strong black woman Waters interpreted serves a specific ideological function, a definition of "humanity" upon which white America can congratulate itself without acknowledging racism or rage. Yet Waters's charisma and her truculence, her appearance as a "star" in such a role, prevent this seamless functioning. The recasting of the "matriarchal" figure in her roles —with its "ambiguities and contradictions"—which necessitates the return to the "mammy" convention, is connected with female homosociality in both *Pinky* and *The Member of the Wedding*. As these were her most successful film roles, this primary connection to other women strongly inflects Waters's star image.

161

Because of *Pinky*'s status in film historiography as a breakthrough "message movie," the strangeness of its matrifocal plot is often overlooked. The film is organized around a central female triangle (like the maternal melodramas discussed in Chapter 4). This consists of Waters's character, the laundress known to the entire town as Aunt Dicey; the redoubtable Miss Em (Ethel Barrymore), the ailing, impoverished white woman who lives in the big house visible from the porch of Dicey's shack; and Pinky, Dicey's light-skinned granddaughter who, at the beginning of the film, returns from the North, where she was educated as a nurse. Dicey persuades Pinky to care for the white woman, almost as atonement for her having passed as white. Pinky is then bequeathed the house and grounds upon Miss Em's death. When the will is upheld in court after being contested by Em's relatives—and despite opposition to her struggle from black and white residents—Pinky breaks with her white fiancé and opens "Miss Em's Clinic and Nursery" on the property (fig. 29).

What is clearly unthinkable to the film on one level is also its very premise; "Miss Em" and "Aunt Dicey," lifelong companions, love each other. Dicey's feeling for her employer was objected to for good reason by Hansberry and others, yet the difference introduced by the film's presenting its "social contract" as one between women (though its terms remain unequal) is overlooked. The black woman is the white woman's double, crucial to her existence. Their relationship, with its rewriting of the Old South through white female benevolence that can embrace the "progressive" message of the panacea of (segregated) social services and racial uplift is the emotional center of the film and reads as romantic friendship.[21] Yet in its racism and homophobia, the film never shows Dicey and Em in conversation, though each conveys to Pinky what the other means to her—Dicey more eloquently and more problematically. In Em's patronizing gesture of leaving her clothes and shoes to her friend (which she has bought in Dicey's size rather than her own for years), can be seen as a manifestation of the kind of ghosting effect generated by their alternating appearance in the text.[22] Dicey's "offensive" desire to serve Miss Em without pay comes to shield the "offensiveness" of an intimacy between two women that might make such a mutual dependence, though asymmetrical and exploitative in actuality, possible. An erotic explanation is one way of accounting for the anachronism of this relationship—however "repressed," it is pressed into the service of disguising hierarchy as reciprocity.

On another level, Ethel Barrymore and Ethel Waters are an almost perfect match; they project something of the same haughtiness and superiority in their upstaging, grande dame character acting. Barrymore's roles

29. *Aunt Dicey (Ethel Waters) and her granddaughter Pinky (Jeanne Crain) in* Pinky *(Elia Kazan, 1949). Although Waters is in the classic supporting actress pose, gazing at the lead, she dominates the shot.*

were often so vigorously matriarchal as to seem sapphic (see, for example, *Spiral Staircase*). The two women are approximately the same age in the film; neither the accepted maternalism of the white mistress toward her "girl" nor her loyalty to her childhood mammy binds them. Because both are older women character roles and thus "desexualized" according to conventional ideology, most viewers overlook that they are "lovers" in the film's logic. Yet the very "offscreen-ness" of the relationship is odd; why couldn't it be represented? As it represents the "normal," familiar, relation of black servitude, perhaps it is so natural it doesn't need to be depicted. Indeed if it were, it might grate on audiences ready for something more contemporary and believable in the film's "message" about black-white relations. Yet because it is only implied, is "understood," it has unforeseen textual echoes.

All of this is to insist that the film does not, strictly speaking, offer a paternalistic solution to "race relations." Miss Em's experiment with a school for girls, of which we learn, prefigures Pinky's experiment of turning inherited property into an institutional legacy for female fulfillment. Pinky is the black/white woman, object and agent of maternalism, who will remake this feminist vision for a new era. Although it is certainly the right of blacks to inherit and hold property that is contested in the trial (and resolved in Pinky's favor with an unforgivable lack of verisimilitude, according to Hansberry), it is also the fact that property is handed from a white to a black *woman* that is problematic. Pinky is "light-skinned" unto whiteness, but there is no diegetic "explanation" for her skin tone; no prominent white *man* is on hand to explain her parentage, as censors had wished.[23] Rather it is Em who claims her as kin in her legacy, a lesbian familial model that includes Dicey, who sends Pinky to her. Pinky resented not being allowed to play on the lawn of the big house as a child, while her grandmother moved back and forth freely. In the plantation scenario this echoes, Pinky is illegitimate child to Miss Em as master. The white woman is evidently unmarried; her kind is doomed. The accusations of Pinky's exerting undue influence over the white woman that come up at the trial simply strengthen the sense of a female world of affinity or more, a quiet travesty of patriarchal inheritance. Indeed Pinky almost seems adopted by Dicey, the blood tie undercut not only by her extreme whiteness, but by Dicey's improbable relation to procreation—for all that she is metaphorical earth mother there are no men in her life. Dicey resembles Pinky's mammy.[24]

Acting, composition, and lighting codes also marginalize Waters/Dicey in relation to the heroine. Under the insidious operation of racism, the film posits a fundamental bond between grandmother and granddaughter on the level of narrative; but in the interest of the heroine's "whiteness" denies it on the level of narration—outside of a few early embraces that actually might read like intrafamilial lesbian "miscegenation."[25] As with the relationship between Em and Dicey, the film works to keep the affect attached to the women's bond off-screen and in check. This has the effect of making one *notice* Dicey's absence from every scene in which she would logically have a stake. This literalizes the problem of defining the center and the margin (and implied audience) of the narrative of a "message movie" (this one deals with a "tragic mulatta," but the romance/passing storyline is not dominant), the question of the central or marginal status of Waters and/as Dicey. In a disruptive moment, Dicey does reappear in a scene from which she has been excluded, like the return of the repressed.

After an attack, Miss Em is attended by Pinky and an older white doctor who is a friend of both matriarchs. Pinky leaves the room, and Miss Em asks the doctor to witness her will. The lengthy scene ends with an unexpected image of Dicey seated at the foot of the bed, her face impassive and unreadable. By no word or glance from the other characters could we have known she was in the room, participating in the scene. She is the archetypal witness, representing black endurance, as she attends the deathbed. Her bearing witness is later made a mockery of in court, in a scene that retrospectively explains the shot. She is unable to testify whether it was indeed a will that she saw because she cannot read. Yet the shot is not recuperated. It brings sharply into focus the excluded black point of view in the person of the servant as supporting character—her marginality made her presence here possible. The moment in the bedroom condenses the indignity of being treated as if she wasn't there, and her own granddaughter's ignoring of her, with the diegetic significance of her grief and love for the dying woman in a quasi-Brechtian moment of defamiliarization punctuated by Waters's ornery and resistant persona.

While I do not mean to mime melodrama's own operation by translating the film's presentation of social conflict and exploitation back into familial and sexual themes, it would be futile to try and decode the film's "race theme" to get at a single "message"—and wrong to separate race from the way it is embodied and performed. Nor am I suggesting the film is "about" lesbianism. But the fact that it floats its liberal achievement on the affective bond between women should be noted. This works through the deployment of stereotypes, the very stuff of Hollywood's black representation, as well as of their contradictions (stereotypes show the work involved in maintaining hegemony), contradictions generated to a degree by Waters's gendered, "racialized" persona and its reception. The mammy type condenses white fantasies and fears about black women and exploits the historical realities of slavery and domestic service. Waters's presence as star functions as a sign of the practice of subordination in Hollywood narrative. Mammy roles are a way of handling her, even as her star image contributes to the contradictory semiotic work of the film.

In the two images of Waters that illustrate Bogle's book, from *Pinky* and *The Member of the Wedding*, she is depicted in an embrace with a young white woman, captioned: "Black shoulders were meant to cry on" (153) and "Even in the 1950s, black shoulders were still meant to cry on" (163). This iconography of the mammy role is inflected by its being Waters in both instances (and thus a particular mammy), and by the fact that both exceed the requisite intimacy or modify the relationship in some way: in Pinky the "white" woman is her granddaughter (the embrace means something "more"), in the second the child Frankie is marked by her difference as a tomboy (though played by an adult, Julie Harris, in a more benign kind of code-breaking casting than *Pinky*'s), and the embrace is so often repeated as to form the dominant narrative image of the film. As in *Pinky*, in *The Member of the Wedding* the Waters character stands in the place of a non-patriarchally identified desire for the heroine; it is her body upon which the possibility of Frankie's different desire is founded, as I discussed in the introduction. In a formulation that is the other side of Spillers's understanding of the black woman as "mother-dispossessed," Water's character is chosen as sexual "mother" by the white girl-child. Berenice is heterosexualized; yet her consuming love for her dead husband is transformed by her stories to stand as the ideal image for the two deviant white children, Frankie and her cousin John Henry.

This odd film is important as the only instance in which what Bogle calls "the movies' Huck Finn fixation" (140) is explored with two female terms (fig. 30). Indeed Berenice's eyepatch and storytelling make her a full-fledged image of adventure. *Member* encodes spectatorial investment in the resonance of the Waters character entirely through Frankie's narrative and even erotic point of view. Berenice is so three-dimensional, so "human," as to be larger than life. Bogle implies more than he realizes in his judgment that "Because *Member*, with its skinny tomboy heroine and its pint-sized bespectacled leading man, was so unlike the typical Saturday evening movie fare, audiences tended to accept Ethel Waters and her life rather than the lives portrayed in the film" (164). Audiences disavowed these strange, marginal lives, and the fiction itself (as does Bogle by not discussing its content). The action of *Member* takes place for the most part in the back of the house, in "Berenice's" kitchen, and literally takes the point of view of supporting characters, child and servant: hence the significance of the wedding Frankie is excluded from and so desperately wants to join. It is particularly symptomatic that *Member* would be the first studio film to be carried by a black woman star, as if her "otherness" were equivalent with that of children, queer white children to boot. Like them, she is an outsider, but her outsiderness is structurally different from theirs. The projection onto Berenice—by Carson McCullers, a Southern white lesbian, and onto Waters by the film's other "authors," including its spectators—comes full circle in the fact that she is the children's primary agent of socialization. James Baldwin describes the performer's resistance: "The moments given us by black performers exist so far beneath, or beyond, the American apprehensions that it is difficult to describe them. . . . There is the truth to be found in Ethel Waters's face at the end of *Member of the Wedding*" (121–22). He notes that "Black spectators supply the sub-text—the unspoken—out of their own lives" and some lesbian and gay spectators are among them.

166

30. *In a similar two-shot from* The Member of the Wedding *(Fred Zinnemann, 1952) Waters, as Berenice, plays a nurturing role to Frankie (Julie Harris).*

The Image of "Woman" and the "Other" Woman

Since the black mammy functions to signify emotional and physical intimacy with a white woman, the burden is on her physical type to connote not sexuality but "motherliness" and labor. Indeed her bulk seems to be exaggerated in proportion to her narrative devotion to the heroine, so she is not read as "sexual" through dominant cultural codes. Other configurations of "racialized" gender are inflected differently as lesbian in Hollywood films. Black, mulatta, Asian, Latina, and "mixed-blood" supporting female characters are often presented as the sexual double of the white heroine. This operation may be differentiated, with all the not-so-subtle discrimination of Hollywood racism, into the black exotic primitive, the ancient erotic "mystery" of Asian women, and the "natural" sensuality and physicality of Latina or Native American characters. Yet this ostensibly heterosexual projection

167

—the "other" can express the presumptively heterosexual desire the white heroine must keep in check—often serves to figure erotic tension *between* the women, particularly if the white woman's sexuality is presented as enigmatic, in a manner which might affect the status and success of heterosexuality.[26]

Anna May Wong, Marlene Dietrich's traveling companion in *Shanghai Express*, as the most developed female second lead in a von Sternberg–Dietrich vehicle, threatens to give an unprecedented narrative trajectory to the lesbian aura accruing to the Dietrich persona across her films. Here the two women are doubled as mysterious, elegant, disdainful prostitutes (fig. 31). The Dietrich character's very name, Shanghai Lily, crosses codes: her identification with the East and the sexual transgression associated with the Chinese woman contrasts with her whiteness and "purity." The association of lesbianism and prostitution comes about as one kind of illicit sexuality standing in for another, and as an imaginative (or actual) product of the proximity to other sexual women. This association overlays the erotic potential signified in *Shanghai Express* by the similarity and contiguity of supporting and lead actress and their narratives: Dietrich's leading to heavily ironized heterosexual closure, Wong's to her killing of the film's Chinese villain, who attempts to rape her.

Bette Davis (Leslie Crosbie)'s confrontation with her dead (male) lover's Malaysian widow (Gale Sondergaard) in *The Letter* (Wyler, 1940) is a memorable instance of the fatal attraction between the white star and a "woman of color" supporting actress double. The absence of the body of the man who links them is underlined with excessive force in the murder sequence that opens the text and which is re-enacted later, again without the body. The almost spectral presence of the other woman, silent, appearing in the compositional and narrative periphery, is a lure of dread and fascination for Leslie, a trace of the tempestuous desire she keeps in check (like Mrs. Danvers, this widow never seems to be shown moving). Leslie finally goes to her and is stabbed to death, a nighttime tryst played out with the passionate compulsion of the scene that opened the film. Sondergaard, of course, is white. The common practice of casting white actors to play people of color foregrounds the way in which the representation of racial difference turns back against that of whiteness in the classical Hollywood cinema. A white supporting actress thus cast represents a paradoxical difference-from and sameness-to the white female protagonist, visually marking her "supporting" function, and potentially allowing eroticism to be signified.[27]

A different sort of *mise-en-abîme* effect is created by the doubling between Davis's character in *Beyond the Forest* (King Vidor, 1948) and her

31. *Anna May Wong mirrors lead actress Marlene Dietrich in* Shanghai Express
   (*Josef von Sternberg, 1932*).

maid, played by Mexican actress Dona Drake, when the white actress comes
to masquerade as the woman of color within the diegesis. As the notorious
Rosa Moline, Davis bears an uncanny resemblance to her hostile Latina
maid. Both sport long, center-parted, slightly unkempt black hair—to jar-
ring effect in Davis's case because of our familiarity with her visual appearance (fig. 32). Drake's presence, however marginal, is as intense as any other
aspect of a film that is over the top in every way. It is a stand-out impertinent
servant role; she is sullen and sluggish, mirroring Rosa's own contemptuous
attitude and hatred of domesticity. This textual doubling effect functions
throughout the film, but at a crucial point in the story, Rosa disguises herself
as her maid in order to leave town. Rosa dons the flannel shirt and jeans she
resented her servant's wearing to work. This is one of Hollywood's most self-
conscious constructions of the expropriation of the supporting actress/wom-

an of color's image, perhaps because Davis is unable or unwilling to register it subtly. While diegetically Rosa capitalizes on the fact that servants, women of color, and women in trousers are "invisible," it is a veritable performance of the visible to the spectator—as the lead actress tries to move to a supporting role. That the masquerade involves an element of gender inversion ironically makes visible the irreducible difference between women—race, class, and power—that appears to give such doubling its frisson.

In her discussion of Dorothy Arzner as a lesbian author, Judith Mayne analyzes iconographic contrast and "lesbian looks" in two-shots of women. She cites Sarah Halprin's point that secondary characters in Arzner's *Dance, Girl, Dance* (for example, Maria Ouspenskaya as the dance instructor, or the secretary who attends the burlesque show) sport the butch dress and manner that the director herself affected, thereby making lesbianism visible in the films, however marginally.[28] Mayne looks at photographs of Arzner—often

32. *Dona Drake mimics star Bette Davis in* Beyond the Forest *(King Vidor, 1948).*

depicting her looking at a conventionally feminine actress—that have been used to illustrate feminist analyses from Pam Cook and Claire Johnston's essays in *The Work of Dorothy Arzner*, a founding text of feminist film theory, to Constance Penley's anthology, *Feminism and Film Theory*. When these configurations of the gaze between contrasting female types are repeated in Arzner's films, Mayne argues, they constitute a kind of lesbian authorial signature. Yet despite the visual insistence of the photographs in their texts, feminist film critics have rarely mentioned lesbianism in relation to Arzner, much less made it a starting point for reading.

Raoul Walsh's *The Revolt of Mamie Stover* (1956) is also the subject of an influential early piece by Cook and Johnston. Although they read the commodification of the woman's image and the circulation of capital in the film, they basically ignore Agnes Moorehead's function as madam of the brothel (or rather, manager of the dance hall) where Flaming Mamie (Jane Russell) creates her fame and fortune, and thus the supporting actress's important role in both of these discourses. A classic still from this film depicts Mamie (Jane Russell) and Agnes Moorehead in her bathrobe, an image of star and supporting actress whose gaze conveys, to my mind, something of the same effect as the two-shots Mayne discusses (fig. 33). Although this film's authorial discourse would seem to quash a lesbian reading, I think one is possible. Besides the iconographic properties visible in the photograph: the bathrobe, Russell's sexual coding, and the figuration of anyone's gaze at such an image of woman as an erotic one, it is Moorehead's star persona that provides this image's lesbian "signature." In another two-shot Agnes Moorehead and Debbie Reynolds personify a supporting actress "type" and a bona fide female star (fig. 34). Moreover their relationship—off-screen as well as on—can be read though the stereotype of older, sapphic sophisticate who preys upon innocent younger woman, in this case the singing nun.

How to Read a Dyke

Not surprisingly, it is not only in straight, psychoanalytically oriented feminist film theory that lesbian images are misrecognized. Gay male critics have often "claimed" particular supporting players as progressive, disruptive, or resistant without necessarily pointing to them as gay or lesbian representations. Inasmuch as character actresses are enjoyed, admired, or pressed into camp service by a "queer" mode of reading, it is apparently "character" itself that is supported.

Russo asserts that female gender-role transgression is acceptable in our society and cinema, whereas male gender-role transgression is both despised

171

33. *Agnes Moorehead as madam stares at one of her girls, played by star Jane Russell, in* The Revolt of Mamie Stover *(Raoul Walsh, 1956).*

34. *In a similar two-shot Moorehead looks in the same manner at sister Debbie Reynolds in* The Singing Nun *(Henry Koster, 1966).*

and disruptive (13). While Dietrich was indeed "allowed" to wear a tux, and Debbie Reynolds could play a tomboy with impunity, Russo's claim does not account for the (hetero)sexualization of the image of femininity in Hollywood, nor for the extent of its misogyny. In the chapter "Hollywood Homosense" in his book on the gay (male) sensibility, Michael Bronski singles out the woman friend that "many top female stars were paired off with . . . before they ended up getting the leading man"—played by the likes of Joan Blondell and Eve Arden—as a character type with specific gay appeal:

> The sidekick's role was generally to act as a confidante and to give the audience a pungent analysis of the plot. Sidekicks were sarcastic, unromantic, and sensible. They were cleverly self-deprecating . . . but could also turn the wit on men. Too smart ever to get the man, sidekicks had to settle for being funnier than everybody else. For gay men who would never walk off into the sunset with a leading man, the sidekick was a dose of real life. (102)

I think Bronski is right in attributing a sort of metacritical role to confidante characters and a self-conscious reading practice to their fans, but he understands these images only in relation to male spectators (which admittedly is his subject) and male roles, despite the fact that it is the heroine with whom they are paired.[29] Bronski cites Russo's work on sissy roles and the actors who portrayed them in films of the 1930s and early 1940s: "Prissified and officious, they were effeminate, and foils to the film's *real* men." Bronski avers: "Woman sidekicks were never played as lesbians, just 'old maids,' but the non-romantic male was always implicitly gay" (102). Bronski is insightful in pairing the sissy with the old maid (rather than with the tomboy) as the type whose gender-role deviation is disempowering and makes of them an object of derision. If the misogyny attributed to the camp sensibility seems to be operative in the persistent failure to recognize the old maid as a lesbian type, it must also be stated that it is misogyny that constructs the type itself.

Given the virtual conceptual blank that is lesbianism in the culture at large, it is no accident that the social types standing in for lesbians in Hollywood cinema are coded as "asexual." They are also trivialized, rendered comical or threatening. Although the ideology of gender certainly marks the stereotypes of sissy and old maid differently, Bronski's statement compounds the invisibility to which lesbians are already consigned. One lesbian writer, in contrast, attributes sexuality to a later popular cultural incarnation of the "old maid" type. In a cover article for *Lesbian News* entitled "The Truth about Miss Hathaway," Marion Garbo Todd takes issue with *The Television Collector's* recent assessment of the *Beverly Hillbillies* character played by Nancy Kulp: "Miss Jane Hathaway could have been the prototype for the term 'Plain Jane.' Tall and lanky, with an asexual manner, the epitome of a spinster" (40).[30] Todd retorts:

> Where does this "plain Jane" stuff come from? How can the word plain be used to describe the handsome Miss Hathaway? "Tall and lanky" is not the right phrase for her body; "long and sensuous" is much more accurate. Her long neck, aquiline nose, wavy hair, and large bright eyes made her very beautiful. She had smile lines to swoon over, and her voice was a delight. . . . The question of Jane Hathaway's sexuality seems to hit a nerve with every television reviewer. . . . In fact there's fairly good evidence that Miss Hathaway had no interest in men at all, because she was a lesbian. She definitely had the clothes for it, tailored outfits. In her tasteful skirt suit, short hairdo, and horn-rimmed glasses, she could have been the lead character in any lesbian pulp novel. (40)

The widespread apprehension of this type as asexual, or worse, man-starved —precisely invisible as lesbian—has to do, perhaps paradoxically, with the visual overdetermination of "woman" as sexual in film. The supporting character necessarily diverges from this "ideal" (a white one), or place, of the woman in film. Feminist film theory has analyzed the manner in which the cinematic system of the look constructs woman as image of masculine desire. As images of a different version of femininity than that of female stars, supporting characters may not ultimately be so supportive of the status quo. As noted above, they can draw the image of "woman" embodied in the female lead, with whom they are contrasted iconographically, into a lesbian visual economy.

Some Dames

It is impossible to grasp the ambivalence of narrative "support" and the function of (lesbian) typification apart from a consideration of the star text. Many a supporting character would fade into the background were it not for spectatorial affinity and the vestiges of the star system working even for character actresses, so that particular performers become visible in these roles. It is Kulp's Miss Hathaway, Ritter's nurses, Arden's sidekicks, Franklin Pangborn's sissies, and McDaniel's maids that capture the imagination. A single role might be unmistakably lesbian, if the writing and wardrobe and performance of the actress add up—such as in the case of Grayson Hall's Miss Fellowes, the chaperone in *Night of the Iguana*.[31] This apprehension of a role or of a physical type as lesbian is reinforced if an actress is familiar from a similar role in another film. And the more roles she appears in, the more unforeseen the effects that are introduced in a given text by her casting. It is in this sense that I speak of the queer careers of these actresses.

Dyer has written extensively about the signifying work of stars, considering not only film appearances but promotion, publicity, and critical commentary as discourses shaping their images (*Stars* 68; see also *Heavenly Bodies*). In narrative films, novelistic conceptions of character are articulated with stars as already-signifying images—which essentially function within the same bourgeois ideology of the self-consistent individual. How might Dyer's approach apply to character actresses, who, however recognizable, are not strictly "stars"? As Dyer notes: "Type characters are acknowledged to have a place . . . but only to enable the proper elaboration of the central, individuated character(s). In this respect, no star could be just a type, since all stars play central characters" (*Stars* 117). By the same token, a character actress might retain a marginal, subversive edge that does not get "rounded off." Agnes Moorehead, for example, does not have a fully individuated star image (at least not before *Bewitched*), yet her on-screen type cannot be considered merely as an extension of her off-screen "self" (which would reintroduce the category of the individual in another way). What was distinct was the fact of her *acting*, which allowed her to represent and to "quote" a type at the same time. In a sense, such a character-star's persona is even more vivid, insofar as she is seen to play the same role from one film to the next.

Moorehead entered films in 1941 and her deviant female characterizations spanned several decades and their shifting ideological demands on femininity.[32] In the 1940s her bitchy and imposing persona was constituted in "literary" roles, gothic- and noir-flavored pictures expressing some of the wartime anxiety about women's roles. The 1950s backlash against women could be read right off her panoply of pioneer mothers, frivolous aunts, and comic foils; yet during this era she also established the archness and camp that would carry her into *Bewitched* in the mid-1960s. Two performers with whom she seemed to divvy up a certain terrain in the 1940s were Gale Sondergaard—"typically cast as a catty, cunning, or vicious woman," "well established as Hollywood's number one female screen villain" (Katz 1071), recipient of the first supporting actress Oscar ever awarded and first choice for the Wicked Witch of the West in *The Wizard of Oz*—and Dame Judith "unsympathetic and at times sinister" Anderson (Katz 29). Both carried more weight as villains than did the shrewish Moorehead. While Anderson was famous for playing classic tragedy on-stage—Gertrude, Lady Macbeth, and Medea—on-screen she was considered as well cast as "Lady Scarface" as Sondergaard was as "The Spider Woman." Sondergaard's career was cut short in 1949 by the Hollywood blacklist (her husband Herbert Biberman was one of the Hollywood Ten); a specialist in sinister on-screen otherness was finally rendered unemployable on account of her private life. Anderson remained active, playing Big Mama in *Cat on a Hot Tin Roof* (Richard Brooks, 1958) and the matriarch on the daytime soap *Santa Barbara* in the 1980s. But by the 1950s, both Anderson and Moorehead had been pressed into service as stooges in Jerry Lewis movies (*Who's Minding the Store* also offered Nancy Kulp a big-screen role); but as the movies themselves were gender-inverted comic revisions of Hollywood standard fare, these women were aptly cast. Moorehead, Sondergaard, and Dame Anderson were actresses of "character."

Thelma Ritter and Mercedes McCambridge both made their screen debuts in the late 1940s and left extremely vivid marks on the American cinema in the 1950s. They were character actresses in that they played one intensely vivid thing. Arguably, they both could be read as working-class butch types of the 1950s—Ritter a less boorish forerunner of Sister George and McCambridge straight from the cover of a pulp novel. According to Esther Newton's research, Ritter was part of the lesbian community of Fire Island in the 1950s. An extraordinary actress, "typically in cynical, wise-cracking, disarmingly outspoken roles" (Katz 976), Ritter is perhaps too easily recuperated by enthusiastic mainstream endorsement of her warm-hearted persona. And yet, the fact that she appeared in fare such as the Doris Day–Rock Hudson romantic comedy *Pillow Talk* by no means reduces her queer quotient. In one of her first film roles, in *A Letter to Three Wives* (Joseph Mankiewicz, 1949), she is the classic servant who sees through the pretensions of her employers. She spends her free time drinking beer and playing cards with another famous character actress, Connie Gilchrist. When she remarks to the suitor who awaits the latter's daughter (Linda Darnell), "Girls always got something to do. Or so they tell me," she both distinguishes herself from the category "girls" and inscribes herself as someone to whom girls are wont to make excuses. In *All About Eve* (Mankiewicz, 1950) she sees through Eve Harrington even before the crypto-homo Addison de Witt (George Sanders) can claim that Eve and he are "two of a kind." Birdie (Ritter) and Eve are two of a kind in their structural relation to Margo (Bette Davis). Inexplicably, Birdie disappears about midway through the film, her function made redundant by that of Eve, a less benign lesbian personal assistant (fig. 35). When she is sent out of the room by Margo for scoffing at her manner toward Eve, Birdie agrees to stay away "till you get normal." Yet it is precisely the fact that Margo does "get normal," deciding to

35. *Thelma Ritter is Bette Davis's companion before being ousted by Eve in* All About Eve *(Joseph Mankiewicz, 1950).*

work at "being a woman" in marriage rather than at being a star, that makes Birdie's exit a definitive and necessary one.

Mercedes McCambridge

McCambridge is described in *The Film Encyclopedia* as an "intense" character player who "appeared intermittently in films, usually in intense, volatile roles"—author Ephraim Katz is uncharacteristically at a loss for a sufficient number of adjectives to describe her (748). Hard and urban as Ritter, she hides no warm heart or "motherly" solicitude and makes no wisecracks. The threat of her persona, derived from homophobic discourses of sexual pathology, is thrillingly transformed by her bravado. Almost every one of McCambridge's appearances could be mentioned as a reading of her deviant female persona. She's as butch in her supporting actress Oscar-winning debut in *All the King's Men* (Robert Rossen, 1949) as she is in *Johnny Guitar* (Nicholas Ray, 1954). Her black-clad villain in this dyke western makes her co-star Joan Crawford look femme as she wreaks twisted vengeance and dies the requisite homo-death.[33] The climactic shoot-out with Crawford turns up the heat even higher than that other classic Arizona scene (Davis and Astor in *The Great Lie*) in which female rivalry signifies desire. Here the hostility is taken to suggestive extremes: "I'm going to kill you," McCambridge hisses. "I know."

In the western setting of the melodrama *Lightning Strikes Twice* (King Vidor, 1951) Liza's (McCambridge) jeans and boots and hand-rolled ciga-rettes seem appropriate. But her attitude toward newcomer Ruth Roman does not. In a rather convoluted gothic plot, Roman finds herself falling in love with Trev, a man who is the prime suspect in the wedding-night murder of his bride Lorraine. Like the heroine of *Rebecca*, Roman is full of curiosity about the dead woman — "What was she like?" "Beautiful, full of laughter — and completely evil!" McCambridge and Roman share several moments of odd affect and butch-femme fashion coordination (from mirroring McCam-bridge's western wear [fig. 36] Roman goes to wearing New Look dresses), before Roman finally marries Trev. Like a good gothic heroine, she's struck with terror on her wedding night and flees in fear — to Liza! "I'd been going out of my mind ever since you left," she confesses to the other woman, ostensibly referring to her fear after McCambridge's tale of witnessing the events of the murder night. But then Liza confesses that *she* killed Lorraine: "She was there with her red hair," Liza explains. She had confessed her own purported love for Trev (though her line "I couldn't even look at her as I talked" doesn't really convince us of her heterosexual motivation); and Lorraine had laughed. "I made her stop!" Liza cries. As Liza, McCambridge is both Mrs. Danvers to the dead woman — "Red mouth, sidelong glance, and her figure!" she describes her — and Maxim who murders the sexual woman when she laughs with the confidence of her autonomous desire. Moreover, there's reason to believe McCambridge is playing a role that is literally a projection of a masculine conception onto a female character. Between two drafts submitted to Hays Office, Lorraine's murderer changes from the wolfish neighbor Harvey to Liza. The logic is much more excit-ing — the film finds a narrative use for the character (and Vidor leaves an auteurist mark with this transgressive woman in pants, kin to the heroines of *Duel in the Sun*, *Beyond the Forest*, and *Ruby Gentry*).

When McCambridge plays "feminine" it is to disturbing effect: as an evangelist in *Angel Baby* (1961), she steels herself to consummate her marriage to George Hamilton, but it doesn't happen. In an ostensibly "straight" role as Elizabeth Taylor's mother in *Suddenly, Last Summer* (Mankiewicz, 1959), a very queer film, she looks like she's in drag in a flowered hat and gloves. Her TV "guest" appearances drew on the deviant connotations of her persona and demonstrated the fact that she could not be incorporated by the text. She played the mother of an effeminate warlock on *Bewitched*, conspiring with her cousin Endora to unite their children, although Samantha already had her cover marriage in place. She is memorable as the woman who wanted to marry television's perhaps most memorable villainous/scapegoat/camp queer, Dr. Smith on *Lost in Space*. McCambridge finally played the requisite sadistic lesbian prison warden that her earlier roles had signaled in *99 Women*, a.k.a. *Isle of Lost Women* (1969), a Spanish-German-British-Italian coproduction.

Perhaps most telling of all is McCambridge's uncredited role in Orson Welles's *Touch of Evil* (1958) as a member of the Chicano gang who ter-

36. *Star Ruth Roman dressed similarly to supporting actress/ villain Mercedes McCambridge (foreground) in* Lightning Strikes Twice *(King Vidor, 1951).*

rorize and rape Susan (Janet Leigh). Two other women are present, but McCambridge wears the slicked-back hair and leather jacket of the men. Though drawing on the immediate recognizability of an ethnic stereotype, what her character signifies is something else. According to her autobiography, she declined Welles's suggestion that she pencil in a mustache for the sequence. Thus although she is unbilled, she refused to be *disguised* (unless we are to believe in her "ethnic" mask). It is McCambridge's voice that tells Susan through the hotel room wall what the "boys" are trying to do, but even if her voice weren't recognizable, she would be definitively placed as a lesbian (thus simultaneous as a woman and not a woman) by her remark just before the fade-out: "I wanna stay—I wanna watch." Thus her incapacity to "participate" is revealed, and voyeurism and sexual violence are used to signal lesbianism, although twisted to represent something lesbians are subjects of, rather than to. McCambridge's role depends on the type's being readable, as well as on its being disavowed as too threatening. (The gang rape itself is monstrously disavowed by the film; supposedly Susan was simply drugged and framed for a narcotics rap. In part, the presence and participation of the other women enable this erasure.) A star cameo depends on the immediate recognizability of the star's person and name (e.g., Zsa Zsa Gabor in this same film), but McCambridge is not technically a star. She is simply familiar, perhaps known as an associate of Welles (like Moorehead, or Joseph Cotton, who plays an unbilled bit here too). The *Touch of Evil* "appearance" is nothing other than a "lesbian cameo" that turns on McCambridge's physical type, previous roles, and performance style.[34] Finally, something of the paradox of the use of McCambridge is recapitulated around another uncredited "cameo." She provided the "vocal effects" of the devil in *The Exorcist* (William Friedkin, 1973). (Her voice was thus "matched" to the body of one of the memorable deviant supporting actress personas of the 1970s, Linda Blair as the possessed girl.) The use of a *woman's* voice is an apparent attempt to appear perverse; the fact that it is McCambridge's plays out the Hollywood logic of the demonized deviant character actress in spectacular and acoustic fashion.

These "dames"—a designation which encompasses both the upper-class types like Anderson, who actually received a title from the Queen of England, and women like Ritter's characters who would use the word to describe themselves—share a certain representational ground with Agnes Moorehead in the 1940s, 1950s, and beyond. That Ritter and McCambridge were radio performers like Moorehead (and the original Sister George) suggests an interesting dialectic between lesbian representability and literal on-screen visibility.[35] Agnes Moorehead's image can be received at a particular intersection of the "spinster" type and an upper-class sapphic stereotype. As a promotional item describes the lady: "Rated as one of the best dressed stars of screen and radio, her preference runs to tailored suits"—in Lynde's words, she was "classy as hell" (fig. 37). We should not underestimate the number of lesbian contenders for the only apparently ironic title of "best dressed radio star." This chapter concludes with a case study of Moorehead.

The Queer Career of Agnes Moorehead

Agnes Moorehead's long career encompassed a gallery of types connoting female difference. Her early success was achieved on radio as, among other things, a stooge to male comics. After she went to Hollywood with Orson Welles and the Mercury Theater she continued her radio work as an all-purpose female voice, impersonating scores of women (from Eleanor Roosevelt on down) on the *March of Time* and playing The Shadow's girlfriend. Outside of the Hollywood regime of the gaze, it seems a deviant

37. *Portrait of Agnes Moorehead.
Paul Lynde described her as
"classy as hell—but one of the
all-time Hollywood dykes."*

version of femininity could represent the norm. On-screen she never portrayed a central character, receiving top billing only in the posthumously released horror flick *Dear Dead Delilah* (1975). Instead, she played second fiddle, variations on the unmarried woman: nurses (*Magnificent Obsession*, 1954), nuns (*Scandal at Scourie*, 1953; *The Singing Nun*, 1966), governesses (*The Youngest Profession*, 1943; *Untamed*, 1955), ladies' companions (*Mrs. Parkington*, 1944; *Her Highness and the Bellboy*, 1945), busybodies (*Since You Went Away*, 1944; *All That Heaven Allows*, 1956), hypochondriacs (*Pollyanna*, 1960), maids (*Hush, Hush . . . Sweet Charlotte*, 1965) and, of course, aunts.

In *The Magnificent Ambersons*, Jack Amberson rebukes his nephew for tormenting the Moorehead character: "You know George, just being an aunt isn't really the great career it may sometimes seem to be." But this, her second film, launched the actress on a trajectory that proved otherwise. Despite her fifth-billed role, she was named Best Actress by the New York Film Critics, and went on to play aunts again in *Jane Eyre* (1944), *Tomorrow the World* (1944), *The Lost Moment* (1947), *Summer Holiday* (1948), *Johnny Belinda* (1948), *The Story of Three Loves* (1953), and on Broadway in *Gigi* just before her death. For variety she portrayed women in professions lesbians might suitably pursue: a WAC commander (*Keep Your Powder Dry*, 1945), a prison superintendent (*Caged*, 1950), a literary agent (*Main Street to Broadway*, 1953), a drama coach (*Jeanne Eagels*, 1957), a mystery writer (*The Bat*, 1959), a judge (*Bachelor in Paradise*, 1961) and, in a blond wig, a "sort of school marm and madam rolled into one," offering firm support to Jane Russell in *The Revolt of Mamie Stover*. (Hortense Powdermaker's comment that character actors are a "brassiere for the star, literally holding him or her up," is too tempting to resist quoting in this case [cited in King 179].) When she played married women, Moorehead was generally a nagging wife, characteristically so in the radio play *Sorry, Wrong Number*, written expressly for her talents. Critics note the "waspish and neurotic," "mean-spirited, shrewish," "possessive, puritanical, and vitriolic," "bitter, nasty, frustrated," "exacerbating," and "meddlesome" traits of her "old crones", "harridans, spinsters and bitches," "termagants and passionate viragos." The role of the Nazi war criminal in hiding that Welles himself plays in his 1946 film *The Stranger* is said to have originally been intended for her. While the title was indeed appropriate, the top billing may not have been. In her many mother parts, she did not always evince maternal qualities. Besides Samantha, her screen offspring included Citizen Kane, Jesse James, and Genghis Khan. Her brief role in *The Story of Mankind* (1957) was that of Queen

Elizabeth I; she commissioned a portrait of herself costumed as the red-haired virgin queen.

The Agnes Moorehead of the *Bewitched* era (1964–1972) can aptly be summed up with the title of her one-woman show, which she toured extensively in the 1950s—*The Fabulous Redhead*. On *Bewitched* she was a flippant, vividly costumed, outrageously made up, impeccably coiffed, castrating witch with a mortal hatred for her daughter's husband, whose name she refused to recall. This is the Moorehead-as-character association the contemporary viewer brings to her earlier film roles. Moorehead turned her Actress-with-a-capital-A stage image—regal bearing, exaggerated gestures and enunciation, and taste for high fashion—to high camp effect, foregrounding performance with her interpretation of Endora. She was nicknamed "Madame Mauve" because of her fondness for lavender, which she insisted upon having everything "done" in—from her luggage and Thunderbird to her dressing room lightbulbs and maids' uniforms (Sherk 72).[36]

Before the 1950s stage and 1960s TV brought color to her roles, Agnes Moorehead was considered an actress of "character." Her imposing name—which calls up the specter of her stern minister father—her "aristocratic" profile, penchant for accents and other vocal trademarks, her manners, even manneredness, contributed to the public perception of Moorehead as a serious actress. As James Robert Parrish notes, she is associated with "heavy dramatics on the grand scale. For many, Agnes' performances represent the near epitome of screen theatrics." Although she was typecast, versatility was regarded as part of her artistry.[37] A studio publicity item among her clippings raved: "The accomplished character actress of stage, screen and radio is given here one of her rare opportunities to bid for romantic interest. The result is a revelation of a new facet of the versatile actress's many-sided repertory, strikingly effective." The implication is that her ability to portray a heterosexual is a true sign of talent. Yet it is just a "bid," presumably an unsuccessful one, for romantic interest; and indeed we are not told exactly what facet of Moorehead is revealed in the attempt.

Moorehead was distinguished by four Academy Award nominations for best actress in a supporting role, although she never won the Oscar. As six-time loser Thelma Ritter cracked, in her inimitable way, "always the bridesmaid and never the bride" (Wiley and Bona 241). A nostalgia profile in the collectors' magazine *Classic Images* muses about the fact that Moorehead never snagged the award: "It is an interesting speculation that one of the reasons she always lost was that she played neurotic aunts, stepmothers, spinsters who reflected the dark side of the human condition" (Oct. 18,

1986, 136). That the old maid should evoke such a grandiose conception as the dark side of the human condition attests to Moorehead's considerable achievement—she makes the spinster positively sinister (fig. 38). Writing on the "functions of feminist criticism," Tania Modleski admonishes a marxist literary critic who, "casting about for an example of the trivial, strikes irresistibly upon the image of the spinster." "From a feminist point of view," Modleski argues, "nothing could be *more* 'historically and ideologically significant' than the existence of the single woman in patriarchy, her (frequently caricatured) representation in patriarchal art, and the relationship between the reality and the representation" (*Feminism Without Women* 50). Moorehead's image captured this significance, if only in the mirror of anxiety. The *Classic Images* profile reveals how well the spinster image "stuck" to the actress: "Never married, she, nevertheless, had an adopted son; a close friendship with Debbie Reynolds, with whom she co-starred in several of her last pictures; and a religious faith as a methodist." This "nevertheless" means to blur over a logical relationship between spinster and lesbian that the syntax sets up: "Never married, she had a close friendship with Debbie Reynolds." The statement is interesting for another reason: its blatant, symptomatic, contradiction of fact. For Agnes Moorehead was married at least twice (Reynolds mentions three unions).[38] I presume the actress's much-vaunted privacy and cultivated "mystery" were not intended to conceal this socially and professionally useful facet of her "many-sided repertory." Even Moorehead's death can be read through the template of "supporting character sacrificed to the Hollywood plot"; like several other members of the cast and crew of *The Conqueror*, shot on location near a nuclear testing site, she died of lung cancer.

Moorehead's image reconciles the serious with the trivial—having "character" with being "a character"—and thus occupies the domain of camp. As Susan Sontag notes, "Not all seriousness that fails can be redeemed as Camp. Only that which has the proper mixture of the exaggerated, the fantastic, the passionate, and the naive" (283). Moorehead meets another of Sontag's criteria: "Camp is the glorification of 'character'. . . . Character is understood as a state of continual incandescence—a person being one, very intense thing. . . . Wherever there is development of character, Camp is reduced" (286). Camp is a far from trivial dimension of the constitution and reception of the Moorehead image. As her "character" developed, became recognizable, camp increased. She became a *star* when she "came out" as camp. In such "straight" dramatic performances as *Don Juan in Hell* (directed by Paul Gregory with Sir Cedric Hardwicke, Charles Boyer, and

38. *Agnes Moorehead's "spinsterish" look. Publicity image for* Citizen Kane *(Orson Welles, 1941).*

Charles Laughton), she cut "a striking figure, with a tiara atop her elaborate hairdo and a flowing mauve-colored gown." Moorehead was conscious of the effect. While performing a camp reading of Moorehead's style, I also undertake a "serious" feminist consideration of what is at stake in the content of her stylized image—the wide cultural understanding, deployment, and placement of deviant femininity.

An analysis of how the Moorehead image was articulated and utilized in certain of her films can illuminate the contradiction she embodies as a figure simultaneously necessary to the Hollywood system and suppressed by it. She is taken seriously, featured in so many films as to seem ubiquitous. At the same time, her parts are marginal ones, the characters she portrays are trivialized or vilified. If her roles as written often smack of misogyny, as performed they suggest a different negativity—a negativity that cannot be represented within the terms of classical cinema, a negativity that shares the semiotic field of lesbianism.

Fanny Minnafer in Orson Welles's *The Magnificent Ambersons* (1942) is the role that established at once Moorehead's spinster image *and* the difficulty of reconciling that image with the Hollywood plot. Lacking economic independence, Aunt Fanny lives with the fading Amberson clan as an observer rather than as a participant. Her restlessness and discontent contribute greatly to the film's mood. *The Magnificent Ambersons* is a self-conscious film, nowhere more evidently than in its awareness of the character of Fanny as reviled spinster. She accuses her nephew George (Tim Holt): "You wouldn't treat anybody in the world like this, except old Fanny. 'Old Fanny,' you say, 'It's nobody but old Fanny so I'll kick her. Nobody'll resent it, I'll kick her all I want to.'"

The movie explicitly thematizes the way Fanny is "used" as a cog in a heterosexual plot. She is relentlessly mocked for her affection for Eugene Morgan (Joseph Cotten), who comes to call not on her but on George's mother Isabel (Dolores Costello). But the film inscribes Fanny's position on the periphery—lurking in the shadows to whisper her suspicions to George, looking on from the edge of the frame or the background of the composition—as a vantage point for the spectator. She actually prevents the formation of the couple by provoking George's objections to his mother's romance, thus contributing to his break with Eugene's daughter Lucy. In material excised from the film's release version, Fanny is shown at the end among a veritable colony of spinsters at the boarding house. Her discourse pervades the film, even if she triumphs only as the representative of its themes of frustration and barrenness.

Parrish characterizes the challenge for Moorehead as an actress as the effort "to channel her tremendous energy so that it would emerge in accord with the film rather than as an intriguing distraction" (122). Elements of her tour de force characterization of Aunt Fanny erupt as fascinating "distractions" in such later roles as Mrs. Reed in *Jane Eyre* and Countess Fosco in *The Woman in White*. The question of Moorehead's discordant difference and of her relation to the fulfillment of the romance plot is marked in another literary film, *The Lost Moment* (1947). In this adaptation of Henry James's *The Aspern Papers*, Moorehead plays the elderly aunt who in her youth was the recipient of love letters from a famous poet. A mere octogenarian in the novella becomes a hideously made-up 105-year-old in the film: "Beneath these eyes, a deathless secret of the past. Behind these walls, no love has lived for years." It is as if the plausibility of Moorehead's participation in such a romance even in the past demands extremes of disguise.

Moorehead thoroughly embraced that inexplicable quality of her characters that prompted others to react with dislike, even phobia. In *Since You*

Went Away (directed by John Cromwell, 1944), David O. Selznick's sentimental story of women on the homefront during World War II, Agnes
portrays a local busybody, a character who embodies a displaced anxiety
about the unheroic activities that women might become involved in while
the menfolk are away at war. Joseph Cotten's character repeatedly insults
her, joking that the memory of her voice grates on him even when he's far
away from her. The penetrating, persecuting female voice signifies here not
only as a quality of Moorehead's character, Emily Hawkins, but of Moorehead as an actress (who often worked with Cotten). Ultimately the disparate
desires and interests of the women of the family — mother Claudette Colbert,
daughters Jennifer Jones and Shirley Temple, and Hattie McDaniel as the
maid — are rallied into patriotic solidarity when they castigate the Moorehead character for not pitching in for the war effort. The film uses her as a
scapegoat to consolidate both nationalist and gender ideology. Indirectly
serving to reinforce Moorehead's difference, the most notorious Hollywood
lesbian actress of all, Alla Nazimova (who was rumored to have been lovers
with Natasha Rambova, Valentino's wife, and with Dorothy Arzner), is the
mouthpiece of the film's most heavy-handed patriotic message. In a bit role
as a Jewish refugee, her last film appearance, Nazimova recites the poem
inscribed on the Statue of Liberty.

The only treatment of the phenomenon of cinematic supporting actresses of which I am aware is a movie buff's book on five female "character
stars" by James Robert Parrish, a prolific author in the genre. Parrish is
keenly perceptive about comparative personae, commenting on Moorehead's performance in *Since You Went Away*:

> The role itself was a variation of the cinema type portrayed throughout the
> 1940s by the very adept Eve Arden. The difference in these two actresses'
> approach to such a part is that whenever Agnes is required to make a flip
> remark on the screen, it comes across in total seriousness as a reflection of
> her character's basic, unregenerate meanness. Her piercing eyes and over-
> all body movements provide the viewer with no other interpretation. In
> contrast, Arden can toss off the most devastating remark, and it emerges as
> a pert observation, juicy and smart, but essentially nonvicious. (90)

Although Moorehead did play essentially nonvicious roles she was more
convincing — and less recuperable — in her moments of unregenerate mean-
ness. The subversiveness of the best character stars, such as Arden and
Ritter, can be neutralized by their being enthusiastically adopted as cuddly
curmudgeons. Moorehead's unlikeableness, on the razor-thin edge of misogynist dismissal, contravenes this tendency. It is hard to embrace Moorehead without being spattered with acid. Yet as she willingly portrayed hateful

women, her vituperative characters can also be identified with as rare screen outlets for women's justifiable hatred—of men, of their lot in life, of everything.

Madge Rapf in the Bogart-Bacall noir vehicle *Dark Passage* (1947), directed by Delmar Daves, is a curious sort of femme fatale, whose fate is a telling example of the retribution the Moorehead character could bring down. Moorehead's being cast against character in a "sexual" role is in part responsible for the film's surreal effects.[39] As Dana Polan comments in an important analysis: "The narrative of *Dark Passage* is one in which dramatic coincidences occur so often as to break down any question of plausibility" (195). When Madge happens to knock at the door of the apartment where, through an unlikely chain of circumstances, escaped convict Vincent Parry (Bogart) is hiding, he instantly recognizes the voice of his nemesis. Madge had testified against him at his murder trial. As he observes, "she's the type that comes back, and back again." This not only indicates how she functions in the film as the return of the repressed, but is also a fitting comment on Moorehead's career.

Madge's character is attributed with the evil, inconsistency, and unintelligibility of motive of an ordinary femme fatale, without the movie conceding that sexuality is her tool for leading men to destruction. Instead her fatal quality seems to be the simple fact of her existence, rendered as "interference" through Moorehead's "nagging" connotations. As Vincent describes her: "Madge knows everybody, pesters everybody." Her ex-fiancé, Bob, snaps at her: "You're not satisfied unless you're bothering people. I'm annoyed whenever I see you." Responding to her concern that Parry will try to kill her, Bob remarks, with an extraordinary mixture of outright malignance and contemptuous dismissal: "You're the last person he wants to see, let alone kill. . . . You're not the type that makes people hate." Her insignificance is thus marked in rather significant terms.[40] It is as if the other characters recognize the difficulty of integrating her in the narrative. Vincent muses: "Maybe she'll get run over or something." And his wish is granted.

For in this profoundly illogical film, the logic of misogyny works with classic simplicity; it can only be placated by Madge's abjection, by the spectacle of her death. When Vincent comes to her apartment to accuse *her* of murdering his wife, she defies him to prove it. (Although the film viciously establishes that she is "in love" with him—so much so that she frames him for a murder she apparently has committed—her relationships with both his wife and the Bacall character are comparably intense and convoluted.) At her crowning moment of Moorehead histrionics, she "accidently" and quite improbably falls through a picture window, with a flounce of floor-length drapes. The camera dwells on her body's descent, a markedly excessive cinematic flourish. Polan has commented on the ambiguity and threat embodied in domestic space in 1940s films: "Significantly, in several films, murder, suicide, and accidental death through windows blur (and not only for the characters but also for the spectator), thereby suggesting the ambivalence of sense." He captures something of the spectator's bewilderment in this instance: "[I]n *Dark Passage*, for example, it is never clear (even with motion-analyzing equipment and freeze-framing) how Madge manages to fall through her apartment window to her death" (274).

Madge, as a "bad," superfluous woman, is marked for death from the beginning. But for all that it is an almost mundane exigency of plot, her killing seems to require a supernatural force, thereby foregrounding the ideology that demands it. And Madge's fall doesn't immediately benefit the hero; it has something of the quality of a self-willed disappearance. Madge threatens, "You will never be able to prove anything because I won't be there." *Dark Passage* plays out the film noir's generic fear of feminine difference. The hero is vindicated, and the woman is both criminal and victim. However here it is not the alluring but the annoying woman who is punished, an extreme case of the anxiety the Moorehead character could provoke. Bacall, straight girl to Moorehead's twisted one, escapes to live happily ever after with Bogart, somewhere in South America.

In the all-girl environment of a women's prison, among female deviates, Moorehead's persona is not pitted against other women but appears at its most benign. John Cromwell's *Caged* (1950) is the Moorehead film that can most readily be construed as lesbian. Eleanor Parker is the charming leading lady, and Agnes Moorehead is second billed, fittingly presiding over a cast of extraordinarily talented character actresses. Like *The Killing of Sister George*, or the lesbian classic *Maedchen in Uniform* with its conflict between stern headmistress and compassionate teacher, this feminist drama opposes two "dyke" types in a struggle for control over the young heroine. Moorehead plays Mrs. Benton, the sympathetic, reform-minded prison superintendent in a tailored suit who tries to protect innocent Marie Allen (Parker) from the corruptions of life inside (fig. 39). "You'll find all kinds of women in here, just as you would outside," she promises. Hope Emerson portrays Evelyn Harper, the sadistic matron in uniform who provides small comforts for her girls in exchange for payment. Of this remarkable 6-foot 2-inch, 230-pound character actress, gay porn editor and film critic Boyd McDonald writes: "Perhaps only members of a sexual elite—that is, outlaws—can instinctively appreciate the grandeur of an Emerson" (21, fig. 40).

In one scene Harper, grotesquely dressed up for her night off, describes

39. *In the central triangle of* Caged *(John Cromwell, 1950), Eleanor Parker is comforted by Agnes Moorehead . . .*

40. *. . . . and threatened by Hope Emerson. Note the similar positions of the supporting actresses.*

in detail her upcoming "date" in order to taunt the imprisoned women. This attribution of heterosexuality, like the photograph of a "husband" displayed on Moorehead's desk, can easily be read as an out-and-out charade. When Benton attempts to fire Harper for her cruelty and excesses, the latter leaks a scandalous tale to the press. "Matron Charges Immorality," headlines blare, "Blames Superintendent." The article is accompanied by a singularly apt sketch of Benton/Moorehead's face encircled by a huge question mark. The unspoken questions dogging Moorehead's persona are here explicitly tied to a story full of "filthy lies" that euphemistically signify lesbianism.

In the denouement of this classic struggle between good and evil, Harper is stabbed by a prisoner. But in the meantime Marie has gone beyond the turning point marked when her kitten is crushed in a riot provoked by Harper's attempt to snatch Fluff from her. Marie finally succumbs to the attentions of an inmate with influence who arranges for her parole. Forced to relinquish her wedding ring when she entered prison, Marie tosses it away when it is returned upon her release. Benton tells her devoted secretary to keep Marie's file active: "She'll be back." Ultimately the forces of lesbian nurturing and domination, represented by Moorehead and Emerson respectively, work in consort to keep the female community intact. In *Caged*, the Moorehead character acts as the film's moral measure, rather than, as in many of her films, the one who undermines the status quo. But these are the morals of a female-gendered world, which she tirelessly and benevolently governs.

In Robert Aldrich's 1965 *Hush, Hush . . . Sweet Charlotte*, Bosley Crowther ranted, "Agnes Moorehead as [Bette Davis's] weird and crone-like servant is allowed to get away with some of the broadest mugging and snarling ever done by a respectable actress on the screen. If she gets an Academy Award for this performance the Academy should close up shop." The slatternly Velma Cruther significantly reverses an important element of Moorehead's image—her fastidiousness. In a cycle initiated by *Whatever Happened to Baby Jane?* in which bona fide female stars travestied their former images, it is appropriate for one of the great supporting actresses to play a classic supporting role, the loyal servant, in a spectacularly unsupportive manner—to indulge in upstaging and scenery-chewing that puts Davis herself in the shade. Velma is killed off for her snooping—and for her devotion to her mistress—by a fall nearly as dramatic as Madge's in *Dark Passage*.

One of Moorehead's last films, scripted by Henry Farrell, who wrote *Baby Jane*, continues this self-conscious exploitation of her image. Set in the 1930s, *What's the Matter with Helen?* (directed by former experimental filmmaker and future *Dynasty* helmer Curtis Harrington, 1971) features

Debbie Reynolds and Shelley Winters as the mothers of two convicted thrill killers in the Leopold and Loeb mode, who move to Hollywood to escape their past. Reynolds, intrigued by the story, which was originally titled *Best of Friends*, persuaded her friend Moorehead to portray powerful radio evangelist Sister Alma. The "matter" with Helen concerns not only her psychopathic murderous tendencies, but her fanatical devotion to the evangelist's message and — surprise — her lesbian love for her "best friend." The role and the project thus summed up a number of strong components of the Moorehead persona: radio, religion, the famous personality, the pivotal supporting role, lesbianism, the relationship with Reynolds.

Endora represents the culmination of Moorehead meddlesomeness. In the premiere episode of *Bewitched* she repeatedly evicts Samantha's husband from the honeymoon suite, and she literally casts a dark shadow over heterosexual relations each week when her credit "and Agnes Moorehead as Endora" appears on a black cloud of smoke blotting out "Derwood" and Samantha's embrace. "What's-his-name's" anxiety about his wife's powers are well founded: she belongs to a matriarchal order of superior beings. *Bewitched* supported a veritable gay subculture among its "funny" witch and warlock character actors: from Maurice Evans as Endora's estranged husband to Paul Lynde as Uncle Arthur, to Marion Lorne's Aunt Clara, Alice Pearce's Gladys Kravitz, and Alice Ghostley's Esmerelda. One of the twins who played the little witch Tabitha even grew up to be a lesbian (Pilato 281).

If Moorehead's earlier characters were outside the central action, Endora is transcendently ex-centric. She has an enunciative role. Casting spells, she disrupts the couple's petty suburban lives and generates the weekly plot. She appears and disappears with a theatrical flutter of the wrist — her ability to materialize when least expected or to drop out of the picture altogether is almost a commentary on the disappearing act "incidental" characters performed in countless Hollywood films.

From stern spinster to fabulous redhead to silly goose, Agnes Moorehead's queer career attests to the ideological and narratological congruence among old maid, witch, and lesbian. Her star image appeals to lesbian and gay audiences because it connotes acting itself — artifice and impersonation. I by no means wish to suggest that the characters Moorehead portrayed "really were" lesbians, nor to imply that lesbians can simply recover our presence in Hollywood cinema by identifying actresses who really were lesbians, although gossip in and of itself is another text to be read (fig. 41). Rather, the peculiarities of Moorehead's image and the enthusiasms it has generated illustrate how supporting characters were essential but also poten-

41. Agnes Moorehead with
unidentified companion.

tially disruptive to the construction of sexual difference in classical cinema. They were the types who were meant to remain invisible so that the codes of Hollywood's heterosexual contract would also remain invisible. Gay male criticism and culture have been alert to the pleasures and resistances embodied in stars as signs; feminist film theory has explicated the patriarchal construction of woman as sexual image. An exploration of the conditions of lesbian representability in cinema might fruitfully draw on both approaches. Whether playing it straight or camping it up, Agnes Moorehead is quite a character, "the type that comes back, and back again" as an insistent reminder of the price of heterosexual presumption.

6

On Retrospectatorship

In *The Devil Finds Work*, a memoir as well as a critique of race and American movies, James Baldwin tells the following origins story:

> [M]y first conscious calculation as to how to go about defeating the world's intentions for me and mine began on that Saturday afternoon in what we called *the movies* but which was actually the first entrance into the cinema of my mind.
>
> I read *Uncle Tom's Cabin* over and over and over—this is the first book I can remember having read—and then I read *A Tale of Two Cities*—over and over and over again. Bill Miller takes me to see *A Tale of Two Cities* at the Lincoln, on 135th Street. I am twelve. (10)

The topography of "the movies" is both inside the narrating subject and outside on 135th Street. "The cinema of my mind" is a place of "conscious calculation" for Baldwin, but also a place where identification ("me and mine") and oppositionality ("defeating the world's intentions") are experienced—through a very particular text at a very particular sociohistorical, biographical, and geographical conjuncture. On the way to his tale about the movies, Baldwin lingers over a scenario of reading—movie viewing is a revisiting of a prior, similar encounter. Baldwin's return to these literary classics belies the control of "conscious calculation": "I had no idea what [they were] really about, which is why I had read them both so obsessively: they had something to tell me. It was this particular child's way of circling around the question of what it meant to be a nigger" (12). *Uncle Tom's Cabin* comes into his story of the movies metonymically—for despite its many screen adaptations none defined Baldwin's childhood encounter with the cinema—to figure "the question" of (dis)identification. Naming *Uncle Tom's Cabin* refracts the national-political fantasy of the historical romance of *A Tale of Two Cities* through the prism of American race relations and racism.[1] The affinity between *Uncle Tom's Cabin* and *A Tale of Two Cities*, and Baldwin's with them in the scene of childhood culture consumption, turns on a question of identification.

In "A Child Is Being Beaten" Freud observed that *Uncle Tom's Cabin* has something of a reputation as a masturbation novel. While the unconscious associations between two texts about injustice that Baldwin's text traces may be far removed from the questions of sexual identity that Freud argues his patients are confronting in their re-reading practices, the experience of being "hung up" on a text is quite similar and suggests that erotics and knowledge, cultural and sexual difference, are subjectively and temporally entangled. Freud writes:

> In my patients' milieu it was almost always the same books whose contents gave a new stimulus to the beating phantasies . . . such as what was known as the "*Bibliothèque rose*," *Uncle Tom's Cabin*, etc. The child began to compete with these works of fiction . . . by constructing a wealth of situations, and even whole institutions, in which children were beaten . . . because of their naughtiness and bad behavior. (180)

Baldwin remembers a prohibition associated with his early reading of Stowe's novel: "I had read *Uncle Tom's Cabin* compulsively, the book in one hand, the newest baby on my hipbone. I was trying to find out something, sensing something in the book of immense import for me. . . . My mother got scared. She hid the book" (16). The compulsive reading Baldwin recalls, and then carries over into film viewing, suggests a homology with the compulsion to fantasize of Freud's subjects, while making explicit the social and cultural dimensions of textual encounters that Freud's reduction of "outside" fictions to the oedipal scenario forecloses. The children prone to such imaginative uses of the classics in Freud's middle-class European milieu were girls and gay boys.[2] While Baldwin is not as explicit about the erotics of his movie encounters as he is about their revelations about the subjective effects of American racism, in the context of recounting their import he indicates that they marked him as queer: "I was considered by everyone to be 'strange.'" His movie-enlightenment leads him consciously to calculate: "Well, if I was strange—and I knew that I must be . . . perhaps I could find a way to use my strangeness" (9). Baldwin's "strangeness" is put to use in his writer's voice, which reshapes his queer encounters with the movies into communicable, counterhegemonic social truths.

In *Cinema and Spectatorship*, Judith Mayne traces a shift in film studies of spectatorship away from the idea of a disembodied subject positioned by a monolithically conceived cinematic apparatus to the current emphasis on local and audience studies, on "real" viewers with specific cultural identities and histories. The latter approach, arising from cultural studies, acknowledges lesbians and gay men and others as devoted viewers of popular culture; it might make use of testimony such as Baldwin's, or that of the women in Whitaker's study discussed in Chapter 2, as ethnographic evidence. Clearly such a departure from the textually constructed spectator is necessary in order to account for oppositional viewing. But Mayne cautions against abandoning the psychoanalytic and semiotic inquiry that explains the efficacy of the movies. She doubts the political claim that reception studies sometimes imply, that "all unauthorized uses of film, and therefore spectatorial positions that depart from the presumed ideal of capitalist ideology, are virtually or potentially radical" (99). Indeed, Baldwin's memoir accounts as much for the unconscious seductions of popular culture artifacts as for their conscious "uses" or "negotiated" meanings, as Stuart Hall defines negotiation in "Encoding, Decoding." Moreover, Baldwin's narrative testifies that specific texts have subjective and cultural efficacy. Clarifying the usefulness of psychoanalysis at the juncture of the social and the psychic, Teresa de Lauretis writes: "[F]antasy is the psychic mechanism that governs the translation of social representations into subjectivity and self-representation, and thus the adaptation or reworking of public fantasies in private fantasies" (*Practice of Love* 285). Baldwin's narration preserves the element of chance in the encounter with the movies within the ideological overdetermination of mass media consumption. His memoir conveys social criticism and/through a reconstructed spectatorial fantasmatic.

As we have seen, the concept of fantasy developed in film theory complicates the reductive, mimetic understanding of spectatorial positioning put forward in apparatus theory and in much early psychoanalytic feminist film theory. Fantasy can also complicate the views of audience response prevalent in lesbian and gay cultural studies of reception, which are often overly voluntaristic in their accounts of viewers' agency. The idea of the "appropriation" of mass media by spectators for their own purposes endows viewers with a problematic degree of self-consciousness and intentionality and ignores the temporal dimensions and *experience* of spectatorship. The concept of fantasy acknowledges the irreducibility of each viewer's experience and the complexity of the viewing process. As Laplanche and Pontalis note: "[T]he subject's life as a whole . . . is shaped and ordered by what might be called, in order to stress this structuring action, a fantasmatic" (*Language* 317). Cultural texts "outside" the subject participate in this structuring, and each new textual encounter is shaped by what's already "inside" the viewer. I call this kind of film reception, which is transformed by unconscious and conscious past viewing experience, retrospectatorship.

The term evokes the structure of psychical temporality and causality Freud called *Nachträglichkeit*, deferred action, or retrospection. As Laplanche and Pontalis explain: "[E]xperiences, impressions and memory traces may be revised at a later date to fit in with fresh experiences or with the attainment of a new stage of development. They may in that event be endowed not only with a new meaning but also with psychical effectiveness" (111). All spectatorship, insofar as it engages subjective fantasy, revises memory traces and experiences, some of which are memories and experiences of other movies. "Retrospectatorship" also recalls the viewing practice attached to film retrospectives, through which texts of the past, reordered and contextualized, are experienced anew in a different filmgoing culture. Classical Hollywood cinema belongs to the past but is experienced in a present that affords us new ways of seeing. Although its modes of production and reception have been historically superseded, it preserves a structuring role culturally and frequently marks individuals and subcultures with its texts and characteristic modes of consumption. The term retrospectatorship helps us theorize the fantasmatic in the cultural and the cultural in the fantasmatic, a formulation that the chapters of this book have engaged in different ways.

In "A Child Is Being Beaten," Freud acknowledges that "phantasies have an historical development which is by no means simple" (184), and in interpreting the fantasy at hand he shuttles back and forth from adolescent to infantile fantasy. His mention of *Uncle Tom's Cabin* introduces to his account of this non-linear development a crucial, if underacknowledged, question about the role of *specific* cultural artifacts in subjective fantasy. Todd Haynes's 1993 short film *Dottie Gets Spanked* is a fictionalized queer "pop culture" autobiography that memorably visualizes the cultural contingency of subjective fantasy by "filming" Freud's essay as an encounter with *I Love Lucy*. Like Baldwin's text and *The Member of the Wedding*, the film dramatizes *exclusion* from hegemonic structures as *fascination* with their formal qualities and shapes this experience as a narrative of retrospective self-making.

The film opens with the credits to *The Dottie Show* (an *I Love Lucy* clone) depicting its versatile star in various male, female, and infantile disguises; we see 6-year-old Stevie sitting before the looming TV screen intently drawing Dottie, exaggerating signifiers of her feminine masquerade: cleavage, eyelashes, high heels.[3] Behind Stevie stand his mom and the mother of his schoolmate Sharon, talking about their own and their kids' enjoyment of *The Dottie Show*—and their husbands' antipathy to it. Stevie, already located on the wrong side of sexually differentiated spectatorship, pricks up his ears as he hears tell of Sharon's misbehavior and the spankings she receives at the hands of her father. In a spatial trope that will recur throughout the film, Stevie is physically positioned between Dottie's regressive on-screen antics and the oedipal "prestructure" behind him—the adult discourse on desire, prohibition, and permission within the nuclear family. The complex relationship between public and private, both represented here by female bodies, is spatialized for our view.

Stevie wins a visit to the set of *The Dottie Show*, there to witness his idol playing iron authority on set. The matter at hand is a spanking scene: the actress stops the action just as her male co-star's hand is about to fall on her rear end—and asks her stand-in to position herself over his knee instead while she gets up to adjust the camera angle. Again, positions of power are spatialized in ways that transgress boundaries of fantasy and reality, public and private, by showing the apparatus of the domestic sitcom's production. When the diegetic camera begins to roll on the "real" Dottie, Stevie becomes more and more excited in the studio audience. Haynes's rapid cutting between different temporal and pictorial registers mimics the rhythm of the spanking itself. Intercut images from the rehearsal, the full-dress performance of the scene on set, and its later broadcast finally come to rest with an image of Stevie frenetically drawing Dottie—who is being spanked "on her naked bottom" by an unidentified adult male figure.

Freud recounts that in the course of their development "beating phantasies . . . are changed in most respects more than once—as regards their relation to the author of the phantasy, and as regards their object, their content, and their significance" (184). Behind the terse fantasy that gives the essay its title, which a number of his patients, male and female, report indulging in, Freud reconstructs a more revealing unconscious fantasy: "I am being beaten by my father," which represents both desire for the father ("I am being loved by my father") and attendant guilt (symptomatized in regression to the anal-sadistic phase). The fantasy is thus characteristic of the negative or inverted—"gay"—oedipal attitude in boys and the "positive"—but perverse—Oedipus complex in girls.

Haynes works back to the "unconscious" version of Stevie's fantasy through two dream sequences linked to the boy's television viewing and drawings. In both, Stevie is perched on a throne, recalling "His Majesty the Ego," whom Freud recognizes as the "hero alike of every daydream and of every story" ("Creative Writers" 150), and Dottie is his subject. The first dream introduces a spanking tableau featuring an agent very like Stevie's father administering punishment to what at first appears to be a boy, and then is replaced by his schoolmate Sharon. "A child is being beaten on its naked bottom"; an intertitle makes the reference to Freud explicit.

In the second, climactic dream, which occurs after his father's discovery of his bare-bottomed Dottie drawing, Steve is toppled from his throne and comes to occupy the desired position in relation to the father previously represented by the punished girl. As its title and Stevie's drawing suggest, *Dottie Gets Spanked* envisions the female star as a stand-in for Stevie—even for young "Toddie" Haynes—but it thereby entails the spanking of the *adult* figure, which doesn't happen in Freud's cases. Gilles Deleuze revises Freud's interpretation of the male masochistic fantasy and foregrounds "the transference of the law onto the mother" in the beating fantasy (79). Freud had argued that the mother doing the beating covers for the boy's homosexual desire for the father. The scenario of *Dottie Gets Spanked* would seem to stress the homosexual position and the difficulty of subverting patriarchal law. Dottie is also a stand-in for Daddy—Stevie looks up at "the strongest man in the kingdom" spanking him and sees Dottie in circus strongman disguise. "Where is the father hidden?" in the female-as-agent-of-beating scenario, Deleuze asks. "Could it not be in the person who is being beaten?" (53). Haynes thus illustrates the homoeroticism of Freud's version and the subversiveness of Deleuze's and suggests that the father is hidden in the spanked and the spanking Dottie. As David Rodowick writes, "[T]he uncanny recurrence of phantasy always represents an attempt to restage the Oedipal drama of desire and identity, to rewrite it and to have it conclude differently" (94). Haynes's film is a canny version of the wish to rewrite patriarchal law enunciated from the (gay) male point of view, a wish that grants power to the female acculturating agent. Freud does not admit this wish to his interpretation.

Stevie's ecstatic dream ends in repression—he wakes up and buries his drawing in the backyard. It is up to Haynes's film to unearth it, to use the child's shame in a process of cultural production. *Dottie Gets Spanked* is much more than a filmic gloss on Freud; the film not only thematizes the structuring role of popular culture in perverse desire, it *performs* it. It addresses its queer audience from within the idiom of television (the film was commissioned by the Independent Television Service series "TV Families" for PBS broadcast). Notably, the film's representation of the "deepest" levels of oedipal fantasy is its most saturated with kitsch cultural reference—the first dream even has a laugh track. Haynes's formal work reveals television as an apparatus of perverse implantation, a mise-en-scène of desire on a literally oedipal stage, that of the nuclear family—since TV is a medium consumed in the domestic realm. Within this insistence on the authority of popular culture, the Lucy/Dottie figure exceeds the father's law. Haynes's film is no simple "gay male appropriation" of a female star to say something about male sexuality. Dottie is no mere replacement of the parental figures; in a sense they stand in for her. She signals a female authority that Stevie's mother, however sympathetic, never attempts to wield (she only suggests "Why don't you watch something Daddy wants to watch?"). We are asked to associate popular culture with a female/feminized cultural authority. Hierarchies of consumption and production, performance and reception, public and private, internal and external, are questioned in the process.[4] All spectators are subjected to this regime to some degree. Its authority is empowering to particular disenfranchised viewers—here, specifically, a boy teased for being a "feminino"—but may be insufficient to make daddy watch.

Before concluding with an elaboration of the female star's relation to fantasy, eroticism, and cultural authority in regard to lesbian spectatorship, I'd like to look at another example of how it is configured through James Baldwin's unexpected identifications. Early in his text Baldwin recounts another originary moment of cinematic recognition, one perhaps less mediated by "conscious calculation," but nevertheless the source of crucial knowledge. The anecdote shows both the (mis)recognition of the mirror stage and a revision of patriarchal law to be at work in the movies. Baldwin's father had always called him ugly and mocked his "frog eyes." But one day, Baldwin writes, "I caught my father, not in a lie, but in an infirmity."

> So here, now, was Bette Davis, on that Saturday afternoon, in close-up, over a champagne glass, pop eyes popping. I was astounded. For here, before me, after all, was a *movie star: white*. And if she was white and a movie star, she was *rich* and she was *ugly*.

Baldwin, poor and black and a boy, forms an identification with a rich white woman on the basis of her ugliness. The cross-gendered identification is facilitated by a familial one: "I have my mother's eyes."

> When my father called me ugly, he was not attacking me so much as he was attacking my mother. (No doubt, he was also attacking my real, and unknown, father.) . . . I didn't really too much care that my father thought me hideous. . . . I thought that he must have been stricken blind if he was unable to see that my mother was absolutely beyond any question the most beautiful woman in the world. (7)

The special (though clichéd) way Baldwin sees his mother (to which his father is blind) is embedded in an account of the clarity of vision and immediacy ("here, now") he experiences at the movies. His mother's "ugliness" is disavowed, and Davis and his biological father, previously identified with that ugliness, come into uncanny association. Baldwin continues to undermine binary categories through the play of (dis)identifications: "Out of bewilderment, out of loyalty to my mother, probably, and also because I sensed something menacing and unhealthy (for me, certainly) in the face on the screen, I gave Davis's skin the dead-white greenish cast of something crawling from under a rock, but I was held, just the same, by the tense intelligence of the forehead, the disaster of the lips: and when she moved, she moved just like a nigger" (7). The star is decomposed into a set of characteristics "dead-white greenish" skin, forehead, lips, movement, that are disengaged from binary (sexual or racial) difference—characteristics that have been insistently recomposed in impersonations of the star. Although the film Baldwin is invoking through the description is *20,000 Years in Sing Sing*, the image of "Bette Davis, over a champagne glass, pop eyes popping" is emblematic of her famous performance in *All About Eve*. Davis's camp iconicity is evoked through this description and by her very appearance in Baldwin's discourse as a signifier of his gayness. At the same time, that iconicity is defamiliarized through an association with a blackness not available to non-black spectators—Bette Davis "moved just like a nigger" in the cinema on 135th Street.[5]

It is only in the beginning of *The Devil Finds Work* that Baldwin dwells on the impressions made on him by Bette Davis and Joan Crawford and Sylvia Sidney—white female stars in the canon of camp. Haynes's film marks the end of a childhood spectatorial practice that had been sheltered by the mother as a distinct loss, and it illustrates the transformation of oedipal fantasy elaborated in "A Child Is Being Beaten" through a particular female star image. Baldwin's memoir recasts his childhood identification with female stars in a much less explicit relation to the seduction fantasy lingered over by the subjects of Freud's essay; his narration relates a spectatorial experience grasped in part in terms of masochism (the mob and the guillotine of *A Tale of Two Cities* as much as the Christian martyrdom of *Uncle Tom's Cabin*) to the apprehension of identity in a world characterized by poverty and racist violence and white patriarchal authority. While Haynes re-enacts the stigma of the queer boy's subversive tastes and the family's role in implanting pleasures and prohibitions, Baldwin's project to locate identity in networks of social power uses mass culture to articulate racial and gender codes, suggesting the importance of eroticism without making it part of the autobiographical narration. Both depict a regulatory and polymorphously perverse mass culture, identified with female authority, in "constructing a wealth of situations, and even whole institutions," for re-envision-ing the marginal subject's desire.

Freud puts little emphasis on the encounter with popular culture in his essay, but the single mention is decisive. *I Love Lucy* and *Uncle Tom's Cabin* are massively popular for good reasons; it is not their popularity alone that accounts for their influence over the boys in these texts. I've noted that the theory of fantasy de Lauretis and other film theorists have derived from Freud's essay and from Laplanche and Pontalis's elaborations helps us to understand how representation is subjectively engaged, how it transforms consciousness and the unconscious and shapes the ways our desire is struc-tured and lived. Baldwin and Haynes have produced vivid texts of retro-spectatorship that invite intellectual and affective involvement and iden-tifications (such as my own) across race, gender, and sexuality. However decisive the female star is in their accounts, they precisely inscribe the sub-ject position as male—both the boy's viewing and the (gay) male author's retrospection. If Haynes and Baldwin tell different boy's stories about fe-male stars, what might a girl's story be? If their texts are "creative writing" that transforms daydreaming, recasting "His Majesty the Ego" as dreamer, can the spectatorial fantasmatic be reconstructed in criticism? In the section below that concludes this book I frame its concerns by taking off from the sexually differentiated spectatorial scenario in Freud's essay. I explore how the "nostalgia" for classical Hollywood in general, and for one very special film and its female star in particular, can function as a seduction fantasy and revision of cultural authority for a contemporary lesbian spectator.[6]

A Star Is Beaten

If asked who stars in Joseph Mankiewicz's 1950 film *All About Eve*, you'd surely answer Bette Davis although she doesn't play the eponymous heroine. You also might know that the film was a comeback for Davis; that it swept the Oscars; that Marilyn Monroe appears in it; even that George Sanders, who played Addison de Witt, left a suicide note as pithy as the film's dialogue—some of which you surely know by heart. *All About Eve* is an American Movie Classic, source of trivia and cultural practice. To para-phrase Addison's opening voice-over: "Time has been good to *All About Eve*. It's been profiled, talked about. . . . You all know all there is to know about *All About Eve*—what can there be that you don't know?"

But what about Eve herself does popular memory preserve? While Margo Channing is remembered almost as a brand name for "star" (with Norma Desmond a keen competitor), Eve is a curious cipher—even Addison breaks off abruptly—"But more of Eve later."[7] Why does this film's title promise thorough and exhaustive knowledge about a woman—about Eve— about Woman—and then keep her waiting in the wings while Bette Davis, Margo Channing, takes all the bows? The epistemological overdetermination that Addison invokes in his cynical introduction provokes anxiety in the fandom. "What can there be that we don't know?" Is an ambivalent and divided epistemology of stardom a model of the experience of cinema for lesbian viewers? (Is she or isn't she? How about *her*? Am I or am I not?) *All About Eve* is a metonym of classic Hollywood, both of it (most Academy Awards until *Titanic*) and about it (it opens with a dig at the "awards given annually by that film society"). Viewers return, despite their overfamiliarity. This phenomenon, I argue, can in part be attributed to the fact that the film is *about* repetition, return, and replacement. Can it be only to find out more about Eve that we go back?

The film offers a behind-the-scenes look at a great star—in the film's own rhetoric, at the woman behind the star (as in Margo's homily: "[S]ooner or later we all go back to being a woman"). Twenty-some years of theoretical debate in the wake of Laura Mulvey's "Visual Pleasure and Narrative Cinema" has concluded that the image, the enigma, of Woman is at the center of classical Hollywood representation, its codes of looking, storytelling, and identification. *All About Eve*, with its fascinating star-heroine, would appear to be no exception. However strenuously the Lacanian model of sexual difference insists that "the Woman" does not exist, feminist film work informed by such a model has nevertheless tended to speak of masculinity and femininity in the abstract—of the Woman in the impossible singular, produced by heterosexual narrative logic. Insofar as we remember the film this way, Margo would be simply a version of "Eve"—a figure of Woman. And yet we are likely to remember the film as all about Margo—not as avatar of the feminine, but as a career-defining role for Bette Davis, a very particular woman. "Bette Davis" is the star persona behind the woman and the star presented in the text—we don't even see Margo perform on stage; her greatness is made plausible by Davis's performance in the film (and in past films). The film lets us know that she is playing "herself." Bette as Margo, woman and star, is queerly insistent in our cultural image-repertoire, most notably in decades of gay male camp practice. The role of Margo Channing is so closely identified with Bette Davis's peculiar cultural performance that the film can hardly be received without intertextual dimensions.

But now *I've* left Eve backstage. It is well known that in *All About Eve* there is literally another woman behind the great star, a woman waiting to take her place. It is the classic tale of protégée paranoia, and there may even be a true story behind it. The film makes room for two women (indeed for more than two, as I'll discuss below) and makes their intensely invested relationship its subject. The epistemological challenge *All About Eve* poses is that of a largely unbroached subject—what goes on "between women." It cannot tell us all there is to know about Eve, because Eve's enigma and Margo/Bette's larger-than-life status are inextricably related.

Addison describes Margo as "a great star, a true star. She'll never be anything less or anything else"; this quality depends, of course, upon her fans, whom Eve is taken to represent. But Eve is a singular kind of fan (and in fact the only representative of Margo's public whom we see in the film). She resists Karen's attempt to introduce her to Margo for the first time: "I'd be just another tongue-tied gushing fan." Karen (Celeste Holm) insists that she renounce her anonymity: "There *couldn't* be another like you." *All About Eve* is compelling viewing not only because Mankiewicz's dialogue suits Davis as perfectly as does her Edith Head gown, but because Eve's stealthy itinerary is so like our own appearance in our favorite movies as "Her Majesty the Ego."

"You must have spotted her by now, she's always there," says Karen, in Margo's dressing room, trying to convince Margo to give Eve an audience. Margo, slathering her face with cold cream, pauses and turns: "The mousy one with the trenchcoat and funny hat? How could I miss her! Every night, every matinee." Eve is emphatically nondescript. "You *must* have noticed her," Karen speaks in the imperative, "she's *always* there." Margo admits that despite the girl's mousiness and her costume of anonymity she has indeed noticed her, every time. She's even made note of the "trenchcoat and funny hat," a kind of disguise. The other women's recognition implies that Eve Harrington's secret is not a private matter; it is not hers alone.

If I'm implying that the content of Eve's secret is lesbian, that *All About Eve*'s epistemological challenge circulates around lesbian representability, then I will also insist, mindful of the complicated forms of knowing that surround the closet, that this is just the beginning of the story. Eve Sedgwick famously writes, "A whole cluster of the most crucial sites of the contestation of meaning in twentieth-century Western culture are consequentially and quite indelibly marked with the historical specificity of homosocial/homosexual definition, notably but not exclusively male . . . [and] among these sites are . . . the pairings secrecy/disclosure and private/public" (*Epistemology* 72).[8] The cinema's specifically twentieth-century form of publicity engages such "private" processes as identification, desire, viewing habits, and memories through the notably but not exclusively *female* phenomena of stardom and fandom. As I've indicated throughout this book, female stars, the women's pictures and related practices that constructed their images, the women who attended those films, and the varied cultural legacies of star images work together to draw and redraw the lines of female homosocial/homosexual definition. In the semi-public performance space of Margo's dressing room, Eve comes out with her fan's tale, and it is a whopper of a lie. Although a lie and a cliché of female ambition, it is a successful seduction: "That same night, we sent for Eve's things. . . . The next few weeks were like something out of a fairy tale and I was Cinderella in the third act. Eve became my sister, mother, lawyer, psychiatrist, and cop," Margo's voice-over recounts. While textual evidence and even authorial intentionality allow us to attribute lesbianism to Eve's character, they also allow us to assimilate her lesbianism to her qualities as a "killer."[9] Yet this unimaginative and somewhat misogynist reading of the film is complicated by the other women's complicity with Eve's seduction.

As I've argued throughout this study, the epistemological project of lesbian and gay readings of "dominant" films is not simply a decoding process, the revelation of queer subject matter, the restoration of coherence and meaning. Rather it is an encoding process, a textual re-vision with the reader-critic as subject of its fantasy, as de Lauretis's account of spectatorship in Chapter 3 of *The Practice of Love* suggests. This is what *All About Eve*'s Eve is all about. This lesbian figure—you must have spotted her—is to be found at the displaced center of one of Hollywood's most celebrated films, upstaged by her star but not invisible. Yet her visibility is paradoxical; it is not the "to-be-looked-at-ness" of Woman, but the "always-hanging-around-ness" of the spectator. A big cliché—the stage door groupie, pathetic in her raincoat and funny hat—she manages to project herself into the picture. Eve's relation to Margo figures the relationship of the spectator to the cinematic seduction (and the possibility of new forms of desiring and identifying) that the female star promises. Even though the seduction of *All About Eve* is generalizable, the seduction of Eve is a lesbian seduction. Not only does Eve attend every performance of the play, she studies Margo "as if she were a play or a book or a set of blueprints." We may never find out all about Eve—or all Eve knows—but she teaches us how to read, to recognize ourselves through what I am calling retrospectatorship.

Teresa de Lauretis distinguishes a film like *All About Eve* from contemporary, lesbian-made works that succeed in representing desire between women *as sexual*, reading Eve's relation to Margo—and the viewer's by proxy, as "a terminal case of identification" (*Practice of Love* 117) and further suggesting that "the pleasures afforded the lesbian spectator by oedipal rivalry in *All About Eve* . . . are those of a sadomasochistic maternal fantasy *made safe* by the film's heterosexual narrative logic" (121). She continues: "The incentive or incitement to fantasy that such representations yield is finally at the cost of a representation of lesbian sexuality in its instinctual, fantasmatic, and social complexity" (122). I will not argue that *All About Eve* provides this complex representation of sexuality; this would be asking it to be, precisely, ahead of its time. Yet I believe that classical Hollywood depictions of affectively charged and symbolically significant relations between women such as those depicted in exceptional star vehicles such as *All About Eve* are retrospectively constitutive of lesbian representability of the kind de Lauretis advocates—not only in the public sense of intertextual possibility, but in the "private" sense of spectatorial history. A scenario of popular culture can itself function as a fantasmatic "prestructure," a cultural organization of possibilities of signifying desire.

De Lauretis argues that Sheila McLaughlin's independent film *She Must Be Seeing Things* (1987), through its narrative's recasting of the primal scene within the specific codes and contexts of late twentieth-century lesbian life as a "lesbian fantasy of origins" marks a new "place of the look" for the lesbian spectator. The film is not a ready-made fantasy, she shows, rather it shifts the existing codes of cinematic representation to enable the "visualization . . . of a *lesbian* subject of viewing" within the film's text (100). In my view *All About Eve*, while working textually within the codes of Hollywood film, embeds its seduction fantasy—on the banal level, Eve's going home with Margo that first night—within the public and private experience of a cinematic institution characterized by unpredictable intersections of female stardom and fandom. Eve's waiting outside the theater figures the "reflexive" gaze ("I am looking on") necessary to the fantasmatic participation of a lesbian spectator in the seduction.

Today *All About Eve* is literally viewed retrospectively. As I suggested above, a virgin viewing is virtually impossible, because it is embedded, with its generic relations (women's pictures, pictures about stars such as *Sunset Boulevard, Sweet Bird of Youth, The Star, The Legend of Lylah Clare*) and the constellation that is Bette Davis, in cultural memory. The lesbian reading of *All About Eve* is thus not purely textual, for the encounter between spectator and text is not a first encounter—a lesbian film festival or friend might bring them together. While early viewing of *All About Eve* is not a necessary precondition for adult identity as a pervert—a number of other films could serve as pretexts—the film does provide a representation of this acculturating, fantasmatizing process in that the only concrete details of Eve's "case history" are that she has been a compulsive spectator at Margo

Channing's performances. The incompleteness of the circuit of desire in the film (as Vermeule writes—and de Lauretis would concur—"the desire *for* is replaced by the desire *to be*" [67]; we can't finally say that Eve wants Margo), is answered by a return, a revisiting, a repetition of desire's ignition. In a similar temporal structure, the spectator provides the affective, lived inflections of the seduction fantasy. Add to this the film's common function as rite of passage and the ritual dimensions of its viewing ("every night, every matinee"). The spectator can know a lot more about Eve than the film itself provides for.

This is the structural importance of Eve's secret—it is interrogated retrospectively, *après coup*. It is important that this film does not give us a conventional protagonist to identify with in Eve, in the sense of a central figure with psychological depth pursuing a course of cause and effect, investigation and discovery. If her identity were less hazy, if she didn't manage to keep her secret, even while giving it away, her story might be as safely contained within a (female) oedipal narrative of identification with the mother as de Lauretis finds it to be. Instead, the film's flashbacks and returns leave a gap at its heart where its ostensible object of knowledge ought to be, frustrating the drive to closure of the classic text. Addison interrupts his initial narration—"More about Eve later, all about Eve in fact"—without picking up the thread again. This gap is made meaningful through "retrospectatorship"; our viewing classical Hollywood from a contemporary position, one shaped by classical Hollywood as a cultural and historical experience and by particular stars or genres or well-loved texts as concrete signifying instances, by the social and cultural, and, for some, personal meanings of lesbianism today.

In *All About Eve*, Margo/Bette is given as spectacularly available to all viewing subjects—yet the text marks Eve's as a particular vantage from which to see her anew. The heterosexual logic at work in the film—the one that asks Margo to prefer "being a woman" to being Margo Channing—does not manage to contain Eve within the heterosexual closure that governs most Hollywood films. Eve remains what Karen says the French would call "de trop." Take for example the threesome formed when Eve accompanies Margo to the airport to bid Bill farewell. Eve's trenchcoat and funny hat contrast tactilely with Margo's lush fur and hair; the image resembles one of Deborah Bright's photomontages of a butch in a Hollywood romantic scene discussed in Chapter 2. Here the film does allow for the "*visualization* of the subject of fantasy" and "affective participation *at a distance*" (99) that de Lauretis argues is the result of the formal and narrative work of *She Must*

Be Seeing Things. This distance can be understood as internal to the subject, the temporal distance of retrospectatorship, and as the distance between "heterosexual" public fantasy and its queer revision.

The scene also inverts the female oedipal script de Lauretis sees underwriting the film ("the daughter becomes like the mother, Eve becomes Eve, the first and only woman" [*Practice of Love* 121]). Bill turns around as he's about to board the plane: "Hey Junior, see that she doesn't get lonely." He hails Eve as his oedipal heir and asks her to mother Margo, whom he calls "a lost lamb." These substitutions of subject and object positions, together with the sadistic form the film's narrative takes, prompt a reconsideration of *All About Eve* in terms of the beating fantasy. This stretches Freud's structure a bit, for "It is not with her relation to the mother that the girl's beating fantasy is concerned," he states emphatically. The girls he analyzes (including his daughter Anna) are producing seduction fantasies involving a positive oedipal attitude. While the beating fantasy allows for cross-gender identifications (a source of its appeal in spectatorship theory), the vicissitudes of the boy's fantasy are distinct from those of the girl, which are peopled exclusively by masculine figures. Freud elaborates: "The boy . . . changes the figure and sex of the person beating, by putting his mother in the place of his father; but he retains his own figure. . . . By the same process, on the other hand, the girl escapes from the demands of the erotic side of her life altogether. She turns herself in phantasy into a man . . . and is no longer anything but a spectator of the event which takes the place of a sexual act" ("A Child Is Being Beaten" 199). This gendered dissymmetry in access to the means of representing one's desire is depressingly familiar doctrine.

But what to make of the fact that it is the daydreams of Freud's *female* patients that rise "almost to the level of a work of art," that she's more than spectator, she's an author? In "Creative Writers and Daydreaming," his earlier essay on the topic of fantasy, Freud implies that daydreams are by no means an erotic renunciation: "In young women erotic wishes dominate the phantasies almost exclusively, for their ambition is generally comprised in their erotic longings" (147). Read retrospectively through the visualization in *Dottie Gets Spanked* of the female star's role in perverse fantasy—as stand-in for the subject and for the parental object of desire and aggression *and* as a female cultural authority—*All About Eve* could be seen as a version of the girl's fantasy that works through erotic and ambitious wishes not, indeed, in relation to the mother, but to another figure—call her Bette Davis. In other words, the revision of patriarchal law that we saw in the gay male (masochistic) fantasies of female-authorized popular culture discussed in the beginning of this chapter is enacted in *All About Eve* and made available to a lesbian spectator.

That first night in Margo's dressing room, Eve's rendering of her pathetic, though fake, life story rises almost to the level of a work of art. Thelma Ritter, Margo's maid Birdie and another proto-lesbian onlooker, reacts with the immortal line: "What a story! Everything but the bloodhounds snapping at her rear end" (a bit of stage business indelibly associated with *Uncle Tom's Cabin*). If Birdie and gay gossip columnist Addison de Witt know all about Eve at a glance, Margo is taken in by the fairy tale—a willing suspension of disbelief. The film's fantasy involves the dethroning of one diva to make room for another, a process put in motion by what Karen refers to as "the boot in the rear" that Margo has coming. To put Eve in Margo's shoes—indeed in her wig and her costumes—a story (what a story!) has to unfold. That narrative movement passes through several intermediate positions that *stage* the question of desire and identification, of Eve's position vis à vis the star, the construct "Woman." In the end (which recalls the beginning) the two women remain *distinct*; the film clarifies Eve's lesbian difference from Margo. What happens "behind the scenes" comes to include the spectator's process of identification and retrospection.

Eve's spectatorial fantasy is in fact an exhibitionist one; she literally desires to be mise-en-scène. The film figures the simultaneity that is possible only in fantasy by repeatedly disarticulating the viewing public from the performing star. (For example, Margo's biggest performance is at her private party, and her breakthrough private moment with Bill—in which she actually gets spanked—takes place on the set of the empty theater. Eve's reading for the part of Margo's understudy, and her debut in the role, take place on stage but are not shown on-screen.) Thresholds, vestibules, bathrooms—public/private spaces—are a defining trope, associated in particular with Eve's liminal status. In the film's beginning, Karen asks Eve whether she spends all her time huddling in doorways, and indeed her dowdy raincoat is soiled from leaning against the wall outside the stage door. When Karen proposes to introduce her to Margo, the star snorts her disdain for "autograph hounds" who "travel in packs." "They never see a play or a movie, even. They are never indoors long enough." Eve waits just outside and overhears the remark: "There's one indoors now," Karen tells Margo. Birdie is banished to the dressing room bathroom for making wisecracks; Karen is later summoned to a ladies'-room tryst where she is blackmailed into betraying Margo (fig. 42).

Thus the film's many behind-the-scenes scenes are often—if less explic-

42. *"Meet me in the ladies' room." Karen (Celeste Holm) is manipulated behind the scenes by Eve (Anne Baxter) in* All About Eve *(Joseph Mankiewicz, 1950).*

43. *Eve watches Margo (Bette Davis) from her position backstage, in an image staged with fantasmatic significance from* All About Eve *(Joseph Mankiewicz, 1950).*

itly than in *Dottie Gets Spanked*—also "behind" scenes, associated with the sadism, exhibitionism, and exchange relations of anality. The circulation among positions of command of the gaze, solicitation of the gaze, and exposure to the gaze—all marked as female—is illustrated in a protracted sequence from the "honeymoon" period that is meant to give us our first sign of Eve's ambition. Eve occupies a post behind the curtain as the cast take their bows before an unseen audience. We regard Margo from Eve's position (fig. 43), then observe Eve's expression of intense, almost erotic, excitement in several alternating reaction shots. Our point of view shifts to a frontal view of the stage as the curtain rises a third time on Margo's solo bow—lifting the back of Margo's skirt as it goes up!—framing the spectacle, highlighting its presentational aspect like the spanking tableau in *Dottie Gets Spanked*.[10] The costume's contrast with the Margo we've seen smeared with cold cream is as immediately apparent as is its resemblance to the frocks a younger Bette Davis had worn in films like *Jezebel*. Eve, in her place in the wings, is presented almost abstractly as spectator. "In reply to pressing inquiries" as to where they were in the beating fantasy, Freud's female patients would only declare: "I am probably looking on." But in the reverse angle Eve is also a spectacle—if not to the diegetic audience then at least to those of us who know she's acting a part. Margo exits backstage, catches sight of Eve, and teases her for crying at the performance yet again. Then the star is defrocked of her wig and hoop skirt and crinolines, with Eve's help, before she even reaches her dressing room.

Moments later, we come upon Eve, who has volunteered to return the costume to wardrobe, on stage *behind* Margo's dress, clasping it to her, superimposing its form on hers (fig. 44). The applause Eve bows to is her fantasy; the diegetic audience is no longer there. This absence might remind us of the absence the cinematic performance is based upon; the empty dress Eve clutches is, like the image, a fetish for the body of the absent star (fig. 45). But the sequence allows us to share the star's gaze. For now Margo is watching Eve—from a position like that from which Eve had watched her. We suspect her reaction will be anger; but her smile is as indulgent as that of Stevie's mother in *Dottie Gets Spanked* and answers Eve's earlier tears. It is not (only) Eve's ambition that she sees, but Eve's erotic fantasy involving the dress, and she's pleased. Under Margo's gaze Eve tenderly returns the dress, carrying it in her arms as if she were bearing a bride over a threshold.

When next we see Eve with the dress, it is not just the wardrobe mistress she's put out of work. She's in her dressing room after her triumphant debut, scheming her next move. She takes her bows as Margo's understudy on the precise condition that Margo cannot be present to watch her. But the film

44. *In a change in roles, Margo watches Eve's private performance from a similar position in* All About Eve *(Joseph Mankiewicz, 1950).*

45. *Caught in the act, Eve clutches Margo's costume.* All About Eve *(Joseph Mankiewicz, 1950).*

also closets her talent by withholding her exhibitionism from our view. We've seen her acting offstage of course, but there her performance must go unrecognized as a performance. And as I noted above, in the film's memory it is Margo who displaces Eve, Bette who upstages Anne Baxter, not the other way around.[11] These related scenes of observing and performing, triumph and downfall, do not imply that Margo and Eve are interchangeable. Nor do the women come together—although they are mutually dependent. It is no simple "star is born" scenario in which one career's meteoric rise is accompanied by the other's decline. Who is in charge? Who is gratified? Who wins? Who is beaten?—The film makes us look again.

To trace the vicissitudes of eroticism and ambition in this fantasy, it remains only to turn to the woman behind Eve. Returning from the awards ceremony that frames the film's flashback narration, Eve is startled to find a strange young woman in her apartment. But not so startled that she misses the opportunity to invite her to spend the night. The poor kid lives in Brooklyn—"You won't get home till all hours," Eve says, an invitation in her voice. At this moment, Eve's secret is out—it is one thing to love and emulate Bette Davis; it is another thing entirely to succumb to the charms of Barbara Bates. The very anonymity of this scene between the ultimately unknowable and pseudonymous Eve and a young woman who "calls herself" Phoebe, underscores its sexual motivation and invites our projection into the scenario. Telling yet another girl's story, the film appears to displace Eve, but it is precisely Eve's fantasy that she acts out. *All About Eve* stages queer spectatorship as command performance.

As president of her school's Eve Harrington club, "Phoebe" knows a thing or two about Eve—enough, perhaps, to expect this welcome?[12] Stevie won the trip to *The Dottie Show*, Eve's impossible wish was fulfilled by being invited indoors and backstage to meet Margo, and "Phoebe's" desire is staged in Eve Harrington's bedroom. Put at once on the scene (mise-en-scène) and backstage, we are supplied with the props and costumes that represent the texture of film viewing and the means of our impersonation. Lest we mistake the plot's *mise-en-abîme* structure of upstagings in *All About Eve*, it finds its perfect condensation, its visualization, in the last shots of the film. Phoebe slips into Eve's evening cape and, holding Eve's award "where her heart oughtta be," stands before the three-way mirror in long shot. The film dissolves to a medium close-up, and Phoebe's figure is multiplied, filling the frame resplendently. She turns and bows three times to her many subjects (fig. 46). Jackie Stacey privileges this shot as exemplary of the cinema's "intra-feminine fascinations" ("Desperately Seeking Difference" 57), a term that de Lauretis finds symptomatic of this film's assimilation of all women to one Woman, of desire to identification. Similarly, Blakey Vermeule notes that in the previous scene a "chiastic succession of mirror shots . . . [in which the two characters first see each other] reads purely as a narrative of the collapse of difference between Eve and Phoebe" so that in the last scene "[t]he sheer pressure of a thousand, or a million, proximate Phoebes continues to push the metonymic signifying chain into an infinite regress" (69).

Rather than reading in this tableau the female spectator's narcissistic overidentification with the image, I find in the play of sameness and difference, original and copy, a superimposition of the spectator on the spectacle, one that figures the lesbian in both positions, and as at once unique and *legion*. If it takes two women to make a lesbian, as de Lauretis reiterates (*Practice of Love* 92), it takes many more to make an audience. Although all of *these* "Phoebes" are the same, each spectator fills her shoes differently. The shot's exploitation of the reflective screen space ("we" are seen) succeeds in visualizing the ambitious and erotic fantasies tied to the figure of the female star without her body's being present. At this moment, Phoebe

46. Phoebe (Barbara Bates), having secretly borrowed Eve's cloak
and her award, is reflected endlessly.

occupies all of the places in the fantasy at once; and any one of us might call herself Phoebe. But even this shot remains all about Eve, insofar as the desire in looking she has inscribed so insistently in this film is mimicked as Phoebe tries to seduce her. Phoebe's props recall Stevie's royal paraphernalia in his dream sequence. But we know this girl isn't anyone in particular; she admits they have Eve Harrington clubs "in most of the girls' high schools." The film invites us all to become members of the club, even as Eve gets her boot in the rear.

The film ends with this staging before the mirror, which recasts in advance our future viewings of the film in terms of lesbian seduction. Spatially the scene as screen or mirror space might be imagined as reflecting the audience in the cinema — in a film that, as I have noted, underrepresents its diegetic audience. The space of pure visuality, the mirror melding with the screen, recalls the self-conscious "other scene" of the dream sequence in *Dottie Gets Spanked*. It takes place, in fact, in Eve's closet. If *All About Eve* didn't end exactly here, Eve might come up behind Phoebe, just as Margo did before, and catch the younger woman with the fetish, the piece of the star's theatrical clothing. Subtly the film has given us the standard Code-era Hollywood ending — the fade-out before the love scene — here an erotic, ambitious lesbian fantasy. This is why I watch the film again and again. It has something to teach me.

The film's flashback begins with Karen's voice-over: "I found myself looking for a girl I'd never spoken to" and the camera mimes her searching gaze. Such an uncanny feeling keeps a lesbian gaze fixed on Hollywood movies, searching for women in the shadows. It invites us to re-encounter something we've seen before but didn't yet know what the encounter could mean to us.

Notes

Introduction

1. Laplanche and Pontalis, in "Fantasy and the Origins of Sexuality," return psycho-analytic attention to the structure, temporality (deferred, *nachträglich*), and topology (inside/outside) of Freud's seduction theory to explain the function of parental fantasy as a prestructure for the emergence of sexuality in the subject (8). See de Lauretis, *Practice of Love*, for a discussion of these ideas and their significance for film studies and lesbian subjectivity. I am suggesting that the film is a cultural prestructure which can give meaning to and thus in a sense call forth a lesbian identity, in a temporal movement in which the affective memory of a text is perceived through a later understanding of the cultural codes and practices in which it and the subject are embedded.

2. Friends have cited *The Boy with Green Hair, To Kill a Mockingbird*, and of course *Mary Poppins. The Wizard of Oz* is described by Salman Rushdie as a "a hymn—*the* hymn—to Elsewhere" (23). I must thank my students from four years of American Narrative Cinema who have written riveting film "testimonials." See Sedgwick, "Queer and Now," and Martin, "The Quarterback, the Hobo, and the Fairy," for eloquent readings of the significance of queer childhood encounters with literary texts. I resume this argument in Chapter 6 of this volume.

3. In particular, my work over the past ten years with the New York Lesbian and Gay Film Festival, especially in retrospective programming, has challenged my thinking about audiences and address.

4. See Cowie; Rodowick; and de Lauretis's *The Practice of Love*. For a helpful synthesis of theories of spectatorship see Judith Mayne, *Cinema and Spectatorship*.

5. Production Code Administration file on *The Member of the Wedding* in the collection of the Margaret Herrick Library, Academy of Motion Picture Arts and Sciences, Los Angeles.

1. Reading the Code(s)

1. Motion Picture Producers and Distributors of America (MPPDA) 333. As my brief discussion below indicates, the process by which the Production Code was adopted and enforced is a complicated one, which excellent historical scholarship (Black, *Hollywood Censored*; Maltby, "The Production Code"; Couvares, *Movie Censorship*; Jacobs, *Wages of Sin*) has addressed. The Code was drafted by Father Daniel Lord and adopted by the industry in 1930. After the formation of the Catholic Legion of Decency and its public relations campaign against the movies in 1933–34 threatened the self-regulatory authority of the studios, the Code became enforced more rigorously under lay Catholic Joseph Breen's Production Code Administration. On October 3, 1961, with *The Children's Hour* and several other films in production that had lesbian and gay themes, the Code was amended to permit the tasteful treatment of "sexual aberrations" (Gardner 193; Russo 121–22). The current ratings system was finally adopted in place of the Code in 1968.

2. I draw here upon the revisionary sense Stuart Hall gives to the terminology of communications theory in his influential essay "Encoding, Decoding."

3. See Terry Castle's *The Apparitional Lesbian* for even more extensive claims about the spectral presence of female homosexuality in modern culture *tout court*.

4. Work on women and early film audiences represents some of the best synthesis of theory and history in feminist film studies. See Jacobs, *The Wages of Sin*; Staiger, *Bad Women*; Peiss, *Cheap Amusements*; and Hansen, *Babel and Babylon* for particularly germinal accounts.

5. "So *correct entertainment raises* the whole standard of a nation. *Wrong entertainment lowers* the whole living condition and moral ideals of a race," stated the general principles of the Motion Picture Production Code of 1930 (MPPDA 321).

6. The classical Hollywood narrative cinema's construction of a male spectator position (Mulvey, "Visual Pleasure"), and the institution's simultaneous reliance on women audience members and fans (Stacey, *Star Gazing*; Hansen, *Babel and Babylon*), has been a generative paradox for feminist film studies, one which has shaped debate between psychoanalytic, textual approaches and cultural and historical ones. See *Camera Obscura* 20–21 (May–September 1989) for one framing of this debate. This is not the place for an extensive summary of work on female representation and spectatorship; these issues will be taken up throughout this volume.

7. *Babel and Babylon*, esp. Chapter 3. For the move from homosocial leisure among immigrant communities to heterosocial mass culture consumption see Peiss. Feminist historians and historians of sexuality document the "heterosexualization" of female sexuality in this period. See D'Emilio and Friedman.

8. See Jeanine Basinger, *A Woman's View*, for an entertaining and comprehensive characterization of the woman's film and the world of women. See also Haskell; Walsh; and Doane, *The Desire to Desire*.

9. *Cahiers du cinéma* contributors Comolli and Narboni drew attention to a certain class of Hollywood films that "present" the ideology within which they are constructed in their editorial "Cinema/Criticism/Ideology." The Althusserian concept of "structuring absence" is used in the *Cahiers* discussion of Ford's *Young Mr. Lincoln*. Barbara Klinger's "'Cinema/Criticism/Ideology' Revisited" and her book *Melodrama and Meaning* explore the implications of the concept of the "progressive text" in film studies.

10. The dreamwork has been used by psychoanalytic film theorists such as Thierry

Kuntzel as an apt analogy for how films signify through visual and sensory means (and often express "censored" sexuality). For film and dream more generally see Kracauer.

11. D. A. Miller provides a powerful model of connotation and contagion in his reading of Hitchcock's *Rope*.

12. The section of the code entitled "particular applications" was added by former Postmaster General and MPPDA head Will Hays to the document drafted by Father Daniel Lord and Martin Quigley. The list was derived from the many local censor boards with which the Hays Office had been dealing since its institution in 1922—a major objective of the Code was to consolidate the objections of the different boards in order to prevent expensive cuts; sex perversion prohibitions were prevalent.

13. Letter from Joseph I. Breen to Louis B. Mayer, January 8, 1934. PCA file on *Queen Christina*, Margaret Herrick Library, Academy of Motion Picture Arts and Sciences. The scenes that were objected to were sexually suggestive: the remarks of a serving girl that she is good "when she does not like a man" and the clear implication that Don Antonio and Garbo's character have spent the night together in a scene when they speak from behind drawn bed curtains. The first line is addressed as a proposition to Garbo in drag, the second is conveyed through the shock of Don Antonio's valet, who believes his master to be in bed with "the other gentleman." I will return below to the question of how the signifiers (of homosexuality) relate to the signified (heterosexual activity) in this instance.

14. Chauncey's is the most influential among historical accounts of shifts in these paradigms. See also Faderman, *Odd Girls* and Terry, *An American Obsession*.

15. And of course Garbo's own gender inversion was announced in her preference for everything from pants to masculine pronouns. See Paris for biographical information.

16. For excellent readings and contextualizations of this exceptional film see Villarejo and Landy; Gaines, "The *Queen Christina* Tie-Ups"; and Erkkila.

17. The Broadway production of *The Old Maid* reviewed February 26, 1936. *Mildred Pierce* reviewed September 26, 1945. *Rebecca* reviewed in *Film Daily*, quoted in Berenstein 1998, 35 n22. The entertainment trade press adopted a general slang usage of the term "femme." *The Historical Dictionary of American Slang* cites *Vanity Fair* in 1927, "A 'femme' is a girl" (Lighter 737). The earliest reference cited in this sense is from 1871. "Femmie" is cited from 1934 in reference to a male homosexual, and the first example given for gay women is from 1957 (738).

18. Christine Holmlund dubs the 1990s examples of lesbian chic films "mainstream femme film[s]," which are not necessarily addressed to female audiences. It would be extremely interesting to trace the continuities between these paradigms. The relationship between contemporary women's genres and lesbianism has been mediated historically by feminism.

19. Margaret Goldsmith's "psychological biography" of Queen Christina (1933) critiques the squeamishness of previous treatments of the queen's life: "Most of Christina's biographers . . . even serious modern writers . . . have shrunk from admitting her sexual abnormality, even though many contemporary documents, and Christina's own letters, make it quite clear that she was attracted by her own sex" (67). One could read the biography—and thus the film—as part of the period's discursive interest in lesbianism.

20. See Freud's "Psychogenesis of a Case of Homosexuality in a Woman," Deutsch, and Lampl-de Groot. For commentary by present-day lesbian theorists, see Merck, *Perversions*; Hamer; Hart; and de Lauretis, *The Practice of Love*.

21. If invoking a "*Maedchen in Uniform* angle" was a way of referencing lesbianism

without naming it among producers and critics, the usefulness of intertextuality doesn't stop there. The lesbian theme of the German film was alluded to by a reviewer by citing yet another precedent "femme" text and scandal: "The New York State Board of Censors at first frowned upon the suggestion in this film of the 'Captive' theme, but recently they reconsidered their refusal to grant it a license." Mordaunt Hall, "'Girls in Uniform,' a German-Language Picture Concerned with Life in a Potsdam Girls' School." *New York Times* September 21, 1932, 26:2. Edouard Bourdet's *The Captive* (*La Prisonnière*) had been shut down on Broadway in 1927. Sherrie Inness argues that for American audiences unfamiliar with the lesbians populating French decadent literature, the feminine lesbians of the play presented "a greater threat to heterosexual order than does the mannish lesbian"—Hall's easily identifiable and "othered" invert (31). I don't think we need to rank the subversiveness of these figures and I'm not convinced about her historical claim. Yet *The Captive* is another metonymy for lesbianism and an influential example of the "femme" (intergenerational, domestic, "artificial") lesbian representational paradigm within which the crypto-lesbianism of Code-era Hollywood films tends to operate.

22. *Ann Vickers* (John Cromwell, 1933) and *Dracula's Daughter* (Lambert Hillyer, 1936) are two other pre-war texts that encountered problems with the PCA about lesbian inferences. They explored other contexts of female homosociality—prison and vampirism. On the latter film see Burns.

23. Lea Jacobs charts the emergence of Hollywood's system of self-regulation in reference to the popular genre of the fallen women's picture and the accompanying discourse on female "deviance" (*The Wages of Sin* 85). The deviance she speaks of is heterosexual activity outside marriage—engaged in by the 1930s gold digger who turned the sexuality of the 1920s "flapper" to economic advantage.

24. I'm greatly simplifying this historical argument (a version of what Terry Castle calls the "no lesbians before 1900" school [*The Apparitional Lesbian*]) to point out that women's culture is a controversial topos in queer historiography. Generally taken to connote a desexualized realm, female homosociality is set up against the homosexual identities that emerged in a new public realm. I doubt that it was sexologists such as Havelock Ellis who "put" the lesbian in boarding schools or the sexuality in romantic friendship. For the purposes of my argument about the 1930s, I suggest that women's culture had already entered the public realm of mass culture and that sexual definitions were in circulation that inevitably informed the revived Victorianism attempted in the women's film genre.

25. For example, a review of *These Three* in *Time* refers to the Hays organization's "mild attack of frenzy" over the planned acquisition: "[T]his seemed to the guardians of the cinema industry's morals so appalling that they not only banned both the title of the play and its plot but refused to allow Producer Goldwyn even to announce that he had bought such a thing. Last week Miss Hellman's adaptation of her own play made the perturbation of the Hays organization look as silly as it made Producer Goldwyn look shrewd" (PCA file clipping, March 30, 1936).

26. Goldwyn to Hays, July 24, 1935. Breen to Goldwyn, July 31, 1935. Production Code Administration files on *These Three* are in the collection of the Margaret Herrick Library, Academy of Motion Picture Arts and Sciences, Los Angeles.

27. Mary's fabrication is whispered, not spoken aloud; communicated to all of the parents while the teachers remain in ignorance of its substance; declared a lie; contested in a court case that remains offstage; and negated by suicide. Erhart persuasively argues for the signifying resonance of the silences around lesbianism in the 1961 film version.

28. Under an agreement called The Formula, the industry compensated a writer for a story that was rewritten and advertised under a different title—a purely economic recognition of the writer's role in a studio's "properties."

29. In a widely told story, Goldwyn purportedly responded to studio personnel who told him the play couldn't be filmed because the women were lesbians with: "All right, we'll make them Albanians!" Russo tells a different version, that Goldwyn wanted to film *The Well of Loneliness*—he planned to get around objections by making Stephen Gordon an American (62).

30. In *Hollywood in the Thirties*, John Baxter notes: "[A]lthough the dialogue states frequently that it is Joel McCrea whom Miriam Hopkins loves and not her companion Merle Oberon, the Hellman script implies at every turn that this love is based on jealousy and a wish to destroy that which has broken up the friends. Aside from a key confession of love for McCrea, delivered by Hopkins with her back to the camera, she acts throughout as if her desire was for her companion and not the man whom Oberon loves, the audience finding itself led inescapably to a conclusion at variance with the script but not with the mood and style of the film, nor the original play" (116).

31. The fact that it makes little difference whether an inference is true or false can be illustrated by the concern at the top of the MPPDA's list of problems with the property: "I: the insinuation the two girls are degenerates." If the worry is that Mary's insinuation is reprehensible, the censors are on the side of the teachers working to clear their names. If the worry is that Hellman's text insinuates that the two girls are degenerates, then the Code is reading with the most wishful of queer spectators who would include Karen in the film's contagion too.

32. Lillian Faderman in *Scotch Verdict* and Lisa Moore have emphasized how central the source of the accuser's knowledge was in the case of Pirie and Woods upon which Hellman's play was based. Moore analyzes the imperialist and racist constructions surrounding references to the student's Indian origins.

33. Fuss's excellent discussion of sexual contagions in Chapter 4 of *Identification Papers* is based on Dorothy Strachey Bussy's *Olivia*, a text written the same year as *The Children's Hour* though not published until 1949. The spreading of lesbianism has a much more beneficial result as "Olivia's identification with her teacher's desires thus provides the protagonist with conduits for her own, as desire is carried along the currents of a contagious passion for learning" (125). Significantly, this novel is the source of Jacqueline Audry's 1951 film, released with considerable cuts in the United States as *The Pit of Loneliness*—the only other lesbian film to appear in the United States until *The Children's Hour* (1961) and a deliriously "femme" film. See Noriega for an interesting commentary on critical reception of Audry's film. The title change once again showed the importance of intertextuality to the inscription as well as the inference of lesbianism.

2. Lesbian Cinephilia

1. See Doty; Doty and Creekmur; and Mayne, *Cinema and Spectatorship*, for considerations of gay, lesbian, and queer consumption of popular media.

2. A number of other works might be cited. Cecilia Dougherty's videotapes (*Grapefruit, Coal Miner's Granddaughter*, and *Joe-Joe*, made with Leslie Singer) draw heavily on popular culture without quoting actual footage. Pratibha Parmar's *Khush* (1991) quotes a production number from a Bombay musical to suggest a lesbian interpretation. The works of Joan Braderman (*Joan Does Dynasty* [1986] and *Joan Sees Stars* [1993]) and Mark Rappaport

(*Rock Hudson's Home Movies, The Silver Screen: Color Me Lavender* [1997]) are important non-lesbian works that employ similar revisionist strategies. Most of these works are distributed by Women Make Movies, New York, New York or Video Data Bank, Chicago.

3. Elizabeth Cowie makes a similar remark about this line. I take up the line and Cowie's reading in a discussion of *Now, Voyager* in Chapter 4.

4. Leo Handel's *Hollywood Looks at Its Audience*, which surveyed 1940s research, notes: "The erroneous assumption that the majority of the film audience is composed of women resulted in the fact that some motion picture companies catered to the tastes of female patrons" (99). The study also documents that audiences preferred players of their own sex.

5. Michael Bronski is one of several astute commentators on the general importance of movie divas to gay male culture. For a different kind of reading of one of Davis's signature roles in relation to AIDS and gay culture, see Jeff Nunokawa. Among the most interesting tributes is James Baldwin's description of his own cross-race, cross-sex identification with the pop-eyed star, which is discussed in Chapter 6.

6. Just how related the "appropriation" of dominant culture by lesbians and the appropriation of lesbians by dominant culture are was brought home to me when, at the height of the lesbian chic phenomenon, I received a call from Catherine Deneuve's lawyer. I was asked to be a paid expert witness for the actress's lawsuit against the San Francisco lesbian magazine *Deneuve*. At issue was not homophobia—Catherine was on the cover of *The Advocate* that very week as "the ultimate lesbian icon"—but money. Her own line of perfume might be hurt financially if consumers could buy something else with her name on it, her lawyer explained. No matter that lesbians are not a huge market for expensive perfume, or a huge market for anything for that matter, even *Deneuve*. Whether lesbians even knew who Catherine Deneuve was proved to be the very question for which my so-called expertise was being solicited. If I could provide a bibliography indicating how U.S. lesbians have followed Catherine Deneuve's career and paid homage to her, it would support her argument that the magazine was being bought and sold with her in mind. I hope to have given some indication in this chapter of how hard it is to prove what a particular star means to lesbians now. I could transform trivia into truth before a court of law. But by legitimating the practices I was writing about, I would be helping to stop them. The clips of Deneuve in these videos might not be considered "fair use." But the incident reminded me that as lesbians become visible as consumers of popular culture we have to think about the equivalence of woman and commodity all over again. We have to be careful not to overvalue, so to speak, our "appropriations." There is nothing inherently transgressive about the consumption of popular culture. But the economics of Hollywood and its national film industry equivalents are very different from those of independent video such as the works discussed here, where our dollars really matter. *Deneuve* settled and became *Curve*.

7. Carlomusto's exploration of the intersection between cultural icons and cultural activism continues in her autobiographical tape, *To Each Her Own*: "Anna Magnani is where I begin my journey."

8. Lesbian theorists such as de Lauretis, Mayne, and Roof have objected to a frequent assimilation of lesbian sexuality to female bonding in feminist theory, from Adrienne Rich's "lesbian continuum" to Eve Sedgwick's blurring of the distinction between the female homosocial and homosexual in her introduction to *Between Men*.

9. In relation to the heterosexual scenario, the star couple that plays it out, and the

terms of narration that support it she undergoes what de Lauretis identifies in "The Technology of Gender" as "the movement in and out of gender as ideological representation . . . a movement between the representation of gender . . . and what that representation leaves out or, more pointedly, makes unrepresentable" (26).

10. This is not to say that cross-gendered identifications are not a crucial part of lesbian viewing experience—but perhaps to suggest that Spencer Tracy is a less appealing figure of identification than, say, the suave and well-dressed Cary Grant, Hepburn's co-star in several 1930s comedies.

Sue-Ellen Case discusses the phenomenon in the context of the theatrical work of Split Britches and its exploration of butch and femme identifications:

> Weaver uses the trope of having wished she was Katherine [sic] Hepburn and casting another woman as Spencer Tracy, while Shaw relates that she thought she was James Dean. The identification with movie idols is part of the camp assimilation of dominant culture. It serves multiple purposes. One, they do not identify these butch-femme roles with "real" people, or literal images of gender, but with fictionalized ones, thus underscoring the masquerade. Two, the history of their desire, or their search for a sexual partner becomes a series of masks, or identities that stand for sexual attraction in the culture, thus distancing them from the "play" of seduction as it is outlined by social mores. Three, the association with movies makes narrative fiction part of the strategy as well as characters. ("Towards a Butch-Femme Aesthetic" 67–68)

While I have been arguing that Hollywood cinema's reliance on aestheticized femininity suggests ways in which queer theory has been insufficiently concerned with the lesbian relation to femininity, Eve Sedgwick suggest the opposite in a rare reference to the movies: "The irrepressible, relatively class-nonspecific popular culture in which James Dean has been as numinous an icon for lesbians as Garbo or Dietrich has for gay men seems resistant to a purely feminist theorization. It is in these contexts that calls for a theorized axis of sexuality as distinct from gender have developed" (*Epistemology of the Closet* 38).

11. For discussions of "A Child Is Being Beaten" and film spectatorship see Berenstein, "Spectatorship as Drag"; de Lauretis, *Practice of Love*; Doane, "The 'Woman's Film'"; Hansen, "Pleasure, Ambivalence"; Rodowick, *The Difficulty of Difference*; and Silverman, *Male Subjectivity at the Margin*.

In "Some Psychical Consequences of the Anatomical Distinction Between the Sexes," Freud asserts that in the girl's masturbation fantasy the "child" that is being beaten is in fact the clitoris. The active clitoral masturbation of the phallic phase (presumably directed toward the mother) is disguised by the regressive anal-sadistic and passive beating fantasy in which the child is male. The beating fantasy is homosexual in boys (the mother appears as agent of beating to disguise this). The little girl is said to turn herself into a "man"; it is not clear whether her fantasy is then gay male, lesbian, or heterosexual.

12. "Meyer's remarks fail to honor the specificity of the struggles of woman-identified women who are . . . heterosexual. . . . In taking over the categories of bourgeois thought, Meyer also inherits their oppressiveness" (*Katharine Hepburn* 40). See Watney for a discussion of Britton's investment here.

13. For example, Molly Haskell's groundbreaking 1974 study of women in cinema, *From Reverence to Rape*, both identifies the key scenes and recuperates their transgressiveness. She writes that the great 1930s stars

are so immensely secure in their sexual identities and in the aura of mutual attractiveness that they can afford to play with their roles, reverse them, stray, with the confidence of being able to return to home base. Hence, the flourish of male impersonators: Dietrich in white tie and white tails, Garbo as the lesbian Queen Christina . . . Eleanor Powell in top hat and tails, and Katharine Hepburn as the Peter Pan–like Sylvia Scarlett; all introduce tantalizing notes of sexual ambiguity that became permanent accretions to their screen identities. (132)

For an actively lesbian reading see Cheryl Clarke's poem "Greta Garbo."

14. Lesbian critic Andrea Weiss argues that elements of these three "androgynous" stars' personae and performances were appropriated by 1930s spectators for use in the formation of lesbian identity. In "'A Queer Feeling When I Look at You,'" she writes that "the process of selecting certain qualities from certain stars was especially important for lesbian spectators in the 1930s, who rarely saw their desire given expression on the screen" (288). Weiss makes reference to changing women's roles and the backlash against the New Woman of the early twentieth century, emerging definitions of sexual deviance influenced by sexology, and signifiers of lesbian style adopted by the sapphic aristocracy as contexts to which the image of these stars and their recognition by (sub)cultures (reinforced by gossip about the sexuality of the stars) might be related. I think Weiss is correct in noting that these images were circulating in popular culture at a moment when female social identities, including that of lesbianism, were the subject of ideological negotiation and stress. But I'm not sure Weiss succeeds in historicizing *spectatorship*. While I'm sure lesbians were pleased when they saw the kiss in *Morocco*, what I think Weiss's essay describes more accurately is the documented interest in these images on the part of lesbian spectators *today*, of which her own critical project must be considered an example. Contemporary appropriations of "sapphic" stars draw on specific aspects of what Dyer calls the star image's career to emphasize its diachronic dimension, which have subsequently been codified by subcultural and popular memory (*Stars*). In short, Weiss's examples are overdetermined.

15. Appropriately enough, this coveted Lola-Lola postcard does exist as a very material fetish. Gladys couldn't have it because it remained in the collection of another cinephile—Dietrich herself. *The New York Times* reported the donation, after the star's death, of her personal collection of thousands of pieces of memorabilia to found a museum in Berlin. The newspaper printed a photo of the artifact and described a tantalizing detail—invisible in the newspaper as in the film—that the feather is pink.

16. Although she does not mention the trajectory of the look in this still, Mayne discusses this character and the thwarting of the male gaze in an essay on the film. Mayne argues that Guste is strongly associated with the club's carnivalesque realm of female performance (for example, she looks on as Lola drops her panties on the professor), a realm which is gradually subordinated to the teleological narrative of male desire and destruction. Indeed, "[Guste's] heterosexual identity . . . become[s] visible only when the opposing worlds of Rath and Lola intersect," Mayne asserts ("Marlene Dietrich" 36–37).

17. See Doane, "Film and the Masquerade," for these tropes, and White, "Madame X"; Case, "Butch-Femme Aesthetic"; and de Lauretis, "Film and the Visible," for lesbian critiques.

3. Female Spectator, Lesbian Specter

1. As one contemporary reviewer summarized the doctor's thesis: "The occurrences, according to Markway, are 'brought on by the people whom they affect'" (*Film Quarterly* 17 [Winter 1963/4]: 44). The film's press book recounts how Wise was posed with the

problem of how to film "nothing," and how he devised an ingenious effect for filming a "cold spot." The language here suggests a connection between the haunting and sexual pathology.

2. Richard Dyer notes that the leopard-spotted dress Theodora wears is a visual signifier of lesbianism ("Seen to Be Believed" 18). Further examples of the lesbian-in-predatory-animal-fashions motif are given in Brooke and Cottis's *Dry Kisses Only* (1990).

3. In "Tracking the Vampire," Sue-Ellen Case writes of Williams's woman: "Hers is an en-tranced look, and the fascination in it could be read as a response to lesbian desire" (10). Yet, in Williams, Case notes, "the same-sex taboo is still safely in place."

4. Carol Clover's work shifted the paradigm in feminist studies. Berenstein (*Attack of the Leading Ladies*), Halberstam (*Skin Shows*), and Benshoff (*Monsters in the Closet*) approach different historical moments of the articulation of queer sexuality and horror.

5. For a fascinating account of how questions of cinematic technique are implicated with homosexual subject matter, both as symptom of blindness on the part of critics and as semiotic elaboration within the film text, see D. A. Miller's "Anal Rope."

6. Films in this cycle include: *Rebecca, Jane Eyre, Gaslight, Suspicion, Undercurrent, Sleep My Love, Secret Beyond the Door, Experiment Perilous, Dragonwyck, Whirlpool, Dark Waters, Spiral Staircase, The Two Mrs. Carrolls,* and *Under Capricorn.* Gothics are characterized by an intense and often diegetically justified fear of heterosexuality, and many that do not have lesbian connotations do involve the investigation of the death of a previous wife. Even in *Gaslight* Alicia's desire is held by the image of her dead aunt. On particular films or the genre as a whole see Doane, *The Desire to Desire,* 123–75; Modleski, *Loving with a Vengeance,* 59–84, and *The Women Who Knew Too Much,* 43–72; Waldman, "'At Last I Can Tell It to Someone!'"; Berenstein, "I'm Not the Sort of Person Men Marry"; Walsh, *Women's Film and Female Experience*; Walker, *Couching Resistance*; and Mulvey, "Myth of Pandora." This criticism often laments the films' critique of heterosexuality. Walsh suggests that the films "provided outlets for female anger rooted in demobilization of Rosie the Riveter, the multiple strains of wartime separation, and a broader historical oppression of women, manifesting itself in the overcommitment of women and the undercommitment of men to heterosexual relationships" (190). Waldman comments on the second male character who steps in and rescues the heroine: "[T]he presence of such a character at least held up the possibility, however utopian, for a model of male sexuality based on something other than brutality, a heterosexual relationship based on something other than male power and dominance, and female danger and distrust" (38).

7. My work on this group of films has been enormously enriched by Rhona Berenstein's parallel studies. Since the essay on *Rebecca* quoted herein, Berenstein has published a definitive study of the interrelatedness of censorship and lesbianism in *Rebecca* and *The Uninvited,* consulting the PCA files on these films.

8. PCA file on *Rebecca,* Margaret Herrick Library, Academy of Motion Picture Arts and Sciences, Los Angeles.

9. Breen argues that in Maxim's speech "we get the quite definite suggestion that the first Mrs. De Winter was a sex pervert" (letter to Selznick, September 25, 1939, PCA file).

10. "The place and object of a female active desire" is also symbolized by the last image of *Rebecca,* which is not the heterosexual couple's embrace. The camera seeks out, in a movement that strikingly prefigures the track in to the burning sled Rosebud in the final moments of *Citizen Kane,* the lingerie case that Danvers embroidered for Rebecca as it is licked by the flames that are consuming Manderley. The large angular "R" on the case is the film's lesbian signature.

11. The daughter in *Curse of the Cat People* forms a similar exclusive attachment to a female ghost. The film is a sequel to *Cat People* (Jacques Tourneur, 1940) only in the loosest sense. After the death of his panther-wife Irena at the end of the justly celebrated original film, *Curse* opens when the hero has settled down with the nice girl from the office he should have married in the first place. But Irena comes back to haunt their domestic life — however, her persona is different. No longer is it her "curse" that she avoid all contact with men lest she turn into a murderous predator. Here she is simply a charming ghost, albeit one with no interest in her former mate. Instead, she becomes the "special friend" of the couple's little girl.

This cycle of horror films produced by Val Lewton at RKO is full of rich queer resonances. *The Seventh Victim* (Mark Robson, 1943) is a female gothic in which a woman seeks her elder sister in Greenwich Village among a cult of Satanists, headed by a lesbian-coded Mrs. Danvers–type cosmetics tycoon who threatens her when she's in the shower in a chilling proto-*Psycho* predatory lesbian scene.

12. There is often a doubling of secondary female characters in the gothic. In *The Uninvited* Pam is tweed-suited, practical, joke-cracking (an Eve Arden sort) and Miss Holloway (a Mrs. Danvers clone, as I discuss below) is a New Woman in terms of career (head of a female institution she herself has founded). She wears the eccentric garb of the hysterical spinster. In *Secret Beyond the Door*, there is a "tweedy" sister-in-law and a villainous, unmarried, eccentrically dressed hysterical woman played by Barbara O'Neil. There's even a tweedy sister-in-law Bea (Gladys Cooper) in *Rebecca*. See Chapter 5 for further discussion of supporting characters.

13. In *The Unseen*, Paramount attempted to repeat the success of *The Uninvited* by casting its young star Gail Russell in the quintessential gothic role of a young governess who arrives at an eerie house whose master behaves suspiciously. But Ray Milland is not in the follow-up film; he does not seem essential to the formula. The actress retained a relation to another of her co-stars from *The Uninvited*, however, when she starred as the young Cornelia Otis Skinner (the actress who played Miss Holloway) in the film based on the memoirs Skinner wrote with a girlfriend, *Our Hearts Were Young and Gay*, also directed by Lewis Allen in 1944.

14. A special issue of *Camera Obscura*, "The Spectatrix" (May–September 1989), lays out a range of positions. For influential lesbian critiques of "sexual difference" theory in feminist film studies see, for example, Merck, "Difference and Its Discontents," and Stacey, "Desperately Seeking Difference."

15. Freud expands on the connection between paranoia and homosexuality: "Distrusting my own experience on the subject, I have during the last few years joined with my friends C. G. Jung of Zurich and S. Ferenczi of Budapest in investigating upon this single point a number of cases of paranoid disorder which have come under observation. The patients whose histories provided the material for the inquiry included both men and women, and varied in race, occupation and social standing. Yet we were astonished to find that in all of these cases a defense against a homosexual wish was clearly recognizable at the very centre of the conflict which underlay the disease, and that it was in an attempt to master an unconsciously reinforced current of homosexuality that they had all of them come to grief" ("On the Mechanism of Paranoia" 29).

Freud notes that the same homosexual fantasy can be detected at the root of all of the principal forms of paranoia, which constitute an exhaustive set of "contradictions of the single proposition: '*I* (a man) *love him* (a man)'" (33). What follows is his schema, including the kind of paranoia, the element that is contradicted in the "root-language" proposition, and its conscious projection "in distorted form."

kind of paranoia	contradiction	conscious projection
a) persecution:	I do not *love* him.	I *hate* him, because he persecutes me.
b) erotomania:	I do not love *him*.	I love her, because she loves me.
c) jealousy:	It is not I who love the man.	She loves him.
d) megalomania:	*I do not love at all.*	*I do not love any one.* I love only myself. (33)

I present these permutations to give a sense of the range of scenarios that are generated as a response to a homosexual fantasy and to remark how very similar they seem to be to film "plots" against the emergence of lesbian desire. Consider, for example: "I do not love Mrs. Danvers, I hate her, because she persecutes me"; "It is not I who love Rebecca, Maxim loves her"; and the paranoid accommodation to the demands of heterosexual narrative closure: "I do not love her, I love him"—which indeed only becomes conscious as "he loves me."

To be sure, Freud denies that *female* paranoia involves any but the delusion of jealousy: "It is not *I* who love the women—but *he* loves them" (34).

16. In the Lacanian definition of paranoia, which is the concept Doane draws upon in *The Desire to Desire* (by way of Guy Rosalato's work), the homosexuality "criterion" is irrelevant: paranoia is defined as the foreclosure of the paternal signifier, the phallus, and thus of any sexual position. Yet Lacan's work on paranoia included his early study of the folie à deux of the Papin sisters, who notoriously murdered the family for whom they worked. The story of the sisters, who were also lovers, was the basis for Genet's *The Maids* and the recent film *Sister, My Sister*. In "Paranoia and the Film System," Jacqueline Rose introduces into film theory's work on the Lacanian imaginary the paranoia and aggressivity characteristic of that register.

17. Thus "throwing away her pleasure" describes the process of female spectatorship: "[T]o possess the image through the gaze is to become it. And becoming the image, the woman can no longer have it. For the female spectator, the image is *too* close—it cannot be projected far enough. . . . What she lacks, in other words, is a 'good throw'" (Doane, *The Desire to Desire* 168–69).

18. In *Rebecca*, the heroine's paranoia shows evidence of the "struggle against a homosexual attachment" and certainly is under the sway of the "influence of a woman." As Hitchcock describes her persecutor:

Mrs. Danvers was almost never seen walking and was rarely shown in motion. If she entered a room in which the heroine was, what happened is that the girl suddenly heard a sound and there was the ever-present Mrs. Danvers standing perfectly still by her side. In this way the whole situation was projected from the heroine's point of view; she never knew when Mrs. Danvers might turn up, and this, in itself, was terrifying. To have shown Mrs. Danvers walking about would have been to humanize her. (quoted in Truffaut 93)

19. Several lesbian critics have isolated this passage. Jackie Stacey quotes it in her critique of film theory's reigning "gendered dualism of sexual desire [that] maps homosexuality onto an assumed antithesis of masculinity and femininity" ("Desperately" 53). Valerie Traub, in tracing from Freud to Kristeva "a continuous lineage of thought that has become . . . an ideological commonplace," namely that "'lesbian' can only be thought of as opposition (to women, to heterosexuality) or similarity ('as a man')" (307), cites the Kristeva passage in reference to Mulvey's work on female spectatorship, but not to Doane's.

Judith Roof offers a different rhetorical reading of Doane's use of Kristeva: "Doane brings up a lesbian moment as that which confuses gendered positions and reveals 'the convolutions of female spectatorship.'" While identifying the heterosexual logic at work in the passage in question, Roof regrets that "Doane reduces the excessiveness of the 'convolutions' introduced by the possibility of lesbian desire to a version of a very stable sexual difference" (50).

20. See Elsaesser, "Tales of Sound and Fury," for a definitive discussion of film melodrama's symptomatizing of domestic space. Laura Mulvey in "Pandora" touches on the relation of the melodramatic topos to the female body with reference to another Hitchcock gothic, *Notorious*.

21. Jackson apparently read more than Freud in preparation for the book. In an essay on the novel, Tricia Lootens locates an interesting phantom intertext for the terrifying picnic the two women take, a scene which did not survive the book's translation to film (187). Jackson intended it as a parody of an account with which she was preoccupied. In *An Adventure*, Charlotte Moberly and Eleanor Jourdain, two respected English women educators, describe their sighting of the ghost of Marie Antoinette on a visit to Versailles in 1901. Moberly and Jourdain's (lifelong) lesbian adventure and the connections manifested among folie à deux, the supernatural, and female homosexuality in their case are discussed in Castle, "Contagious Folly."

22. In *Questions of Cinema*, Stephen Heath defines the narrative image as "a film's presence, how it can be talked about, what it can be sold and bought on, . . . in the production stills displayed outside a cinema, for example" (121). De Lauretis's discussion develops the overdetermined association of the narrative image with femininity.

23. In *The Celluloid Closet*, Vito Russo documents the homophobic (and commercial) tendency to claim gay-themed movies are about "something else" (126). Yet Russo's preference for overt and positive representations of homosexuality leads him to misrecognize what's at stake in *The Haunting*:

> Unconscious lesbianism is its own punishment . . . for Claire Bloom's neurotic Greenwich Village lesbian in *The Haunting* (1963). She gets her psychosexual jollies by hugging Julie Harris and blaming it on ghosts. But she is not predatory; she is just out of life's running. She professes no interest in actively seducing either Harris *or an attentive Russ Tamblyn*. The lesbianism is entirely mental, and her sterility leaves her at a dead end. . . . Lesbianism is rendered invisible because it is purely psychological. *And since most lesbians were invisible even to themselves*, their sexuality, *ill-defined in general*, emerged onscreen as a wasted product of a closeted lifestyle. (158, emphasis added)

Bloom's character's mental characteristic is ESP, not neurosis. I read the very "invisibility" of lesbianism in the film as a strategy of representation. Parker Tyler regards the "hugging" more generously: "It might seem to both readers of the novel and viewers of the film . . . that lesbianism had a role in drawing these unusual ladies closer in the frightening, macabre situation to which they commit themselves and where they must 'cling' to each other" (*Screening the Sexes* 190).

24. The companion recalls the lesbian-coded supporting roles in the gothic. Theo is of course a chic but unmistakable version of the type, with her lesbianism and her dark coif. In *The Haunting* the heroine also identifies with this role. The heroine of *Rebecca* begins the film precisely as a lady's companion, "a friend of the bosom," as she defines it. I shall discuss the figure of the companion in more detail below.

25. The spectator/auditor is allied with Theo in our ability to "read Eleanor's mind" through the voice-over. Theo's mental gift also affiliates her with the hypnotic powers attributed to Danvers and Miss Holloway.

26. The lesbian significance of Theo's "reading" of Eleanor is underlined when she repeats this phrase later. The two women are asked to share a bedroom, but Eleanor protests. "We'll have fun," Theo assures her, smiling, "like sisters."

27. Eleanor's desire for Theo and its prohibition is projected and dispersed across the effects of the haunting, even unto the use of language. The group discovers, written on the wall, the legend: "Help Eleanor come home." She accuses Theo of having written it, Theo accuses her of writing it herself—yet the haunting, like lesbianism, is not confined to a single character. Eleanor is upset because "it knows [her] name"; it is as if she has been outed—or interpellated. The writing is reminiscent of the "R" inscribed on Rebecca's effects throughout Manderley. The "trace" is opposed to the regimes of knowledge represented by Dr. Markway and Maxim in the two films (their names are utterly significant in this context).

28. The MPPDA correspondence on the film pertains exclusively to the treatment of Theo's attraction to Eleanor and goes through most of the moments I have used as evidence in my reading. For example:

> In all circumstances we think that it would be plainly unacceptable under the Code to have a scene of Theo painting Eleanor's toenails. This is a physical intimacy which we are reasonably sure would be distasteful to audiences and subject to the accusation of an infringement on taste. . .
>
> We doubt that we could approve a picture under the Code in which a woman, with Lesbian intentions, is indulging in physical intimacies with, or bedroom proximities to another woman, even though these things are done with tact and refinement. (Geoffrey M. Shurlock to Robert Vogel, May 28, 1962)

29. Eleanor's death is ambiguous in both the film and the novel, though in the original the doctor's wife does not materially influence it. Even as she sharply turns her car toward a tree, Eleanor seems to struggle against the action. Tricia Lootens reads Eleanor's death as a wasted sacrifice, a feminine fate, but there is the suggestion that the house offers her some kind of transcendence. It is Theo who reminds us "it's what she wanted, to stay in Hill House."

30. *We Walk Alone—Through Lesbos' Lonely Grove* is a 1950s collection of first-person case histories.

31. It is significant that it is with the revision of her earlier essay to include mention of lesbian desire that the word "haunted" also appears in Modleski's text. Here again is the

quotation, with the added phrase highlighted: "[T]he heroine continually strives . . . to win the affections of Mrs. Danvers *who seems herself to be possessed, haunted, by Rebecca and to have a sexual attachment to the dead woman*" (*The Women Who Knew Too Much* 51).

4. Films for Girls

1. The novel is one of a series on the Vales of Boston: *White Fawn* (1936), *Lisa Vale* (1938), and *Home Port* (1947). In some regard it is "one of the lesser ones" (as Charlotte responds when Jerry asks her whether she's one of the Vales of Boston)—the novel failed to sell as well as Warner Bros. anticipated with their early acquisition. The film was, however, a strong box office and critical success. See Allen.

2. *Now, Voyager* is an interesting test case for the assumption that weepies are devalued because of their association with female audiences. Basinger cites Richard Corliss on the quandary of the (male) critic's ten best list: "'*Potemkin* (which I admire but don't really like) is the very stuff of cinema—but *Now, Voyager* (which I love but am afraid to admire) is only a movie!' As a result, the typical ten best list wound up looking like screening selections for an undergraduate course in Seminal Cinema 101. And the *Now, Voyagers* of the film world were relegated to a mind-closet containing all of the critic's secret sins" (439n). On the reification of melodrama and the woman's film as critical categories in contemporary film theory see Neale, "Melo Talk."

3. In her essay on the film, Lea Jacobs writes, "In a gloriously perverse gesture the narrative does not bring Charlotte's desire to fruition and an even more perverse sub-text would lead one to suspect that she likes it that way" ("Some Problems of Enunciation" 103). It is the "perverse" subtext in the maternal melodrama as a genre addressed to women and taken up by a lesbian spectator (who "likes it that way" too) that concerns me here. Yet lesbian analysis cannot be convincing if reduced to the willful "appropriation" of consciously identified, inert meanings, which the word "subtext" implies. Something like Jacobs's stress on enunciation must be incorporated to yield an understanding of the "perverse" as a deflection from normative narrative aims. It is the way desiring is played out in the interaction between text and spectator that Elizabeth Cowie's reading of the film in terms of fantasy foregrounds. She acknowledges Jacobs's conclusion as an explicit point of departure for a reading that, she promises, "gives different analysis and emphasis to Charlotte's desire through taking up the 'subtext'" ("Fantasia" 195 n8). "No, indeed, why ask for the moon when you want the stars?" Cowie asks, a question my reading echoes from a lesbian perspective.

Gay critic Andrew Britton writes: "It is the burden of *Now, Voyager*, in fact, that a sexual relationship with a man is *not* the supreme good, and that in the circumstances the stars, far from being an inadequate substitute for the moon, are distinctly to be preferred to it. . . . *Now, Voyager* endorses this decision, which it offers as the only rational one, and the final scene moves triumphantly, not towards the heterosexual embrace but towards Charlotte's refusal of it, celebrated on the soundtrack by Max Steiner with a delirious dissonant interval" ("A New Servitude" 58).

For Maria LaPlace, "In the last scene of the film the miserable matriarchy of the film's beginning has been substituted by an ideal one," although she regrets that "a complete expression of sexuality" is not permitted (164). I am not aware of any specifically lesbian readings of the film or its ending.

4. I borrow this designation "something else besides a mother" from another Olive Higgins Prouty maternal melodrama, *Stella Dallas*, and from the title of feminist film critic

Linda Williams's influential essay on King Vidor's film adaptation (1937), both of which I discuss in more detail below.

5. An important exception is Stacey's study of female audiences and female stars, *Star Gazing*.

6. For feminist readings of the maternal see Chodorow, Garner, Hirsch, Kristeva, and Rich. The classic psychoanalytical accounts of the relationship between female homosexuality and the maternal are Deutsch, Jones, Freud ("A Case of Homosexuality" and "A Case of Paranoia") and Lampl-DeGroot. In Chapter 2 of *The Practice of Love* de Lauretis thoroughly reviews and re-evaluates this psychoanalytic literature to formulate a new account of lesbian sexuality. The approaches of feminist film theory are discussed below.

7. The Freudian scenario Kaplan recapitulates to characterize women's identification with the maternal position in the oedipal drama actually dates to the same period as this cycle of maternal melos. Freud's "Femininity" (1933), his notorious attempt to tell the oedipal tale from the "other"—this time the girl's—direction, produced a narrative whose twists and turns are worthy of the plot convolutions of the best women's pictures. Viennese director von Sternberg's *Blonde Venus* might well have been playing in a theater near him when Freud concluded, with an almost palpable sigh, that "One gets the impression that a man's love and a woman's are a phase apart psychologically" (134). That the mother-son "couple" formed at the end of *Blonde Venus* conforms so closely to Freud's perception of heterosexual dissymmetry indicates that masculinity and femininity, normality and perversion are far from stable in this period.

8. See the influential exchange between the two critics in *Cinema Journal* (Winter 1985).

9. This crucial text of twentieth-century U.S. women's culture lived on as a long-running radio soap, and in the 1980s returned as a Bette Midler vehicle and, obviously, a staple of feminist criticism.

10. See Mayne, *Woman at the Keyhole* 153–54; Roof; de Lauretis, "Sexual Indifference" and *The Practice of Love* for compelling critiques of the erasure of lesbian specificity attending the feminist reclamation of the pre-oedipal.

11. See Byars and LaPlace for appropriations of Chodorow for definitions of female spectatorship.

12. For example, the resolution of the 1934 *Imitation of Life* presents a romantic reworking of mother-daughter intimacy similar to *Stella Dallas*. The film opens with the naked little girl in the bathtub asking mommy for her "quack-quack"—an evocation of pre-oedipal oceanic bliss. It ends with mother and adult daughter walking in the moonlight, having rejected the male suitor who came between them, repeating this private dialogue. If the man is given up (rather like in *Now, Voyager*) as a superfluous mediator of their desire, there remains a structurally important third term. Delilah (Louise Beavers), Bea's (Claudette Colbert) partner and servant and in a sense Jessie's mammy (as literal representative of the "domestic," her relation to [white] domestic ideology is both overdetermined and denaturalized), though radically excluded from the twosome by her death, is represented by the enormous neon sign that bears her face, illuminating the sky behind them. In *Femmes Fatales* Doane suggests that the black mother is closer to pure ideology of nurture and body (240), but the neon sign would seem to ironize this equivalence (see Berlant on the use of the trademark, embodiment, and citizenship in this film). The white mother also seems to represent the symbolic through her authority and money.

13. Lea Jacobs explains that in ambiguous strategies of the early 1930s maternal

melodramas, if the initial female sexual transgression was mitigated by its embodiment in the appearance of a child to suffer over, getting rid of the child could be seen as a noble sacrifice and allow for the film's penchant for rendering the fate of the fallen woman as upward class mobility (*The Wages of Sin*). This paradox was not ignored at the time, when the Depression was a very real force breaking up families. Tino Balio notes that a full 22 percent of MGM's productions in 1931 were maternal melos and quotes *Variety*, "More babies were wrenched from their mothers' arms in 1931 than in any previous film year; more tears were shed over unofficial motherhood and the final renunciation that washed records clean. Every infant torn from a sobbing mother brought a happy smile to the box office" (Balio 236).

Molly Haskell recognizes of the woman's picture's obsession with children: "[L]ike all obsessions, this one betrays a fear of its opposite, of a hatred so intense it must be disguised as love. . . . in true having-your-cake-and-eating-it-too fashion, the underlying resentment will have its say" (169).

14. Cavell's reading of the film in *Contesting Tears* is explicitly concerned to reverse the idea of Stella's "eradication," and his primary reference is this final shot: "Her walk toward us, as if the screen becomes her gaze, is allegorized as the presenting or creating of a star, or as the interpretation of stardom" (219). In contrast, in Prouty's book Stella lives the destiny—marrying the repulsive and drunken Ed Munn—that she only performs (in order to alienate Laurel) in the Vidor version, which thus appears more radical.

15. *That Certain Woman* provides an example of the insistence of this motif of maternal "sacrifice" as female triumph, one that prefigures the more complex negotiations of pairs of mothers in the later Davis films on which Goulding worked (discussed below). The film's heroine (Davis) is separated from the society man she loves (Henry Fonda) the day after their elopement by the revelation that she is none other than the notorious Mary O'Donnell, a gangster's widow. Their marriage is annulled. She raises their young son, with the help of her female best friend in a domestic partnership not uncommon to films of the 1930s, and Fonda marries a virtuous woman (Anita Louise). When the wife is crippled in an accident and she comes to Mary, the "other woman," in order to offer her her husband, Mary outdoes her in the sacrificial sweepstakes. In a flash of sympathy, she relinquishes any claim to the man and donates the baby to the couple to boot. Her recognition and her emotional reaction are instant and sublime.

16. Veda's flirtation with her mother is quite obvious, and the novel is even more explicit about the incestuous nature of their relationship. The novel and film of *The Bad Seed* (Mervyn LeRoy, 1956) take the pathologization of the mother-daughter relationship to its extreme. The way Rhoda (Patty MacCormack) manipulates her mother with caresses is almost as chilling as her cold-blooded murders. The original bad seed of *These Three*, Mary Tilford (Bonita Granville), also gets her way through caressing her grandmother.

17. There are also extratextual lesbian pleasures in this case. The white mother-daughter relationship in the film is part of Turner's cycle of mothers-with-troubled-daughter films during this period that resonate with real-life events: namely her daughter Cheryl Crane's stabbing to death Turner's lover Johnny Stompanato in her mother's bedroom. Knowledge of Crane's lesbianism is available to contemporary viewers through her autobiography *Detour*.

18. The grouping of these films as the Davis motherhood cycle is Andrew Britton's (*Katharine Hepburn*). Both he and LaPlace compare Davis's persona with nineteenth-

century literary heroines. In "Ugly Duckling, Funny Butterfly," Cavell refers to Freud's hysterics.

19. Feminist analyses of Davis as exemplary career woman tend to distance themselves from those of her gay male followers, an implicitly homophobic gesture in response to the perceived "misogyny" of camp discourses. At the same time, the centrality of passion among women is often minimized by gay male cultural appropriations that are attuned to its frequent appearance as rivalry. I am suggesting that a queer feminist reading that is attentive to collaborations in meaning production across gender and sexuality can be less willfully selective of elements of the Davis star image.

My debt to Britton's meticulous feminist readings of these Davis melodramas in *Katharine Hepburn: The 30s and After* and to his more recent essay on *Now, Voyager* is considerable. Judith Mayne's chapter on Davis in *Cinema and Spectatorship* also considers lesbian inflections in the cycle of "rivalry" films. Her critique of certain feminist appropriations of Davis's "independence" is particularly valuable.

20. As Nina Auerbach argues, the Victorian spinster carries misogynist connotations of asexuality, yet has considerable power, even in her negativity, as a feminist heroine. What is hidden even in this feminist interpretation is how often she is a figure of lesbian existence and of its discursive erasure. See Franzen, *Spinsters and Lesbians*, for links among Progressive-Era U.S. spinsters and contemporary lesbian identities.

21. In Hopkins's interpretation of the role, Delia is both selfish and flirtatious. Judith Anderson originated the role and apparently played her very differently, and Helen Menken, who starred as the younger woman who falls under the spell of an older lesbian in the controversial play *The Captive*, played Charlotte.

22. MPPDA file on *The Old Maid*, Margaret Herrick Library, Academy of Motion Picture Arts and Sciences.

23. Terry Castle, in "Marie Antoinette Obsession," writes of the sapphic connotations of the cult around the doomed French queen and the Princesse de Lamballe, the most famous inhabitants of the Concièrgerie, prevalent among nineteenth-century English women and girls (14).

In *Bio/pics*, George Custen discusses the relation between what a star is famous for and the famous people she might be asked to play—thus the questions of greatness and uniqueness in star personas, noting that both Hepburn and Davis "were frequently showcased in films that showed them as existing outside the normal bounds of heterosexual desire, to the extent that marriage was not an option in their scripts" (193). The compatibility of an "unhappy ending" with the personas of these stars may even lead to the expectation of one, and to their casting in such "real-life" stories. I suspect it is with no lack of appreciation for the compensatory pleasures the Davis character achieves that Custen writes that her Queen Elizabeth and the heroine of *All This and Heaven Too* "end up bereft of happiness, though Elizabeth has her nation, and Henriette has her class of adoring schoolchildren" (193).

24. While Henriette's real-life prototype married Reverend Field, such a resolution is by no means unequivocally presented in the film. The young minister begins the narration, encountering the heroine shipboard bound for France. He later visits her in prison and arranges her post in America. The final shot of the film portrays the two of them at the window of her schoolroom. Yet she looks out beyond him—toward the stars—in a shot that prefigures the last shot of *Now, Voyager*.

Allison McKee's fine essay on the film reads it as an "example of the manner in which issues of historical representation and gendered subjectivity collide in . . . films of the 1940s." McKee consults the previous accounts of "L'affaire Praslin" as well as the court proceedings that Field's novel drew upon.

25. In "A New Servitude," Britton addresses the trope of the "mother as governess" in *Now, Voyager* and the debt to *Jane Eyre*.

26. I've developed these ideas with reference to some of the feminist literature on Freud's governesses (Gallop, Cixous/Clement) in "Governing Lesbian Desire: *Nocturne's* Oedipal Fantasy."

27. The spectator may recognize the actress playing the Duchesse as the "square-shouldered, handsome" woman who portrayed Helen Morrison in *Stella Dallas*. Another of Barbara O'Neil's important characterizations is the maniacally jealous governess in *Secret Beyond the Door* (Fritz Lang, 1946).

John Brahm's *The Locket* (1946) is another woman's film in which the erotics of household relationships among women are explored. In the film's innermost flashback, the secret of the heroine's kleptomania is uncovered in the complex relations of exchange, prohibition, and fetishism among mistress, daughter, and servant's daughter (the heroine).

28. See my "Governing Lesbian Desire." *The Sound of Music* is the key contemporary text.

29. If this diagnosis seems tailor-made for Puddle and heroines of the woman's picture, it also, according to Anna Freud's biographer Elizabeth Young-Breuhl, suits her subject, who was the prototype of the altruistic character described in the case history (128–130, 210). Young-Breuhl speculates that there may be a connection between the altruistic surrender of the autobiographical case history and female homosexuality (328). I am indebted to Teresa de Lauretis for pointing out this text and Young-Breuhl's remarks on it.

30. Prouty herself was a patron of women's institutions, notably Smith College, where she funded Sylvia Plath's scholarship. Her fictional analogue in *The Bell Jar*, Philomena Guinea, takes a special interest in the heroine, removing her from the state hospital after her suicide attempt and sending her to a Cascade-style New England sanitarium, and Prouty similarly assisted Plath.

31. See the argument in Chapter 5 about the narrative queering effected by supporting characters/actresses such as Cooper; Cooper (whom Kaplan misidentifies as Gladys Young) was Oscar-nominated for this performance. Kaplan considers the mother in *Marnie* a more redeemable representation: "She does not fall neatly into the usual mythic opposite of the 'evil' or 'possessive' mother like Mrs. Vale; or, in Hitchcock's own oeuvre, the surrogate-mother figure Mrs. Danvers (Judith Anderson) in *Rebecca*" ("Motherhood and Representation" 136). This symptomatic statement recruits a character whom Kaplan admits is at best a "surrogate," as an archetype of the evil mother. "Lesbian" comes more easily to mind than "mother" in identifying Danvers's valence in *Rebecca*, and Kaplan is comparing Cooper's character in *Now, Voyager* with her.

32. When Tina says she wishes Charlotte were her mother, Charlotte rebukes her. In the book, in fact, Tina says she's unhappy when people make this error in identifying their relationship, designating Charlotte as something else. Since the screenplay otherwise conforms quite closely with the novel's dialogue, divergences such as this may be significant.

33. MPPDA file on *Now, Voyager*. Letter from Breen to Hal B. Wallis (April 14, 1942).

34. I'm not suggesting Jerry is marginal to the film. He mirrors Charlotte; he represents her secret love; and her refusal of what he has to offer is definitive of her self-realization. Both Britton and Cavell's readings of Jerry's position are quite detailed.

35. Fans relish the information that it was Davis who first insisted on Astor for the role (for which the supporting actress won an Oscar) and then drafted her co-star's services in rewriting and intensifying their scenes together. Lawrence Quirk's gossipy biography of Davis, *Fasten Your Seat Belts,* reports that Goulding worried that the Arizona hideaway sequence was "'too—well, lesbian in tone, Bette,'" and that the Hays Office and more sophisticated audiences would "pick up on it." She is said to have answered: "Well let them! . . . There's enough strangling, nitpicking censorship as it is, and if it adds a little paprika so much the better!" (223). See Mayne, *Cinema and Spectatorship* for the discourse surrounding the actresses' collaboration.

36. A later maternal melodrama, *Three Secrets* (Robert Wise, 1950), introduces lesbianism into a scenario of triangular female "parenting." A young boy is orphaned in a plane crash and stranded on a mountainside. While waiting for the search party to reach him, three women, each of whom could be his biological mother (all having relinquished for adoption boys born on his birthday—that very day—at the very same agency), spend the night together in the lodge and recount their stories in flashbacks. Phil (Patricia Neal), a mannish war correspondent covering the rescue attempt, was divorced by her husband for her careerism and for "not being a woman" (we know she's a lesbian because she wears a leopard-spotted kerchief and muff to the adoption agency). Ann (Ruth Roman) killed her cruel boyfriend and her child was born in prison and removed. Susan (Eleanor Parker) is a meek homemaker who seems miserable, ostensibly because she's keeping the secret of the illegitimate child.

At dawn, Phil finds out the child is Ann's, but Ann gives it up to Susan to raise and we can't tell whether Susan suspects the truth. The film ends with Phil repeating to Ann a pick-up line she had used first on Susan: "Come on, I'll buy you a cup of coffee." Thus the film leaves us with the suggestion of a female couple (who are vindicated in choosing childlessness), the pathos of female "sacrifice," and ambiguous solidarity. As Ann says, in a way we are all this kid's "mother."

37. As Mayne points out, Violet's position complicates the film's vision of surrogate motherhood in its primary plot (139). See also my discussion of Hattie McDaniel in Chapter 5.

5. Supporting "Character"

1. Reprinted in Twomey and McClure 21.

2. For an influential critique of the politics of "rejecting" stereotypes and a discussion of *Sister George* see Dyer, "Stereotyping" 30–31.

3. Quoted in Sherk 73. This book about Moorehead was clearly written by a fan.

4. While filming *How Sweet It Is* on an ocean liner, Lynde recounts, "At night, we'd sit around and dish. [Director] Jerry [Paris] told me those rumors that everybody's heard about Debbie [Reynolds] and her *close friend* Agnes Moorehead. . . . I'd heard those rumors, but Jerry filled in some details that . . . Oh, I'd better not, I'm not even sure if the story's really true" (Hadleigh, "A Hollywood Square Comes Out" 26).

Reynolds's autobiography actually reports the rumor that she and Moorehead were lovers without explicitly denying it (388). Moorehead repeatedly discussed "why I adore Debbie Reynolds" (interview with Sidney Skolsky, *New York Post,* Aug. 2, 1964); "It's really the loneliest sort of life . . . I did become good friends with Debbie Reynolds," (*New York Post,* Jan. 11, 1969). The friendship is generally considered a salient fact about Moorehead: The two women "became close friends, in a mother-daughter type relationship" (Parrish 122).

As corroboration goes, there is no more than ample documentation of the *rumor* in the gay press, motivated in part by a recent *Bewitched*-kitsch revival. "Hollywood knew her as its reigning lesbian, queen of Sapphic love. ('Who was Carrie Fisher's mother?' the old joke went. 'Debbie Reynolds. Who was her father? Agnes Moorehead.')" (NYQ, Dec. 22, 1991, 41). Dick Sargent, the second actor to play Samantha's husband on the show, who came out in the early 1990s, was unable to confirm the tales about Moorehead's lesbianism. The knowledge that Darrin, the representative of put-upon normalcy at the center of the show, was played by a gay actor literalizes what *The Advocate* calls *Bewitched*'s "gay allegory" (July 30, 1992, 69). In a gracious interview with the lesbian and gay news weekly on the occasion of her serving with Sargent as grand marshal of the Los Angeles pride parade, star Elizabeth Montgomery responded to the reporter's assertion, "It's the ultimate closet story": "Don't think that didn't enter our minds at the time. We talked about it on the set . . . that this was about people not being allowed to be what they really are . . . and all the frustration and trouble it can cause. It was a neat message to get across" (69).

In follow-up questions, Montgomery was asked to respond to rumors that Moorehead was a lesbian: "I've heard the rumors, but I never talked with her about them. . . . It was never anything she felt free enough to talk to me about. I wish . . . that Agnes had felt she could trust me. . . . We were very fond of one another, but it never got personal."

Outside of a gay context, what often appears in place of any remarks about Moorehead's sexuality is an emphasis on her religious beliefs. For example, the section on Moorehead in *The Bewitched Book* is entitled "Agnes of God" (Pilato 24–26). Religious conviction seems to put as efficient a shield around one's behavior and intimacies as the closet door. That Moorehead was devout is not in question. But religion appears almost as a defense against a homosexual reading, as the very emblem and safeguard of spinsterishness.

Ann B. Davis, who played Alice, the housekeeper who resembled a phys ed teacher, on *The Brady Bunch* (and before that Schultzy on *The Bob Cummings Show*) has also enjoyed a surge in appreciation. A profile in *People* reported her as having shared a home since 1976 with an Episcopal bishop and his wife. "The three are dedicated to prayer and Bible study." She "never married," and admitted, "I basically don't do that well with children, although my sister [identical twin Harriet] says I'm a great aunt" (June 1, 1992, 86).

In characteristically grande dame fashion, Moorehead herself wrote: "I have played so many authoritative and strong characters that some people are nervous at the prospect of meeting me. . . . There is a certain amount of aloofness on my part at times, because an actor can so easily be hurt by unfair criticism. I think an artist should be kept separated to maintain glamour and a kind of mystery. . . . I don't believe in the girl-next-door image. What the actor has to sell to the public is fantasy, a magic kind of ingredient that should not be analyzed" (quoted in *New York Times* obituary May 1, 1974, 48).

Agnes Moorehead material was found in clippings files at the New York Public Library for the Performing Arts and the Museum of Modern Art Film Study Center.

5. Kron's biographical note for "101 Humiliating Stories" (performed at P.S. 122, Jan. 7–31, 1993) reads in part: "At college . . . Lisa was consigned to four years of walk-on roles as grandmothers, neighbor ladies, and the occasional animal. She was advised to lose 20 pounds or gain 200 and told that her professional prospects are good if she can just hold on until she is sixty when there will be plenty of work playing someone's mother. She loses one role because . . . 'you don't really convey any sexuality on stage.' She is told she is a character actress. . . . [S]he is encouraged by a friend to visit the lesbian theater collective, the WOW

Cafe. This turns out to be an East Village storefront packed with other wayward 'character actresses' who have recast themselves as ingenues."

6. I am using Dyer's term from *Stars*, "star image," to refer to the complex of meanings derived from a star's films, publicity, promotional and critical discourses, what is known of their "real life," the commonsense apprehension of their "type," etc. The term star text will refer more specifically to the signifying function(s) of the star image within a specific film text or discourse.

7. For a tour-de-force reading which contrasts Propp's historical understanding of the function of the princess in relation to moments of power transition with the more reductive or gender-blind schemas of other studies of narrative and narrativity, see de Lauretis, *Alice Doesn't*, Chapter 4.

8. Dyer's essay "Homosexuality and Film Noir" is particularly relevant to these considerations of homosexuality and narrativity, genre, and typing. He observes that it is their association with work that differentiates lesbian characters in these films from those in the traditional female roles of mother or wife (20).

9. Isaac Julien's *The Attendant* is a particularly moving and inventive rendition of the dynamics of racial and sexual marginalization. It depicts the sadomasochistic "high art" fantasies of a middle-aged Black museum guard in tableaux that stage interracial, subversive variations on the "old masters." The film casts the uniformed Black man, an archetypal "attendant" of others' stories, as the lead, showing his subjectivity and erotic imagination to be bound up with, and an appropriation of, dominant representation. Significantly, he still has no lines. In Cheryl Dunye's *The Watermelon Woman*, the filmmaker-protagonist takes on an identification with a black lesbian who worked as a supporting actress in studio-era Hollywood and as a lead in race movies. The "watermelon woman" leaves a visual trace of a lost history. Ironically, the actress's lesbianism—her relationship with a white woman director—allows her paradoxical (stereotyped) visibility in mainstream cinema. See Leonard.

10. "Sapphire"—the backtalking woman on Amos and Andy (hooks refers to her as a "man in drag, castrating bitch" 120), the eponymous character of the British "social problem" film (in which the perpetrator of racist murder is revealed as a white spinster), the contemporary black lesbian poet whose name recalls that of Sappho—names an intersection of stereotypes and potentialities of black female agency and sexual transgression. (See also Bobo 74–75.)

11. All of these commentators include significant discussion of Sarah Jane, the "passing" black daughter in the Sirk film, and the film's "split" character, to use Sirk's terminology. Her definition of her sexuality through relation to white womanhood figures sexual agency as a question of representability.

12. See Heung on *Imitation of Life* as well as Katzman and Rollins, whom she cites. Judith Rollins writes in *Between Women*, "While any employer-employee relationship is by definition unequal, the mistress-servant relationship—with its centuries of conventions of behavior, its historical association with slavery throughout the world, its unusual retention of feudal characteristics, and the tradition of the servant being not only of a lower class but also female, rural, and of a despised ethnic group—provides an extreme . . . example of a relationship of domination in close quarters" (8).

13. For a recent discussion of appropriations of the mammy see Phyllis Jackson and Darrell Moore's review of Cheryl Dunye's *The Watermelon Woman*. This film imagines the lesbian private life of an actress specializing in mammy roles.

14. Tallulah Bankhead's claim that Hattie McDaniel was her "best friend" generated rumors that McDaniel was bisexual, according to McDaniel's biographer Carlton Jackson, who gives Carlton Moss as source for the Tallulah "source." (Kenneth Anger famously reported the linkage of the two stars in his *Hollywood Babylon*.) Jackson notes judiciously that "there is no evidence to support these beliefs, but the rumors continue to this day" (134) and cites a group of interviewees attesting to her fondness for homosexuals — though she was "not personally bisexual."

15. Bogle discusses Mae West's maids on pages 45–46. See also James Snead's chapter "Angel, Venus, Jezebel." Cripps notes "By the 1930s Mae West's maid, the accomplished actress Libby Taylor, played her role both on and off screen, fussing over the bathwater, the breakfast, and her employer's moods" (96).

16. Doane reads this "shadowing" of white heroine with black supporting actress in *The Great Lie* as ideologically typical and invisible (*Femmes Fatales* 239). Mayne attends to the force of McDaniel's persona, performance, and plot codes (*Cinema and Spectatorship* 139).

17. James Baldwin writes of the "loyal nigger maid": "The inclusion of this figure is absolutely obligatory — compulsive — no matter what the film imagines itself to be saying by means of this inclusion. How many times have we seen her! She is Dilsey, she is Mammy, in *Gone with the Wind*, and in *Imitation of Life*, and *The Member of the Wedding* — mother of sorrows, whore and saint" (*The Devil Finds Work* 86–87).

18. Baldwin takes the linked but not overlapping episodic narrative structure of *Tales of Manhattan*, in which Paul Robeson and Waters are featured in a separate segment, as instructive of the role of African Americans in Hollywood narrativity more generally: "What the black actor has managed to give are moments — indelible moments, created, miraculously, beyond the confines of the script; hints of reality, smuggled like contraband into a maudlin tale, and with enough force, if unleashed, to shatter the tale to fragments. The face of Ginger Rogers, for example, in *Tales of Manhattan*, is something to be placed in a dish, and eaten with a spoon — possibly a long one. If the face of Ethel Waters were placed in the same frame, the face of Little Eva would simply melt: to prevent this, the black performer has been sealed off in to a vacuum" (*Devil* 121–122).

19. In his essay on Bentley, Garber argues that the bulldagger black lesbian type she embodied circulated widely in images of Harlem culture in the 1920s. The bulldagger provides one possible cultural translation for the requisite physical bulk of the mammy.

20. " Ethel Waters came into my life when I was a timid young woman groping for an identity. I was a new bride, freshly graduated from nurses' training" writes Juliann DeKorte (24). The nature of their relationship echoes the scenario of *The Member of the Wedding*: "We were as mother and child from the beginning. . . . Recently we were patient and nurse. But all along, she was instructing me in a different relationship — that of teacher and student" (24). Twila Knaack's book testifies to a "beautiful relationship" with Waters, "first as good friends and then as her 'Girl-Saturday'" (10) and she draws the parallel to Waters's relationship to Julie Harris during the Broadway run of *Member*, quoting the younger actress: "I loved her immediately. . . . I belonged to Ethel, to Brandon. They were the we of me" (quoted 108).

21. Although I suggest that an erotic dimension of the mistress-servant relationship exists on the imaginary level from the dominant position, either as an exercise of power, a projection of sexuality onto the other, or as an inflection of the emotional devotion expected as the mistress's due, it is more the province of melodrama's translation of social relations to

familial, and by extension sexual, logic than a sociological phenomenon. Yet David Katzman provides equivocal reference to the latter: "Not all mistress/servant love . . . was maternal; an occasional glimpse of sisterly or womanly love made its way into the literature as well. It might have entailed the concern of one woman for another within the bonds of woman-hood. Or a lonely woman searching for platonic companionship. . . . In seeking love in the mistress/servant relationship, a mistress would have had a greater chance of satisfaction than her servant. Womanly love— 'the long-lived, intimate, loving friendship between two wom-en,' the close emotional relationships which Carroll Smith-Rosenberg has described, re-quired the sharing of common experiences even on a mother/daughter level" (158–59). Hollywood films express the imaginary of the dominant culture, which if it even approxi-mates that of white femininity, certainly does not foreground the point of view of black servant women.

22. Judith Rollins notes that the ideology of maternalism in mistress/servant relation-ships invariably entails the giving of old clothes as a "reading" of the relationship to and the status of the other (189).

23. Cripps notes a Southern censor's favoring this explanation (*Making* 239). Accord-ing to the PCA file on *Pinky*, Francis Harmon of the New York censor's office recommended making Pinky the daughter of one of Miss Em's relatives and even amended the script. On March 30, 1949, Fox head Darryl F. Zanuck replied that "representatives of many different Negro points of view" had been consulted and "without exception they have objected to the suggestion of miscegenation."

24. The way the mammy stereotype overlays the black mother's role in the relationship between light-skinned daughter and dark-skinned mother is exploited to full melodramatic effect in *Imitation of Life*. In the first version Delilah tells Peola, "I ain't no white mother, I's your mammy," implying that her depth of feeling and capacity for sacrifice is greater. In the Sirk version, Annie embraces Sarah Jane in front of her daughter's roommate, who doesn't know her "secret." "So you had a mammy." Sarah Jane responds, "All my life."

25. Breen wrote to former Hays Office censor, who was then at Fox, Colonel Jason S. Joy: "[F]rom the standpoint of general good and welfare, we strongly urge that you avoid physical contact between Negroes and whites, throughout this picture" (PCA files, February 28, 1949). It is ambiguous whether this applied strictly to the heterosexual couple, and indeed whether it was black and white characters or actors who were forbidden physical contact. Joy responds "a great deal of research has been made concerning the probable acceptability of PINKY. It is our intention to have many instances of physical contact between Dr. Hester and Pinky. We believe these contacts to be absolutely necessary. . . . We sincerely believe that this is the proper way of handling this subject. Incidently, you know, of course, that the actress who will play the part of Pinky will in fact be a white girl" (March 3, 1949).

26. In *The Devil Finds Work*, James Baldwin writes of the othering function of the sexual mulatto in *The Birth of a Nation*: "[T]he merciless plot . . . is entirely controlled by the image of the mulatto . . . one male and one female. All of the energy of the film is siphoned off into these two dreadful and improbable creatures. . . . Both are driven by a hideous lust for whites, she for the master, he for the maid: they are, at least, thank heaven, heterosexual, due, probably, to their lack of imagination" (57–58). The very improbableness of black people in the white racist imagination, Baldwin implies, would make homosexuality seem a probable attribute of their image.

27. See Doane's discussion of blackface in *The Birth of a Nation* (*Femmes Fatales* 228). Agnes Moorehead played a pipe-smoking "octoroon" in *The Adventures of Captain Fabian* and her portrayal of the treacherous wife of the Third Cousin in the all-Anglo Chinese epic *Dragon Seed* is a important determinant of her persona. See Shohat and Stam on casting in *Unthinking Eurocentrism.*

28. Halprin 32, cited in "Lesbian Looks" 115. Mayne's argument about Arzner also appears in Chapter 3 of *Woman at the Keyhole,* "Female Authorship Reconsidered" and has been extended in *Directed by Dorothy Arzner.*

29. The sidekick's self-deprecation is a "metatextual" example of her acting as the agent of her own containment. Despite the delightfulness of Eve Arden's looks, voice, and dress, and her popularity with lesbian spectators, her persona is so often put down by her characters and by others that I find Moorehead a less painful, though perhaps less obvious, example of the lesbian type.

30. *Roseanne,* whose cast consisted almost entirely of women who in another era would have been pressed into service as lesbian-coded supporting actresses (and who, in the case of Estelle Parsons and Shelley Winters, as Roseanne's mother and grandmother, respectively, actually had been) featured a classic nod to sitcom icons when Nancy, a recurring character played by Sandra Bernhard—a notorious real-life, role-playing queer—declared that she was, in fact, a lesbian. Yet, like *The Killing of Sister George,* in putting forward an overt lesbian characterization, the show drew on a covert one. At first surprised by her friend's announcement, Roseanne then invoked a code through which the coming-out message was intelligible: "Nancy always did like that Miss Jane Hathaway on *The Beverly Hillbillies.* That about says it all."

31. But even this is an example of intertextuality, because it established an eccentric or "queer" image that informed Hall's casting in future roles, such as in the campy supernatural soap opera *Dark Shadows,* and her Miss Fellowes *resembled* other suspect supporting roles.

32. A discussion of Hollywood before the 1940s, especially in the pre-Code period, which would offer fertile ground for decoding lesbian types in character actresses' repertoires, will have to be left for another study.

33. The *Johnny Guitar* take-off is one of the highlights of *Dry Kisses Only.* See also Pamela Robertson's discussion of this extraordinary film in *Guilty Pleasures.*

34. The notion of a "lesbian cameo" could be applied to one pleasurable moment in *Basic Instinct.* Toward the end of the film, an aged but unmistakable Dorothy Malone (best supporting actress Oscar winner for *Written on the Wind*—as Sirk said, "the eccentric role like the Stack or Malone parts certainly is always more rewarding to play than the straight one" [114]), comes down Sharon Stone's stairs. Her gaze, her intimacy with the other woman, bespeak the "lesbianism" that appears preposterous elsewhere in the text.

35. Hattie McDaniel starred in the number-one radio hit *Beulah.* Again, it is not only lesbianism that works the margins of the representable in U.S. popular culture.

36. In Charles Laughton's blurb on Moorehead for *Don Juan in Hell,* with which they both toured extensively in the early 1950s, he writes about her days as a drama student in New York: "She was kind of mad around this time, not because she had to pull in her belt notches, but because she hadn't enough money to buy mauve lace, and mauve taffeta and mauve velvet and mauve feathers and geegaws which are a necessity to Agnes Moorehead's breathing."

37. The Agnes Moorehead fan club's publication was originally called "Versatility," as noted in an issue of "Moorehead Memos," a later incarnation of the club's newsletter.

38. The son, who was indeed adopted, by some accounts was later disowned; others report that he simply disappeared.

39. Parrish notes that *Dark Passage* gave Moorehead an "opportunity to portray . . . a woman close to her own age without disguising costumes, makeup or foreign accents. . . . Here was a jealous, sex-starved characterization that the electric Dame Judith Anderson would have been proud to play in her heyday" (122). Higham and Greenberg acknowledge that "Agnes Moorehead's prying, vicious Madge Rapf is a definitive portrait of bitchery" (39).

40. Confirmation of this reading, and a sense of the intensity of the performance and the resonance of the type, can be derived from these comments by the legendary underground gay filmmaker Jack Smith: "Acting in movies is the essence of the art of acting because it gets more detailed. Yes, I think so, because I'm being haunted now by a performance in a movie. It was in *Dark Passage*. Agnes Moorehead plays this pest, and fills out the character in detail. In a huge close-up you see the twitch of her little purse of a mouth. And that couldn't have been rendered on stage. You can reveal a certain personality type—a certain kind of pest or what have you—and then you have something to remember when you see a person in life that this reminds you of. That happened to me just recently. This raging pest from the Gay Men's Health Crisis just called and said she'd be right over. And she has no right to go to anybody's home, but she just came over. The poor creature, her life was so empty that she had to join the Gay movement to pester AIDS victims in order to have a social life. Right away I looked at her and thought of Madge in *Dark Passage*" (133–35).

6. On Retrospectatorship

1. Stowe's novel was the most popular literary work of the nineteenth century; adaptations were performed somewhere on the American stage well into the 1930s, and it was filmed repeatedly (1903, 1911, 1927, etc.) The power of its persistent fantasy of national identity had by the 1940s begun to lose its grip after long-standing African American criticism of the "Tom" stereotype. Baldwin himself contributed one of the novel's most withering critiques, though interestingly he doesn't mention his childhood encounter with the book in "Everybody's Protest Novel."

2. See Martin's "The Hobo, the Quarterback, and the Fairy" for a moving invocation of the power of childhood reading and its irreducibility to questions of *sexual* identity alone. Eve Sedgwick eloquently describes what is at stake here: "I think that for many of us in childhood the ability to attach intently to a few cultural objects, objects of high or popular culture or both, objects whose meaning seemed mysterious, excessive, or oblique in relation to the codes most readily available to us, became a prime resource for survival. We needed for there to be sites where the meanings didn't line up tidily with each other, and we learned to invest those sites with fascination and love. This can't help coloring the adult relation to cultural texts and objects. . . . For me a kind of formalism, a visceral near-identification with the writing I cared for, at the level of sentence structure, metrical pattern, rhyme, was one way of trying to appropriate what seemed the numinous and resistant power of the chosen objects" ("Queer and Now" 3).

3. Some of the drawings used in the film were made by director Todd Haynes as a child, a revealing authorial inscription.

4. However dissimilar in their content and in their political and cultural legacies, *I Love Lucy* and *Uncle Tom's Cabin* represent somewhat analogous cultural products for their times. They both reached an unprecedented national (eventually international) audience with exemplary female uses of a genre often thought of as itself feminized (TV, the novel).

5. Later in the book, Baldwin pursues representations of race in Davis's films (*In This Our Life*), moving from the encounter with the image to the critical engagement with the text.

6. In her account of the seduction fantasy's role in sexual structuring, de Lauretis explains the temporal structure that I am associating with retrospectatorship: "[T]he psychoanalytic explanation of sexual subjectivity rests on the structure of deferred action (*Nachträglichkeit*), a distinctive articulation of present, past, and future by which a forgotten event can be recovered and understood only after some other event has acquired a causative function. The chronologically first event, whether real or fantasized, is of the nature of a seduction; the second event, whatever its nature, becomes understood (as attached to the first) through a particular form of discursive interaction between patient and analyst which is itself a kind of seduction" (*The Practice of Love* 149).

7. Interestingly, the character is referred to as Eve Butler rather than Eve Harrington in one of the best feminist analyses of the film, Jackie Stacey's "Desperately Seeking Difference," a reading that considers the fan's homoerotic desire for the star. In a brilliant essay on *All About Eve*, Blakey Vermeule employs Abraham and Torok's notion of cryptology in directly addressing this issue of Eve's unknownness, even closetedness, and the correspondingly spectacular appeal of Margo.

8. Vermeule raises the epistemology of lesbianism in *All About Eve* as a direct engagement with Eve Sedgwick's work and my thinking has clearly been marked by her formulations.

9. Mankiewicz agrees that the character was conceived as a lesbian. Besides the final scene, discussed below, Eve is seen with her arm around her female roommate—whom she has manipulated into assisting in her seduction of Lloyd Richards. "Killer" is Addison's epithet—he claims he and Eve are two of a kind; homosexuality might be the basis of that identification. I discuss Eve's lesbianism briefly in Chapter 1 in the context of *Dry Kisses Only*'s skit on the film.

10. See Eve Sedgwick's "A Poem Is Being Written" for a vivid evocation of the presentational arrangement of a fantasized childhood spanking scene and its relation to artmaking. My analysis has been enriched by her essay.

11. If Margo usurps Eve's place, does this mean *she* could be in the lesbian position? It is interesting to entertain the question of whether Bette Davis could play Eve Harrington. One could easily describe her in numerous films as "the mousy one in the funny hat." She appeared in *Jezebel* only by taking the place of Miriam Hopkins, who had played the lead on stage. Eve is ambitious, Eve is a bitch; these are two salient components of Davis's star image. Indeed, as Judith Mayne points out in her chapter on the star in *Cinema and Spectatorship*, Davis's rivalry—with female stars such as Hopkins and Joan Crawford and Tallulah Bankhead (whom Margo appears to be fashioned after), with the women of her family, and certainly within the plots of her films, as we saw in Chapter 4—was a crucial dimension of her construction as a star of the woman's film. It is apt that since both Baxter and Davis were nominated for Academy Awards in the category of best actress for *All About Eve*, neither took home the award.

12. To indulge the overreading that is the prerogative of fan and theorist alike, I note that Phoebe speaks of "the Eve Harrington clubs they have in most of the girls' high schools"—she doesn't call them Eve Harrington *fan* clubs. I imagine these as clubs where everyone has to be an "Eve Harrington" (it is a fake name, after all) and that girls' schools are full of them.

Works Cited

Affron, Charles. *Star Acting: Gish, Garbo, Davis.* New York: Dutton, 1997.

Allen, Jeanne, ed. *Now, Voyager.* Madison: University of Wisconsin Press, 1984.

Anger, Kenneth. *Hollywood Babylon.* New York: Bell, 1975.

Auerbach, Nina. *Woman and the Demon: The Life of a Victorian Myth.* Cambridge: Harvard University Press, 1982.

Babuscio, Jack. "Camp and the Gay Sensibility." *Gays in Film.* Ed. Richard Dyer. London: BFI, 1977. 40–57.

Baldwin, James. *The Devil Finds Work.* New York: Dell, 1976.

Balio, Tino. *Grand Design: Hollywood as a Modern Business Enterprise, 1930–1939.* History of the American Cinema. Vol. 5. Berkeley: University of California Press, 1995.

Barthes, Roland. "The Face of Garbo." *Film Theory and Criticism.* Ed. Gerald Mast and Marshall Cohen. 2nd ed. New York: Oxford University Press, 1979. 720–21.

———. "The Third Meaning." *Image/Music/Text.* Trans. Stephen Heath. New York: Hill and Wang, 1977. 52–68.

———. "Upon Leaving the Movie Theatre." *Apparatus.* Ed. Teresa Hak Kyung Cha. New York: Tanam, 1980. 1–4.

Basinger, Jeanine. *A Woman's View: How Hollywood Spoke to Women, 1930–1960.* Hanover: Wesleyan University Press, 1995.

Baxter, John. *Hollywood in the Thirties.* New York: AS Barnes, 1968.

Baxter, Peter. "On the Naked Thighs of Miss Dietrich." *Wide Angle* 2.2 (1978): 18–25.

Becker, Edith, Michelle Citron, Julia Lesage, and B. Ruby Rich. "Introduction to Special Section on Lesbians in Film." *Jump Cut* 24-25 (March 1981): 17–21.

Benshoff, Harry M. *Monsters in the Closet.* New York: Saint Martin's Press, 1997.

Berenstein, Rhona J. "Adaptation, Censorship, and Audiences of Questionable Type: Lesbian Sightings in *Rebecca* (1940) and *The Uninvited* (1944)." *Cinema Journal* 37.3 (Spring 1998): 6–37.

———. *Attack of the Leading Ladies.* New York: Columbia University Press, 1996.

———. "'I'm Not the Sort of Person Men Marry': Monsters, Queers, and Hitchcock's *Rebecca.*" *CineAction* 29 (Fall 1992): 82–96.

———. "Spectatorship as Drag: The Act of Viewing and Classic Horror Cinema." *Viewing Positions: Ways of Seeing Film.* Ed. Linda Williams. New Brunswick: Rutgers University Press, 1995. 231–70.

Bergstrom, Janet and Mary Ann Doane, eds. "The Spectatrix." Special issue of *Camera Obscura* 20-21 (May–September 1989).

Berlant, Lauren. "National Brands/National Body: Imitation of Life." *Comparative American Identities.* Ed. Hortense Spillers. New York: Routledge, 1991. 110–40.

Black, Gregory D. *Hollywood Censored: Morality Codes, Catholics, and the Movies.* New York: Cambridge University Press, 1996.

Blumer, Herbert. *Movies and Conduct.* New York: Macmillan, 1933.

Bobo, Jacqueline. "Black Women in Fiction and Nonfiction: Images of Power and Powerlessness." *Wide Angle* 13.3 (July 1991): 72–81.

Bogle, Donald. *Toms, Coons, Mulattoes, Mammies and Bucks: An Interpretive History of Blacks in American Films.* New York: Viking, 1973. New York: Continuum, 1989.

Bordwell, David, Kristin Thompson, and Janet Staiger. *The Classical Hollywood Cinema: Film Style and Model of Production to 1960.* New York: Columbia University Press, 1985.

Bourdet, Edouard. *The Captive.* Trans. Arthur Hornblow, Jr. New York: Brentano's, 1926.

Bright, Deborah. "Dream Girls." *Stolen Glances.* Ed. Tessa Boffin and Jean Fraser. London: Pandora, 1991. 144–54.

Britton, Andrew. *Katharine Hepburn: The Thirties and After.* Newcastle upon Tyne: Tyneside Cinema, 1984.

———. "A New Servitude: Bette Davis, *Now, Voyager* and the Radicalism of the Woman's Film." *CineAction* 26/27 (1992): 32–59.

Bronski, Michael. *Culture Clash: The Making of Gay Sensibility.* Boston: South End, 1984.

Burns, Bonnie. "*Dracula's Daughter*: Cinema, Hypnosis, and the Erotics of Lesbianism." *Lesbian Erotics.* Ed. Karla Jay. New York: New York University Press, 1995. 196–209.

Butler, Judith. *Bodies that Matter: On the Discursive Limits of "Sex."* New York: Routledge, 1994.

———. *Gender Trouble: Feminism and the Subversion of Identity.* New York: Routledge, 1989.

———. "Lana's 'Imitation': Melodramatic Repetition and the Gender Performative." *Genders* 9 (Fall 1990): 1–18.

Byars, Jackie. *All That Hollywood Allows: Re-Reading Gender in 1950s Melodrama.* Chapel Hill: University of North Carolina Press, 1991.

Cahiers du cinéma. "Morocco." *Sternberg.* Ed. Peter Baxter. London: BFI, 1980. 81–94.

———. "Young Mr. Lincoln." *Movies and Methods.* Vol. 5. Ed. Bill Nichols. Berkeley: University of California, 1976. 493–529.

Case, Sue-Ellen. "Towards a Butch-Femme Aesthetic." *Discourse* 11.1 (Fall/Winter 1988/1989): 55–73.

———. "Tracking the Vampire." *Differences* 5.2 (Summer 1991): 1–20.

Castle, Terry. *The Apparitional Lesbian: Female Homosexuality and Modern Culture.* New York: Columbia University Press, 1993.

———. "Contagious Folly: *An Adventure* and Its Skeptics." *Critical Inquiry* 17 (Summer 1991): 741–72.

———. "Marie Antoinette Obsession." *Representations* 38 (Spring 1992): 1–37.

Cavell, Stanley. "Ugly Duckling, Funny Butterfly: Bette Davis and *Now, Voyager*" and "Postscript (1989): To Whom It May Concern." *Critical Inquiry* 16 (1990): 213–89.

———. *Contesting Tears: The Hollywood Melodrama of the Unknown Woman.* Chicago: University of Chicago Press, 1996.

Chauncey, George, Jr. "From Sexual Inversion to Homosexuality: Medicine and the Changing Conceptualization of Female Deviance." *Salmagundi* 58–59 (1982–83): 114–146.

Chodorow, Nancy. *The Reproduction of Mothering: Psychoanalysis and the Sociology of Gender.* Berkeley: University of California Press, 1978.

Cixous, Helene and Catherine Clément. *The Newly Born Woman.* Trans. Betsy Wing. Minneapolis: University of Minnesota Press, 1986.

Clark, Danae. "Commodity Lesbianism." *The Lesbian and Gay Studies Reader.* Ed. Henry Abelove, Michèle Aina Barale, and David M. Halperin. New York: Routledge, 1993. 186–201.

Clarke, Cheryl. *Experimental Love.* Ithaca: Firebrand, 1993.

Clover, Carol. *Men, Women, and Chainsaws.* Princeton: Princeton University Press, 1991.

Comolli, Jean-Louis and Jean Narboni. "Cinema/Criticism/Ideology." *Movies and Methods.* Vol. 1. Ed. Bill Nichols. Berkeley: University of California, 1976. 22–30.

Cook, Pam and Claire Johnston. "The Place of Woman in the Cinema of Raoul Walsh." *Feminism and Film Theory.* Ed. Constance Penley. New York: Routledge, 1988. 25–35.

Couvares, Francis G. *Movie Censorship and American Culture.* Washington: Smithsonian Institution Press, 1996.

Works Cited

Cowie, Elizabeth. "Fantasia." *m/f* 9 (1984): 70–105.

———. *Representing the Woman: Cinema and Psychoanalysis.* Minneapolis: University of Minnesota Press, 1997.

Creed, Barbara. "The Position of Women in Hollywood Melodramas." *Australian Journal of Screen Theory* 4 (1978): 27–31.

Crimp, Douglas. "Right On, Girlfriend!" *Fear of a Queer Planet: Queer Politics and Social Theory.* Ed. Michael Warner. Minneapolis: University of Minnesota Press, 1993. 300–320.

Cripps, Thomas. *Making Movies Black: The Hollywood Message Movie from World War II to the Civil Rights Era.* New York: Oxford University Press, 1993.

———. *Slow Fade to Black: The Negro in American Film, 1900–1942.* New York: Oxford University Press, 1977.

Curry, Ramona. *Too Much of a Good Thing: Mae West as Cultural Icon.* Minneapolis: University of Minnesota Press, 1996.

Curtin, Kaier. *"We Can Always Call Them Bulgarians": The Emergence of Lesbians and Gay Men on the Stage.* Boston: Alyson, 1987.

Custen, George. *Bio/pics: How Hollywood Constructed Public History.* New Brunswick: Rutgers University Press, 1992.

Cvetkovich, Ann. *Mixed Feelings: Feminism, Mass Culture, and Victorian Sensationalism.* New Brunswick: Rutgers University Press, 1992.

De Acosta, Mercedes. *Here Lies the Heart.* North Stratford, Conn.: Ayer Company Publishers, 1975.

DeKorte, Juliann. *Finally Home.* Old Tappan, N.J.: Fleming H. Revell Company, 1977.

De Lauretis, Teresa. *Alice Doesn't: Feminism, Semiotics, Cinema.* Bloomington: Indiana University Press, 1984.

———. "Film and the Visible." *How Do I Look? Queer Film and Video.* Ed. Bad Object Choices. Seattle: Bay, 1991. 223–76.

———. *The Practice of Love.* Bloomington: Indiana University Press, 1994.

———. "Sexual Indifference and Lesbian Representation." *Theatre Journal* 40.2 (May 1988): 155–77.

———. *Technologies of Gender: Essays on Theory, Film and Fiction.* Bloomington: Indiana University Press, 1987.

Deleuze, Gilles. *Masochism: An Interpretation of Coldness and Cruelty.* Trans. Jean McNeil. New York: George Braziller, 1971.

D'Emilio, John and Estelle B. Freedman. *Intimate Matters: A History of Sexuality in America.* New York: Harper and Row, 1988.

Deutsch, Helene. "On Female Homosexuality." *The Psychoanalytic Reader.* 1948. Ed. Robert Fliess. New York: International Universities, 1973. 208–30.

Diawara, Manthia. "Black Spectatorship: Problems of Identification and Resistance." *Screen* 29.4 (Autumn 1988): 66–79.

Doane, Mary Ann. *The Desire to Desire: The Woman's Film of the 1940s.* Bloomington: Indiana University Press, 1987.

———. *Femmes Fatales: Feminism, Film Theory, Psychoanalysis*. New York: Routledge, 1991.

———. "Film and the Masquerade: Theorising the Female Spectator." *Screen* 23 (1982): 74–87.

———. "The 'Woman's Film': Possession and Address." *Home Is Where the Heart Is: Studies in Melodrama and the Woman's Film*. Ed. Christine Gledhill. London: BFI, 1987. 283–98.

Doty, Alexander. *Making Things Perfectly Queer: Interpreting Mass Culture*. Minneapolis: Minnesota University Press, 1993.

Doty, Alexander and Cory Creekmur, eds. *Out in Culture: Lesbian, Gay, and Queer Essays on Popular Culture*. Durham: Duke University Press, 1995.

Douglas, Ann. *The Feminization of American Culture*. New York: Knopf, 1977.

Duggan, Lisa. "The Social Enforcement of Heterosexuality and Lesbian Resistance in the 1920s." *Class, Race, and Sex: The Dynamics of Control*. Ed. Amy Swerdlow and Hanna Lessinger. Boston: G. K. Hall, 1983. 75–92.

Du Maurier, Daphne. *Rebecca*. 1938. New York: Avon, 1971.

Dyer, Richard. "Entertainment and Utopia." *Movies and Methods*. Vol. 2. Ed. Bill Nichols. Berkeley: University of California Press, 1995. 220–32.

———. *Heavenly Bodies: Film Stars and Society*. New York: St. Martin's, 1986.

———. "Homosexuality and Film Noir." *Jump Cut* 16 (1977): 18–21.

———. *Now You See It: Studies of Lesbian and Gay Film*. New York: Routledge, 1990.

———. Review of Vito Russo, *The Celluloid Closet: Homosexuality in the Movies*. *Studies in Visual Communication* 9.2 (Spring 1983): 52–56.

———. "Seen to Be Believed: Some Problems in the Representation of Gay People as Typical." *Studies in Visual Communication* 9.2 (Spring 1983): 2–19.

———. *Stars*. London: BFI, 1979.

Dyer, Richard, ed. *Gays and Film*. London: BFI, 1977. Revised 1984.

Eckert, Charles. "The Carole Lombard in Macy's Window." *Movies and Mass Culture*. Ed. John Belton. New Brunswick: Rutgers University Press, 1996. 95–118.

Ellis, Havelock. "Sexual Inversion in Women." *Alienist and Neurologist* 16 (1895): 141–58.

Ellis, John. "Star/Industry/Image." *Star Signs*. Ed. Christine Gledhill. London: BFI Education, 1982. 1–12.

Ellsworth, Elizabeth. "Illicit Pleasures: Feminist Spectators and *Personal Best*." *Wide Angle* 8.2 (1986): 45–56.

Elsaesser, Thomas. "Tales of Sound and Fury: Observations on the Family Melodrama." *Home Is Where the Heart Is*. Ed. Christine Gledhill. London: BFI, 1987. 43–69.

Erhart, Julia. "She Could Hardly Invent Them! From Epistemological Uncertainty to Discursive Production in *The Children's Hour*." *Camera Obscura* 35 (1995): 87–106.

Erkkila, Betsy. "Greta Garbo: Sailing Beyond the Frame." *Critical Inquiry* 11.4 (June 1985): 595–619.

Faderman, Lillian. *Odd Girls and Twilight Lovers: A History of Lesbian Life in Twentieth-Century America.* New York: Columbia University Press, 1991.

———. *Scotch Verdict: Dame Gordon vs. Pirie and Woods.* New York: William Morrow, 1983.

———. *Surpassing the Love of Men: Romantic Friendship and Love between Women from the Renaissance to the Present.* New York: William Morrow, 1981.

Field, Rachel. *All This, and Heaven Too.* New York: Macmillan, 1939.

Fletcher, John. "Versions of Masquerade." *Screen* 29.3 (Summer 1988): 43–70.

Foster, Jeannette H. *Sex Variant Women in Literature.* Tallahassee: Naiad, 1985.

Foucault, Michel. *The History of Sexuality. Volume 1: An Introduction.* Trans. Robert Hurley. New York: Vintage, 1978.

Franzen, Trisha. *Spinsters and Lesbians.* New York: New York University Press, 1996.

Freeman, Elizabeth. "'The We of Me': *The Member of the Wedding*'s Novel Alliances." *Queer Acts.* Ed. José Muñoz and Amanda Barrett. *Women and Performance* 16 (1996): 111–36.

Freud, Anna. "A Form of Altruism." *The Ego and the Mechanisms of Defense. The Writings of Anna Freud.* Vol. II. New York: International Universities, 1966. 122–34.

Freud, Sigmund. "A Case of Paranoia Running Counter to the Psychoanalytical Theory of the Disease" (1915). *Sexuality and the Psychology of Love.* Ed. Philip Rieff. New York: Collier, 1963. 97–106.

———. "'A Child Is Being Beaten': A Contribution to the Study of the Origin of Sexual Perversions" (1919). *The Standard Edition of the Complete Psychological Works of Sigmund Freud.* Vol. 17. Trans. James Strachey. London: Hogarth Press, 1955. 175–204.

———. "Creative Writers and Day-Dreaming" (1908 [1907]). *The Standard Edition of the Complete Psychological Works of Sigmund Freud.* Vol. 9. Trans. James Strachey. London: Hogarth Press, 1955. 141–53.

———. *The Ego and the Id.* Ed. James Strachey. New York: Norton, 1960.

———. "Femininity" (1933). *The Standard Edition of the Complete Psychological Works of Sigmund Freud.* Vol. 22. Ed. James Strachey. London: Hogarth, 1955. 112–35.

———. "Fetishism" (1931). *Sexuality and the Psychology of Love.* Ed. Philip Rieff. New York: Collier, 1963. 214–19.

———. *Group Psychology and the Analysis of the Ego.* Trans. James Strachey. New York: Norton, 1959.

———. *Interpretation of Dreams.* New York: Avon Books, 1965.

———. "On the Mechanism of Paranoia" (1911). *General Psychological Theory.* Ed. Philip Rieff. New York: Collier, 1963. 29–48.

———. "The Psychogenesis of a Case of Homosexuality in a Woman" (1920). *Sex-*

uality and the Psychology of Love. Ed. Philip Rieff. New York: Collier, 1963. 133–59.

——. "Some Psychological Consequences of the Anatomical Distinction Between the Sexes" (1925). *Sexuality and the Psychology of Love.* Ed. Philip Rieff. New York: Collier, 1963. 183–93.

——. *Totem and Taboo.* New York: Vintage, 1946.

——. "The Uncanny" (1919). *The Standard Edition of the Complete Psychological Works of Sigmund Freud.* Vol. 17. Trans. James Strachey. London: Hogarth Press, 1955. 217–56.

Fuss, Diana. "Fashion and the Homospectatorial Look." *Critical Inquiry* 18 (Summer 1992): 713–37.

——. "Sexual Contagions: Dorothy Strachey's *Olivia.*" *Identification Papers.* New York: Routledge, 1995.

Fuss, Diana, ed. *Inside/Out: Lesbian Theories, Gay Theories.* New York and London: Routledge, 1991.

Gaines, Jane. "The *Queen Christina* Tie-Ups: Convergence of Show Window and Screen." *Quarterly Review of Film & Video* 11.1 (1989): 35–60.

Gaines, Jane and Charlotte Herzog, eds. *Fabrications: Costume and the Female Body.* New York: Routledge, 1990.

Garber, Eric. "A Spectacle in Color: The Lesbian and Gay Subculture of Jazz Age Harlem." *Hidden from History: Reclaiming the Gay and Lesbian Past.* Ed. Martin Duberman, Martha Vicinus, and George Chauncey, Jr. New York: New American Library, 1989. 318–31.

——. "Gladys Bentley: Bulldagger Who Sang the Blues." *Out/Look* 1.1 (Spring 1988): 52–61.

Garner, Shirley Nelson, Claire Kahane, and Madelon Sprengnether, eds. *The (M)other Tongue: Essays in Feminist Psychoanalytic Interpretation.* Ithaca: Cornell University Press, 1985.

Giddens, Gary. "Ethel Waters: Mother of Us All." *Village Voice* (October 10, 1977): 63, 92.

Gilbert, Sandra M. and Susan Gubar. *The Madwoman in the Attic: The Woman Writer and the Nineteenth Century Literary Imagination.* New Haven: Yale University Press, 1979.

Gledhill, Christine, ed. *Home Is Where the Heart Is: Studies in Melodrama and the Woman's Film.* London: BFI, 1987.

——. *Stardom: Industry of Desire.* New York: Routledge, 1991.

Goldsmith, Margaret. *Christina of Sweden: A Psychological Biography.* Garden City: Doubleday, 1933.

Grosz, Elizabeth. "Lesbian Fetishism?" *Differences* 5.2 (Summer 1991): 39–54.

Hadleigh, Boze. "A Hollywood Square Comes Out: Interview with Paul Lynde." *Out/Look* (Fall 1989): 24–27.

Halberstam, Judith. *Skin Shows: Gothic Horror and the Technology of Monsters.* Durham: Duke University Press, 1995.

Works Cited

Hall, Radclyffe. *The Well of Loneliness*. 1928. New York: Avon, 1981.

Hall, Stuart. "Encoding, Decoding." *Culture, Media, Language*. Ed. Stuart Hall, Dorothy Hobson, Andrew Lowe, and Paul Willis. London: Routledge, 1992. 128–38.

Halliday, John. *Sirk on Sirk*. London: Secker and Warburg, 1972.

Halprin, Sarah. "Writing in the Margins." Review of E. Ann Kaplan, *Women and Film: Both Sides of the Camera* and Annette Kuhn, *Women's Pictures*. *Jump Cut* 29 (February 1984): 31–33.

Hamer, Diane. "Significant Others: Lesbians and Psychoanalytic Theory." *Feminist Review* 34 (Spring 1990): 134–51.

Hamilton, Marybeth. *When I'm Bad, I'm Better: Mae West, Sex, and American Entertainment*. Berkeley: University of California Press, 1997.

Handel, Leo A. *Hollywood Looks at Its Audience: A Report of Film Audience Research*. Urbana: University of Illinois Press, 1950.

Hansberry, Lorraine. "The Case of the Invisible Force: Images of the Negro in American Films." *Celluloid Power: Social Film Criticism from "Birth of a Nation" to "Judgment at Nuremberg."* Ed. David Platt. Metuchen: Scarecrow, 1992. 457–67.

Hansen, Miriam. *Babel and Babylon: Spectatorship in American Silent Film*. Cambridge: Harvard University Press, 1991.

———. "Pleasure, Ambivalence, Identification: Valentino and Female Spectatorship." *Stardom*. Ed. Christine Gledhill. London: BFI, 1991. 259–82.

Harper, Sue. "Historical Pleasures: Gainsborough Costume Melodrama." *Home Is Where the Heart Is*. Ed. Christine Gledhill. London: BFI, 1987. 167–96.

Hart, Lynda. *Fatal Women: Lesbian Sexuality and the Mark of Aggression*. Princeton: Princeton University Press, 1994.

Haskell, Molly. *From Reverence to Rape: The Treatment of Women in the Movies*. New York: Holt, Rinehart, 1973.

Heath, Stephen. *Questions of Cinema*. Bloomington: Indiana University Press, 1981.

Hellman, Lillian. *The Children's Hour*. In *Four Plays by Lillian Hellman*. New York: Modern Library, 1942.

Heung, Marina. "'What's the Matter with Sarah Jane?': Daughters and Mothers in Douglas Sirk's *Imitation of Life*." *Cinema Journal* 26.3 (Spring 1987): 21–43.

Hirsch, Marianne. *The Mother/Daughter Plot: Narrative, Psychoanalysis, Feminism*. Bloomington: Indiana University Press, 1989.

Holland, Norman and Leona Sherman. "Gothic Possibilities." *New Literary History* 8.2 (Winter 1977): 279–94.

Holmlund, Christine. "When Is a Lesbian Not a Lesbian? The Lesbian Continuum and the Mainstream Femme Film." *Camera Obscura* 25–26 (Jan.–May 1991):145–78.

hooks, bell. "The Oppositional Gaze." *Black Looks: Race and Representation*. Boston: South End, 1993. 115–32.

Inness, Sherrie. *The Lesbian Menace: Ideology, Identity, and the Representation of Lesbian Life*. Amherst: University of Massachusetts Press, 1997.

Irigaray, Luce. *This Sex Which Is Not One*. Trans. Catherine Porter with Carolyn Burke. Ithaca: Cornell University Press, 1985.

Jackson, Carlton. *Hattie: The Life of Hattie McDaniel*. Lanham, Md.: Madison Books, 1990.

Jackson, Phyllis J. and Darrell Moore. "Fictional Seductions." Review of *The Watermelon Woman*. *GLQ* 4.3 (1998): 499–508.

Jackson, Shirley. *The Haunting of Hill House*. 1959. New York: Penguin, 1987.

Jacobs, Lea. "*Now, Voyager*: Some Problems of Enunciation and Sexual Difference." *Camera Obscura* 7 (1981): 89–110.

——. *The Wages of Sin: Censorship and the Fallen Woman Film, 1928–1942*. Madison: University of Wisconsin Press, 1991.

Johnston, Claire. "Women's Cinema as Counter Cinema." *Notes on Women's Cinema*. Ed. Claire Johnston. London: SEFT, 1973. 24–31.

Jones, Ernest. "The Early Development of Female Sexuality." *International Journal of Psycho-Analysis* 8 (1927): 459–72.

Jones, Lisa. "The Defiant Ones: A Talk with Film Historian Donald Bogle." *Village Voice* (June 1991): 69.

Kaplan, E. Ann. "Dialogue: Ann Kaplan Replies to Linda Williams's 'Something Else Besides a Mother: *Stella Dallas* and the Maternal Melodrama'." *Cinema Journal* 24.2 (Winter 1985): 40–43.

——. "Motherhood and Representation: From Postwar Freudian Figurations to Postmodernism." *Psychoanalysis and Cinema*. Ed. E. Ann Kaplan. New York: Routledge, 1990. 128–42.

——. *Motherhood and Representation: The Mother in Popular Culture and Melodrama*. London: Routledge, 1992.

——. "Mothering, Feminism and Representation: The Maternal in Melodrama and the Woman's Film, 1910–40." *Home Is Where the Heart Is*. Ed. Christine Gledhill. London: BFI, 1987. 113–37.

Katz, Ephraim. *The Film Encyclopedia*. New York: Crowell, 1979.

Katzman, David M. *Seven Days a Week: Women and Domestic Service in Industrializing America*. New York: Oxford University Press, 1978.

Kay, Karyn and Gerald Peary. *Women and the Cinema*. New York: E. P. Dutton, 1977.

Kear, Lynn. *Agnes Moorehead: A Bio-Bibliography*. Westport, Conn.: Greenwood Press, 1992.

King, Barry. "Articulating Stardom." *Stardom: Industry of Desire*. Ed. Christine Gledhill. New York: Routledge, 1991. 167–82.

Kirihara, Donald. "The Accepted Idea Displaced: Stereotype and Sessue Hayakawa." *The Birth of Whiteness: Race and the Emergence of U.S. Cinema*. Ed. Daniel Bernardi. New Brunswick: Rutgers University Press, 1996. 81–99.

Klinger, Barbara. "Cinema/Criticism/Ideology Revisited: The Progressive Genre."

Film Genre Reader II. Ed. Barry Keith Grant. Austin: University of Texas Press, 1995. 74–90.

——. *Melodrama and Meaning: History, Culture, and the Films of Douglas Sirk.* Bloomington: Indiana University Press, 1994.

Knaack, Twila. *Ethel Waters: I Touched a Sparrow.* Word Books, 1977.

Koch, Gertrude. "Why Women Go to Men's Films." *Feminist Aesthetics.* Ed. Gisela Ecker. London: Women's Press, 1985. 108–19.

Kracauer, Siegfried. *Theory of Film: The Redemption of Physical Reality.* New York: Oxford University Press, 1965.

Kristeva, Julia. *Desire in Language: A Semiotic Approach to Literature and Art.* New York: Columbia University Press, 1982.

Kuhn, Annette. "*Mandy* and Possibility." *Screen* 33.3 (Autumn 1992): 233–43.

Kuntzel, Thierry. "The Film-Work." *Enclitic* 2.1 (Spring 1978): 39–62.

Lacan, Jacques and the école freudienne. *Feminine Sexuality.* Ed. Juliet Mitchell and Jacqueline Rose. New York: Norton, 1985.

Lampl-de Groot, Jeanne. "The Evolution of the Oedipus Complex in Women." *The Psychoanalytic Reader.* Ed. Robert Fliess. New York: International Universities Press, 1948. Reprinted 1973. 180–94.

Lang, Robert. *American Film Melodrama: Griffith, Vidor, Minelli.* Princeton: Princeton University Press, 1989.

LaPlace, Maria. "Producing and Consuming the Woman's Film 1910–1940." *Home Is Where the Heart Is.* Ed. Christine Gledhill. London: BFI, 1987. 138–66.

Laplanche, Jean and J.-B. Pontalis. "Fantasy and the Origins of Sexuality." *International Journal of Psycho-Analysis* 49.1 (1968). Reprinted in *Formations of Fantasy.* Ed. Victor Burgin, James Donald, and Cora Kaplan. London: Methuen, 1986. 5–34.

——. *The Language of Psycho-Analysis.* Trans. Donald Nicholson-Smith. New York: Norton, 1973.

Leff, Leonard J. and Jerold L. Simmons. *The Dame in the Kimono: Hollywood, Censorship, and the Production Code from the 1920s to the 1960s.* New York: Grove Weidenfeld, 1990.

Leonard, Zoe. *The Fae Richards Photo Archive.* Zoe Leonard, photographer; Cheryl Dunye, filmmaker. San Francisco: Artspace Books, 1996.

Lighter, J.E., ed. *Random House Historical Dictionary of American Slang.* Vol. 1. New York: Random House, 1994.

Lootens, Tricia. "'Whose Hand Was I Holding?' Familial and Sexual Politics in Shirley Jackson's *The Haunting of Hill House.*" *Haunting the House of Fiction: Feminist Perspectives on Ghost Stories by American Women.* Ed. Lynette Carpenter and Wendy Kolmar. Knoxville: University of Tennessee Press, 1991. 166–92.

Maltby, Richard. "'To Prevent the Prevalent Type of Book': Censorship and Adaptation in Hollywood, 1924–1934." *Movie Censorship and American Culture.* Ed.

Francis G. Couvares. Washington: Smithsonian Institution Press, 1996. 97–128.

——. "The Production Code and the Hays Office." *Grand Design: Hollywood As a Modern Business Enterprise, 1930–1939.* Ed. Tino Balio. Berkeley: University of California Press, 1995. 37–72.

Marcus, Frank. *The Killing of Sister George: A Comedy.* New York: Random House, 1967.

Marks, Elaine. "Lesbian Intertextuality." *Homosexualities and French Literature.* Ed. George Stambolian and Elaine Marks. Ithaca: Cornell University Press, 1979. 353–77.

Martin, Biddy. *Femininity Played Straight.* New York: Routledge, 1996.

——. "Lesbian Identity and Autobiographical Difference(s)." *The Lesbian and Gay Studies Reader.* Ed. Henry Abelove, Michele Aina Barale, and David Halperin. New York: Routledge, 1993. 274–93.

——. "The Hobo, the Quarterback, and the Fairy." *Femininity Played Straight.* New York: Routledge, 1996. 33–44.

Mast, Gerald. *The Movies in Our Midst: Documents in the Cultural History of Film in America.* Chicago: University of Chicago Press, 1982.

Matthews, Peter. "Garbo and Phallic Motherhood—A 'Homosexual' Visual Economy." *Screen* 29:3 (Summer 1988): 14–39.

Mayne, Judith. *Directed by Dorothy Arzner.* Bloomington: Indiana University Press, 1994.

——. "Lesbian Looks." *How Do I Look?* Ed. Bad Object Choices. Seattle: Bay, 1991. 103–44.

——. "Marlene Dietrich, *The Blue Angel,* and Female Performance." *Seduction and Theory: Readings of Gender, Representation, and Rhetoric.* Ed. Diane Hunter. Urbana: University of Illinois Press, 1989. 28–46.

——. *Cinema and Spectatorship.* London: Routledge, 1993.

——. *The Woman at the Keyhole.* Bloomington: Indiana University Press, 1990.

McDonald, Boyd. *Cruising the Movies.* New York: Gay Presses, 1985.

McKee, Alison L. "'L'affaire Praslin' and *All This, and Heaven Too*: Gender, Genre, and History in the 1940s Woman's Film." *The Velvet Light Trap* 35 (Spring 1995): 33–51.

Merck, Mandy. "Difference and Its Discontents." *Screen* 28.1 (Winter 1987): 2–9.

——. *Perversions.* New York: Routledge. 1993.

Metz, Christian. *The Imaginary Signifier.* Trans. Celia Britton, Annwyl Williams, Ben Brewster, and Alfred Guzzetti. Bloomington: Indiana University Press, 1982.

Miller, D. A. "Anal Rope." *Inside/Out: Lesbian Theories, Gay Theories.* Ed. Diana Fuss. New York: Routledge, 1991. 119–141.

Miller, Nancy K. *The Heroine's Text: Readings in the French and English Novel, 1722–1782.* New York: Columbia University Press, 1980.

Modleski, Tania. *Feminism without Women*. New York and London: Routledge, 1991.

——. *Loving with a Vengeance: Mass-Produced Fantasies for Women*. 1982. New York: Methuen, 1984.

——. "'Never to Be Thirty-six Years Old': *Rebecca* as Female Oedipal Drama." *Wide Angle* 5.1 (1982): 34–56.

——. "Some Functions of Feminist Criticism, or The Scandal of the Mute Body." *October* 49 (Summer 1989): 3–24.

——. *The Women Who Knew Too Much: Hitchcock and Feminist Theory*. New York and London: Methuen, 1988.

Montgomery, Elizabeth. Interview. *The Advocate* 608 (July 30, 1992): 66–69.

Moore, Lisa. "'Something More Tender Still than Friendship': Romantic Friendship in Early Nineteenth-Century England." *Feminist Studies* 18.3 (Fall 1992): 499–521.

Motion Picture Producers and Distributors of America. "The Motion Picture Production Code of 1930." *The Movies in Our Midst: Documents in the Cultural History of Film in America*. Ed. Gerald Mast. Chicago: University of Chicago Press, 1982. 321–33.

Mulvey, Laura. "Afterthoughts on 'Visual Pleasure and Narrative Cinema' Inspired by *Duel in the Sun* (King Vidor, 1946)." *Framework* 15/16/17 (1981): 12–25.

——. *Fetishism and Curiosity*. Bloomington: Indiana University Press and London: BFI Publishing, 1996.

——. "The Myth of Pandora: A Psychoanalytical Approach." *Feminisms in the Cinema*. Ed. Laura Pietropaolo and Ada Testaferri. Bloomington: Indiana University Press, 1995. 3–19.

——. *Visual and Other Pleasures*. Bloomington: Indiana University Press, 1989. 177–200.

Neale, Steve. "Melo Talk: On the Meaning and Use of the Term 'Melodrama' in the American Trade Press." *The Velvet Light Trap* 32 (Fall 1993): 66–89.

——. "Melodrama and Tears." *Screen* 27.6 (Nov.–Dec. 1986): 6–22.

Nestle, Joan, ed. *Persistent Desire: A Femme-Butch Reader*. Boston: Alyson, 1992.

Newton, Esther. "The Mythic Mannish Lesbian." *Signs* 9.4 (Summer 1984): 557–75.

Noriega, Chon. "Something's Missing Here!: Homosexuality and Film Reviews during the Production Code Era, 1934–1962." *Cinema Journal* 30.1 (Fall 1990): 20–41.

Nunokawa, Jeff. "'All the Sad Young Men': AIDS and the Work of Mourning." *Inside/Out: Lesbian Theories, Gay Theories*. Ed. Diana Fuss. New York: Routledge, 1991. 311–23.

Oppenheimer, Judy. *Private Demons: The Life of Shirley Jackson*. New York: Ballantine, 1989.

Paris, Barry. *Garbo*. New York: Knopf, 1995.

Parish, James Robert. *Good Dames*. South Brunswick: A. S. Barnes, 1974.

Parker, Alison M. "Mothering the Movies: Women Reformers and Popular Culture." *Movie Censorship and American Culture.* Ed. Francis G. Couvares. Washington: Smithsonian Institution Press, 1996. 73–96.

Peiss, Kathy. *Cheap Amusements: Leisure in Turn-of-the-Century New York.* Philadelphia: Temple University Press, 1986.

Perkins, T. E. "Rethinking Stereotypes." *Ideology and Cultural Production.* Ed. Michèle Barrett, et al. New York: St. Martin's, 1979. 135–59.

Peterson, M. Jeanne. "The Victorian Governess: Status Incongruence in Family and Society." *Suffer and Be Still: Women in the Victorian Age.* Ed. Martha Vicinus. Bloomington: Indiana University Press, 1972. 3–19.

Pilato, Herbie J. *The Bewitched Book.* New York: Delta, 1992.

Plath, Sylvia. *The Bell Jar.* Cutchogue, New York: Buccaneer Books, 1971.

Polan, Dana. *Power and Paranoia: History, Narrative, and the American Cinema, 1940–1950.* New York: Columbia University Press, 1986.

Poovey, Mary. "The Anathematized Race: The Governess and Jane Eyre." *Feminism and Psychoanalysis.* Ed. Richard Feldstein and Judith Roof. Ithaca: Cornell University Press, 1989. 230–54.

Prouty, Olive Higgins. *Now, Voyager.* 1941. New York: Triangle, 1943.

Quirk, Lawrence. *Fasten Your Seat Belts: The Passionate Life of Bette Davis.* New York: Morrow, 1990.

Reynolds, Debbie with David Patrick Columbia. *My Life.* Pocket Books, 1988.

Rich, Adrienne. "Compulsory Heterosexuality and Lesbian Existence." *Signs* 4.4 (Summer 1980): 631–60.

———. *Of Woman Born: Motherhood as Experience and Institution.* New York: Norton, 1976.

Rich, B. Ruby. "From Repressive Tolerance to Erotic Liberation: *Maedchen in Uniform.*" *Re-Vision: Essays in Feminist Film Criticism.* Ed. Mary Ann Doane, Patricia Mellencamp, and Linda Williams. Frederick, Md.: University Publications of America/AFI, 1984. 100–130.

Robbins, Bruce. *The Servant's Hand: English Fiction from Below.* New York: Columbia University Press, 1986.

Roberts, Shari. "'The Lady in the Tutti-Frutti Hat': Carmen Miranda, a Spectacle of Ethnicity." *Cinema Journal* 32.3 (Spring 1993): 3–23.

Robertson, Pamela. *Guilty Pleasures: Feminist Camp from Mae West to Madonna.* Durham: Duke University Press, 1996.

Rodowick, D.N. *The Difficulty of Difference.* New York: Routledge, 1991.

Rollins, Judith. *Between Women: Domestics and Their Employers.* Philadelphia: Temple University Press, 1985.

Roof, Judith. *A Lure of Knowledge: Lesbian Sexuality and Theory.* New York: Columbia University Press, 1991.

Rose, Jacqueline. "Paranoia and the Film System." *Screen* 17.4 (Winter 1976–77): 85–104.

———. *Sexuality in the Field of Vision.* London: Verso, 1986.

Rubin, Gayle. "Thinking Sex: Notes for a Radical Theory of the Politics of Sexuality." *Pleasure and Danger.* Ed. Carole Vance. Boston: Routledge, 1984. 267–319.

Rushdie, Salman. *The Wizard of Oz.* London: BFI Film Classics, 1992.

Russo, Vito. *The Celluloid Closet: Homosexuality in the Movies.* New York: Harper & Row, 1987.

Schatz, Thomas. "'A Triumph of Bitchery': Warner Bros., Bette Davis and Jezebel." *Wide Angle* 10.1 (1988): 17–29.

Sconce, Jeffrey. "Narrative Authority and Social Narrativity: The Cinematic Reconstitution of Brontë's *Jane Eyre.*" *Wide Angle* 10.1 (1988): 46–61.

Sedgwick, Eve Kosofsky. "A Poem Is Being Written." *Tendencies.* Durham: Duke University Press, 1993. 177–214.

——. *The Epistemology of the Closet.* Berkeley: University of California Press, 1990.

——. "Queer and Now." *Tendencies.* Durham: Duke University Press, 1993. 1–20.

Sheldon, Caroline. "Lesbians in Film: Some Thoughts." *Gays in Film.* Ed. Richard Dyer. London: BFI, 1977. 5–26.

Sherk, Warren. *Agnes Moorehead: A Very Private Person.* Philadelphia: Dorrance, 1976.

Shohat, Ella and Robert Stam. *Unthinking Eurocentrism: Multiculturalism and the Media.* London: Routledge, 1994.

Silverman, Kaja. *The Acoustic Mirror: The Female Voice in Psychoanalysis and Cinema.* Bloomington: Indiana University Press, 1988.

——. *Male Subjectivity at the Margins.* New York: Routledge, 1992.

——. *Threshold of the Visible World.* New York: Routledge, 1996.

Sirk, Douglas. *Sirk on Sirk.* Ed. Jon Halliday. New York: Viking Penguin, 1972.

Smith, Jack. "The Perfect Filmic Appositeness of Maria Montez." *Historical Treasures.* Ed. Ira Cohen. New York: Haumann, 1990. 67–107.

——. "Remarks on Art and the Theatre." *Historical Treasures.* Ed. Ira Cohen. New York: Haumann, 1990. 111–36.

Smith-Rosenberg, Carroll. *Disorderly Conduct: Visions of Gender in Victorian America.* New York: Oxford University Press, 1985.

Snead, James A. *White Screens, Black Images: Hollywood from the Dark Side.* New York: Routledge, 1994.

Sontag, Susan. "Notes on 'Camp.'" *Against Interpretation.* New York: Farrar, Straus, 1965. 275–92.

Spillers, Hortense J. "Mama's Baby, Papa's Maybe: An American Grammar Book." *Diacritics* 17.2 (Summer 1987): 65–81.

Stacey, Jackie. "Desperately Seeking Difference." *Screen* 18.1 (Winter 1987): 48–61.

——. "Feminine Fascinations: Forms of Identification in Star-Audience Relations." *Stardom: Industry of Desire.* Ed. Christine Gledhill. London: Routledge, 1991. 141–63.

——. *Star-Gazing: Hollywood Cinema and Female Spectatorship*. London: Routledge, 1994.

Staiger, Janet. *Bad Women: Regulating Sexuality in Early American Cinema*. Minneapolis: University of Minnesota Press, 1995.

Straayer, Chris. *Deviant Eyes, Deviant Bodies: Sexual Re-Orientations in Film and Video*. New York: Columbia University Press, 1996.

Studlar, Gaylyn. *In the Realm of Pleasure: Von Sternberg, Dietrich, and the Masochistic Aesthetic*. Urbana and Chicago: University of Illinois Press, 1988.

Terry, Jennifer. *An American Obsession: Science, Medicine, and Homosexuality in Modern Society*. Chicago. University of Chicago Press, 1999.

——. "Theorizing Deviant Historiography." *Differences* 3.2 (1991): 55–74.

Todd, Marion Garbo. "The Truth about Miss Hathaway: The Fascination of Television's Perennial Spinster." *The Lesbian News* 16.10 (May 1991): 40+.

Traub, Valerie. "The Ambiguities of 'Lesbian' Viewing Pleasure: The (Dis)articulations of *Black Widow*." *Body/Guards*. Ed. Julia Epstein and Kristina Straub. New York: Routledge, 1991. 305–28.

Truffaut, Francois. *Hitchcock*. New York: Simon & Schuster, 1985.

Turk, Edward Baron. "Wartime Hollywood and the Racial/Musical Other, or Ethel Waters in Egypt." Unpublished ms., 1991.

Twomey, Alfred E. and Athur F. McClure. *The Versatiles*. South Brunswick and New York: A. S. Barnes, 1969.

Tyler, Parker. *Screening the Sexes: Homosexuality in the Movies*. New York: Holt Rinehart, 1972.

Vermeule, Blakey. "Is There a Sedgwick School for Girls?" *Qui Parle* 5.1 (Fall/Winter 1991): 53–72.

Viertel, Salka. *The Kindness of Strangers*. New York: Holt Reinhart, 1969.

Villarejo, Amy and Marcia Landy. *Queen Christina*. London: BFI Publishing, 1995.

Viviani, Christian. "Who Is Without Sin? The Maternal Melodrama in American Film, 1930–39." *Home Is Where the Heart Is*. Ed. Christine Gledhill. London: BFI, 1987. 83–99.

Waldman, Diane. "'At Last I Can Tell It to Someone!': Feminine Point of View and Subjectivity in the Gothic Romance Films of the 1940s." *Cinema Journal* 23.3 (1983): 29–40.

Walker, Janet. *Couching Resistance: Women, Film, and Psychoanalytic Psychiatry*. Minneapolis: University of Minnesota Press, 1993.

Walkerdine, Valerie. "Video Replay: Families, Films and Fantasy." *Formations of Fantasy*. Ed. Victor Burgin, James Donald, and Cora Kaplan. London: Methuen, 1986. 167–99.

Walsh, Andrea. *Women's Film and Female Experience, 1940–1950*. New York: Praeger, 1984.

Waters, Ethel, with Charles Samuels. *His Eye Is on the Sparrow*. New York: Doubleday, 1951.

Works Cited

———. "The Men in My Life." *Ebony* 7.2 (January 1952): 24–38.

Watney, Simon. "Katharine Hepburn and the Cinema of Chastisement." *Screen* 26.5 (Sept./Oct. 1985): 52–62.

Weiss, Andrea. "'A Queer Feeling When I Look at You': Female Stars and Lesbian Spectatorship in the 1930s." *Stardom: Industry of Desire.* Ed. Christine Gledhill. London: Routledge, 1991. 283–99.

———. *Vampires and Violets: Lesbians in Film.* New York: Penguin, 1992.

Weldon, Michael. *The Psychotronic Encyclopedia of Film.* New York: Ballantine, 1983.

Wharton, Edith. *Old New York.* New York: Scribner, 1952.

Whitaker, Judy. "Hollywood Transformed." *Jump Cut* 24–25 (1981): 33–35.

White, Patricia. "Governing Lesbian Desire: *Nocturne's* Oedipal Fantasy." *Feminisms in the Cinema.* Ed. Ada Testaferri and Laura Pietropaolo. Bloomington: Indiana University Press, 1994. 86–105.

———. "Madame X of the China Seas." *Screen* 28.4 (Autumn 1987): 80–95.

Wiley, Mason and Damien Bona. *Inside Oscar.* New York: Ballantine, 1986.

Williams, Linda. "'Something Else Besides a Mother': Stella Dallas and the Maternal Melodrama." *Cinema Journal* 24.1 (1984): 2–27.

———. "When the Woman Looks." *Re-Vision.* Ed. Mary Ann Doane, Patricia Mellencamp, and Linda Williams. Frederick, Md.: University Publications of America/AFI, 1984. 83–99.

Wilton, Tamsin, ed. *Immortal/Invisible: Lesbians and the Moving Image.* London: Routledge, 1995.

Wittig, Monique. "On the Social Contract." *The Straight Mind.* Boston: Beacon, 1992. 33–45.

———. "The Straight Mind." *Feminist Issues* 1 (Summer 1980): 103–11.

Young-Bruehl, Elizabeth. *Anna Freud: A Biography.* London: Macmillan, 1988.

Index

Index

Index

Marcus, Frank, 12, 139
Marks, Elaine, 18
Martin, Biddy, 37
Masquerade, 35–36, 54, 56–58, 117, 128, 170, 197
Maxwell, Lois, 89
Mayer, Louis B., 10
Mayne, Judith, 47–48, 52, 117, 142, 170–171, 195–196, 224n16
McCambridge, Mercedes, xxii–xxiii, 141–142, 176–180
McCarthy, Joseph, 147
McCullers, Carson, xi–xii, 62, 166
McDaniel, Hattie, 130, 134, 144, 147, 152, 155–157, 174, 187, 238n14
Meeting of Two Queens (Cecilia Barriga, 1991), xx, 30, 34, 53–58
Melodrama: maternal, xxi, 94–111, 118, 130–131. *See also* Woman's picture
The Member of the Wedding (Carson McCullers, 1946), xi–xii
The Member of the Wedding (Fred Zinnemann, 1952), xi–xv, xxiii–xxiv, 4, 62, 157–161, 165–167, 197
Mercury Theater, 181
Metro-Goldwyn-Mayer (MGM), 20, 112, 158
Metz, Christian, 29–30, 60
Meyer, Janet, 45, 47
Mildred Pierce (Michael Curtiz, 1945), 15, 101, 109
Miller, D. A., 110
Miller, Nancy K., 95
Miranda, Carmen, 32
Modleski, Tania, 64–67, 71, 184
Monroe, Marilyn, 37, 202
Moorehead, Agnes, xxii, 139–142, 144, 146, 171–172, 175–176, 180–193, 235n4
Morocco (Josef von Sternberg, 1930), 44, 46–47, 53, 55, 108
Motion Picture Producers and Distributors Association, 8, 10, 14, 20–22, 25, 127, 178, 218n1. *See also* Hays, Will; Production Code Administration
Motion Picture Production Code, xviii, 1–

3, 6–24, 27–28, 100, 136, 139, 141, 147, 215, 218n1
Mulvey, Laura, xvi, 29, 41, 50, 63, 72, 203

Names Project AIDS Memorial Quilt, xiv
Narrative closure, xii, 27, 79, 91, 94–95, 115, 123, 133–135, 143–144, 146, 150, 168, 177, 186, 189, 215
National Association for the Advancement of Colored People, 157, 161
Nazimova, Alla, 187
Nestle, Joan, 56
New Woman, 11, 104, 131, 147
Newton, Esther, 14, 175
Night of the Iguana (John Huston, 1964), 174
Nochlin, Linda, 155
Noriega, Chon, 22–23, 25
Now, Voyager (Olive Higgins Prouty, 1941), 94
Now, Voyager (Irving Rapper, 1942), xviii, xxi, 31, 94–97, 101, 112, 117, 121, 124–129, 131, 133–134, 144, 130nn2–3

Oedipal drama, 195, 198, 200–201; female, xii, 64–69, 71–72, 79, 82, 88, 90–93, 97, 100, 102–107, 111, 126–128, 134, 198, 205–208; governess in, 96–97, 119, 122–124, 129–130; negative, 106–107, 198–199
Old Acquaintance (John Van Druten, 1941), 131
Old Acquaintance (Vincent Sherman, 1943), 112, 117, 131–135
The Old Maid (Edith Wharton, 1924), 113, 115, 117
The Old Maid (Zoë Akins, 1935), 113
The Old Maid (Edmund Goulding, 1939), 15, 107, 112–118, 123–124, 127, 130–131, 133–134
Oliver, Edna May, 141

Pangborn, Franklin, 142, 174
Paramount Studios, 112, 118
Paranoia, xxi, 61, 72–75, 85–88, 112

PATRICIA WHITE is Assistant Professor of English and Film
Studies at Swarthmore College. Her articles have appeared in *Screen,*
The Oxford Guide to Film Studies, and in numerous collections
of feminist and lesbian/gay film studies. She is a member of the
editorial collective of *Camera Obscura.*